# THE PANTHAY REBELLION

T0281779

# The Panthay Rebellion

ISLAM, ETHNICITY, AND THE DALI
SULTANATE IN SOUTHWEST CHINA, 1856–1873

*David G. Atwill*

Foreword by Tariq Ali

VERSO

London • New York

This edition published by Verso 2023
First published as *The Chinese Sultanate: Islam, Ethnicity, and the Panthay Rebellion in Southwest China, 1856–1873* by Stanford University Press
© 2006 by the Board of Trustees of the Leland Stanford Junior University
Foreword © Tariq Ali 2023

All rights reserved

The moral rights of the authors have been asserted

1 3 5 7 9 10 8 6 4 2

**Verso**
UK: 6 Meard Street, London W1F 0EG
US: 388 Atlantic Avenue, Brooklyn, NY 11217

versobooks.com

Verso is the imprint of New Left Books

ISBN-13: 978-1-80429-054-5

**British Library Cataloguing in Publication Data**
A catalogue record for this book is available from the British Library

**The Library of Congress has catalogued the 2005 edition as follows:**
Atwill, David G.
    The Chinese sultanate : Islam, ethnicity, and the Panthay
  Rebellion in southwest China, 1856–1873 / David G. Atwill.
        p. cm.
    A Mandarin's Tale—South of the Clouds: The World of
19th Century Yunnan—Shades of Islam: The Muslim
Yunnanese—Rebellion's Roots: Hanjian-ism, Han Newcomers,
and Non-Han Violence—Spiraling Violence: The Rise of Anti-
Hui Hostilities—All the Fish in the Pond: The Kunming
Massacre and the Panthay Rebellion—Ambiguous Ambitions:
Ma Rulong's Road to Power, 1860–1864—Rebellious Visions:
Du Wenxiu and the Creation of the Dali Sultanate—Ethereal
Deeds: The Struggle to Reclaim Yunnan, 1867–1873—Epilogue:
The Aftermath of Rebellion.
    Includes bibliographical references and index.
    ISBN 0-8047-5159-5 (cloth : alk. paper)
    1. Yunnan Sheng (China)—History—19th century.
2. Yunnan Sheng (China)—Ethnic relations—History—19th
century.  I. Title: Islam, ethnicity, and the Panthay Rebellion
in southwest China, 1856–1873. II. Title.
DS793•Y8A79 2005
951'•3S'03 3—dc22                                    2005012304

Printed and bound by CPI Group (UK) Ltd, Croydon, CR0 4YY

*For Yurong, my favorite Lolo*
*and for Dru C. Gladney (1956–2022) who continues to inspire me*

# Contents

# Maps, Figures, and Tables

# Acknowledgments

This book is the end result of a long process that began for me during a graduate seminar taught by K.C. Liu, who suggested to me that a paper on the Panthay Rebellion might be worth my time. Later, after a chance encounter with Dru Gladney, who had just arrived at the University of Hawaii, Manoa, this book began to take shape in my mind. While writing it, I have incurred many debts.

One of the greatest joys of researching a topic as broad as the Panthay Rebellion is that it allowed me to travel across three continents in search of books and archival materials. Especially important were the libraries of Yunnan University, the University of Hawaii, and the University of Washington as well as the Fu Sinian Library at the Academia Sinica. Several archival centers—namely, China's No. 1 Historical Archive in Beijing, the National Palace Archives in Taipei, and the archives of the Société des missions-étrangères de Paris—all provided essential documents at crucial junctures in my research. I especially thank the staff at each of these institutions for their patience and assistance.

I could not have visited these depositories of history without the financial support of the following: a Foreign Language and Area Studies Fellowship at the University of Hawaii; a *China Times* Young Scholar Fellowship; a Fulbright-Hays grant; grants from the Pacific Cultural Foundation and the Working Group Modernity and Islam Berlin Seminar; and many smaller grants from Juniata College and Pennsylvania State University.

Some parts of this book have been published in journals and edited volumes. Sections of "Blinkered Visions: Islamic Identity, Hui Ethnicity, and the Panthay Rebellion in Southwest China, 1856–1873," *Journal of Asian Studies* 62(4)(2003), appear in chapters 3, 6, 8, and 10. Parts of "Trading Places: Resistance, Ethnicity and Governance in Nineteenth-Century Yunnan," in Robert J. Antony and Jane Kate Leonard, eds., *Dragons, Tigers, and Dogs: Qing Crisis Management and the Boundaries of State Power in Late Imperial China* (Ithaca: Cornell East Asia Series, no. 114, 2002), appear in chapters 4 and 5. I thank both presses for allowing me to use portions of these articles, and I am grateful for the insights the editors and reviewers offered.

Several people were generous enough to read various incarnations of this book prior to its publication and offered honest and useful comments:

Leonard Andaya, Ned Davis, John Stephan, Rebecca Weiner, and Jackie Armijo-Hussein, as well as an anonymous reviewer for Stanford University Press. Laura Clark Hull pored over multiple iterations of this book and helped me understand that writing is a process and thereby made the end product far better. Of course, any remaining errors, imperfections, and quirky language are entirely my own.

As with most tasks in my life, other people have nourished me intellectually, emotionally, and physically with thoughtful conversations, shared pitchers of beer, and kind words at decisive moments. All of them helped me greatly while I was writing this book. Here I must acknowledge Peter Worthing, David Sowell, Russ Motter, Anne Hattori, Bill Cummings, Li Donghong, Lin Chaomin, Lu Ren, Joshua Howard, Bill Coleman, Chas McKhann, and Donald P. King. All members of my extended family, on both sides of the Pacific, have helped me by guiding me through rural parts of Yunnan province, by providing a bed during a conference, by offering a key ride to the airport, and so on—I thank them all. One of my greatest resources has been those ties that bind.

Finally, there is that random multitude of cohorts who ushered me through multiple moves, responded to countless e-mails, facilitated last-minute research ventures, and helped me negotiate various crises. I must mention Keith Schoppa, who at various stages tendered his objective judgment and advice; and David Sowell, Elisabeth Allès, and Ingeborg Baldauf, all of whom continue to serve unselfishly as sounding boards for many of the ideas in this book. However, my heaviest debt is to Dru C. Gladney, who served as my advisor throughout this project (long before he officially "gained" that title) and who has been my professional and personal mentor ever since. With grace and generosity, he has seen me through my graduate program and beyond. I hope he finds this book worthy of the field he helped establish.

But my chief companion in the study of Yunnan and the Panthay Rebellion has been Yang Yurong, whom I first met while exploring Yunnan. She has never lost patience or confidence through all of the twists and turns that this journey has taken (even when it has taken me far from her). Without her love, laughter, and support this book would have been a far less enjoyable endeavor and, indeed, a far inferior product. It is fitting, then, that this book is being finished where it all began . . . south of the clouds in Yunnan.

D.G.A.
Kunming, China (Summer 2006)

# Foreword

*"The mountains are high and the Emperor is far away."*

Three huge rebellions swept Manchu-ruled China in the nineteenth century. The two best-known and much written about are the Han-led, semi-Christian, mildly reformist, Taiping revolt (1850–1864) and the anti-colonial Boxer Rebellion (1899–1901). The third is the subject of this indispensable account by David Atwill. The Panthay Rebellion (1856–1873) has been bracketed as a Muslim revolt and largely ignored, both inside and outside China. It was, in fact, much more complicated than that, and while it would be stretching the facts to describe it as progressive in the modern sense of the word, its leaders were open-minded and tended to avoid superstitions that were the curse of Chinese culture. A spiritualist tendency within the Chinese intelligentsia regularly prayed to the Confucian philosopher Mencius appealing for advice to help solve the country's problems. Du Wenxiu, on the other hand, the instigator of the Panthay revolt, chose to rely on the people of the Yunnan, and his message was essentially political.

All three revolts, in different ways, were harbingers of the coming fall. An atrophied Qing dynasty, the longest in Chinese history, was on its last legs. Its decision to collaborate with European imperialist powers provided the trigger for the Boxer upheavals. Ten years after their suppression, the dynasty fell and was replaced by a confused Republic.

I had no idea that there had been a Muslim Sultanate in Yunnan. When I began the last novel of my Islam Quintet, *Night of the Golden Butterfly*, I decided that it would be set in Lahore and London, but with reference to China since the heroine was a Lahori from a Chinese family. This involved a lot of research that included reading most of the translated Chinese classics and some histories. One of these was W. J. F. Jenner's *The Tyranny of History: The Roots of China's Crisis* (1992). Bill Jenner was fluent in Chinese, had worked for the Foreign Languages Publishing House in Beijing, was an ardent Maoist during his younger days and later a distinguished scholar. There was much of value in his book of disillusionment, even though I didn't appreciate the note of European condescension that sometimes crept in and disfigured his thought processes, leading him to over-stress the continuities in Chinese history. What I found in the first few pages of *The Tyranny of History* astonished me, as it had astonished Jenner:

> From Chinese accounts, contemporary or modern, one would never imagine of the Muslim rebellion in Yunnan in the third quarter of the nineteenth century that one of its leaders wrote to Queen Victoria requesting, in language rich in purely Chinese references to uprisings and sage rulers of antiquity, to be allowed to become a subject of hers. (I would never have believed this if I had not been shown a photograph of the letter by Mr Joe Ford who found it in, as I remember, India Office archives in London.) It is much harder to find indications in Chinese sources of the full diversity, ethnic and other, of the 'China' of any period than it is for a European country.

Rarely have I been so excited by such a discovery. The reason was purely instrumental: it was perfect for my novel. Work on the *Night of the Golden Butterfly* had been interrupted by the jihadi attacks on the United States in September 2001, my energies consumed by writing on the wars of the twenty-first century. I now transformed the Chinese family in Lahore that I had invented from economic to political refugees: a universal condition that follows every long war. I searched for more material in diverse publications in the Muslim world but found virtually nothing. It was the same in Europe. There was more in the United States, but nothing else in terms of quality or research that came near to David Atwill's work. I quarried it shamelessly, but with great pleasure. Today I am shocked that *Night of the Golden Butterfly* is cited in more than a few reference works on Islam in China, as though it were a history. It is not. My fictional reconstructions in the Islam Quintet never fool around with historical facts; they simply construct a scaffolding around them.

David Atwill's book is the real history of the dual power created in Yunnan by Du Wenxiu, later know as Sultan Suleiman. Atwill underlines how the outbreak of the Taiping Rebellion had shaken the Chinese Empire, whose main forces were henceforth occupied in crushing that insurgency. In Yunnan, meanwhile, 1,500 miles to the west, a series of atrocities by the Manchus and Han Chinese against the Muslim Hui Chinese and other minorities laid the basis for another resistance movement, which in due course became the Panthay Rebellion. Du Wenxiu's strategic plan was not just to inflict a temporary defeat on the Manchu Governor-General imposed on the region, but to take the entire province and possibly declare independence. An old Yunnan proverb cited by Atwill helps us to understand the self-confidence of the rebels: "The mountains are high and the Emperor is far away."

The Han Chinese had always regarded the Hui people as outsiders, interlopers, even though by the nineteenth century they had been settled in China for almost twelve centuries. The first mosque was built in the Tang capital, Chang'an (today Xi'an), in 742 CE. Muslim traders had arrived shortly after the Prophet Muhammad's death along the Silk Road and in trading vessels, and soon there were thriving Muslim communities in many Chinese port towns, from where they travelled to the interior.* Over the centuries, the Sinicized Muslims (Hui) became part of Chinese history, despite rules designed to prevent intermarriage and confine them to ghettoes. Their distinct identity was mainly a question of differing rituals, such as prohibition of pork and alcohol. The fact that Hui were used by the state as tax-collectors and became moneylenders helped the Han elites to incite popular hatred against them, a fate shared with Jews in Europe and Armenians in Ottoman lands. This came a bit later, however. The early Tang period was much more open and cosmopolitan in outlook, which explains the rapid spread of Muslim communities and a spate of voluntary conversions. In 847 an Arab, Li Yansheng, was permitted to pass the civil service exams and was appointed to a post in the Palace. The open attitude of Qubilai Khan's later Yuan Dynasty opened the Wall for new immigrants of the Muslim faith. It is a rich history.

David Atwill convincingly argues that the Panthay Rebellion was not a "Muslim" revolt as such, but a united front of many ethnic minorities in Yunnan under Hui leadership, hence the Sultanate. Du Wenxiu's political strategy was to unite Yunnan against the Qing court—its relays in the province and the Emperor—and to break the Han officials and their supporters by isolating them from ordinary Han people. The Sultan constantly stressed Hui-Han unity against the Manchu court, not without some success. To appease and please the Han population, a Forbidden City was reconstructed in Dali. The aim was to stress that the Hui were also Chinese. In the early days of the Sultanate, when large numbers of Hui queued in public to have the Manchu-imposed pigtail (or queue) removed from their heads, . many Han people joined them.

The Sultanate lasted for almost eighteen years. And as in many other cases elsewhere in the medieval and modern worlds—Sicily, al-Andalus,

---

* The domains of the Tang Empire extended to Central Asia, where serious clashes between the armies of the Prophet and the Chinese Emperor culminated in 751 when the Arab General Abu Muslim inflicted a heavy defeat on the Tang garrison in Talas, marking the permanent retreat of the Chinese from Central Asia. It was a Poitiers in reverse.

the Arab Middle East—Sultan Suleiman's bold experiment was defeated by
an imperial strategy of divide and rule. A Hui turncoat, Ma Rulong, helped
to restore Manchu rule, denigrating Suleiman for not being a proper
Muslim in order to divide the leadership of the Sultanate and its followers.
Suleiman was accused of eating pork and drinking wine. Military victory
for the Manchu brought a mass emigration of the Hui people from Yunnan
to Thailand, Burma and Vietnam, with some reaching India. It's time for
Chinese historians to study and discuss the Panthay Rebellion, regardless
of the Chinese state's continuing oppression of the Muslims of Xinjiang.

*Tariq Ali*
*July 2022*

# THE PANTHAY REBELLION

## CHAPTER I

# A Mandarin's Tale

## The End of the Beginning

On a warm summer evening in July 1857, Governor-General Heng-chun stood on the city wall of Kunming surveying the chaotic scene all around him.[1] Dragon Gate Temple, carved into the steep cliffs of the Western Hills and normally visible across Dianchi Lake, was obscured by thick columns of smoke rising from the city's burning suburbs and adjacent fields. The wealthy caravansaries, the thriving markets, and the innumerable houses outside the massive city walls had all been looted and were now in flames.[2] Thousands of city residents and refugees from other parts of the province of Yunnan had thought their capital would be safe; all had been caught in the sudden offensive of the rebel army.[3]

Hengchun knew the Chinese Empire was staggering from advances being made by the rebel leader Hong Xiuquan and his Taiping army far to the east in the strategic lower Yangtze valley. Thus, the central government was unlikely to send him either military reinforcements or funds to relieve the siege of Kunming. Yunnan was one of the poorest and most distant provinces of the Qing Empire. Its greatest value to the imperial court had been its mineral reserves, especially copper. But early in the 1800s, many of Yunnan's mines had begun to close as the quality of the copper declined, deposits were depleted, and transportation costs rose. The trade in Yunnan's famous tea was still lucrative, but except for that the province rarely drew the court's already strained attention.

As Hengchun stood on the city wall and stared bleakly at the impending destruction of his capital, perhaps the proverb common among residents of Yunnan came to his mind: "The mountains are high and the emperor is far away." It was tragically appropriate to the devastation he saw that evening and partly explained why the multiethnic rebel forces had risked attacking the provincial capital. At the very least, the proverb underscored his despair:

he had failed to protect the people of his province from the rebel hordes and the chaos that now engulfed Kunming.[4]

With the rebel forces encircling the city, Hengchun often walked the city walls, inspecting its defenses. In this way he saw the devastation firsthand—the corpses, the ransacked shops—as well as the banners of the Muslim Chinese rebels.[5] Witnesses would recount that the governor-general looked disconsolate. He sighed deeply time and again in remorse over the dreadful consequences of his decisions.[6] As a youth, he had absorbed the precepts of Confucius while preparing for his civil service examinations. He measured his worth as an official by the welfare of his people. The weight of their present suffering was thus a direct indictment of his leadership.

Governor-General Hengchun was the Qing government's ranking official in all of southwestern China. He was responsible for all that happened in Yunnan and in Guizhou Province directly to the east. When the news reached Beijing that a rebel force had besieged the provincial capital, the emperor would react swiftly and without hesitation. The central court might show a modicum of leniency over a skirmish along Yunnan's remote border areas. But Hengchun had allowed a rebel army to reach the very walls of the provincial capital and kill scores of the emperor's subjects. This was grounds for censure and perhaps dismissal, and quite conceivably for charges of official negligence.

At Kunming's broad southern gate, Hengchun paused to study the damage to the wealthiest suburbs of the city and to assess the rebels' movements on the level ground between Kunming and Dianchi Lake.[7] From where he stood he would have seen the Eastern Pagoda a few hundred yards from the wall. It was more than one hundred feet high and had been built during the Nanzhao and Dali kingdoms (c. 738–1253), in the tenth century, a time when Yunnan had been free of Chinese central control. The pagoda was a visible reminder of Yunnan's tenuous historical links to the Chinese Empire. Several months earlier Hengchun had received word that Dali, Yunnan's military and commercial center in the west, had fallen to the Yunnan rebels. The top Qing administrators stationed there had been beheaded, and a king appointed.[8] Was he witnessing the beginning of a new era of Yunnan autonomy? Was the rise of a rebel government in Dali, Nanzhao's former capital, an omen? With Kunming now under siege, the end of Qing rule in Yunnan—and his own demise—were all too conceivable. It was little consolation to him that the events that had ignited this violence had taken place the previous year while he was away in Guizhou. Only after his return had he pieced together that sequence of horrifying events.

It had all begun the previous year when the emperor ordered Hengchun to Guizhou to suppress an uprising by members of the Miao ethnic group. He departed from the capital, leaving Yunnan governor Shuxing'a to oversee the provincial bureaucracy in his absence. Shuxing'a, like Hengchun, was of Manchu ethnicity. Unfortunately, he suffered from a debilitating mental condition (*zhengchun chong*) whose symptoms were melancholia, memory loss, and fatigue.[9] His increasingly unstable health prevented him from carrying out more than a small part of his administrative duties in Hengchun's absence. Furthermore, he detested Muslims (which Hengchun did not). He blamed them for his poor health, which he firmly believed was the result of his dealings with Muslim Chinese many decades earlier, when he served in China's predominately Muslim northwestern frontier.[10] That Muslims were only 10 percent of Yunnan's multiethnic population did little to soften his enmity toward the province's Hui community. In his view, their powerful position as merchants, caravaneers, miners, and soldiers lent them, as he put it, "strength far greater than their numbers."[11]

After Hengchun left Kunming in early 1856, a strongly anti-Muslim faction quickly began to take hold in Kunming. Composed of high provincial officials, including the provincial judge (*fansi*), the local elite, and several powerful retired officials, this group fomented a policy of "attacking the Muslims in order to exterminate the Muslims."[12] These people organized and guided a reign of terror against the Muslims in Kunming. Those who opposed this faction's tactics were labeled traitors to the people (*hanjian*) and arrested.[13]

This orchestrated violence peaked on May 19, 1856, when Qingsheng, the provincial judge, issued orders allowing "the authorized slaying [of Muslims] without being held accountable [*gesha wulun*]"—a directive some say was miswritten when posted to read "kill them one and all."[14] As one Chinese official described it: "Then every Muslim family within the provincial capital, regardless if they were men or women, young or old, were all mercilessly killed."[15] The massacre lasted three days and three nights. The city's five mosques were looted and torched. Within seventy-two hours, as many as four thousand Muslims had been slaughtered. Several witnesses would later contend that the numbers were two or three times that.[16]

The governor-general had been detained fighting the Miao through the summer and into the fall and did not return to Kunming until early January 1857, months after the massacre.[17] At first he blamed "the murdering of a few innocent Hui" on Qingsheng's ill-worded proclamation and the excessive vigilantism of "unlawful Han traitors."[18] Slowly, however, he concluded that although violent attacks had been carried out by both Muslims and Han, the violence had escalated as a result of anti-Muslim sentiment among local, regional, and provincial Yunnan officials. Worried that their virulent hatred would only increase the violence, he warned the imperial court in Beijing that "if the extermination of the Hui is the only goal [of the Han Chinese], not only will the Muslims never yield, but it will precipitate

the Han's suffering."[19] Then he acted on his belief by implementing a policy of nonprovocation.[20] Hengchun was correct in stating that the Han had
led the attacks, but he was ignoring the fear and hostility the massacre had
generated among the Muslim Chinese and other Yunnanese ethnic groups.

Now, on July 19, 1857, fourteen months after the massacre of the city's
Muslims, Hengchun watched hopelessly from atop the southern gate as his
last attempt to break the siege failed.[21] The Hui Islamic rebels, led by Ma
Dexin and two of his former students, Xu Yuanji and Ma Rulong, routed
Hengchun's remaining troops.[22] With his defeated soldiers in front of him
and the destroyed Muslim quarter directly behind him, Hengchun knew his
fellow officials had deceived him, and despair overwhelmed him.[23]

Hengchun sighed again, grief-stricken that he had been deceived. Only
after his return to Kunming had he realized that his closest aides had been
undermining his work. In particular, Shuxing'a despite his illness had ex-
ploited Hengchun's absence from Kunming and Yunnan's growing instability to promote a more combative solution to the Muslim violence. "If we
do not use force there is no way to bring an end to the Muslim bandits'
wrath," he had insisted in a memorial to the emperor, "and in particular no
way to calm the Han Chinese's heart."[24] For many years the imperial court
had emphasized, specifically with regard to Yunnan's ethnic violence, "distinguishing between good and bad [character], not between Han and Muslim." Hengchun had tried to follow this policy in his pursuit of peace.[25]
However, given the choice between Hengchun's approach and that of Shuxing'a, the young Xianfeng emperor (or those court officials acting in his
name) now preferred action. He demoted Hengchun one official rank and
rebuked him, allowing him to retain his office but informing him that it was
not enough to "simply sit and protect the provincial capital while doing
nothing else."[26]

Hengchun gazed sadly over the consequences of his foolish optimism,
the emperor's words weighing heavily on his mind. In spite of the emperor's
stern admonition, he had continued to deploy his troops sparingly. In the
spring of 1857, it seemed to him that his strategy was beginning to work. In
and around Dianchi Lake and the broad plain surrounding Kunming, an
uneasy calm had returned.[27] Many Kunming residents had begun to venture
outside the city walls during the day to work their fields and tend to their
businesses, returning to the safety of the city walls at night. Then on July 12
the tranquility ended: a Muslim force ten thousand strong burst onto the
Kunming plain, to the complete surprise of provincial officials and Kunming
residents. Hengchun, who had done almost nothing to prepare for such an
event, immediately ordered the city gates closed. In doing so he was abandoning tens of thousands to the rebels' wrath and ensuring that thousands
would die.[28]

The city had now been under siege for a week, and the failed sortie by his troops had been Hengchun's last hope. He could see no way to extricate himself or his city from this crisis. Shoulders slumped, he climbed down from the city wall and returned to his official residence (*yamen*) in the Wuhua district in the center of Kunming. That evening the city's residents watched the flames and listened to the shouts of the Muslim rebels, whose plundering continued through the night.[29]

Late that night, in despair that his misguided efforts had failed to lift the siege, Hengchun sat down at his desk and wrote his last official communication. He apologized to the emperor for his failures and stated repeatedly that the situation in Yunnan was overwhelming. He then wrote "that by dying I hope I might compensate for my inabilities as governor-general."[30] He set down his brush and placed the letter on his bed. Then, side by side, he and his wife hanged themselves.[31]

Hengchun's suicide on that July night in 1857 brought to an end any hope for a peaceful end to the conflict in Yunnan between Muslim and Han Chinese. More critically, the court and the empire now realized belatedly that the hostilities in Yunnan could no longer be treated as a series of isolated incidents. The Qing Empire was facing a rebellion—the Panthay Rebellion.

## The Foundations of Resentment

The strong response of the Muslim Yunnanese to the Kunming Massacre caught Qing officials off guard, perhaps because Han-led massacres of the Hui were nothing new to nineteenth-century Yunnan. The scale of the anti-Hui violence perpetrated by Han Chinese officials in the fifteen-odd years leading up to the rebellion was staggering. In 1839 a local military official organized a Han militia that, with the implicit consent of ranking civil officials, killed 1,700 Hui in the border town of Mianning. Six years later, in the early morning of October 2, 1845, local Qing officials, with the covert assistance of bands from the Han secret societies, barred the gates of the city of Baoshan in southwestern Yunnan and carried out a three-day cleansing (*xicheng*) of the Hui populace.[32] More than eight thousand Muslim Yunnanese, men and women, young and old, were slaughtered.[33]

It is perhaps not surprising that these and other massacres heightened Han antagonisms rather than assuaging them. As described earlier, the government's collusion in these massacres culminated in early 1856 when, in the absence of Governor-General Hengchun, the Han elite and ranking civil and military officials in Kunming set into motion a plan to eradicate the Hui.[34] The causes of the anti-Hui sentiment that fueled these massacres are unclear; that said, one obvious factor was that more and more Han immigrants were flowing into the province.

In the latter part of the eighteenth century, Yunnan underwent a dramatic transformation. With population growth placing immense pressure on China's already overpopulated interior, Han Chinese, encouraged by incentives from the central government, began migrating in ever increasing numbers to Yunnan. Between 1775 and 1850 the province's population increased from an estimated four million to roughly ten million.[35] Immigration *per se* was not new to the region: ever since its integration into the Chinese Empire under the Yuan, Yunnan had been a magnet for internal migrants. However, this new wave was composed almost entirely of Han immigrants; in this, it was profoundly dissimilar to preceding waves, which had been ethnically diverse.

These new Han settlers differed from the local Han, who for generations had lived alongside the Muslim Yunnanese (Hui) and the indigenous non-Han groups. The new immigrants tended to be far more assertive than the Han who arrived earlier.[36] For example, they occupied non-Han lands illegally, appropriated productive mines by force, and both submitted to and helped enforce the economic and political strictures of the Qing government. Yunnan's transregional ties had traditionally been with Tibet and Southeast Asia; the new Han were seeking to turn the region toward China.[37]

This influx of Han settlers led to widespread violence between the newcomers and the established Yunnanese, and the Han directed most of their animosity toward the Hui. Why this was so is unclear. Perhaps it was because the Hui dominated the same occupations (mining, trading, agriculture) sought by the Han and were more numerous than other non-Han in the Han-dominated urban centers. Perhaps it was because the Hui were well familiar with Chinese laws and with their rights as Qing subjects, and thus were able to defend themselves more effectively than the other ethnic groups the Han encountered. The new Han arrivals would have resented this. Whatever the reasons, by the early nineteenth century, disputes between the Han settlers and the Hui had escalated into large-scale confrontations during which Qing officials sided more and more with the Han.[38] This rising anti-Hui sentiment culminated in the Kunming Massacre of 1856, which led to the Panthay Rebellion and, after Hengchun's death, the loss of imperial control over much of the province.

One of the many paradoxes of the Panthay Rebellion is that while many Han actively despised the Muslim Yunnanese, the Yunnan Hui were arguably the most sinified non-Han group in Yunnan. This is especially ironic given that Yunnan was home to a broad spectrum of ethnic groups—groups far less "civilized" as well as less tolerant of Chinese society and governance. Despite this, the Han consistently differentiated the Hui both from the indigenous non-Han population and from themselves. Chinese documents (both popular and imperial) routinely divided the population of Yunnan into three categories: Han, Hui, and *yi*. The Hui were not included in the non-Han indigenous category in large part because of the prominent and well-documented role they had played in the Mongol Conquest of 1254, which had fully integrated Yunnan into China after several centuries of independence under the Nanzhao (738–902) and Dali (937–1253) kingdoms. The central court of the Yuan had at first considered Muslims more trustworthy than either the indigenous Yunnanese or the Chinese; as a consequence, the Muslim Yunnanese often attained the highest local and regional offices in the Ming and early Qing bureaucracies.[39]

The Hui had retained a strong sense of identity over the centuries and tended to live together in their own villages or neighborhoods and to work together in occupations such as mining and the caravan trade. Perhaps because of their success in these ventures, the Hui were described by the Han in some rebellion-era accounts as "full of strength and able to endure hardship, full of vitality, fierce and brave."[40] However, terms applied to the Hui more often than not expressed disapproval: fierce (*han*), combative (*xidou*), and assertive (*qiang*). Such terms inevitably led to the Hui being characterized as having "a propensity to stir up trouble."[41] Also, the Hui prohibited the eating of pork. The Han found this incomprehensible and often used it as the differentiating marker between Han and Hui.[42]

Despite these perceived differences and the liminal status of the Muslim Yunnanese, to be Hui was never seen as antithetical to being "Chinese" or a Qing subject. The state did not see it that way and neither did the Hui themselves. In addition, the elements that defined one as Hui were not necessarily the same as those that defined one as Muslim. Many nineteenth-century Hui did not base their identity solely on religious faith; they also based it on occupation, community solidarity, and putative common origins.[43] Significantly, Han antagonism toward the Hui in the nineteenth century was based more on assumed behaviors or "customs" and specific practices (violence, cross-border trading, and the like) than on religion. As will soon be clear with regard to the Panthay Rebellion, the boundaries of religion, ethnicity, and other salient categories—boundaries that today are often perceived as sharply etched—were at the time considerably more fluid.

## Reframing the Panthay Rebellion

The Panthay Rebellion, more than any other event in Yunnan's history, has dominated both Chinese and Western representations of the Yunnan Hui in historical treatises. The theoretical frameworks employed in these narratives diverge in many ways, but they all filter the insurrection through the political and military lenses of the Chinese center; they also perpetuate two fundamentally false assumptions. The first is that the rebellion was rooted solely in Hui hatred of the Han Chinese. The second is that the rebellion was primarily Islamic in orientation. Both assumptions have had the effect of dismissing out of hand the significant contributions to the rebellion's success of Yunnan's myriad indigenous groups and their local Han Chinese allies.[44]

I challenge both assumptions. In doing so I am deliberately positioning this study of the Yunnan Hui and their role in the Panthay Rebellion at the intersection of two contentious debates in Chinese and Islamic studies. The controversy in Chinese studies centers on the utility of the terms "ethnicity" and "ethnic groups" when discussing the peoples of various cultures in nineteenth-century China.[45] In their studies of the Manchu culture and Qing rule, Evelyn Rawski and Pamela Crossley have recently asserted that to apply the term "ethnicity" "to earlier periods is anachronistic and distorts the historical reality."[46] Challenging this stance, Mark Elliot proposes that "thinking about the Manchus in ethnic terms is helpful because it enables us to . . . understand Manchu ethnic coherence in spite of apparent cultural incoherence."[47]

Similarly, within Islamic studies in China there has been an ongoing dispute, at times vociferous, over whether the Hui should be viewed solely as an ethnic or religious group in the late imperial era.[48] In this study, a primary concern is the manner in which the Hui expressed their faith, identity, and resistance during the Panthay Rebellion and how that expression challenges assumptions that are fundamental to both debates. The Panthay Rebellion marked the zenith of Hui dominion in Yunnan, yet few accounts of the rebellion focus on the Yunnan Hui and Yunnan society.

Yunnan Province is in the southwest corner of China, bounded by the Tibetan Plateau to the northwest, tropical Southeast Asia to the south, and the mountainous Chinese provinces of Sichuan, Guizhou, and Guangxi to the north and east. For centuries this area constituted the outermost zone of imperial control. Yunnan's varied topography, and its unique geographical position at the confluence of Tibetan, Chinese, and Southeast Asian cultures, made for an ethnically diverse population unlike any other in China. This multiethnicity, more than any other factor, would set the course of the Panthay Rebellion.

Conventional accounts too often overemphasize the part played by the Muslim Yunnanese in the decades of violence that led up to the rebellion and in the rebellion itself. Yet even a cursory reading of the sources reveals that many indigenous groups besides the Muslim Yunnanese were resisting the rising economic, cultural, and political pressures generated by increased Han immigration to Yunnan. Indeed, perhaps the greatest miscalculation made by the anti-Hui faction in Kunming related to the degree of non-Han support the Hui would receive: there was much more than expected. In almost every memorial he submitted to the throne, Hengchun tried to impress on the court that the Hui enjoyed widespread support among other non-Han groups; yet the emperor continued to believe that his other non-Han subjects would remain loyal to the Qing.[49] In his memorials, Hengchun stressed the fact that in every region of Yunnan, non-Han ethnic groups were collaborating with the Hui. His warnings were all too prescient. In the 1857 siege of Kunming non-Han troops would constitute a large proportion of the rebels and ultimately drive him to suicide.[50]

By downplaying the role of the non-Han peoples, later Chinese and Western narratives have perpetuated two myths: that the Panthay Rebellion was purely a Han–Hui conflict; and—an even greater error—that the uprising was launched entirely by the Hui. The most widely read account of the rebellion is the one by Taiwanese scholar Wang Shuhuai; his conclusion has become the standard explanation offered by Western historians for the rebellion: "The misunderstanding between the Han and the Hui, was originally based on mutual enmity and hostility, beginning with simple misconceptions and discord and then eventually evolving into a battle between the two groups, which was compounded by government officials improperly handling [the situation] with the Manchu and Han becoming one, causing the Hui to hate the Han and oppose the officials."[51]

Although not entirely false, this interpretation is exceedingly deceptive in that it overemphasizes ethnic and religious divisions. In fact, various Han, Hui, and non-Han groups fought both for and against the Qing.[52] A variant of this dualistic misconception is that ethnic tensions were heightened by economic tensions in Yunnan's mines.[53] What both of these now-standard depictions disregard is that the rebellion flowed out of a decade-long campaign of violence orchestrated by Han militias and Qing officials whose goal was to exterminate the Hui. Thus we cannot unearth the rebellion's foundations if we focus exclusively on the Hui to the point of ignoring Yunnan's multiethnic context.

Even the names given to the rebellion preserve this misconception. Chinese works on it have generally referred to it as the Hui Rebellion (*Huimin qiyi*).[54] Many historians in the People's Republic of China make this distinction even more precise by labeling it the Du Wenxiu Rebellion (*Du Wenxiu qiyi*)—Du Wenxiu being the leader of the Hui, who established a government in the western Yunnan city of Dali.[55] This label further muddles the picture by implying that the rebellion was limited to those acts committed in Du Wenxiu's name. This assertion is inaccurate: many rebels associated themselves only indirectly with Du and his government or spurned his leadership entirely.

Such labels are especially misleading because they reflect a tendency to equate the Panthay Rebellion in Yunnan with Muslim uprisings in northwestern China during the same era.[56] In fact, the Panthay rebels maintained their independence from Qing oversight for a longer time than the north-western rebels; furthermore, there was little or no substantive contact be-tween the two centers.

The most common term in English for the insurrection, "Panthay Rebel-lion," is a slightly more nettlesome affair. Even before the uprising ended in 1873, British travelers had baptized it the "Panthay Rebellion."[57] Yet the term "Panthay" is unknown to almost all Muslim Yunnanese. Most schol-ars agree that it came from a Burmese term—"*pa-ti*," meaning Muslims.[58] Even while it was entering common parlance, use of the term was being questioned. Many British travelers returning from Burma and Yunnan dur-ing the rebellion asserted that the term was "utterly unknown in the coun-try that was temporarily under the domination of Sultan Suliman [Du Wenxiu]."[59] In the decades after the rebellion the use of "Panthay" to mean Muslim Yunnanese faded from English-language treatments, yet it is still the most common name given to the rebellion itself.

Yet the term "Panthay Rebellion" still has its uses. First, it highlights the multifaceted nature of the Muslim Yunnanese and of their and Yunnan's strong ties with Southeast Asia. Second, it prevents any inadvertent con-flation between the Muslim-led resistance in Yunnan and the Muslim up-risings in northwestern China. Finally, although a misnomer in some re-spects (like the "Boxer Rebellion"), the term is now so widely recognized that coining a new one would result in more ambiguity than clarity.

Above all, this study seeks to shift the analysis of the Panthay Rebellion from the concerns and worries of the imperial court to the multitudinous complexities of the transregional, multiethnic world of Yunnan. Because of the prominent role the Muslim Yunnanese played in it, most studies of the rebellion and of the Hui have myopically ignored the complexities of this multiethnic region. To focus exclusively on the violent incidents involving the Han and the Muslim Yunnanese is to ignore the broader context: the multiethnic frictions that infested Yunnan throughout the early 1800s. What makes the Muslim-led Panthay Rebellion (1856–73) so compelling is the ambivalence of the various peoples of Yunnan toward one another and the intricate web of actions and reactions among them.

CHAPTER 2

# South of the Clouds:
# The World of Nineteenth-Century Yunnan

Framed by the remote upper reaches of the Yangtze River to the north, by the lofty Himalayan peaks of Tibet to the west, and by the steamy highlands of Southeast Asia to the south, Yunnan Province marked the southwestern limit of Qing control in the mid-nineteenth century. Chinese imperial sources dating back more than two thousand years have consistently labeled this region Yunnan—literally, the land "south of the clouds." According to traditional lore, the name "Yunnan" denoted the region's position just south of the misty, humid, and often overcast Sichuan Basin. "South of the clouds" suited the image of the region held by outsiders; figuratively speaking, Yunnan was obscured by drifting clouds that allowed only enigmatic glimpses of a distant horizon. Indeed, this region "south of the clouds" was dramatically different, both in its external realities and in people's minds.

The view of nineteenth-century Yunnan from the north—that of the Manchu imperial court in Beijing and of most of China's Qing subjects—was strongly influenced by the cultural, ethnic, and climatic differences between Yunnan and the rest of the empire. For Chinese outside the province, simply uttering the two characters—*yun nan*—immediately conjured up a multitude of fantastic images. Illustrated albums depicting menacing tribesmen wielding clubs and titillating "courtship meetings" between ethnically non-Chinese couples circulated widely among the Chinese. Epic stories such as the *Three Kingdoms*—repeated for centuries and familiar to most Chinese—reinforced the notion that Yunnan was a distant place inhabited by "savages."[1]

Yunnan was notorious for other reasons. Widely circulated travelers' tales reported mysterious blue, green, and red *zhangqi* (poisonous clouds), which caused bleeding from one's ears, nose, eyes, and mouth. And then there were stories of seasonal *shuyi* (rat epidemics), which were always preceded by the appearance of dead rats. An infected person could wake up healthy and be dead before nightfall.[2] These two diseases are now known as malaria and bubonic plague; both continue to afflict Yunnanese. Finally,

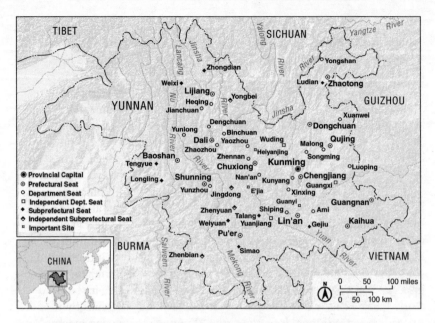

MAP 2.1. Yunnan Province (with administrative seats), circa 1800

there was the fact that Yunnan was among the more dreaded destinations of Chinese convicts sentenced to internal exile. This last detail sealed the province's sinister reputation throughout the Chinese heartlands.

The view from the south—from the lowland kingdoms of Ava (Burma), Siam (Thailand), and Vietnam—although less vivid than the one from China, was equally otherworldly. Malarial valleys and the fierce reputation of the multiethnic peoples of the mountainous Shan States acted as a potent barrier between lowland Southeast Asians and Yunnanese. The lowland kingdoms gleaned most of their knowledge of Yunnan from the thriving caravan trade—a trade that provided highly desirable goods such as silk, tea, and medicines. The overland route also offered a means for Southeast Asia to market its cotton and salt as well as (by the nineteenth century) a growing array of British manufactured goods.[3]

Dealings between Yunnan and Southeast Asia were conducted mainly through the ethnic groups inhabiting the borderlands between the two. Several of these groups established semiautonomous states (such as Lanna and the larger Shan States); others (such as the Kachin, Dai, and Miao) were more loosely associated. These groups controlled the region's commercial and mineral resources. Intimate, and often illicit, political alliances and trade networks bound Yunnan to Southeast Asia. Though quite conspicuous at the local level, the interregional links were often beyond the administrative reach of both the lowland Southeast Asian political centers and the Qing court in faraway Beijing.[4]

Relations between Yunnan and Tibet to the northwest were heavily dependent upon the strong ethnic affinities that facilitated the commercial dealings with the eastern Tibetan state of Kham. Every year, attracted by Yunnan's salt wells and famous tea and by its many commercial fairs, Tibetan traders plied the long-distance trade routes that stretched deep into Yunnan—even as far as Xishuangbanna, to which "several thousand Tibetan traders annually" traveled to purchase tea.[5] Official Chinese sources often overlooked or simply ignored the fact that Yunnan played a prominent role in Tibetan Buddhist traditions because of its many pilgrimage sites. Every year, sacred Buddhist mountains in western Yunnan attracted countless Tibetan Buddhists.[6] In the late nineteenth century, one European observer remarked that the Tibetans' "first visit is to Jizu Mountain situated a day's march northeast of Dali, where some celebrated Buddhist temples are situated. From thence they visit Weibaoshan, near Menghua, where the Taoist temples are, and they pass through Dali again on their return. There are seen here often amongst them many Fakirs—called Lamas by the Yunnanese as well as Tibetans—with their pointed caps, praying machine and double-faced drum."[7]

Yunnan's relations with eastern Tibet were similar to those it had with Southeast Asia. The distant political centers were only dimly aware how the religious and commercial networks seamlessly linked the two regions to each other.

At the intersection of China, Tibet, and Southeast Asia, Yunnanese society reflected overlapping ethnicities, polities, and cultures. Yunnan's multiple and often illicit commercial, ethnic, and political connections evaded official Qing channels and called into question traditional representations that placed the imperial court at the center of all of China's interactions with neighboring political centers. This court-centered perspective—which by the nineteenth century was also an outmoded one—disregarded the multilateral and transnational nature of the Yunnan world, a world that heeded the Qing presence but often circumvented its centralized bureaucracy.

A closer approximation of this local reality might be Stanley Tambiah's conception of a "galactic polity." As he conceived it, this model emphasizes distant centers that exert a "gravitational pull" on a variety of regional peoples, communities, and polities. Tambiah's model offers a more nuanced alternative to the traditional center/periphery perspective of the sort the Qing court employed to support its notion of hierarchical tributary relations.[8] By emphasizing the multiple ties of border communities, Tambiah's notion of "galactic polities" substitutes the Qing court's static notion of a steady and perpetual imperial presence with a concept that reflects more closely the fluctuating attractions between nominal tributary states and the various political centers. His model inserts the prevailing autonomy of peoples and territories into our schema of frontier societies; however, it does little to acknowledge the perspective from the periphery and from those who live there.

Tambiah is not alone in failing to acknowledge this perspective. Most conceptual approaches that attempt to factor in the roles played by the "borderlands" in early modern China and lowland Southeast Asia have adopted externalist frameworks (such as galactic polity, concentric circles, or zones of authority) that consider these borderlands only in relation to their centers. In doing so, they adopt a bipolar perspective that disregards the pervasive notions of centrality exhibited by the peoples of Yunnan. At the same time, they minimize both the multiplicity and the significance of the commercial, political, and cultural projects present in the Yunnan world. These projects, although they interacted with multiple polities, did not "orbit" any single state exclusively; more often, the Yunnanese juggled their relations with multiple dominant albeit distant powers.[9]

Only after we adopt a regionally informed perspective can we begin to discern that the primary concerns of Yunnan were not inextricably linked to the interests of the distant imperial center; rather, they were balanced with matters of regional and local significance. Once we take this path— that is, once we step outside the dualistic framework—we can begin to understand the actions of the Yunnanese. These people were not simply for or against the Chinese state; they were not simply functioning inside or outside state-proscribed channels of interaction. Rather, their actions were often motivated and shaped by local contingencies. Having decentered our perspective in this way, we can begin to enter the hazy world south of the clouds, the world of nineteenth-century Yunnan.

## Yunnanese Landscapes

Chinese tourist brochures today promote Yunnan's southern location and reputation for mild weather by quoting the first line of a poem that describes the province as a paradise where *siji ruchun* ("the four seasons are all like spring"). In many ways, this reputation is justified. With its average elevation of six thousand feet, Yunnan suffers neither the punishing winters of northern China nor the sweltering summers of the southeast. Yunnan's mile-high elevation alters the climate in other, unanticipated ways, as is apparent in the (rarely mentioned) remaining three lines of the poem:

> When the sun shines, it is like summer;
> With the slightest shadow, it is like autumn;
> As soon as it rains, it is like winter.[10]

When read in its entirety, the poem offers a hazy, rather ambiguous portrayal of Yunnan and hints at the complexities of its physical landscape.

## REGIONAL LANDSCAPES

Topographically, Yunnan resembles a swath of rippled silk pinned to the eastern end of the Tibetan Plateau; it cascades precipitously down to the tropical lowlands of the south and less dramatically to the Yunnan–Guizhou Plateau in the east. The land is rugged, serrated, and unforgiving. Its towering mountain ranges are divided by temperate valleys and scored by deep gorges.[11] Yunnan's topography profoundly influenced its people's conceptions of their land. Indeed, the major topographical variations resulted in the province being rendered by most Yunnanese as being composed of three regions: western, southern, and eastern.

Western Yunnan, bordered by Tibet to the north and Burma to the south, is characterized by deep river gorges and lofty mountain ridges. In this region four of Asia's greatest rivers—the *Dulong jiang* (Irrawaddy), *Nu jiang* (Salween), *Lancang jiang* (Mekong), and *Jinsha jiang* (Yangtze)—flow within sixty miles of one another. Yet they never converge, nor are they navigable until well beyond Yunnan's borders. In addition to this ruggedness, western Yunnan has abundant forests and many fertile valleys with rich soil and plentiful rainfall. Western Yunnan was not as isolated as many borderlands in central China. In its northern and southern corners, two of the province's most prosperous cities, Lijiang and Baoshan, benefited enormously from their proximity to Tibet and Burma, respectively. The main trade routes from these two cities to the center of Yunnan converged in Dali, the administrative capital and trading emporium for the region.

Eastern Yunnan is dominated by the massive Yunnan Plateau; however, it can hardly be called flat. One nineteenth-century traveler described the plateau as "everywhere broken by hills and cut through by rivers, and in some parts even traversed by mountain ranges."[12] The provincial capital, Kunming, is in the middle of this region, on a fertile plain beside Dianchi, Yunnan's largest lake. In the nineteenth century, Dongchuan northeast of the capital was the hub of the copper-mining industry; Zhaotong served as the gateway to Sichuan and the Yangtze River. Today, roads and rail lines in eastern Yunnan snake back and forth over the defiant topography; journeys of one hundred miles as the crow flies are epic day-long journeys.

In great contrast, southern Yunnan is mostly tropical and subtropical lowlands. This region lies entirely south of the Tropic of Cancer. It resembles eastern Yunnan except that the pine forests give way to palm trees and rain forests. Because it drops steadily in elevation, southern Yunnan serves as a natural causeway linking the province commercially to the highlands of Southeast Asia. In the nineteenth century, Lin'an, the region's prosperous administrative center, gained prominence as Yunnan's intellectual center. Far to the south, in the tea-growing districts, the market town of Pu'er profited from the demand for tea and from its proximity to the trade routes to Burma and Thailand.

By the nineteenth century the three regions were highly distinct entities, to the point that the people viewed their province largely as the sum of its three parts. When the Qing gained control of Yunnan in the late seventeenth century, the triadic administrative structure they implemented mirrored the local realities of the area. In addition, the Qing grouped together the prefectures and counties in each of the three regions and appointed a military commander for each. The new administrative divisions reinforced the physical, ethnic, and cultural realities that affected all aspects of Yunnanese life. By the eighteenth century, the term *sanyi* (three regions) was used as a shorthand term for the province as a whole among Qing officials and local residents alike.

### COMMERCIAL LANDSCAPES

Yunnan's imposing terrain decisively shaped its commercial networks. These networks connected the province's three regions with one another and with neighboring polities. That Yunnan's topography had a strong impact is seen in the fact that distances were measured not by standard units of length but rather by the number of stages (or days) it took to travel from one point to the next. And even this system was contingent on the direction and gradient of the road the traveler was taking.

Outsiders such as Edward Baber, a nineteenth-century British civil servant sent to Yunnan from Burma to explore trading opportunities, often declared themselves bewildered by the local system for measuring distances between towns. Inevitably, residents of the town where Baber began his day's journey offered estimates of the distance to his destination that differed from those given by the inhabitants of his destination at day's end. Only after he realized that the distances he was being told were calculated according to the difficulty of grade—thus making the journey from a mountaintop village to the valley bottom shorter than the reverse—did he finally arrive at the following scale of conversion: "The scale of distance is something like this:

On level ground 1 statute mile is called 2 li [Chinese mile]
On ordinary hill-roads, not very steep, 1 mile is called 5 li
On very steep roads, 1 mile is called 15 li."[13]

But the impact of Yunnan's ridges and valleys on travel went far beyond making one mile seem like five. What one observer bemoaned as Yunnan's "everlasting hills" indelibly colored the patterns of Yunnan society, culture, and commerce.[14] At the best of times, to traverse the province from southwest to northeast, from the Burmese border town of Bhamô through Kunming to the Yangtze town of Suifu, required at least sixty-six days. A journey from Pu'er in southern Yunnan to Deqin on the Tibetan borderlands required at least sixty-three days.[15]

Historical records for Yunnan make very clear the impact the topography had on the movement of goods and people. To begin with, Yunnan's steep roads precluded wheeled traffic outside the large towns and valley bottoms. At every steep ascent the roads gave way to carved stone steps. In some places these steps were too steep even for mules, which meant that human porters were required to transport goods.[16] Yunnan's many rivers offered no relief from all this since they flowed swiftly through deep gorges and rarely linked population centers of any size.

Another deterrent to trade was the dilapidated condition of the roads. Their state of disrepair validated emphatically the Chinese proverb that "a road is good for ten years and bad for ten thousand." Alexander Hosie, who traveled throughout Yunnan in the 1880s, offered a humorous account of this:

To say that the road was best where there was no road may seem paradoxical. It is nevertheless true, for where the paving had disappeared, fine battened sand or clay gave an excellent foothold except when it rained. In many places paved mounds rose in the middle of the roadway and these were carefully avoided by man and beast. Not infrequently, too, so distorted was the paving that it had every appearance of having been convulsed by an earthquake.[17]

Away from the main trunk roads, traffic snailed along routes that were little more than footpaths. These often skirted plunging cliffs where a single misstep would mean certain death. Well into the twentieth century, bridges consisting of nothing more than two frayed ropes strung hundreds of feet in the air were often the only means of crossing Yunnan's deep river gorges.[18]

However poor their quality, these routes were crucial economic conduits, and they carried considerable traffic between the commercial centers and the smaller towns and markets. Unfortunately, few accounts survive from Yunnanese caravaneers and porters. We do have the account of Augustus Margary, who traveled by sedan chair along Yunnan's main road from Kunming to Dali in 1875, and who captured the daily hazards of Yunnan's heavily trafficked roads:

It is far from being an easy task to describe the incredible obstacles which are suffered to remain unheeded on this track. . . . It is full of steep passes, the chief of which rises 3,500 feet, and the track by which it is surmounted is simply a chaos of deep ruts and broken stones, offering the acme of dangerous footing to animals as well as carriers. Chair-bearers have to be supplemented by six or eight coolies dragging a rope passed round the chair, and even with this aid it is difficult to conceive how they retain their footing at the rate they press up the incline. . . . In many places the steep path has a horizontal slope as well, and to complicate the danger, pack animals passing both ways have to be avoided.[19]

Several months after writing these words, Margary encountered another common hazard of travel in Yunnan: his caravan was attacked by bandits. The young envoy was murdered, which led to one of the most infamous diplomatic incidents of the late nineteenth century, the Margary Affair.[20]

With the roads too steep and badly maintained for wheeled traffic and the rivers unnavigable for any distance, commodities had to be transported by mule caravans.[21] A typical Yunnanese long-distance caravan had between twenty and one hundred animals; some of the larger ones had more than five hundred. The province's muleteers were organized into formal and informal guilds (as was typical for most professions in nineteenth-century China). These guilds, like most organizations in Yunnan society, were divided internally along lines of ethnicity and place of origin.[22]

The Yunnan caravans were colorful affairs. Foreign travelers almost always noted the elaborate decorations of the Tibetan and Muslim Yunnanese caravans. As Edward Colborne Baber observed in the 1870s: "The head of the leading mule was completely hidden in an elaborate ornament of coloured wool and silver buttons, and plumed with a *panace* of the tail feathers of the Amherst pheasant. All the succeeding animals some twenty in number, bore aigrettes of the same description."[23]

These decorations reflected the wealth to be gained from being a muleteer. Clearly, caravans played a crucial economic role in Yunnan. In a province where a livelihood was difficult to earn, caravaning provided one of the best ways available for Yunnanese to scratch out a living.

Shared commercial objectives, widespread reliance on caravans, and the exigencies of Yunnan's rugged topography promoted a sense of "Yunnaneseness" among the province's long-time residents. When a European inquired about their identity, a resident of Kunming told him: "We are not Chinese, we are Yunnanese."[24] The transnational orientation of most long-time Yunnanese did much to forge this identity: the province looked toward Tibet and Southeast Asia. This was evident as early as the seventeenth century, when a Yunnan gazetteer highlighted:

> Yuanjiang, Lin'an, are the gateways for the non-Chinese peoples of Thailand, Laos, Viet Nam.
> Tengyue, Yongchang, and Shunning are the key avenues for the non-Chinese peoples of Burma.
> Lijiang, Yongning, and Beisheng are the strategic outposts for Tibet.[25]

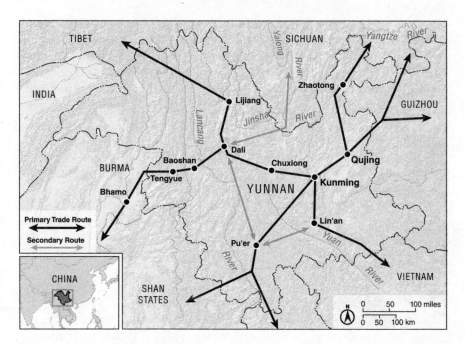

MAP 2.2. Yunnan Trade Routes

Yunnan's transnational orientation was more than a matter of geography. There were diverse other factors, from trade to ethnic familiarity. A map of Yunnan's primary trade routes might suggest that Kunming, the capital, was the province's economic hub and principal entrepôt (see Figure 2.2). In fact, quite the opposite was true. Because it was so expensive to transport goods across Yunnan, most commodities were imported from neighboring polities. In this sense, Kunming was the "end of the line" for most products.

The shipping of goods by caravan across Yunnan was governed by the high-profit / low-bulk principle. In other words, the less bulky the item, the higher the profit obtained. In the equally mountainous neighboring province of Guizhou typically "two days transport was all most agricultural goods could pay."[26] This was likely true for Yunnan as well. In the nineteenth century only Yunnan tea and opium could consistently overcome the substantial markup in price and thereby pay well enough to make shipment outside the region worthwhile. In the nineteenth century the Qing court still looked to Yunnan's mines as its principal source of copper (and to a lesser extent silver and tin), but this was only possible because the price of copper had been pegged artificially low and because the overland transportation of that metal to Beijing was heavily subsidized.[27]

The commercial barriers Yunnan faced because of its topography compelled each of the three regions to import needed goods from the closest adjacent lowland regions, be they Chinese or not. One nineteenth-century observer outlined Yunnan's transnational trade in cotton and tobacco, showing how each region in the province reached outward for the cheapest and closest sources: "Thus, to take two examples, cotton and tobacco, both absolute necessities to Chinese existence, which the [Yunnan] plateau does not produce: cotton is supplied to North Yunnan from Sichuan, to West Yunnan as far east as Kunming from Burma, to Southwest Yunnan as far east as Mengzi from the Shan States and Siam, to Southeast Yunnan from Canton, and to Guizhou from Hankou by the Yuan River."[28]

Only by yielding to topographical realities (and often ethnic ones as well) could Yunnan function. By the nineteenth century, Yunnan had developed extensive commercial ties with its non-Chinese neighbors and was trading with them for goods that would have been far too expensive for most Yunnanese if they had come from China.

In the first years of the nineteenth century, Yunnan's trade routes were dominated by imported cotton and exported tea. The top-grade tea was Pu'er, which was grown in the Xishuangbanna region in southernmost Yunnan. It was in demand throughout China and in many parts of Southeast Asia. Also grown in this region was the lower-grade *guzong* tea, which was exported to Tibet. This tea was "fermented and transported by backpack and packhorse to Tibet or markets bordering Tibet"; after that it was repacked and transferred to pack animals for sale throughout Tibet.[29] Finally, an enduring demand in Southeast Asia and Tibet for porcelain, tobacco, silk, and a variety of Chinese medicines ensured that these goods made up a fair portion of Yunnan's cross-border trade.[30]

Often overshadowed by the cotton and tea trade was the flourishing "short haul" trade in salt, gems, and other sundries, which was carried out with non-Chinese peoples and polities clustered along the trade routes. This often illicit trade heavily influenced the profitability of the caravans as well as the routes they took.[31] Salt was an alternative currency and was "exchanged everywhere for grain [and] horses . . . in western [Yunnan] for musk and medicine, and in the east for tea."[32] In theory, salt was taxed within Yunnan at one of the fifty-six authorized salt wells where it was produced, "after which salt became a free-trade commodity within the region."[33] In reality, the salt trade was a far more fluid venture.

Along Yunnan's porous borders, and even in the interior, there were many unmonitored salt wells.[34] The strong demand for salt and the state's control of Yunnanese salt production generated a highly profitable "illicit" trade that revolved around sources the state did not control. This problem was exacerbated by the fact that in western and southern Yunnan the caravan trade often imported sea salt from Burma and rock salt from the Tibetan borderlands.[35] Because salt was taxed at the site of production and not at the time of sale, the state faced a heavy burden of enforcement.[36]

As with cotton and tobacco, each of Yunnan's regions gravitated toward the cheapest sources of salt. This created strong ties between regions that derived their salt from a common source. Consider as an example those areas of Yunnan that imported their salt from Sichuan. Sichuan produced salt by pumping brine from deep wells and then evaporating it; the resulting product was dingy black in color. Yunnanese salt was produced the same way but contained fewer mineral impurities, so it was whiter in color.[37] In between these two spheres was the urban center of Dongchuan. Markets north of Dongchuan sold the black salt of Sichuan; south of Dongchuan only the white salt of Yunnan was consumed.[38] Similarly, there were occasional reports that the sea salt being sold in Burmese border towns was also for sale in western Yunnan.

Because these salt wells were widely scattered and because many of them were in "peripheral" and ethnically non-Han Chinese regions, many caravaneers supplemented their profits by trading salt along their routes. It is perhaps not surprising, then, that one Qing official declared that "of all the sources of mischief in Yunnan, there is none that surpasses salt."[39] Throughout the nineteenth century, officials posted to Yunnan complained that wells "which were located in indigenous areas along the border [yijiang] were difficult for soldiers and officials to patrol."[40] It is clear that the salt trade, with its state-imposed proscriptions, oriented many parts of Yunnan away from China and further entwined them both economically and socially with neighboring polities.[41]

Not all transnational trade was conducted outside provincial borders. Yunnan was the site of many trade fairs. The largest and most famous of these was Dali's Third Month Fair (sanyue jie), which attracted traders from as far away as Tibet, Burma, Thailand, and a number of distant Chinese provinces. The British traveler Arthur Davenport remarked on the cosmopolitan flair of the fair when he passed through Dali a few years after the end of the Panthay Rebellion: "We were fortunate to arrive while the famous yearly fair was going on which years ago was attended by Lamas from Tibet, aborigines from Weixi, Burmese, Cochin-Chinese, and, in short, people from all the adjacent countries, and from eleven out of eighteen of the Chinese provinces."[42]

Lesser fairs—such as the Horse Bazaar (luoma hui), held in Lijiang on the Yunnan–Tibet border—and other smaller annual markets in the south were largely commercial in nature. However, they were timed to coincide with local indigenous festivals.[43] The Qing tried to regulate the commercial dimensions of these fairs; however, the deeply embedded multiethnic and

transnational orientation of the province made such gatherings rich junctures of ideas, cultures, and religions. For this reason, they largely escaped
the court's understanding and control.

From the perspective of the imperial court, Yunnan's greatest asset was
its mineral reserves—principally copper. In the early eighteenth century,
after Japan sharply reduced copper exports to China, Yunnan quickly became the central government's single most important source of copper for
the metropolitan mints in Beijing.[44] Yunnan's annual quota of 4,106,880
catties of copper (almost 10,000 tons), which was set by the Board of Revenue, remained constant throughout the latter eighteenth and early nineteenth centuries, although yields from the thirty-nine officially sanctioned
mines were falling steadily throughout those decades.[45] By the early nineteenth century, Yunnan was beginning to exhaust its richest and most accessible veins. Officials frequently reported that the "mines are old and the deposits depleted" (donglao shanhuang) and that the quality of the copper was
declining.[46] Moreover, because the imperial court had pegged the price of
copper artificially low, there was little motivation to seek out new sources.

Significantly, the largest of Yunnan's imperially designated mines lay in
eastern Yunnan. This strengthened that region's already close ties with Sichuan and imperial China. So did the fact that the mines drew considerable
numbers of Han miners from other parts of the empire. Yunnan's mines
were a microcosm of broader Yunnan society, in that the miners tended to
be divided into groups based on either ethnicity or (if Han) province of origin.[47] Among the miners of Yunnan there were three principal groups: Muslim Yunnanese (Hui), Han Chinese from Lin'an, and Han Chinese from
Hunan.[48]

The approach to administering these mines was a hybrid of the baojia
registration system, which had three primary elements: registering the resident miners, ensuring that the requisite taxes were collected, and establishing a hierarchy to facilitate production while maintaining order.[49] Each
work team had a boss who reported directly to the mine supervisor (kuangguan).[50] Perhaps these teams fostered cohesion among their own miners,
but they did little to promote an understanding among the migrant Han Chinese of the highly charged ethnic environment of Yunnan. The teams com-
peted constantly for the richest veins, the highest ore prices, and better
working conditions, and their bosses often played on ethnic rivalries to spur
their miners to work harder and longer.[51] The above description highlights
the fact that ethnicity was an inescapable dimension of Yunnanese society.
It could be argued that for any venture to succeed in Yunnan—be it commercial, political, or even religious—it had to accommodate Yunnan's complex
ethnic mosaic.

ETHNIC MOSAIC

In the nineteenth century, Yunnan was the most ethnically diverse area in all of China.[52] This is still the case today. "We ordinarily count Yunnan among the provinces of the Chinese empire," noted a French missionary living in Yunnan, "but if one leaves the main lines of communication, entering the interior, traveling through the deserts and mountains, you are always in the territory of Yunnan, but you are no longer in China; you are in an uncivilized country [*pays sauvage*] without roads, without inns, surrounded by thieves who want your purse or your life, and sometimes both."[53]

The contrasting worlds within Yunnan were not perceived as a simple, bipolar division of Han and non-Han (as was typical in Tibet and Xinjiang and in China's other border regions), for Yunnan was home to an astonishing mix of ethnic groups, especially from the perspective of the in-migrating Han Chinese.

The province today is home to twenty-six of China's fifty-six officially recognized nationalities; but a late-Qing gazetteer listed more than 140 different ethnic groups. These ranged from the "Kawa" (Wa) headhunters of southwestern Yunnan to the highly assimilated Bai around Erhai Lake to the powerful Lolo (Yi) tribes of northern Yunnan, who often swooped down on isolated Han settlements to capture slaves. Nineteenth-century Yunnan was a mosaic of ethnic groups. The non-Chinese population of southwestern China had been a topic of interest for the Chinese for several millennia, at least since the Warring States Period (403–221 BCE). Figure 2.3 suggests that the Chinese of central China were becoming more familiar with these groups. Over time and ever more selectively, the original and broadly applied ethnonyms were beginning to delineate the ethnic divisions of southwest China. This figure accurately reflects the genealogy of the ethnic labels employed by the Chinese but does not indicate how the ethnic groups perceived themselves.

In the nineteenth century, Qing officials and recent Han immigrants did not always grasp the finer distinctions between the different ethnic groups, but they were probably aware of the general divisions between diverse peoples such as the Miao, the Yi, and the Dai, who populated large areas of Yunnan. Despite this awareness, Chinese documents routinely reduced the population to three categories: yi, Hui, and Han. In doing so, the Qing was following its tendency to impose an "us–them" framework on the region, just as they did elsewhere in the empire.

One consequence of this reductionistic approach was that all of Yunnan's diverse ethnic populations were lumped into a single category. From the perspective of the Qing, the non-Han category made it easier to maintain a

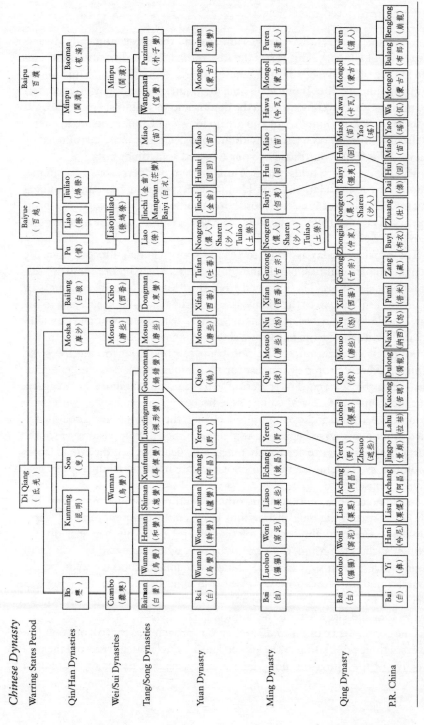

TABLE 2.1  Historical Evolution of Chinese Terms for Yunnan Ethnic Groups (Adopted and Modified from Zhang Pengyuan, "Yun-Gui shaoshu minzu de shehui bianqian jiqi xianzhi," in *Zhongguo xiandai hualun wenji*, 1991. p. 241).

system largely based on a blinkered dualism, one that placed the imperial court at the center. But that category also perpetuated a model of statecraft predicated on dealing with only one ethnic group at a time in isolation from its multiethnic context. This, in an province that was profoundly fluid and multifaceted.

Yunnan's ethnic diversity defied this simplistic "us–them" binary. To begin with, there were large numbers of Hui, who fit in neither the yi nor the Han category; for another, the other non-Han groups were often completely unrelated ethnically, linguistically, and culturally. The Qing would pay heavily for the stance it took. This misrepresentation of Yunnan society's complex interethnic realities encouraged the Qing court to overlook a multitude of significant commercial, cultural, and even political contacts between ethnic groups. These contacts not only circumvented the Qing administrative framework but also, often, entirely excluded contact with Han Chinese.

Furthermore, the imposition of this triadic division strengthened the assumption that Chinese culture was superior to non-Chinese culture. The term *yi*, often translated as "barbarian" in English, is the same character the Qing court employed when referring to the increasing numbers of Westerners who were arriving in China in the nineteenth century. The term's use in southwestern China predated its application to Westerners by many centuries, but the same ethnocultural and sinocentric undertones applied in both cases.[54]

In the context of Yunnan, the term *yi* (to be distinguished from the more modern ethnonym Yi) referred to any indigenous group that was not Han.[55] The strongly negative connotations of this definition have prompted me to translate the term as "non-Han," although it could be understood generally as "indigenous peoples" as well.[56] Groups as dissimilar as Tibetans, Hani, and Dai were all thrown into a single classification by the Han, even though in many parts of Yunnan one of the indigenous groups could easily be double or triple the size of the resident Han population.

As will be discussed in more depth in chapter 3, the Hui, or "Muslim Chinese," were considered neither yi nor Han Chinese of the Islamic faith; rather, they were perceived by all parties in this Yunnan context as distinct from both Han and yi. The term "Hui" for the Muslim Yunnanese[57] was not explicitly derogatory; however, the implication was that they were distinct from the Han and thus likely inferior.

The broader ethnonyms of yi and Hui were not openly derogatory. However, the Chinese characters employed to designate specific ethnic groups explicitly articulated Chinese cultural chauvinism and perpetuated the engrained belief that non-Han and Hui were both less than civilized and less than human. The most obvious manifestation of this was the practice of appending a "dog radical" (*quanzi pang*) or "insect radical" to the group's Chinese ethnonym (examples: *luoluo, dulong, zhongren, manzi*). These non-Han groups were routinely described in one of two ways. Either the terminology was highly condescending—"easily duped," "slow-witted," "uncivilized," and so on—or it made them sound threatening, as in "strong," "fierce," "bold."[58] As if these labels were not explicit enough, one nineteenth-century provincial gazetteer interspersed them with descriptions of grotesque and unmistakably nonhuman "ethnic groups." For example, the "Flying Head tribe" was said to come "at night and throw their heads into people's homes and feast on small children."[59]

The reliance of Han Chinese and Qing officials on a tripartite division of ethnicities in nineteenth-century Yunnan had yet another consequence: it perpetuated a variety of ethnic fallacies. In particular, this framework insinuated that there was a parity in numbers among the three groupings when in fact there was not. Han Chinese began arriving in Yunnan in large numbers as early as the thirteenth century, during Yuan dynasty. With government encouragement this immigration continued throughout the Ming dynasty and on into the Qing. No precise figures for this immigration wave are available; however, by the late sixteenth century Yunnan's registered population had reached almost 1.5 million (note here that most indigenous groups were excluded from the registration process).[60] These immigrants were still a minority relative to the indigenous population of Yunnan. Moreover, these first immigrants were striking in their diversity. This early influx included Han Chinese from almost every province of China as well as large groups of Mongols, Central Asians, and Manchus. This belies the myth of early Han demographic dominance; it also suggests that the newcomers' impact on the indigenous people of Yunnan was less than has long been assumed.

Still another consequence of the tripartite ethnic framework employed by the Qing as well as by many Han Chinese was that it encouraged a highly reified and sinocentric perspective—one which suggested that there were sharp divisions among the three ethnic groupings. This vision was often contradicted by the reality, especially with regard to those settlers who arrived before the late eighteenth century and who became acculturated to Yunnan. These people seem to have embraced many of the same ideals and perspectives as the Yunnanese, and to have intermarried with them: "There are quite a few Han villages, they migrated from the interior provinces of China [*neidi*] the majority coming more than a hundred years ago . . . who are now the same as many of the mountain people . . . practicing swidden agriculture and similarly abiding by the rule of the local *tusi*."[61]

Apparently, these local Han had few conflicts with their multiethnic neighbors. The instances of Han adopting yi cultural practices, marrying non-Han, and even taking up arms against the Qing contradicted the accepted cultural belief that sinicization was unidirectional.[62]

The assimilation that was taking place can be attributed in part to the fact that the number of Han immigrants was still relatively small and that they were settling in a limited number of areas. It seems that most Han gravitated to the urban centers. One gazetteer put it this way: "In the county seat Han are many and *yi* few, in the rural areas *yi* are many and Han few."[63]

Most accounts date the second wave of Han settlement between 1700 and 1850. Unlike the first, this one fundamentally changed Yunnan society. In the latter half of this period, between 1775 and 1850, Yunnan's population surged from an estimated four million to nearly ten million. As Lee notes in his demographic study of the province, this growth was remarkable: "Whereas the population took 300 years to double in the period between the sixteenth and eighteenth centuries, it required less than 100 years to double between the eighteenth and nineteenth centuries."[64] Most of the Han settlers in this period were from the overpopulated interior provinces of Sichuan, Hunan, Hubei, Guangdong, and Jiangxi. Although not as diverse as the first wave of settlers, they were hardly homogenous. They practiced a wide variety of religions and cultural rituals and often spoke very different dialects. However, these divisions often melted away when they were confronted with the multiethnic and transnational assumptions of Yunnan society. As Dru Gladney has contended with regard to ethnic groups in modern China: "Identities are often seen to coalesce and crystallize in the face of higher-order oppositions."[65] This was the case with Han Chinese in the multiethnic context of Yunnan when they were confronted with non-Han configurations of ethnicity, power, and territorial control.

The impact of this new wave of settlement on the predominantly non-Han areas of Yunnan seems to have been slow to make itself felt. Imperial records suggest that Han immigrants in the mid to late eighteenth century moved first to the core and urban centers of Yunnan, in response to a need for nonagricultural labor. Only around 1800, after these areas became saturated, did other parts of Yunnan begin to feel direct pressure from the newcomers; only then did they begin to notice the consequences of this population movement.[66] Increased contact meant more stringent enforcement of Qing legal codes and a waxing of Chinese cultural influence. For example, wearing of the queue was enforced, and greater fluency in Chinese was now required. Few argue that the Han set out to turn the non-Han into "ethnic" Han; that said, there is little doubt that Chinese officials were trying to turn them into law-abiding subjects of China by instilling basic Confucian values. In nineteenth-century Yunnan this process involved a variety of measures. In 1818, Governor-General Bolin advocated promoting Confucian teachings in order to modify the customs of the yi. The Jiaqing emperor supported this program, adding that if the "program can be carried out over an extended period of time, then you will successfully change their habits and customs."[67] In his study of the prominent eighteenth-century administrator Chen Hongmou, Rowe states that a universalist policy—that is, "the marshaling of Confucian arguments in defense of the views that the empire and its people were unitary"—was launched as early as the Yongzheng reign in the 1730s.[68] However, the effect of the migration went far beyond encouraging outward expressions of "Chinese-ness." More and more settler Han in Yunnan—and this was typical of migrations into imperial borderlands throughout Chinese history—sought nothing less than to transform the transnational and multiethnic Yunnan frontier into a closer approximation of the "China" from which they had come.

Did these campaigns succeed? And what impact did the settler Han have on the multiethnic culture of Yunnan? A key obstacle to answering these questions is that reports on the relative sizes of the various ethnic groups involved are confusing and contradictory. The conventional wisdom among many recent Chinese and Western scholars has been that by the time of the Ming dynasty at the latest, the Han Chinese had become the single largest ethnic group in Yunnan, and that by the nineteenth century the Han were a majority in the province.[69] However, there are several good reasons to doubt the accuracy of these estimates.

Foremost among these is that the figures are based largely on registered population figures—figures that omitted large numbers of non-Han who fell outside the purview of Qing registration efforts.[70] Also, the registered population was not broken down along ethnic lines, which suggests that later observers assumed that many urban-dwelling non-Han were Han.[71] Many eighteenth- and early-nineteenth-century editors of Yunnan gazetteers themselves expressed doubts about the accuracy of the population figures as a whole.[72]

Nineteenth-century methods for registering the non-Han rarely took ethnicity into account; even so, Chinese sources offer considerable evidence that non-Han continued to form the majority of Yunnan's population into the nineteenth century. Governor-General Zhang Liangji, who served for more than a decade in various offices throughout Yunnan, wrote in 1860 that "the yi are a majority constituting seventy percent of the population, the Han constitute only twenty percent, with the Hui barely at ten percent."[73] Several years later, another provincial official familiar with Yunnan altered Zhang's figures only slightly, suggesting that the yi were roughly 50 to 60 percent, with the Han making up 30 to 40 percent and the Hui only 10 to 20 percent.[74]

European travelers in the latter half of the nineteenth century agree that the non-Han were in the majority. Many commented on the province's ethnic diversity. The French adventurer Jean Dupuis in 1868 commented: "In the center of Yunnan, the black and white Lolos [Yi] dominate; in the south and southeast it is the Bai-yi [Dai] and the Dulous [Zhuang] but in all of [Yunnan] there is tremendous variety of tribes and they all have their own unique style, character, [with] customs so different from each other that I cannot speak of each one of them in particular."[75]

At the turn of the nineteenth century, Henri d'Ollone put the Muslim Yunnanese at "about a tenth of the population" and stated confidently that "it would not be an exaggeration to estimate [the non-Han population] at around six million of the approximately ten million inhabitants in Yunnan."[76] George Clarke, a Protestant missionary in Dali, estimated Yunnan's total population in the late 1870s as "quite six-tenths are aborigines."[77]

Although these are at best estimates, both Chinese and European observers of the time agree that non-Han groups predominated in Yunnan. This raises doubts about the official registration figures with regard to the proportion of Yunnanese who were Han. The above observations also suggest that non-Han groups must have played a vital role in that society because they were the majority. However, any discussion of when the Han Chinese achieved a numerical majority over non-Han groups—if they ever did—diverts attention from a more significant question: Exactly *where* did the Han dominate?

A century after the period in question, a 1953 census indicated that more than half the prefectures in Yunnan (mainly in the south and west) had non-Han populations of at least around 50 percent.[78] In the mid-nineteenth century, then, the issue very likely was not whether Han were the outright majority, but *where* they dominated (and, one would assume, their culture, customs, and attitudes). On this point there is little controversy: nearly all extant sources tell us that the Han were the overwhelming majority in cities and in the more urbanized prefectures but quite sparse in Yunnan's more mountainous and peripheral areas. Clearly, Yunnan's physical landscape strongly affected the ethnic landscape in ways that divided Yunnan along deep ethnic faultlines.

## Ethnic Landscape

Nowhere in nineteenth-century Yunnan could one find an ethnic community that did not interact with another group on an almost daily basis. Even in Kunming, the provincial capital, which had the highest concentration of Han Chinese of all the cities in the province, few visitors failed to note the presence of many non-Han in the markets and streets.[79] Specific ethnic groups did predominate in several regions—for example, the Dai in tropical Xishuangbanna in the south, and the Naxi in and around Lijiang in the north—but nowhere in Yunnan did a single group exist in isolation. Specific ethnic groups tended to congregate in distinct climatic regions and ecological niches, which ranged from tropical lowlands to mountain highlands.

There were so many ethnic groups in the province mainly because Yunnan had been attracting migrants continuously right up through the nineteenth century. It is important to note that the many non-Han ethnic groups were not static entities that passively retreated from the incoming Han (a notion forcefully presented by Wien in *China's March Toward the Tropics*).[80] It is more accurate to say that although many non-Han groups had over the centuries been pushed out of Yunnan's fertile valleys up to the less desirable ridgetops by newly arriving Han Chinese, they continued to practice their cultural beliefs. Furthermore, they were not isolated; rather, they coexisted with the Han who had ousted them.[81] In addition, Han and non-Han regularly intermarried throughout this period and in doing so transformed solely "Chinese" cultural and social forms into ones that were uniquely Yunnanese.

Two-dimensional representations of Yunnan's ethnic distribution can only mask crucial altitudinal divisions among the region's indigenous peoples. Attempts to reduce Yunnan's ethnic diversity to a simplistic dichotomy block understanding of the patterns of Yunnanese regionalism. One way to grasp the complexities of Yunnan's ethnic groups is by utilizing the three regional divisions the Yunnanese themselves employed—eastern, western, and southern Yunnan. In general, although the Han were ubiquitous everywhere, each region contained several non-Han ethnic groups that dominated its culture, politics, and commerce through sheer weight of numbers. In addition to this, smaller groups straddling important mountain passes or dominating specific commercial centers tended to have a greater impact than their numbers might suggest. By structuring a study of Yunnan's ethnic landscape along these regional lines, we can more easily elucidate the ethnic faultlines that crisscrossed Yunnan society.

EASTERN YUNNAN

Three main groups inhabited eastern Yunnan during the Qing—the Yi, the Zhuang, and the Miao. The largest ethnic group in all of Yunnan during this period was the Yi (Luoluo or Lolo). They dominated northeastern Yunnan in and around the first slow bend of the Yangtze River; there were also Yi settlements as far west as Dali and as far south as Kaihua and Mengzi.[82] Culturally and linguistically, the Yi were a diverse group; however, imperial documents consistently portrayed them as a single, ethnically homogenous entity.[83]

Chinese and European sources often represented the Yi as a fierce mountain people wreaking destruction on Han settlements. Districts near the Yi were presented as scenes of "frequent Luoluo raids, whole caravans—goods, animals, and men—being swept off and carried into the inaccessible mountains to the east."[84] Despite this reputation for banditry—which was ascribed mainly to the Yi along the border of the Liangshan Mountains in northern Yunnan—many branches of the Yi practiced sedentary agriculture and were active traders.[85] In particular, the lowland Yi in eastern Yunnan near Qujing were less combative. They wore their hair in a queue as a mark of submission to the Qing, and they generally accepted their position as Qing subjects.[86] The Yi were one of the few ethnic groups in Yunnan besides the nonindigenous Han and Hui to have settlements in all three regions of Yunnan.

The largest group in southeastern Yunnan during the Qing was the Zhuang, often referred to by Qing officials as the Sharen or Nongren. They inhabited the subtropical districts of the eastern region around Wenshan, Honghe, and Qujing. The Zhuang were skilled lowland agriculturists who often grew two and three crops a year, including paddy rice. The Zhuang who occupied these coveted lowlands were heavily influenced by Han culture. However, they preferred to live apart from the Han Chinese in their own villages; in these, they practiced their distinctive festivals and retained the customs and rituals that marked them apart from the ethnic Chinese settlers.

Finally, all along the border with neighboring Guizhou were many Miao communities. For the most part, the Miao were culturally, socially, and ethnically oriented toward Guizhou, where the largest concentrations of Miao were to be found. They lived mainly in small mountain villages and tended to depend on agriculture for their livelihood.[87] Much like the Yi and the Zhuang, the Miao were cast as less civilized by the Han, who portrayed them as culturally inferior and often dangerous.

### WESTERN YUNNAN

Because western Yunnan stretches from the mountainous Tibetan Plateau south to the tropical highlands of Burma, it is especially difficult to generalize about the people living there. Along the northern and southern borders of western Yunnan lived two ethnic groups, respectively the Lisu and the Yeren[88] (Jingpo)—literally "savage people." In the nineteenth century, these two dominated the key trade routes in and out of Yunnan, although both were small relative to other Yunnan groups. The Lisu lived in mountain villages above the Salween River in alpine forests between five thousand and nine thousand feet.[89] With other Tibetan groups, the Lisu had

established an autonomous zone that was largely impervious to Qing jurisdiction and in fact often threatened it.[90]

Like the Lisu, the Yeren dominated trade routes, but they did so in the
southwest, in the semitropical Yeren Mountains. In upland Burma, the Yeren
lived in small villages and generally practiced a form of swidden agriculture.
During the nineteenth century many Yeren launched frequent raids on sedentary agricultural settlements; other Yeren used their control of key valleys
between Burma and Yunnan to collect tolls from passing caravans.[91]

Besides the Lisu and Yeren there were many "lowland groups" (a relative
term in western Yunnan, applied to those who occupied valleys, which were
not necessarily at low elevations). By the nineteenth century these groups
were extremely active in trade. The Bai (Minjia) lived in and around Dali at
the foot of the Cangshan Mountains and practiced sedentary agriculture
and husbandry.[92] They were probably descendants of Yunnan's earliest inhabitants and were the most acculturated of its indigenous peoples. A mid-
eighteenth-century Chinese gazetteer described them as "hardworking, sedentary agriculturists, rather studious, Confucianists, good mannered."[93] He
then paid the Bai the highest compliment possible for a Han Chinese chron-
icler: "[The Bai] are no different from Han [*yu Hanren wuyi*]."[94]

Another lowland group, the Naxi, were concentrated in the northwest in
and around the urban center of Lijiang. There, they served as commercial
(and probably cultural) mediators in the trade between the Tibetan borderlands and central Yunnan.[95] Although long familar with Chinese practices,
the Naxi had their own resilient ethnic identity, which was based largely on
their own Dongba script, which they used in their religious and cultural
practices.

Both the Bai and the Naxi played critical roles in cross-border trade. The
Bai hosted Yunnan's largest annual commercial gathering, the Third-Month
Fair in Dali; the Naxi hosted the Horse Fair in Lijiang. Both groups were
active in the caravan trade. The Naxi caravans dominated the trade routes
into Tibet.

### SOUTHERN YUNNAN

The dominant ethnic group in southern Yunnan in the nineteenth
century was the Tai (or Dai), also referred to in Chinese writings as Baiyi.[96]
It is generally believed that the Tai emigrated during the first millennium BC
from south-central China (today's Guizhou and Guangxi). Their slow migration "along the south China coast to the Red River Delta and into what
is now northern Vietnam" and Yunnan was an effort to elude the expanding Chinese Empire.[97] Tai political power was concentrated to the south of

Yunnan Province; however, many Tai communities existed throughout southern Yunnan.[98]

The northernmost of these Tai polities, Xishuangbanna (Sipsongpanna in Thai), began a formal relationship with the Ming court in the fourteenth century and was governed as a pacified administrative region named Cheli.[99] This political relationship was never stable, for the region was only nominally under Chinese authority. The Tai were a potent political force and acted with considerable autonomy from the imperial court throughout the nineteenth century.

The second dominant ethnic group in southern Yunnan, the Woni (Hani), were for the most part dispersed along the northern portions of Xishuangbanna up to Jingdong, Lin'an, and Yuanjiang.[100] They were skilled farmers and had transformed their steep hillsides into highly productive terraces of such beauty that one Chinese gazetteer characterized them as follows: "From a distance [the Woni] terraces look like they could be from a painting."[101] Their territory attracted considerable numbers of Han immigrants, and as a consequence, many Woni became increasingly involved in commercial activities, including the selling of bamboo utensils and other handicrafts in town markets.[102] As we shall see in chapter 4, this led to increasing friction between Han immigrants and the Woni and to extended periods of violence.

The influence of these non-Han groups on Qing efforts to integrate Yunnan Province during the seventeenth and eighteenth centuries is not fully understood. This is partly because records from this period reflect the Qing's efforts to reduce Yunnan's ethnic diversity to a simple "we/they" dichotomy. It is clear, though, that the non-Han remained an important element in the Qing's approach to governing Yunnan.

## CHAPTER 3

# Shades of Islam: The Muslim Yunnanese

## Introduction: Islamic Roots

Yunnan's first contact with the Islamic world can be traced to the Tang and Song dynasties (618–1276). In those eras, Muslim traders were plying the prosperous Southwestern Silk Road, which traversed Yunnan and linked central China with the prospering Indian Ocean trading networks.[1] Islam became firmly established in Yunnan during the Yuan dynasty in the thirteenth century, when Khubilai Khan's armies conquered the region and fully integrated it into the Chinese Empire. This subjugation occurred after Yunnan had experienced several centuries of independent rule under the Nanzhao (738–902) and Dali (937–1253) kingdoms.[2]

The "first tide"[3] of Muslims to enter Yunnan arrived from Central Asia. They served as soldiers and administrators for the Mongol rulers of the Yuan dynasty, who viewed them as more trustworthy than the indigenous Yunnanese or the Chinese. In particular, these early groups of Muslims benefited from Khubilai's appointment of Sayyid 'Ajall Shams al-Din (Ch. Saidianchi Shansiding Wuma'er), a Muslim from Bukhara (in present-day Uzbekistan), as governor of the province in 1274. He held this post until his death five years later.[4]

Traditional imperial histories largely ignore Sayyid 'Ajall's Muslim identity and the role he played in establishing Islam in Yunnan. Armijo-Hussein notes that court historians lauded him for "introducing the most important of the traditional Han Chinese customs, values and rituals" during his six-year reign.[5] According to Rossabi and others, although Sayyid 'Ajall promoted Chinese culture in the region and never set out to convert the multiethnic populace to Islam, Yunnan remained "the one area in early Yüan China in which Muslim jurisdiction was virtually unchecked" by the Mongol court.[6] As a consequence, the region had one of the largest Muslim populations outside the "Quran Belt" of northwestern China.

In contrast to what is recorded in imperial histories, later generations of

Yunnan Hui would remember Sayyid 'Ajall's rule as one that provided them with a useful model for balancing one's obligations as a Muslim with those as a subject of the imperial throne.[7] Sayyid 'Ajall strengthened the growing Muslim community by supporting the construction of at least two mosques, by permitting Islamic education, and by sanctioning the open practice of the Islamic faith. Not all Muslims elsewhere in the empire had it this good.[8] Early in Yunnan's reintegration with the empire, 'Ajall was able to show the central government that the Yunnanese Hui were loyal. Just as important, he served as an essential legitimizing force for Islam in the region for all of Yunnan's population—Muslims and non-Muslims alike.[9]

After Sayyid 'Ajall died, Muslim Yunnanese continued to hold high positions in the imperial bureaucracies of the Yuan, Ming, and Qing dynasties. None of those officials rose higher than Zheng He (1371–1433). Zheng He was born in Yunnan and lived there until he was twenty, when he was captured by an invading Ming army. He came to the attention of a general, Zhu Di, who later ascended the throne as the Yongle emperor. One of Zhu Di's first acts as emperor was to appoint Zheng He an admiral. Between 1405 and 1432, Zheng He led seven naval expeditions that made contact and established trade with kingdoms throughout India, Southeast Asia, and even the east coast of Africa.[10]

Yet despite examples like this of sustained loyalty and illustrious service to the imperial government, and despite the many achievements of Yunnan Hui like Zheng He, the Muslim Yunnanese were perceived even into the nineteenth century as different from both the multiethnic non-Han and the increasingly numerous Han Chinese. The Yunnan Hui's prominent and well-documented role in the Mongol Conquest and the settlement of Yunnan made it quite clear they were not Han Chinese (many Hui families traced their origins to Central Asia). Yet at the same time, neither the imperial court nor the immigrant Han Chinese perceived the Hui as one of the large, indigenous non-Han groups who inhabited Yunnan. The Hui were often treated as separate and unique in part because the Qing court and many of nineteenth-century Yunnan's newly arriving Han Chinese simply were unaware of the Hui's historical place in Yunnan; that or they tended to view Yunnan's ethnic make-up in dualistic terms (that is, there were Han-yi or Han-Hui). Such depictions of Yunnan's ethnic make-up established a false sense that the Han were dominant; at the same time, it distiguished the Hui from both the Han and the yi.

As noted in chapter 2, the non-Han category of yi was highly oppositional and referred to any group that was neither Han nor Hui. The yi classification was all-encompassing, yet the Hui were never included in it. Although the Hui were not considered yi, they did not escape many of the derogatory characterizations employed by the Han when describing the non-Han. The clearest indication of this is that many chroniclers appended a dog radical (quanzi pang) to the Hui character—a practice reserved almost exclusively for ethnonyms of the yi peoples, who were viewed as culturally inferior by the Han.[11]

The Muslim Yunnanese were thus denied both the "us" status and the "them" status, both of which were central to sinocentric perspectives of the borderlands—perspectives predominant both in the imperial court and in other parts of China. Yet in Yunnanese society itself, the Hui were easy to distinguish. This chapter focuses on how the Muslim Yunnanese created a space for themselves as a discrete third category within Yunnan's multiethnic framework.

## Dangerous Dualism: Chinese Muslims or Muslim Chinese

Western scholarly accounts of Islam in China began appearing in the late nineteenth century. Ever since, the standard rendering in English for Hui has been simply "Chinese Muslims" or "Chinese-speaking Muslims." These terms reflect and reinforce the idea that the Hui were and still are "Muslims residing in China." Yet Hui identity has a variety of dimensions besides the religious one. To understand Yunnan Hui identity and the roots of the Panthay Rebellion, it is vital to understand precisely how this Hui identity has been expressed with reference to Chinese cultural symbols and state policies in both modern and imperial China.

A common assumption among Chinese and Western scholars alike is that to be Hui has always been incompatible with the "Chinese Order." Perhaps the strongest proponent of this view is Raphael Israeli, who contends that the Islamic and Chinese cultures are irreconcilable. He asserts that the Hui are more likely to conform to the Chinese culture and abandon their Islamic identity "in isolated places where maintaining one's distinctiveness could become a matter of daily embarrassment and a constant nuisance rather than a source of pride and superiority."[12] Chinese scholar Wang Jianping in a recent historical study of Yunnan Hui adopts a similar reasoning. He suggests that being Hui "was distressing for the Hui [who] lived on the edge of two societies and were forced to have one foot in their Islamic culture and one foot in the 'host' Chinese culture."[13] From these two perspectives, then, the Yunnan Hui, isolated and outnumbered, should have long ago been assimilated. Yet the Yunnan Hui have persisted over the centuries and into the present day as an independent and highly important group.

American scholar Jonathan Lipman in his history of the Hui in northwestern China voices another common supposition. He coined the term "Sino-Muslim" to describe the Hui prior to the emergence of the People's

Republic of China in 1949, and he proposes that until then "the word Hui meant Muslim . . . but they would not have used that name themselves."[14] Few people contend that the highly reified system of ethnic identification employed today in the PRC accurately reflects the myriad permutations in which ethnic identity manifests itself. That said, the historical record makes it clear that both Han and Hui used the Hui ethnonym when referring to the Muslim Chinese. The manner in which it was employed suggests some sense of ethnicity, even if different from the criteria employed in the PRC today. Suggestions that the Hui identity was purely religious reflect a modern interpretation of religion as something completely separate from ethnic and cultural identity.[15]

Israeli, Lipman, and Wang Jianping all deny the existence of any overarching Hui identity beyond a religious one. Implicit in the literature on the Hui is the assumption that Han and Hui have always been separated by their religious beliefs and by nothing else. Yet a study of nineteenth-century Yunnan offers evidence to repudiate all this. There is no evidence that the Hui's "distinctiveness" ever caused the Yunnan Hui to relinquish their Hui-ness; furthermore, there are plenty of indications that the Hui were amazingly resistant to assimilation.[16] They seem to have avoided many of the cultural, moral, and intellectual biases of the Han toward the yi, and they selectively adopted many cultural practices of the Dai, Tibetans, and Bai. Hui communities living near or among these non-Han groups learned their languages and adopted many of their customs even while retaining their Hui identity and remaining part of broader Hui networks.[17]

In contrast to those who de-emphasize the nonreligious identities of the Hui, two anthropologists, Dru Gladney and Elisabeth Allès, offer much less reductionist frameworks for understanding Hui identity. Instead of falling into a binary classification of the Hui as either Muslims or Chinese, Gladney focuses on "the wide ethnographic and religious variety found among the Hui who, despite this diversity, continue to regard themselves as one group."[18] In this way he redefines Hui identity so that Islam is no longer the single defining characteristic of Hui-ness in China; rather, it is "only one marker of that identity."[19] He suggests that Hui identity be approached as "ethno-religious"; when it is, the religious dimension of Hui identity can be seen to vary widely among Hui communities even while retaining its overarching Hui-ness. Taking a somewhat different approach, Allès refutes the assumptions made by Wang and Israeli that Hui are disposed to assimilation. She suggests that Hui identity is "not as much a mixture than it is a juxtaposition" of Chinese and Hui cultures.[20]

Gladney and Allès treat Hui identity as multifaceted, not simply religious. Moreover, they do not see it as the result of China's rise as a nation-state; rather, it is the end product of centuries of acculturation. In this, they concur with the renowned Hui scholar Bai Shouyi. More than forty years ago, Bai offered a characterization of the differences between Hui and Muslim identity that laid bare the problem of thinking about Hui identity in exclusively religious or ethnic terms: "A Muslim may be a Hui, but may also belong to another ethnic group. A Hui is likely a Muslim, but being a Hui does not [inexorably] mean one is a Muslim."[21]

In other words, the elements that defined one as Hui and those that defined one as Muslim were not necessarily coextensive, although they were clearly interrelated. In fact, the Hui's sense of Hui-ness depended on a variety of factors that often fell outside their identity as Muslims. The Hui themselves had a clear understanding of their identity, yet both official and popular perceptions of the Yunnan Hui during the Qing dynasty were often inaccurate and uninformed.

### HUI ETHNORELIGIOUS IDENTITY IN NINETEENTH-CENTURY YUNNAN

Rebellion-era documents written by Han chroniclers apply a number of different terms to the Hui. The ethnic labels employed by the Han for the Muslim Yunnanese were very different from those the Hui employed when referring to themselves. Throughout the nineteenth century, government documents consistently employed four terms when referring to the Yunnan Hui: Huimin, Huiren, Huizhong, and Huizi. Each of these terms contains the Hui ideogram combined with a second ideogram indicating people or group of people. The four resulting compound characters are subtly different, although they were used interchangeably by Qing officials and the Han elite when referring to the Hui.

It is significant that in the nineteenth century, the term "Hui" differed considerably from the terms employed for other religious groups such as the Buddhists (*fojiao tu*), the Confucianists (*rujia tu*), and the Daoists (*daojiao tu*). In these three cases the emphasis was on being a disciple (tu) or on the religion (*jiao*) itself. Important for this discussion, the Chinese characters designating these religions (*fo, ru,* and *dao*) were often employed to refer to a category or class of people (Daoists, Confucianists, and so on), based on their beliefs or adherence to those teachings. In late imperial Yunnan, these characters or terms were never used as single-character designations to describe a people in the same way the terms Han, yi, and Hui—perceived as permanent and fixed—were employed. Specifically, the character "Hui" often appeared either alone or in ways that distinguished the Hui as a group. One example is Huimin—literally, "Hui-people." Another is Huizi, which, as Wellington Chan has pointed out, is remarkably analogous to the derogatory label for the far less assimilated Miao ethnic group, Miaozi.[22] As becomes evident in a study of the Panthay Rebellion, the boundaries of religion, ethnicity, and other salient categories that today are often perceived as mutually exclusive were at that time considerably more blurred.

In documents written by Yunnan Hui for other Yunnan Hui in the nineteenth century, two other terms consistently appear—mumin and Huijiao, meaning "Muslim" and "Hui culture," respectively. These terms are not synonymous with the four terms mentioned earlier, and the differences between the two sets shed light on the ethnoreligious aspects of Hui identity. Although being Hui meant also being Muslim, the shifting relationship between that Muslim-ness and other identities (such as local, regional, and occupational) allowed for the formation and reformation of what it meant to be Hui.

The Chinese word mumin almost certainly comes directly from the Arabic mu'minin, or Muslim, and has the strong religious connotation of "believer."[23] The term Hui has its roots in the Chinese ethnonym for the Uyghur people of Central Asia, Huihu or Huihe; in both meaning and pronunciation, this was transmuted into Huihui, meaning Muslim, at some point after the twelfth century.[24] By the nineteenth century the use of Hui—at least in the multiethnic context of Yunnan—had taken on a broad ethnoreligious meaning whereas mumin retained its narrower religious connotation.

The Hui today generally contend that one should not say Huijiao to mean Islam. Clearly, they differentiate between between religious identity (Muslim) and ethnic identity (Hui). Although ethnicity has only fully emerged as a discursive category of the state in the twentieth century, a clear distinction between ethnic and religious identity does seem to have existed in mid-nineteenth-century Yunnan during the Panthay Rebellion. In other words, when the Muslim Yunnanese distinguished themselves as Hui, they were not simply declaring their religious identity as Muslims. These clashing identities, which will be examined in more detail in chapter 7, became a major point of contention among rival Hui leaders during the rebellion and reveal how the Muslim Yunnanese distinguished between being Hui and being Muslim.

The difference between mumin and Huimin enables us to cast light on an important dimension of late imperial Yunnan Hui identity, yet the term "Huijiao" remains ambiguous. Most Western commentators have suggested that Huijiao, which contains the character for "Hui" and the character for "religion" (jiao), should be understood as "Hui-religion" or more literally "teachings of the Hui."[25] Yet understanding jiao strictly as "religion" in the context of the later empire is somewhat problematic, since the term is also used in the expression Hanjiao to refer to the agglomeration of beliefs ascribed to Han Chinese. The eminent seventeenth-century Yunnan Hui scholar Ma Zhu rather disparagingly noted as a warning to Hui: "Those who do not have religion will become Hanjiao."[26] Ma was concerned here that Hui youth growing up in a Han-dominated culture tended to lack proper training in Islamic teachings. It is significant, though, that Ma was not indicating that without an Islamic upbringing they would become Han. Similarly, in neighboring Guizhou we find references to "Miaojiao" which are indicative not of any specific corpus of religious teachings, but rather of the traits or beliefs of the Miao peoples.[27]

There remains one final and highly suggestive clue to the Hui's ethnic self-awareness. Besides mumin and san jiao, a third term, Huizu (Hui lineage or group), appears fleetingly in both Hui and Qing documents.[28] From a modern perspective, this is the most tantalizing of the three terms, since it mirrors the modern Hui PRC ethnonym—an ethnonym that designates the Hui as one of fifty-six state-recognized nationalities (*minzu*). Du Wenxiu in his "Proclamation from the Headquarters of the Generalissimo" (*shuaifu bugao*), issued during his final offensive in 1867, used the phrase in a generalized fashion, which suggests he meant all the Hui: "This army expedition was caused by the Manchu's taking China from us and staying in power for more than 200 years, treating people as oxen and horses, having no regard for the value of life, hurting my compatriots, and wiping out my fellow Hui [*wo Huizu*]."[29]

The appearance of the term Huizu during the rebellion seems to have reflected something more than the idea of lineages (its traditional meaning); the meaning was something closer to an ethnic consciousness, but without any connotations of a state-imposed politicized framework.

## Redefining the Hui: More Than Muslims

In current scholarly discussions, the concept of ethnicity is highly controversial. In a recent critique of Benedict Anderson's claim that conceptions of ethnicity only came about after colonial conquest, Frank Proschan asserts that "indigenous local peoples had already themselves imagined ethnicity well before the colonial era."[30] Through a nuanced examination of the flood myth of the Kmhmu highlanders of northern Laos, Proschan demonstrates that conceptions of ethnicity—and perhaps even more significantly, interethnic consciousness—were beginning to take shape before colonial contact. The Kmhmu's strong sense of a multiethnic society offers evidence to counter those in Chinese studies who resist the notion of ethnicity in the early modern era, an era free of the trappings of a nation-state. The Kmhmu's participation in the broader Yunnan world of the Hui also provides further historical evidence that the Muslim Yunnanese were active in a "stubbornly ethnoeccentric" society that placed a premium on one's ethnicity.[31]

Just as pertinent is Harrell's examination of the civilizing process in southwestern China in the nineteenth and twentieth centuries. He proposes that we distinguish between an ethnic consciousness—which he defines as "the awareness of belonging to a group"—and an ethnic group, defined as a group that perceives itself as sharing common descent and common customs and as in opposition to other such groups.[32] He contends that a group can come to perceive itself as an ethnic group "in situations where a group is confronted in some way by an outside power with whom it is in competition for resources of some kind whether they be material . . . or symbolic."[33] Such a situation seems rather similar to the one the Hui faced in nineteenth-century Yunnan.

Both Harrell and Proschan raise issues that are critical to our efforts to understand the ethnic identity of the Yunnan Hui in the nineteenth century. Both scholars build from ideas about how a given ethnic group perceives itself, how others perceive it, and how it demonstrates its identity—sometimes forcefully—in the face of conflicting notions of ethnicity and culture. The Yunnan Hui offer a unique historical example of such models in that they sought to participate in the culturally and politically sinocentric world of the Qing as well as in the far more fluid world of Yunnan. This latter world viewed allegiances to multiple sovereign powers as the norm; in Yunnan, a multi-ethnic landscape was typical and cross-boundary trade was indispensable.

### MUSLIM YUNNANESE COMMUNITIES

During the Ming dynasty, the descendents of Sayyid 'Ajall continued to play important roles in administering Yunnan. Many of them received noble titles from the court. Military requirements dictated that most of the earliest Muslim settlements were clustered in western Yunnan. By the middle of the Ming dynasty, however, there were Muslim communities throughout the province in almost every prefecture, from Zhaotong to Baoshan, from Chuxiong to Lin'an.[34] Although widely distributed geographically, Muslim Yunnanese retained highly concentrated settlement patterns. They usually lived in predominantly Hui villages; in large urban centers, they tended to cluster in specific streets or districts.[35]

Because villages were segregated along ethnoreligious lines, it was not uncommon to find towns with names like Hui-hui Village (*Huihui cun*), Huihui Barracks (*Huihui ying*), and Huihui Encampment (*Huizi zhai*)— names which highlighted that the inhabitants were Muslim Yunnanese.[36] But the Hui did not restrict themselves to villages; Shadian, Weishan, and Ludian were among the larger Hui centers. Also, many Yunnanese Hui lived in larger urban centers where they were not the dominant group. In these centers, Hui businesses and homes tended to cluster in distinctive and identifiable Muslim districts. Here the Hui preserved their religious beliefs, practices, and lifestyles with minimal interference.

Large-scale violence was rising in frequency by the mid-nineteenth century, but the Hui were facing underlying tensions and daily discrimination decades and even centuries before that. Han Chinese conceptions of the Hui tended to focus on what to them was the most obvious and perverse fact about the Hui—their religion forbade them to eat pork. Records of Han–Hui interactions in late imperial Yunnan recount a number of disparaging sayings, stories, and epithets that center on the Hui's aversion to pigs. Most often, these jokes insinuated that the Hui refused to eat pork because they either worshipped pigs or believed they were descended from them. Taunts such as "son of a pig" and worse were an inescapable fact of Hui life.[37] A shocking demonstration of this bias in nineteenth-century Yunnan is that the street running past one of Kunming's oldest mosques was called Zhuji Jie (Pig-gathering Road).[38]

Besides openly insulting the Hui in the streets and markets, the Han often disparaged them in their writings. Rebellion-era gazetteers and reports, even when they did not openly insult the Hui, often depicted them as vaguely threatening beings—for example, as "full of strength and able to endure hardship, full of vitality, fierce and brave."[39] Typically, the terms applied to the Hui expressed disapproval: "fierce" (han), "combative" (xidou), and "assertive" (qiang). Inevitably, the Hui came to be characterized as having "a propensity to stir up trouble."[40]

Among the non-Han population, the Yunnan Hui seemed to fare much better. By the eighteenth century, there were Muslim Yunnanese communities throughout the more settled areas of Yunnan and also in the more distant non-Han regions. There were Hui villages in southern Yunnan in the Xishuangbanna region, in the northwest near the Tibetan town of Zhongdian, and in the northeast in the Xiaoliang Shan region—in areas that were heavily populated by the Dai, Tibetans, and Yi respectively, and that were generally shunned by the Han Chinese. The Hui of these remote areas continued to embrace their Muslim beliefs, building mosques and refusing to eat pork. But they also—unlike their Han counterparts—adopted local cultural traditions relating to clothing, language, and so on.[41]

This sort of acculturation was not in and of itself uncommon. Hui were living in almost every border region of the Qing Empire: there were the Mongolian Hui (Meng Hui) in Inner Mongolia, the Tibetan Hui (Zang Hui) in Lhasa, and the Dungan of Soviet Central Asia. All of these groups made similar adjustments: "These Muslims are culturally indistinguishable from the minority group with whom they live, but they identify themselves as Hui and are recognized by the state as members of the Hui nationality."[42] What is significant is that these nineteenth-century Hui straddled multiple communities. Thus they functioned as intermediaries between non-Han and Hui communities within Yunnan and as key nodes along Muslim Yunnanese caravan routes that linked these areas to regions beyond Yunnan.

Equally conspicuous is the absence of Han Chinese communities that functioned in a similar manner. As will be discussed in chapter 4, those Han who did assimilate or who interacted closely with the non-Han were viewed as suspect by the imperial court. By the nineteenth century it was the Yunnan Hui who had established close and enduring relations with many of Yunnan's non-Han regions. Hui communities extended down into highland Southeast Asia and up into Tibet. In this way the world of the Yunnan Hui extended far beyond the ethnocultural and political boundaries of the Qing Empire.

MUSLIM YUNNANESE NETWORKS

The success the Muslim Yunnanese had in maintaining a strong community identity had its roots in their religion and was sustained by their skill in adapting themselves to the province's ethnic, political, and commercial realities. In particular, the Muslim Yunnanese excelled in occupations that allowed them to work in teams. Through such teams they were able to preserve their religious beliefs while meeting the demands of their work. By the nineteenth century, their success in occupations that called for group cohesion—especially mining and the caravan trade—was often deeply resented by less successful Han teams.

It is difficult to ascertain precisely how dominant a role the Muslims played in early Yunnanese trade. We do know that by the nineteenth century, Muslim Yunnanese controlled a large portion of the caravan trade. Many European travelers described Muslim caravaneers in detail. Gervais Courtellemont noted: "The mafou [muleteers] . . . are almost all Muslim. One of my soldier escorts was also, and it was by him that I obtained much of my information about commerce in the province. His parents were mafous and I was able to make their acquaintance as well."[43]

Another account, although written in the early part of the twentieth century, highlights the Muslim caravaneers' reputation as hard workers, as well as their dominance of the province's trade routes: "The Panthays [Muslim Yunnanese] are a virile, sturdy and aggressive race, even more so than the true Chinese. Caravaneers and muleteers on the Yunnan trade routes are very likely to be Panthays. The men who guide the long trains of mules and ponies through the wild mountain passes of Yunnan and the Burmese frontier must be rugged in constitution and resolute in spirit to endure this rough life, filled with hardships and dangers."[44]

The reputation of the Muslim Yunnanese as successful traders gave rise to one of the few positive Han stereotypes of Muslim Yunnanese.[45] Their success as traders allowed them to expand into other occupations that revolved around caravaneering—many became leather workers, furriers, and harness makers. Town-dwelling Hui often carved out occupational niches. There were Hui tanners in Zhaotang and Hui jewelers in Tengyue, across the border from the Burmese jade mines.[46]

The Hui also became expert miners. One source goes so far as to say that "there was no mine [in Yunnan] where there were no Hui."[47] They dominated the lucrative jade trade to the point that that stone came to be known locally as "Huihui gem." There are clear indications that prior to the rebellion, the Hui were often involved in opening and operating mines.[48] Some Hui communities became known for their expertise in mining. Hui from Lin'an—especially those from the village of Huilong—were famously skilled miners and traveled long distances to work mines throughout the province.[49]

Finally, the Hui were successful in obtaining military degrees (*wu juren*). A Yunnan-born official offered a typical Han explanation for why this was so: "Hui do not like to study and rarely own property. They often practice husbandry and are butchers. If they are poorer then they usually become miners, but if they have money typically they are caravaneers traveling back and forth between Burma [and China]—making three times their original investment. They also enjoy archery and riding horses. Because of these skills, two-thirds of Yunnan's military degree holders and military officials are Hui."[50]

The estimate of two-thirds is likely too high. But during the Daoguang reign (1821–1850) more than 12 percent of those who received a military degree did have a typically Hui surname.[51] In the three exams given in the five years just before the rebellion, Muslim Yunnanese constituted almost 19 percent of all graduates.[52]

The Hui also excelled as overland long-distance traders. Their strong commercial and political links with the Southeast Asian highlands and Tibet—through their dominance of the caravan trade—spread their influence far beyond the borders of imperial China. Some Han plied these same routes, but in general they tended not to be as numerous in these areas as in other parts of Yunnan. They were fearful of catching diseases and of passing through non-Han controlled areas.

By the 1800s the Hui had been working the transregional trade routes for centuries. In doing so they had established strong cultural ties with Tibet, Burma, Thailand, and Sichuan.[53] Dali, for example, was the commercial hub for an area far larger than western Yunnan. Through its annual Third Month Fair (Sanyuejie), Dali maintained strong trade relationships with Tibet, Sichuan, and Burma.[54] Southeastern Yunnan's trade was generally limited to Laos, Thailand, and to a lesser extent Burma. In contrast, northeastern Yunnan had its strongest commercial ties (and at times administrative ones) with central China during the rebellion, only rarely interacting with the Muslim Yunnanese of these other areas.[55]

The degree to which these transnational links were dominated by the Muslim Yunnanese communities is open to debate. What is clear, according to nineteenth-century documents, is that the Hui were a prominent part of those links. Throughout much of upland Southeast Asia the Yunnanese Chinese were known simply as Haw, with no distinction drawn between Han and Hui. Although the term Haw is somewhat ambiguous, firsthand accounts from late-nineteenth-century travelers in the region suggest that a large proportion of the Haw were Hui.[56] Haw caravans, which typically numbered between fifty and one hundred mules, carried salt and tea south to the Southeast Asian lowlands and returned with cotton. These caravans were vital to Yunnan's commerce in that they brought needed goods into the province and carried Yunnanese goods to outside markets.[57]

Every year in the dry winter season, Haw caravans passed through and traded with the many diverse Tai, Karen, and other ethnic groups that populated the region separating lowland Southeast Asia from the Yunnan Plateau. Most of the ethnic groups with which the Haw caravans traded lived in communities and loosely bound states (such as Lanna and Sipsongpanna) that enjoyed semiautonomy from their overlords far to the south and north.[58] Forced to negotiate a complex series of tolls and transit permits imposed on the caravans by non-Chinese ethnic groups, the Haw became extremely familiar with the region's networks, allegiances, and political entities.[59] This resulted in a "Yunnan world" comprising the Hui and those ethnic groups affected by or involved in trade with them. This world, which extended far beyond the formal borders of the imperial frontier, had considerable economic, political, and ethnic integrity well into highland Southeast Asia.

Many scholars have suggested that the peoples of the Southeast Asian uplands looked on the Hui and Han Yunnanese as a single undifferentiated group. If they did, it raises the strong possibility that a non-Islamic dimension of the Hui identity emerged as a result of the Haw label. Conversely, the ambiguity of the Haw label, in concert with the Hui's interactions with the ethnically diverse and sensitive ethnoscape of highland Southeast Asia, likely encouraged the Hui to perceive themselves in similar "ethnic" terms. The importance of the Hui ethnic self-identity outside of their self-identity as Muslims is especially significant when we consider what Thongchai, following the observations of Leach and other ethnographers of upland Southeast Asia, calls "negative identification"—that is, the tendency for groups to define themselves by differences rather than through static sets of shared characteristics.[60] In other words, as an apparent consequence of the Hui's role as caravaneers, middlemen, and cultural mediators throughout the

Yunnan world, Islam had by the nineteenth century become only one part of a broader Hui identity.

Furthermore, the Hui's strong trade-based contacts in Burma, Laos, and Thailand accentuated the fact that the boundaries of the Yunnan world and Qing China were not coextensive. There is no doubt that economic tensions resulting from the influx of new Han settlers generated rivalries that led to violence in Yunnan; that said, the differences between the Beijing-centric Qing regime and the multicultural world of Yunnan also led to a certain amount of friction. This friction was especially apparent between the groups most active in these non-Chinese regions and the newly arrived Han settlers—settlers whose ties were to central China. The extent of the Hui religious, commercial, and occupational networks also underscores the degree to which even the remotest Hui villager could be plugged into an array of influences from a variety of non-Chinese sources (such as Southeast Asia, Tibet, and the Muslim world)—sources that distinguished them from the Han and at the same time reinforced their Hui-ness.

## Conclusion

If Governor-General Zhang Liangji and other long-serving officials estimated accurately, in the mid-nineteenth century the Yunnan Hui were roughly 10 percent of the province's population—around one million people.[61] Yet their small demographic presence does little to suggest the strength and organization of the Muslim Yunnanese. Through their intricate web of identities and relationships, the Muslim Yunnanese were able to participate in a wide array of political, commercial, and ethnic arenas. It may be that the highly ethnicized context of the Yunnan world is what enabled the Yunnan Hui to express a more fully developed ethnic identity.

The experience of the Hui in Yunnan seems quite similar to that of Muslims around the world. As Dale Eickelman has suggested so eloquently, throughout the Islamic world Muslims seem able to "juggle local and multiple identities—villager, tribesman, woman, citizen—with the broader identity of believer and to legitimize them all by reference to the idiom of the cosmopolitan community of believers [umma]."[62]

The experiences of the Muslim Yunnanese in the events leading up to and including the Panthay Rebellion offer clear evidence that the Hui were aware of their own ethnicity and were able to articulate the difference between being a Hui and being a Muslim.

The role played by Hui ethnicity in the early modern period, as something discrete from their religious identity as Muslims, has gone practically unacknowledged by Western scholars. This chapter has demonstrated that by the nineteenth century Hui identity was based on belief in a shared history, on collective cultural markers, and on common occupations; furthermore, that identity was constructed in much the same manner that ethnicity is understood in the modern era. At the same time, the events of the Panthay Rebellion would make it clear that this Hui identity was often fraught with regional, cultural, and perhaps religious discord.

As we shall see in the following chapters, the Hui conception of themselves as an ethnic group was defined oppositionally from within—by their occupations, by their non-Yunnan and non-Han origins, and by their Islamic faith. But it was also proscribed from without, often violently by the Han and peacefully by the yi. Only by understanding the multiplicity of ethnic, religious, and political attitudes and actions that formed the Muslim Yunnanese identity can we begin to see that the actions of the Hui during the rebellion were much more than simply a religious reaction against their Han or Qing oppressors.

## CHAPTER 4

# Rebellion's Roots: Hanjianism, Han Newcomers, and Non-Han Violence in Yunnan

## Converting Yunnan

At the beginning of the Qing dynasty in 1651, Yongli, the last known surviving grandson of the Ming emperor, found himself pursued by Qing forces who had overthrown the Ming court in Beijing and who were now consolidating their control across the empire. He and his dwindling group of loyalists swept into Yunnan, where they established a government-in-exile that lasted for nearly eight years before they were forced by Qing troops to flee into Burma. The Burmese king, likely realizing there was little to be gained from such an arrangement, switched his allegiance from the ousted Ming to the emergent Manchu and took the prince and his family hostage. He placed them under virtual house arrest and executed many of their retainers. Yongli's dismal existence ended in 1662, when the Burmese court handed him over to the Qing general, Wu Sangui, who escorted him back into Yunnan. There the prince and his son were executed by strangulation.[1]

The death of the last Ming heir quelled the Qing court's fears of a Ming restoration led by a blood descendent. However, a new danger soon arose, from General Wu Sangui, the same general who had helped the Manchu overthrow the Ming. Wu Sangui was growing increasingly dissatisfied with his subordinate role to the Qing throne and was not content to be even nominally under Qing control, so he dissolved his allegiance to the Qing and in 1678 declared himself emperor of a new dynasty. Only months after this, however, he died of dysentery. Later that same year, Qing forces recaptured Kunming (although remnants of Wu's forces would remain in Yunnan until 1681). Nearly four decades after the Qing dynasty was founded in 1644, Yunnan became the last of the Chinese provinces to be formally brought under Qing authority.

This inauspicious beginning of Qing dominion over Yunnan did little to ameliorate the region's already dodgy reputation as a dangerous frontier province. During the four centuries between Yunnan's reintegration into

China by Mongol forces in 1253 and the rise of the Qing in 1644, Yunnan was of peripheral concern to both the central court and Chinese society. Ming emperors viewed Yunnan as a dangerously unstable multiethnic backwater and handed much of it over to non-Han native chieftains (*tusi*). In the early eighteenth century, partly because the populace had collaborated with the administrations of Yongli and General Wu, the Qing court began to rethink the non-Han administrative institutions it had inherited from the Ming. Court worries over imperial control of the southwest came to a head during the reign of the Yongzheng emperor (r. 1723–35), who launched a program of administrative consolidation (*gaitu guiliu*).

The main purpose of the Yongzheng emperor's consolidation scheme was to end the self-governance of the hereditary tusi and establish direct rule by regularly appointed state officials. Ostensibly, the emperor was seeking to free the non-Han people from rule by the tusi in order "to make their lives safe and happy."[2] The real reason was more likely that by "removing the non-Han officials, the Qing can appraise the property and land and thus increase [the income from] the land tax."[3] To accomplish this, the Qing assigned each tusi a rank in the administrative hierarchy, complete with a seal of office. Given the long-established power of the tusi, the conversion was not without opposition—indeed, it was often violent.

Those tusi who resisted conversion were dealt with summarily by E'ertai, a trusted Manchu official dispatched to the province by the Yongzheng emperor. Many battles were fought; an account described the carnage from one of these as covering "more than ten miles [with] bodies suspended among the trees and stones dripping flesh and blood."[4] More than a century and a half later, gazetteers writing about the consolidation would rank it one of the province's six great military campaigns, alongside Qianlong's Burma campaign and the Panthay Rebellion.[5]

The conversion was an attempt to alter Yunnan's political landscape so as to enhance the Qing's capacity to directly administer Yunnan's multiethnic frontier. Yet the weakening of indigenous rule and the growing presence of the Qing state in Yunnan society (as well as the subsequent increase in the flow of migrants to the province) generated new tensions in Yunnan. In his study of the consolidation process, John Herman concluded that the "reform policies ostensibly designed to bring order and stability to China's southwestern frontier instead brought instability and violence" as the indigenous population resisted the cultural, political, and economic repercussions of consolidation.[6]

By the late eighteenth century, as a result of these dramatic changes, Qing officials were facing serious obstacles to bringing peace and stability to Yunnan. More and more Han were flowing into Yunnan from the overpopulated provinces of the Chinese interior. As their numbers grew, they pushed progressively deeper into the non-Han lands that had once been populated solely by indigenous peoples. At the same time, having removed the tusi administrative framework with great violence, Qing local officials were faced with a dilemma: How were they to govern such a large area, especially one with a culturally and politically alienated populace?

To complicate this picture, many tusi remained in the province and retained a high degree of autonomy over large areas of Yunnan. As late as the 1840s, a French missionary in western Yunnan remarked on the highly independent nature of the tusi: "The small tusi in Yunnan have a certain degree of sovereignty, with fortresses, large homes, and even their own prisons. The only thing they do not have is an army. . . . Because of these aspects in many areas the indigenous tribes still possess something of a society apart, of a distinct *nationalité*."[7]

So the predicament confronting Qing local officials in the first decades of the nineteenth century was how to protect the interests of the state and the Han Chinese when those interests were in conflict with the interests of the non-Han populace (be they under tusi jurisdiction or not), and at the same time strengthen the state commercially and militarily.[8]

During this same period, Yunnan experienced a long string of natural disasters. In a little over fifty years Kunming suffered five severe earthquakes, six calamitous floods, three epidemics, two famines, two droughts, and a major windstorm. In the 1833 Kunming earthquake alone, more than six thousand people were killed and another eighty thousand displaced. Kunming's experience was not unique in the province; in this period every area of Yunnan was struck by a devastating array of natural disasters, extreme weather, and epidemics. Contemporary records state that only in 1818 were there bountiful harvests everywhere in the province.[9]

Man-made disturbances were just as numerous. During the late eighteenth and early nineteenth centuries, Yunnan suffered elevated levels of conflict. Documents indicate that between 1796 and 1851 there were over seventy local disturbances, which touched every region of Yunnan and unsettled its society almost continuously.

It is difficult to pinpoint the cause of this growing interethnic hostility. However, it seems that the growing state presence resulting from the conversion process, the ever-escalating numbers of Han migrants moving into non-Han areas, and the unrelenting succession of natural calamities combined to exacerbate divisions that already existed between the long-term residents (including long-settled local Han as well as the Hui and the non-Han) and the newly arriving settler Han. Yet these conflicts in the early decades of the nineteenth century do not seem to have been the result of rigidly defined ethnic identities and decades-long grudges, as was the case in other parts of China during the same period. Typically, they were described as far more random and spontaneous. A minor official referred to them as clashes between groups who "seeing something they want, banding together; then when they have what they want, disbanding."[10]

### TRAITORS IN THE BORDERLANDS

Yunnan's turbulent transition from Ming to Qing authority and the central court's violent usurpation of administrative control over non-Han areas is an often forgotten prelude to the influx of Han settlers in the eighteenth century. Imperial records of the ethnographic, commercial, and political landscapes of this transition era indicate the ongoing political integration of the province into the Chinese empire. What is often omitted is the deep suspicion of the Qing court and the new settler Han toward the non-Han and those who associated with them. To fully understand the broader implications of Yunnan's integration—and the subsequent violence—it is useful to heed Philip Kuhn when he tells us in his innovative study of the soulstealers that "perceptions matter."[11]

At the turn of the nineteenth century, in memorials to the throne, apprehension over some of the inevitable interactions between Han and non-Han began to appear with more and more frequency. In particular, officials posted to Yunnan increasingly referred to what for them was a worrisome issue: Han Chinese were taking up the causes of the non-Han against the Qing. Some reports described Han involvement in petty disputes or illicit trading. Others pointed to individual Han engaged in efforts to undermine the Qing's carefully laid state-building policies. By the late eighteenth century the Qing court, Qing officials, and many recent Han settlers were beginning to express alarm at the actions of those Han who were associating with non-Han and acting against the state's interests. In the contemporary records, such Han were increasingly branded as traitors to the Han (*hanjian*).

Was this panethnic opposition to Qing governance more than isolated acts of opportunism by a small number of Han? If so, perhaps it meant that the benefits of adopting the transregional and multiethnic model of traditional Yunnan society outweighed any benefits of adopting the sinocentric orientation demanded by the Qing. And in turn, if that was so, then as the Qing's political and military infrastructure in non-Han areas grew stronger, the threat of discontented Han and non-Han joining forces against the Qing would grow apace. This is not completely self-evident, and furthermore, it raises knotty questions: Can the apparent rise in hanjianism be explained by such factors as the Qing authorities' fears that they would fail to integrate Yunnan into the Chinese polity? Or was the rise more properly viewed as a result of the worrisome power of the non-Han to convert Han to their perspective?

Accusations of hanjianism arose most often along the external Burmese and Tibetan borders of Yunnan as well as within internal zones dominated by non-Han. In one of the better-documented cases, a former Buddhist monk named Zhang Fuguo settled in southwestern Yunnan near Mianning in the last years of the eighteenth century. Han immigrants had been settling in this part of Yunnan since the mid-1700s, attracted by the gem and mineral mines. By 1800 they had developed their own enclaves complete with city god temples (imported from their distant hometowns) and merchant associations.[12] Zhang did not take up the same pursuits as his fellow Han; instead he began to associate with the local non-Han in ways that directly contravened the wishes of the state—and that would become increasingly typical across Yunnan.

Early in 1800 Zhang was captured, tried, and punished for his role in a variety of illicit activities. Yunnan officials later petitioned the throne, asking that Zhang be pardoned and indicating that he had admitted the errors of his past and was promising to work with instead of against the imperial government. The Jiaqing emperor well realized how disruptive a Han monk with a troubled past could be in such a distant region, and only reluctantly accepted the recommendation of his provincial officials. Finally, in 1803, he granted Zhang the title of local head (*tumu*), ordering him "to control the [non-Han] and not cause trouble."[13]

In 1811, Zhang returned to his wayward habits. He organized a band of several thousand non-Han, who burned and looted villages, occupied the land of a local tusi, and "secretly recruited other hanjian."[14] Clearly chagrined over the whole affair, the Yun-Gui governor-general, Bolin, ordered three local tusi to organize a multipronged attack on the villages occupied by Zhang. Zhang was finally arrested in 1813, sentenced for his crimes, and publicly executed to "clearly show the power of the law" to the area's residents.[15]

The Qing court now sought to declare actions such as Zhang's as the work of hanjian—an indication of the Qing's awareness of their precarious position in Yunnan. The use of the term hanjian in the context of late imperial Yunnan is striking for its seemingly broad and inconsistent application. In other areas of China it was applied to any Han Chinese who collaborated with non-Han (including Westerners) against Qing interests. In areas of China where Chinese were beginning to work with Westerners (as translators, middlemen, and so on), some Qing officials, including Lin Zexu, who was famous for his role in the Opium War, argued that the key to managing foreigners lay in suppressing the hanjian.[16] Especially in the southeastern province of Guangdong, "the assumption was that these people betrayed their national interest to the foreigners, and as they were of Han Chinese descent, they were therefore termed hanjian."[17]

Hanjianism in nineteenth-century Yunnan seems to have been somewhat different in nature. Most significant is that the non-Han were in the eyes of the central court all Qing subjects. Equally significant is that hanjian were perceived as more than simply bandits active in non-Han areas.[18] Han collaborating with non-Han were beginning to be regarded by the Qing court and by many recent Han settlers as no better than traitors.

It is important to note that during the rise of hanjianism the distinction between banditry and hanjianism continued to be maintained. Banditry in these border areas was common enough, and participants in such illicit activity were labeled, as they were elsewhere in the empire, as just that—bandits (*fei*). Indeed, banditry was so common in Yunnan that different categories of bandits abounded; there were "roving bandits" (*youfei*), "local bandits" (*tufei*), "seditious rebels" (*jiaofei*), and "non-Han bandits" (*yifei*), to name but a few. Clearly, the Qing government feared the consequences of unscrupulous Han bandits interacting with Yunnanese indigenous groups. Indeed, concern about this prompted Yunnan's military commander in 1821 to post notices "forbidding Han to recklessly kill non-Han."[19] However, those Han labeled as hanjian in early-nineteenth-century Yunnan seem to have been, in the eyes of the state, something very different from those who betrayed the state by interacting with foreigners, or those who were bandits. Treason, in the Yunnan context, came to be interpreted not broadly as acts against people but more specifically as Han carrying out acts against the state. Intentions and the court's interpretations of those intentions came to be a significant factor in defining hanjianism. As became increasingly apparent in the first decades of the nineteenth century, hanjian were seen by the state to be those Han who acted in the interests of local non-Han and against the Qing.

Significantly, there seems to have been no strong correlation between hanjianism and any specific ethnic group or region of Yunnan. In 1812, two Han, Kuang Lao and Kuang Hun, were labeled as hanjian, arrested by Qing troops in a Jingpo (*yeyi*) village in southwestern Yunnan, and accused of aiding the non-Han.[20] In 1817, in a case that will be examined in more depth later, hanjian were linked to an uprising in southern Yunnan; they were accused of orchestrating the revolt by hoodwinking its Woni (Hani) leaders.[21] In March 1821, Governor-General Qingbao blamed hanjian in northwestern Yunnan for provoking problems and asked that they be "tried and executed accordingly."[22] These cases suggest that behavior which led to someone being labeled a hanjian involved more than simply a Han flouting the Qing legal code in a predominantly non-Han area; more than that, it involved Han actively supporting non-Han Qing subjects in subversive behavior against state authority.

Yet it is clear from the historical record that a correlation existed between the increasing frequency of contact between non-Han and Han communities and the rise in hanjianism. These contacts provoked spirited reactions among those Chinese who were accustomed to the cultural and political mores of interior China, and they often led to misunderstandings, hostility, and violence. These outbreaks, however, rarely fell along strictly ethnic lines. There was considerable solidarity between Yunnan's diverse non-Han ethnic groups and long-time Han residents whose families had lived in Yunnan for many generations. These were the Han who, by allying themselves with the non-Han, were labeled as hanjian by the Qing government.

## Non-Han Uprisings and Resistance

Between 1796 and 1856 there were at least seventy documented local disturbances involving non-Han and Hui peoples (see Map 4.1). Some of these lasted only one or two days, others well over a year. These clashes tended to occur between long-time residents and newcomers rather than between rival ethnic groups.[23] Although some incidents involved Hui, it was only after 1839 that the violence became increasingly Han-instigated and specifically directed against the Hui.

Sow-Theng Leong's illuminating study of the Hakka in southeastern China offers many parallels to the multiethnic tensions present in Yunnan. In particular, Leong highlights the issues that arose between "natives" and "newcomers." Perhaps some of the issues that triggered the violence in Yunnan had been present for a considerable time; that said, the changing circumstances caused by in-migration seem to have triggered many of the disruptions. The effects of this in-migration into Yunnan in the late eighteenth and early nineteenth centuries were very similar to those in other parts of China, where migration was becoming the "particular context in which ethnic consciousness and conflict emerged in terms of a contradiction between 'natives' and 'newcomers.'"[24]

During the five years on either side of 1800, there were fourteen outbreaks of violence between Qing government forces and Yunnan's multiethnic population. A closer examination of these often overlooked events will bring into sharper relief the nature of these smaller-scale incidents and of Qing attempts to manage a rapidly changing demographic landscape. The non-Han incidents examined next will reveal not only the instability of Yunnan's border society during this period but also the strategies the state followed to address that instability—strategies that differed markedly from those employed later on by Qing officials when handling the Hui.

The following three uprisings occurred within a span of two decades, between 1817 and 1833, in three distinct parts of Yunnan, and were led by people from three different ethnic groups: the Lin'an Uprising of 1817–18,

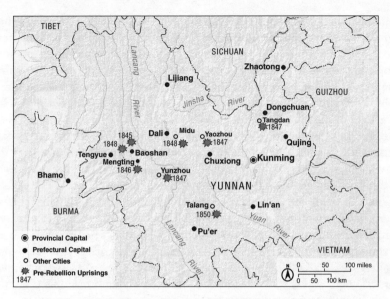

MAP 4.1. Mid-Nineteenth-Century Uprisings in Yunnan

the Lisu Uprising of 1821, and the Dao Shengwu Tusi Affair of 1833. The pattern that emerges from these three insurrections does not reflect ethnic rivalries but rather the animosity felt by long-time multiethnic residents toward Han settlers who were moving into the province in large numbers.

### THE LIN'AN UPRISING OF 1817–1818

In the spring of 1817 a Woni chieftain named Gao Luoyi "attracted over 10,000 people to his cause and proclaimed himself Woni King while conferring titles on his supporters."[25] At first the rebels contented themselves with raids on neighboring non-Han villages and native chieftains. Then, after several months of successful forays, they crossed the Yuan River and threatened the prefectural seat of Lin'an.

This uprising was similar to other Yunnan uprisings of the time in that its causes and events did not reflect ethnic polarization.[26] In 1817, Governor-General Bolin identified Gao Luoyi as a non-Han but also indicated that his followers and high-level supporters included many Han.[27] The uprising is noteworthy because written accounts of it do not describe the events as mere banditry and looting of the sort so often mentioned in official reports of the time. From the outset, this uprising had a clear leader and sought to establish rebel authority over a large area.

Bolin promptly ordered troops to the area and set about overwhelming Gao's forces through superior firepower and organization. Within several months he had dispatched two generals with troops to Lin'an; there, they soon defeated the rebels and executed the principal leaders. The state here was employing a standard Qing tactic relying heavily on a rapid and substantial response to contain resistance early. Such an approach prevented small-scale violence from escalating and garnering widespread support. Bolin's efficient handling of the affair earned him the honorary title Junior Guardian of the Heir Apparent (*taizi shaobao*).[28]

But in this instance the Qing strategy was not entirely effective. A report written less than a year after Bolin's apparent triumph indicates that the local Yunnanese were still committed to a rebellion and that the rebel leadership had been inherited by Gao Luoyi's nephew, Gao Laowu. The official account of the nephew's subsequent actions reads remarkably like that of Gao Luoyi's revolt the previous year. Noteworthy are Bolin's indications that, far from diminishing, rebel support had actually increased in the intervening months: "The Woni from beyond the [Yuanjiang] river led by the nephew of Gao Luoyi, Gao Laowu, again rebelled, and Gao proclaimed himself king. . . . He also coerced and attracted even more people [than the previous year] and gave titles to his followers in resistance against the government. They plundered the region then crossed the river [into the *jiangnei* region] and threatened the prefectural capital, Lin'an."[29] Such sustained resistance, which had been rare in Yunnan, leads one to ask: What motivated a second insurgency after the overwhelming defeat of the first one?

It is directly relevant to the earlier discussion of hanjianism that Bolin at first blamed recent Han immigrants for inciting the rebellions, suggesting that "Han Chinese from Jiangxi, Hunan, and Guangdong were carrying out trade thus taking the profits away from locals and causing hardships."[30] These acts, he added, necessitated "that we more strictly combat the illegal entry of Han Chinese privately entering the border region. By rigorously governing such entry and punishing the illegal immigrants there will not be any further disturbances."[31] Bolin then went on to indicate that hanjian were largely to blame for "teaching" Gao Luoyi how to rebel. The Han he was referring to here were apparently not recent immigrants; in fact they had lived in Yunnan for many generations and had adapted to non-Han ways.

The governor-general's evaluation is striking at several levels. To begin with, the Han were playing two seemingly contradictory roles: as rebel advisors and as catalysts for Woni discontent. Implicit here is that although both groups were Han Chinese, those aiding and abetting the Woni were those who had lived in Yunnan for many years or whose families had immigrated generations earlier. Those who were sparking the unrest were new immigrants whose recent arrival in Yunnan had generated a variety of economic tensions.

Bolin's denunciation of the Han for their complicity in the uprising reveals the prevalent belief among Qing officials posted to Yunnan that the non-Han were passive groups who lacked the capacity to revolt against the state. Thus the state's responsibility was to protect the non-Han by fighting the predatory Han. In this way, provincial officials cast the Han as both the cause and the enablers of the disturbances. Bolin attempted to bolster this line of reasoning by suggesting the "non-Han were dim-witted [*yuchun*]" and thus incapable of carrying out an insurgency without Han assistance.[32]

The non-Han were hardly as obtuse as Bolin portrays them; however, it is equally true that Han old-timers had a hand in the violence. It is likely that Yunnan's long-term Han residents had adopted the local non-Han orientation toward trade (illicit and otherwise) and had forged bonds with the non-Han against the government regulation of trade. This bond would have developed over many generations prior to the actual uprising. This suggests that the Lin'an Uprising was not a matter of non-Han fighting Han.[33] Rather, it was a troubling sign that immigrant Han were playing an increasingly prominent role as instigators of violence.

In a memorial dated February 16, 1819, Bolin offered a twelve-point strategy for addressing what he saw as the causes of the disturbances in Lin'an prefecture.[34] This plan to eradicate undesirables focused on creating a modified mutual surveillance (*baojia*) system for tusi areas. In the standard baojia system, households were organized into decimal divisions; the purpose of these was to provide an added layer of security through mutual surveillance.[35] Instead of the standard baojia system, Bolin envisioned one that would promote "interlinking responsibility between neighboring villages and hamlets—coupling together like a chain, to create stability."[36]

The registration system was largely a preventive measure. To supplement it, Bolin wanted to implement a proactive check on Han who had illegally entered the region and who were potential hanjian. To control these Han, he proposed a more stringent enforcement of the special pass system (*yaopai*). His rationale for this program is significant both for the activities he was ascribing to the hanjian and for how he was seeking to limit those activities. It is worth quoting in full:

These measures are critical because the non-Han disturbances are always caused by Han traitors fleecing (*panbo*) [the non-Han] and always inserting themselves in the middle spreading rumors [*bonong*]. . . . From this time forth Han are not allowed to privately enter non-Han areas for trade. Those traders [given official permission] should be given a special pass [*yaopai*] and are required to return within a specified time. If they fail to return within the proscribed time, it will be considered a crime and punished.[37]

In other words, Bolin wanted to limit the time any Han could trade in a non-Han region and to dictate how many traders could pass into any non-Han area. He specifically identified hanjian bandits as the targets for such a program, believing this policy would "soothe the non-Han groups."[38]

This account of the Lin'an Uprising of 1817–18 points to two factors that were present in most disturbances of the early nineteenth century. First, the hostilities tended to break out between long-term Han residents and Han newcomers, and not as a result of ethnic conflict. Second, the provincial authorities perceived these uprisings as acts of political subversion fomented by hanjian and pursued military solutions. In particular, Qing officials viewed Han immigration and unscrupulous native officials as the main sources of the instability. But although Bolin's fifteen-year tenure as governor-general lent him considerable insight into the trouble caused by the massive influx of immigrants into peripheral areas, he disregarded the way in which Han immigration was altering forever the delicate balance between the indigenous peoples and their land.[39]

### THE LISU UPRISING OF 1821

Bolin had concluded that the Lin'an hostilities were caused by unscrupulous Han as well as by Han immigration. In 1821, the year after he left the province, another outbreak of violence occurred between in-migrating Han and indigenous non-Han peoples. This time, however, the fighting was in northern Yunnan, due east of Lijiang along the border with Sichuan, and involved the Lisu community living there.[40]

This uprising began early in 1821 when several thousand Lisu, demanding the return of their land, looted and burned several Han villages and killed many Han living around Yongbei.[41] From there the violence spread south to Dayao County, where Lahu and Yi joined the attack on several more Han settlements. According to government estimates more than eight thousand Lisu, Lahu, and Yi killed more than five hundred Han settlers.[42]

Investigations by the new governor-general, Qingbao, in the Yongbei and Dayao areas focused on the practice of *dian*, or conditional sales of land. As Huang has pointed out in his study of Qing legal practices, dian was neither an outright sale nor a rental; rather, it "was above all a conditional sale subject to redemption."[43] Dian titles gave the holder the use of the land and even the right to "sub-dian" (*zhuandian*) the property (that is, for example, to pass the conditional ownership for a specified time to a third party). The use of dian in Yunnan came about largely because non-Han lands (under tusi jurisdiction) could not legally be sold outright to Han commoners. To circumvent the letter of the law, the tusi and Han settlers colluded by portraying such transactions as dian.[44] The result, as Qingbao described it, was devastating: "Within the tusi administered non-Han lands there were those who had authorized dian transactions with the Han. From 1756 until the present, some have dian-ed seventy to eighty percent [of the non-Han lands] to Han [settlers] . . . the non-Han do not have enough land to cultivate and thus have a deep-seated hatred towards the Han."[45]

As a direct result of this practice, in 1821 "the indigenous people murdered many of the Han."[46] The incident was exacerbated by the hesitation of the provincial military commander to dispatch soldiers to the area.[47] The actual uprising lasted a relatively short time—only about four months from beginning to end.

The Lisu Uprising of 1821 is exceptional in several ways. First, Chinese accounts of it are among the few that show an understanding of non-Han motives. Second, these government accounts indicate that there was not only tension between indigenous residents and newcomers but also anger over the environmental devastation that had been triggered by the flood of Han settlers. Third, the accounts call attention to an often overlooked dimension of the period: the complicity of the tusi and other native leaders in the Han settlers' actions.

Christian Daniels and Takeuchi Fusaji, environmental historians, have argued separately that the loss of land in the lowlands was not the only cause of the uprising. Both contend that another cause was the massive destruction of the hill lands—destruction brought about by the intensive cultivation of mushrooms by Han settlers.[48] This thesis is substantiated by the fact that the Lisu rarely lived on the valley floors, preferring to inhabit small settlements along the mountain ridges.

The Han did not simply gather mushrooms from the wild; they cultivated them, and for that purpose denuded entire hillsides. *Dayao xianzhi* (1845) described the process this way: trees were cut down and "twenty to thirty holes [were filled with] fine ash and a small quantity of a powder of ground stipes of old mushrooms."[49] After four to five years the mushrooms grew in profusion all over the downed trees. Unfortunately, "after ten years or so, the trees decayed and the mountains were left bare."[50]

Governor-General Qingbao acted on a rather different set of assumptions from those of Bolin, whose overriding concern had been to keep the non-Han and Han separate by raising barriers to interaction. Qingbao sought first of all to establish the foundations for peaceful coexistence between Han and non-Han. He did this by allocating funds to house rebuilding and to food allowances for lost crops, and also by investigating those Han who illegally dianed land.[51] However, Qingbao was not immune from cultural stereotypes. He prefaced his action plan by contending that the underlying problem was that "the non-Han do not know how to make a living from hard work so have often sold or leased their land to Han."[52]

Qingbao's policy struck a careful balance between the unavoidable consequences of migration and the persistent need to maintain some separation between the indigenous and Han populations. Like his predecessor, he believed the Han were provoking the non-Han insurrections by engaging in a variety of illicit and unscrupulous practices. Qing officials felt that the non-Han who actually carried out the attacks were not the main problem, and they sought to identify and address the root causes of the violence.[53]

### THE DAO SHENGWU TUSI AFFAIR OF 1833

In 1833, sixteen years after the Woni uprising, on Yunnan's southern border, a native chieftain of the Dai ethnic group, Dao Shengwu, organized a militia of several thousand men to carry out local raids. Dao was the tusi of Cheli and thus was the area's ranking Qing administrator. Official accounts state that the raids began after Dao fell in with rogues who persuaded him, unwisely, to attack his uncle, a native leader (*tushe*). After that attack was repulsed, he returned to his home district but continued to cause further disturbances. After several reversals, he established an army and offered military positions to those willing to join his band. With this large force, he enriched himself by robbing caravans that were transporting salt, cotton, and other goods.[54] Dispatches from local authorities reported that he had recruited hanjian, indigenous traitors (*yijian*), and non-Han outsiders (*waiyi*) as well. After refusing to surrender to a superior government force, he fled with the seals of his office. The government responded by revoking his status as tusi.[55] Most likely, Dao was motivated by a desire to reestablish a local system of commercial and political autonomy, one that reflected southern Yunnan's powerful ties to the Southeast Asian highlands.

Communications between Beijing and Yunnan provincial officials in the wake of this incident reveal that the central court very much intended to preserve the hereditary system of local Dai leadership. The state wanted to replace Dao rather than attempt to consolidate the area with the empire. This attitude reflected a mature understanding of local politics on the part of Ruan Yuan, the Yun-Gui governor-general, and the Manchu governor of Yunnan, Yilibu; between them, these two men had more than twenty-five years of service in Yunnan. Perhaps their administrative experience is what enabled them to balance the needs of the Qing state with those of Yunnan's non-Han society. Or perhaps this restraint on the part of the Qing simply reflected the provincial authorities' preoccupation at the time with the destruction caused by recent earthquakes, which had destroyed more than one-third of the province.[56]

Ruan Yuan stated that provincial officials, in selecting a new Cheli tusi, had sought a candidate who fell into the patriarchal hereditary line:

The local heads of Cheli's thirteen indigenous districts [*banmeng*] have been ordered to deliberate and equitably select a replacement. Dao Taikang [Dao Shengwu's paternal uncle] has two sons. The public meeting discussed and selected Dao Taikang's elder son, Dao Zhengzong, who is old enough, to take over Dao Taihe's hereditary office. All were direct descendants of Dao Shiwan [Dao Shengwu's paternal grandfather]. The 'indigenous populace' all received this decision happily and enthusiastically. All agreed to submit to his authority.[57]

This conspicuous effort to involve the community in the selection process had a twofold purpose. The native chieftain's jurisdiction was only nominally under Qing control. By ensuring local support for the Qing government's candidate, the provincial officials were not only ending the discord manifested in the uprising but also establishing a basis for future cooperation with the local population. By having local headmen elect him, they were also legitimizing imperial authority in the region.

Yilibu had ordered local troops to pursue Dao Shengwu. After Dao escaped "far across the border" and stopped disturbing the area, he called off the pursuit,[58] although he ordered provincial officials to remain on the alert for him and posted a reward for his capture. Accounts strongly suggest that since Dao had been divested of his office, Yilibu and other officials no longer considered him a threat to the region's order.

The nature of Dao's resistance merits comment. Most likely, he did not feel compelled to adopt a personal title, as Gao had done during the Woni incident, since he held seals of office and a high rank within the Qing power structure. His followers included Han, Dai, and a third indeterminate group referred to as "luo-yi." Official accounts suggest that Dao wanted to build a power base along the border, one that would be unfettered by but not necessarily independent of state control.[59]

In his study of the early modern state of Xishuangbanna Hsieh Shi-chung describes a pattern of resistance that Dao's activities seem to have paralleled. This pattern suited nineteenth-century Sipsongpanna, a region comprising many small kingdoms, allied villages, and local Dai tribes in various galactic orbits. "If an indigenous leader raised armies for purposes such as expanding territories, or avenging a blood feud," Hsieh contends, "he stood only about a fifty percent or smaller chance of causing China to send a punitive expedition."[60] Moreover, because of the very real danger of malaria, Chinese troops rarely remained in tropical southern Yunnan for extended periods. This almost guaranteed that local rebel groups would not face outright extermination.

Dao had first affected deference to the Chinese state and then pursued his own ends. Similar tactics that had been employed by local Dai leaders for centuries. Although Qing officials always suppressed outright sedition, in cases involving native chieftains along remote borders they were mindful of the buffer role that indigenous leaders might play. What the Qing could not accept was Dao's pursuit of power above and beyond what was ascribed to his office—in particular, his attempts to subvert Qing administrative and military authority.

As in the Woni uprising in Lin'an, at least some Han Chinese joined Dao. Predictably, the accounts labeled these men hanjian. Not so predictable was the appearance in these same accounts of the term "indigenous traitors" (yi-jian). The implications of this term are far-reaching, and suggest that even in the not yet fully incorporated Yunnan borderlands a non-Han Dai could, in the eyes of the state, be a "traitor" to the empire (since it seems the imperial court would hardly express concern if a non-Han was acting against his own people). This term in this context implies that besides being marginalized as ignorant savages under the tutelage of local rulers, the Dai were being cast as Qing *subjects* who knowingly chose to oppose imperial rule.

From this time on, all of the indigenous non-Han peoples were generally considered Qing subjects and, as such, bound to baojia regulations and taxation. Furthermore, state officials were delineating precisely the ethnic differences between Han traitors and non-Han traitors. This reminds us that ethnicity was not absent from their analyses of these situations; however, it was rarely the determining factor. The state was adhering to a policy in which ethnicity was not the main determinant of the actions taken; this typified not only the three uprisings discussed here but also the large majority of government responses to conflicts involving non-Han. A valid interpretation of the tempered response to Dao Shengwu's rebellion is that the Qing wanted to control indigenous peoples by maintaining order strategically, but not necessarily territorially.

## Shifting Concerns

Throughout the first three decades of the nineteenth century, Qing officials consistently blamed non-Han violence on the Han. In 1822, Yin Peifen, an imperial censor and a native of Yunnan, filed a report on the general situation in the province: "In the areas along the border, Han are few and non-Han peoples are numerous and diverse. There are also many hanjian who come from central China and dupe the indigenous peoples, making it very easy for problems to arise."[61]

Four years later, in 1826, another censor listed hanjianism as one of the three main problems facing Qing governance in Yunnan.[62] At the same time, officials fretted over the impact of the overwhelming numbers of migrant Han, many of whom had eluded registration in local baojia systems. In 1836 one local official noted that several prefectures in southeastern Yunnan each had more than twenty thousand unregistered immigrants; most of them were "cutting down the trees and burning the mountainsides [bare] . . . generally in remote and secluded areas." Almost identical factors had led to the Lisu Uprising of 1822.[63]

It was quite common for Qing officials posted to Yunnan to perceive Han Chinese as both the cause of and the catalyst for the province's instability. From the uprisings described earlier, it is clear that the non-Han were a concern to the Qing authorities mainly because of the danger that they would fall prey to immigrant Han or come under the spell of devious hanjian. The flaw in this explanation was that it denied any agency to the non-Han and ignored the growing signs of multiethnic resistance to the project of reorienting Yunnan politically and culturally.

All of this seems to suggest that Qing authorities were becoming concerned about *Han* contact with non-Han but not the non-Han themselves. The emphasis on hanjianism perhaps reflected these officials' profound anxieties over how the new Han residents would cope with Yunnan's alien environment—with its diseases, transnational commerce, and cultural differences. These anxieties were reflected in the way the central authorities focused on those Han Chinese who were seeking to defend traditional Yunnanese ways against the assimilationist projects promoted by the Qing court and commonly supported by the new Han immigrants.

Tensions rose during the early decades of the nineteenth century. Logic would suggest that the cause was escalating hanjianism. Yet around this time, without explanation, reports of hanjian activity begin to disappear from official records, until by the late 1830s they have almost vanished. In their place one group stands out more and more as a focus of anxiety for both the state and the newly settled Han. That group is the Muslim Yunnanese. They are different enough from the Han to be identifiable; they are successful enough to be resented; and they tend as a group to support Yunnan's multiethnic and multiregional orientation. In the years to follow, the state's concern shifts from a category of people to a single ethnic group, and from proactive suppression to outright extermination.

## CHAPTER 5

# Spiraling Violence: The Rise of Anti-Hui Hostilities

## The Xiyi Mine Incident of 1800

Early in the spring of 1800, at a small silver mine in Shunning County on the far western border of Yunnan, a quarrel broke out between a Han migrant from Hunan and a Muslim Yunnanese. The exact circumstances are unclear, but according to confessions in the official records, the argument between the two men—a Hui and a Han—quickly led to a street brawl during which Hui damaged several Hunanese shops.[1] In retaliation, more than 180 Hunanese Han formed a band and over the next several days carried out extended attacks on the Hui community, killing a Hui team boss and at least eighteen other Hui. Several Hunanese were wounded in the fighting, but none were killed.[2] Remarkably, the Han from other provinces never joined the fray; they stayed on the sidelines in groups based on their native provinces (Jiangxi and so on).[3]

At the time the clash occurred, the Xiyi mine had been open "officially" for less than two decades (it had been operating outside Qing oversight since at least the early eighteenth century).[4] In 1800, several thousand miners, workers, and merchants were working in or near the mine and living close by.[5] Because of its remote location near upland Southeast Asia, the local population included yi, Han, and Hui.[6]

From the perspective of Qing officials, mining populations were innately unstable and those on the empire's periphery especially so. One official in Yunnan bemoaned that the Yunnan mines were difficult to control: "Everywhere there are covert bandits and hanjian establishing gangs and miners predisposed to fight and rob. . . . What is the method to repress and govern [such behavior]? How can that be easily changed when the majority of the gold, silver, and iron mines are all like this?"[7]

The Xiyi mine was distant from Yunnan's administrative center, yet it had experienced the full impact of Han in-migration. The result was an unstable mixture of lawlessness, ethnic tension, and greed. The incident was similar to many other ethnic flare-ups in Yunnan during this period, and thus seemed like nothing out of the ordinary, so officials were little concerned and took no action.

### BAIYANG MINE INCIDENT OF 1821

Twenty years passed before the next recorded outbreak of violence between Han and Hui in Yunnan. In May 1821 at the Baiyang mine, several days' travel northwest of Dali, a conflict erupted between the Han and Hui miners. The mine population included many Han from outside Yunnan as well as both Han and Hui from within the province. In the communities around the mine the various groups had established Buddhist temples, native place societies (*huiguan*), and mosques. These buildings were central meeting places for their respective groups.[8] Like the hostilities at Xiyi, the Baiyang incident began as a dispute between several Han and Hui miners and quickly degenerated into a series of running street battles between roving bands of more than two hundred Han and Hui. After more than a week of fighting, nearly one hundred people lay dead. Almost 90 percent of them were Muslim Yunnanese.[9]

It is significant that in their later descriptions of the event, both the Han and the Hui repeatedly alluded to the Xiyi incident as a factor in the bloodshed. Put simply, Baiyang was partly about payback. One Han from southern Yunnan recounted that the team boss, "playing on lingering memories of the Xiyi Incident . . . sought to use this animosity to enlist the support of the Hunanese Han by fabricating the rumor that the Hui [strategy] was to first kill those Han from Lin'an and then those [Han] from Hunan and Guangdong to revenge the Xiyi Incident."[10]

These comments tell us two important things. First, even as the violence at Xiyi receded from view in the reports filed by the steady stream of officials posted there, it lingered in the memory of the Han and Hui communities. Second, the Han miner's comment, noted above, indicates an unambiguous attempt to forge a new transprovincial identity vis-à-vis the Hui. This was an ominous turn from the earlier tactics of Xiyi.

The Qing authorities responded very differently to the Baiyang incident. At Xiyi, a local magistrate had captured and tried two Han Chinese for their part in the killings. He had sentenced one to death by slicing and beheading (*lingchi*) and the other to one hundred strokes.[11] The resolution of the Baiyang case was not so straightforward. Zhang Zhixue, the magistrate for Dali district, was ordered by the governor-general to investigate the case. Zhang, aged and ill, delegated the task to the prefectural magistrate, Lei Wenmei. Lei traveled to the mine, where he carried out a purely perfunctory investigation. He would base his account solely on what the local Han Chinese told him. His report, which was filed quickly, concluded that "in the Han-Hui conflict, after my investigation only 5 Han and 23 Hui died."[12]

Had the Baiyang investigation ended there, the meager documentation would have suggested that it, like Xiyi, was a minor affair. However, one of the Hui mine owners, Ma Xingyun, distressed by the death of his relatives, the damage to his mine, and the lack of a serious investigation, traveled to Beijing to present his case before the Qing court. This, even though he had been away in Dali during the violence. As a result of his efforts, the original investigators were demoted one grade and the provincial officials were compelled by imperial edict to reopen the investigation, interview scores of eyewitnesses, and attempt to mediate any remaining disputes.[13]

Surprisingly, Baiyang's Hui did not universally approve of Ma Xingyun's actions. Apparently Ma, in his appeal to the throne, exaggerated both the number of deaths and the amount of property damage. In his statement to the new team of investigators, the mine's Muslim Yunnanese team boss, Zhang Zihong, actually tried to mitigate the acts of the Han: "After the altercation between the Han and the Hui, I carefully investigated [the accusations] and found there were no incidents of looting silver or [mining] materials. . . . If there had actually been incidents of looting by Qin Xianzhong and his group, why would the Hui team boss aid them to conceal it?"[14]

If we are to believe Zhang Zihong, despite the lopsided number of deaths and the apparently biased official investigation, the Hui involved in the violence at Baiyang were not intent on bringing down retribution on their fellow Han miners, even though they now had the opportunity. Some Hui even tried to follow official avenues of resolution and willingly testified on the Han miners' behalf to prevent them from being punished.

Ma Xingyun's petition and the government's timely and evenhanded response suggest that at the provincial and court levels, anti-Hui violence was treated in much the same way as violence against other non-Han people (and, for that matter, Han-versus-Han violence). Thus the Baiyang incident is not especially conspicuous amidst a host of other hostilities recorded in correspondence with the court—although the imperial court's attentiveness to redressing bureaucratic malfeasance is noteworthy. Nowhere are there any indications that Qing officials at any level considered the Muslim Yunnanese any more or less violent than any other group in Yunnan.

This last point is significant. Late nineteenth and early twentieth century analyses of the Han–Hui violence prior to the Panthay Rebellion inevitably point to the Xiyi and Baiyang incidents as irrefutable proof that as far back as 1800, the Muslim Yunnanese had a predilection for committing violence against the Han.[15] A Dali County gazetteer from early in the twentieth century, under the section "The Causes for Hui Provocation of the Rebellion," explicitly linked the 1800 and 1821 incidents with ethnic strife in the

1850s.[16] Because these incidents have been misrepresented as the origins of some unstoppable Muslim juggernaut increasingly intent on rebellion, other factors such as the changing stance of local Qing officials, the growing influence of Han brotherhoods, and repeated efforts by the Hui to cooperate with the Qing state have been either ignored or dismissed entirely.

In light of the many non-Han outbreaks of violence examined in the previous chapter, it is highly significant that the Xiyi and Baiyang incidents, although noteworthy for the role the Hui played in them, were hardly different from numerous other uprisings that were occurring throughout the province in the first decades of the nineteenth century. The two incidents were radically different in tenor and scope, however, from those involving Hui which followed.

### THE MIANNING MASSACRE OF 1839

The small walled town of Mianning lies 130 miles south of Shunning, the prefectural capital. Shunning and its surrounding region had come under direct Chinese administration only in 1746; until then it had been ruled indirectly through a local tusi.[17] Hui and a variety of ethnic groups lived in the area. However, in the early decades of the nineteenth century, more and more Han Chinese were settling there, mainly in the town and the surrounding fertile valley.

In December 1838 a dispute arose between several members of the Muslim Yunnanese and Han communities. It began when a local Hui, Ma Wanju, sought repayment of a debt of a few taels of silver from Zhang Xunzheng, the subprefectural magistrate.[18] Zhang felt insulted by the request and demanded a vacant plot of land opposite a mosque, ostensibly to erect a pavilion commemorating an imperial edict (*shengyu ting*).[19] The Muslim community maintained that there were many other tracts of land within the city walls that were larger and more appropriate, since the mosque would dwarf even the largest shengyu ting.[20] Believing that official channels for resolving this dispute were being obstructed, they tried to block Zhang's project by building a decorative wall (*zhaobi*) on the land in question.[21] Incensed, local officials allied with Zhang ordered construction of the wall halted immediately.

Shortly after this, two local gentry, Yang Yaodou and Zhao Shizhi, solicited the Muslim community for a donation of forty taels toward a ceremonial umbrella to honor the assistant regional commander, Rui Lin.[22] The Muslim Yunnanese balked at such an expensive show of support for an official they scorned. In retaliation for this refusal, local officials alleged that the mosque encroached on the public road and brought the case before the magistrate.

The Muslim Yunnanese showed the magistrate municipal records proving that the ground in question was in fact *waqf*[23] land (property held communally by the mosque) and that they held basic land-owning rights to it. The Hui were exonerated, and Yang and Zhao were publicly humiliated. The latter responded by fomenting anti-Hui sentiment in Mianning. On July 5, 1839, they secretly organized a meeting with the leaders of recent Han immigrants from Sichuan, Hunan, and other Chinese provinces. All who attended "agreed to join forces to destroy the Muslim Yunnanese."[24]

The Hui heard about this and approached Rui Lin to try to diffuse the situation. Rui Lin acknowledged that such a plot existed and suggested they "go and collect two thousand strings of cash to be forfeited to Yang Yaodou and the others who will use it to disperse the people."[25] However, when they returned with the cash, Rui Lin told them that forces were already gathering against them and that he could do nothing to prevent it. Terrified, the Muslim Yunnanese sent local Hui to the prefect in Shunning for assistance. Those who remained fled into hiding with their families.[26]

On July 17, the local magistrate, professing concern for their safety, ordered the Muslim families living outside the city wall into the town. The next day at dawn the company commander, Zhu Zhanchun, silently led the Han militia into the city, where they waited for Rui Lin to give the predetermined signal—the firing of two cannons and the blowing of conch shells from the city walls. On hearing the signal the local militia struck from all sides, massacring more than seven hundred Hui. Later that same day other Han bands moved beyond the city into nearby Hui villages, where the slaughter continued.[27] In the two weeks that followed more than 1,700 Muslim Yunnanese in and around Mianning were murdered. Their houses and mosques were razed.[28]

Almost immediately, Ma Wenzhao, a prominent local Hui, set off for Beijing to petition for an investigation. By the time he reached Beijing several months later, Governor-General Yilibu—the same Manchu official who had been involved in the Dao Shengwu incident described in chapter 4—had heard about the attack. Yilibu recommended that Zhang Jingyi and Rui Lin be dismissed from their posts for their "failure to use soldiers to disperse the disturbances [against the Hui]."[29] The Daoguang emperor immediately took Yilibu's advice and dismissed both. Ma Wenzhao's additional accusation that officials were shielding ringleaders of the massacre prompted the emperor to order Yilibu's successor, Gui Liang, to investigate further. In this way, local officials were brought under intense scrutiny.[30]

The complicity of the local officials with the Han Chinese residents in the Mianning Massacre marked a sea change in the nature of hostilities between ethnic groups. Before Mianning, officials had never sided so openly or actively with one group against another. Moreover, when indigenous peoples had rebelled in the past (see chapter 4), many local Han had sided with the insurgents. The Mianning Massacre was a new development in two critical ways. First, it signaled a shift in the violence from isolated, rural, and often predominantly non-Han areas to urban centers dominated by immigrant Han. Second, local officials were siding with the perpetrators of the violence. In the earlier incidents, these officials had sometimes been inefficient, corrupt, and even prejudiced against the non-Han, but they had never promoted or joined in the violence against either Hui or non-Han. Third, Mianning was the first instance of patently premeditated violence against a single group, the Muslim Yunnanese.

## Things Happen: Notions of Communal Violence

At first glance, the massacre at Mianning might seem the end result of a community feud (*xiedou*). In the nineteenth century such feuds were most common in the southeastern provinces of Guangdong and Fujian, where competition for land was intense and lineage rivalry was commonplace.[31] However, there is little evidence that the violence in Mianning was of the same variety.

Was xiedou at the root of the violence in Mianning? The question is far from academic. In trying to close the case, the Mianning officials—the very ones who had launched the attack—claimed that it had been a case of xiedou violence. These efforts by officials to conceal their own participation in the massacre by calling it xiedou are what drove Ma Wenzhao to travel to Beijing. In his multipage description of the acts committed by Rui Lin and other officials, Ma refuted point by point their untenable claims. In his petition he stated adamantly that he was not arguing that Hui were "incapable of burning and looting"; he was, however, saying that the nature of the violence in Mianning was quite different from xiedou:

But if it were xiedou, why was it that young boys and pregnant women were killed. . . . Why did the Hui ask repeatedly for assistance from the government officials? . . . Why was it that only the Hui homes and villages were demolished while the Han houses and temples of east Mianning escaped any damage? . . . Why did the Western Intendant give relief assistance only to the Muslim Yunnanese? . . . Why was it that Hui men and women, young and old were wounded and killed in the fighting, but not a single Han? Judging from this evidence, it could not have been xiedou.[32]

As Ma was pointing out, the Mianning Massacre was singular because there was no evidence that any Han were killed and no evidence that any Han property had been damaged or destroyed. Just as significant is that the local officials were claiming that the massacre was the result of a feud, yet nowhere in their accounts did they suggest that there had been long-term feuding or even that either side was trying to link the Mianning Massacre with earlier hostilities at the mines.

The central court made immediate inquiries into the massacre but forgot about it soon afterwards; the Opium War and events in other parts of the empire had captured its attention. In hindsight, the Mianning bloodshed marked a profound change in the nature of hostilities in Yunnan and in the state's responses to them. State records indicate that fewer and fewer incidents of indigenous resistance were reported after this time. In fact, only a handful of revolts were noted after 1839, and most of these involved only Muslim Yunnanese and Han Chinese. More and more often, local and provincial reports were casting the Muslim Yunnanese not as victims but as a group predisposed to seditious acts.

The coordinated attempt by the Mianning Han in 1839 to eradicate the local Hui was the first sign that Yunnan's growing Han population was becoming intolerant of the Muslim Yunnanese. It has long been thought that Han–Hui violence grew out of a long history of friction; in fact, the historical record offers little evidence for such a conclusion. Instead, the records indicate a surging intolerance and resentment of the Hui among the Han— an intolerance increasingly encouraged by local Qing officials.

THE BAOSHAN MASSACRE OF 1845

The Baoshan Massacre arose out of a complex web of Han–Hui animosities and mutual resentments. This mutual ill feeling led to specific incidents that sparked the massacre in the spring of 1845.

The first incident was rather minor, and took place near the village of Banqiao, in the broad valley that surrounded the prefectural capital of Baoshan. Specifically, it took place in a rice paddy during the labor-intensive planting season.[33] It was common while planting for workers to sing impromptu rhyming couplets (duichang); one person would sing a line and the other would respond, back and forth, each trying to outdo the other in cleverness. On this occasion, a Muslim Yunnanese sang: "Rice straw binds the seedlings, young next to old." To this a Han responded: "The Hui leads his pig, an old man guiding his grandson."[34] This was a highly public insult against the Hui community and a calculated affront to the Muslim Yunnanese, whose religion forbade the eating of pork. Another verse, also said to have been given in response, was just as incendiary: "Pork being sold in front of the mosque / Seeing it, the Hui buys half a pound."[35]

Imperial records indicate than Han and Hui exchanged taunts in public on a daily basis.[36] Ditties, jokes, and off-color comments aimed at other ethnic groups were hardly new to the multiethnic society of Yunnan; such teasing often served to release tensions before they could brew into large-scale violence. However, official records indicate that from April 1845 onwards, "songs, other trivial jests, and teasing" were becoming increasingly commonplace.[37] In the spring of 1845 such exchanges between Han and Hui in the Baoshan valley began to take on a far more menacing tone.[38]

Early every spring, a local festival celebrating the birthdays of the Five Sacred Mountain Temple gods was held. This festival began at the Wanshou Temple and culminated two days later at the Temple of the East Mountain God outside the city's southern gate.[39] A local Baoshan Han described how this annual event heightened tensions between the Han and Hui communities:

Every year on the 29th day of the third lunar month, there is a festival celebrating the meeting of the Five Great Mountain Gods. [On the 27th] two days prior to the festival eight people would bring a sedan chair to welcome the statues of the Five Gods. They then would carry the five gods to Wanshou Temple. Many [Buddhist] monks and Daoists collect alms, chant and prostrate themselves for two days. On the third day (the 29th), they carry the statues to East Mountain Temple, south of the town, to celebrate. The procession has to traverse the town via Tongfeng Street which passes in front of the mosque gate. . . . Every time this occurs, there are often several dozen [Hui] students who come out and watch—not paying respect to the Han religion [hanjiao]. The rowdy ones laugh and taunt the procession, taking whatever they are chewing (orange peel, sugar cane) and throwing it at the people in front of the sedan and jeering. [This behavior] angers both the Han participants and bystanders who often start quarreling and fighting.[40]

Such heated exchanges and brawls had been a fact of life in Baoshan for many years. In the summer of 1845, however, the minor outbreaks began to escalate into armed confrontations involving one thousand or more participants.[41]

A major contributing factor to this rise in violence, and its tendency to spill out onto the streets of Baoshan, was the increasingly dominant role played by local Han brotherhoods in the Baoshan area. These brotherhoods appeared under a variety of guises ranging from "cattle protection associations" (niucong)[42] to "Incense Brotherhoods" (xiangba hui).[43] The origins of these brotherhoods in Baoshan are obscure, although they appear in reports of local officials as far back as 1808.[44] The societies were officially scorned; imperial sources described their members as primarily "young brawlers, local bullies, and low grade scholars."[45] Other accounts suggest that their members were Han newcomers who were either farmers or small-time merchants. Like many throughout the empire at this time, these newcomers were seeking ways to survive in a world grown complicated because of bureaucratic inefficiencies, population pressure on limited resources, and ethnic rivalries.[46]

The term Incense Brotherhood, uncommon in other parts of Yunnan, referred to the burning of incense prior to the oath-taking ritual during the initiation rite. The following description survives of this particular brotherhood's initiation rites, which were likely similar to those of other societies around Baoshan:

In March of this year, Wan Lingui [the Banqiao head] conspired to draw up an agreement with his Incense brothers to unite in order to control the [Banqiao] village. . . . On April 8 they gathered twenty-nine of their brothers in Zunguang Temple and burned incense before the gods, swearing a pledge of mutual support.[47] Because Wan Lingui was young and strong, they selected him as the head and swore their allegiance to him. . . . At the temple they set up instruments of punishment and vowed that all affairs of Banqiao must be decided and arbitrated by them. They then drank wine and dispersed.[48]

The Incense Brotherhoods had branches in each of Baoshan County's townships (xiang). Each "branch" was referred to as one stick of incense (ba). Since each of the eight townships had a local branch, they were collectively referred to as the Eight-Incense (baba) Brotherhood.[49] The local branches of the Incense Brotherhoods resembled brotherhoods common elsewhere in China, such as the Tiandihui and Gelao Hui; however, there is no indication they had direct ties outside of the Baoshan Valley.[50]

According to official investigations, the incense societies first appeared as cattle protection societies in small communities; they guarded against rustlers. In the 1830s, however, they began to evolve into more powerful organizations that often, instead of killing in defense, "killed out of revenge" or murdered those who opposed their leadership.[51] The brotherhoods do not seem to have been exclusively anti-Hui; that said, the Hui had clearly become the principal target of their activities by the 1840s. They also assaulted Han who failed to follow their lead.[52]

By the mid-1840s, the power, status, and wealth of these societies had grown dramatically throughout the Baoshan Valley. In each village an elder (daye) was appointed.[53] The largest of the branches of the brotherhood was in Banqiao village. It was said that when the head of the brotherhood went out, he was carried in a sedan chair by eight men and escorted by an armed guard. In scale and style, these processions surpassed those of any local official and were said to rival even those of the governor-general. The daye were so powerful that local officials avoided contact with them for fear of creating an incident.[54] Besides being more powerful, the brotherhoods were often more ambitious than the local authorities.

In the early 1840s, an acting district magistrate noted that the Incense Brotherhood's leaders were perceived as more effective than local officials at settling disputes.[55] A formal investigation conducted later on would have this to say about the organization: "Western Yunnan has the evil practice of forming Incense Brotherhoods that frequently use their sheer numbers to tyrannize the region. Not only do they oppress the common people, committing robbery and murder, but they defy arrest and assault officials, making the people become daily more angry and disdainful of government officials."[56]

Hui were not the only victims of the Incense Societies. Many Han also feared them. The authority these brotherhoods wielded was increasingly pervasive. One Han was hounded by them for failing to pay a fine and committed suicide in order to avoid appearing before an Incense Brotherhood tribunal.[57]

Many local officials acknowledged the rising power of the brotherhoods. It is far from clear, though, just how much they bowed to their power or even facilitated their rise.[58] Many officials lacked sufficient resources to counter the brotherhoods, and those seeking promotion were easily coerced by the brotherhoods into delaying investigations and overlooking illicit activities. Only when it was absolutely unavoidable did these officials arrest brotherhood members.[59] Even less clear is the degree to which officials came to agree with the brotherhoods' aims and support their means.[60]

Evidence from the early 1840s suggests that the local bureaucracy was at best ambivalent about the Incense Brotherhoods. Later investigations noted that through displays of force, these groups were able to enforce their will on villagers and officials alike: "For more than ten years [they] have intimidated their rivals and murdered the people—with none of it reported. If an official comes to investigate, there will immediately be a signal given for a crowd to gather, which will then surround and abuse him."[61] By early 1845 the Han brotherhoods had succeeded in intimidating the local authorities, who depended more and more on them to maintain the peace. The brotherhoods could just as easily choose to destabilize the area, in which case the officials might well be dismissed from office.

The Hui were clearly not part of these secret societies and felt the full brunt of this new power structure. At the same time, they were not entirely blameless in the spiraling violence. In the mid-1840s large numbers of Hui from northwestern China were immigrating to the Baoshan region, albeit never on the same scale as the Han. Tensions grew between the Han and the Hui; the violence that followed was largely between Han newcomers and Hui newcomers.

If an incident from May 1845 is any indication, these two groups of recent immigrants hated each other. In the spring of that year four Hui immigrants arrived in Banqiao village from Shaanxi Hui. The four men, "Ma Da, Ma Laoshaan, Hai Laosha'an, and Qin Erlaosha'an entered the village singing songs and then laughed at a group of Han. Enraged, the Han told the Hui they were going to drive them out of town."[62] Ma Da angrily replied: "Having only just arrived and we are already insulted by Han, it will be difficult in the future to live here."[63]

It is unclear whether a scuffle ensued or whether the two groups went their separate ways, although certainly neither side was willing to let the matter end there.[64] Ma Da and several other Hui began teaching martial arts at a local mosque in a neighboring Hui village. The county magistrate, Li Zhengrong, ostensibly enforcing the law forbidding illicit teachings, ordered their arrest, but all escaped except one.[65] Wan Lingui, head of the Banqiao brotherhood, was angry at the state's "incompetence" and decided to take matters into his own hands. The following day, at the head of a band of compatriots, he vandalized the mosque. When the magistrate failed to arrest the Han for the resulting damage, the Hui concluded that the government was applying a double standard in dealing with Han and Hui and began forming their own self-defense corps.[66]

What happened next is difficult to piece together. It seems that the local Hui solicited help from other Hui communities in Mianning, Yunzhou, and Shunning to seek revenge for the Han's actions. They had concluded that the government was powerless to act, or perhaps they were seeking ways to protect themselves against the powerful local societies.[67] In response to their appeal, a band of largely Hui criminal elements from the northwest established a camp in Banqiao village close to Baoshan and began making forays against nearby Han villages.[68] Throughout the month of May, rumors raced through each community about atrocities being committed by the other. One rumor had it that the Hui had captured, killed, skinned, roasted, and eaten the heart of a Han who had warned a village of an impending attack.[69]

The outsider Hui continued to stir up dissent, yet the local Hui's initial concerns seem to have disappeared in the face of escalating tensions. Hui leaders in the area began cooperating with the local officials, who were trying to eradicate the outsider Hui and bring an end to the violence. In their reports to their provincial superiors, these local officials consistently differentiated between the local and northwestern Hui communities, referring to the latter as "*wai*-Hui"—that is, Hui from outside the province. They also praised the local Hui for their efforts to encourage the outsider Hui to return to their homes in the northwest.[70] The joint efforts of the local officials and Baoshan Hui compelled the northwestern Yunnan Hui—now identified by their leader, Ma Da—to retreat to Mengting, a small village three days from Baoshan. There, they attempted to regroup.[71]

On September 30, after a period of calm, Ma Da's band, in a bold and unexpected strike, marched on Bingma, an isolated government outpost thirty miles from Baoshan. Only one Qing officer was killed in that raid; the Qing soldiers inflicted considerable damage in return, "wounding or killing two hundred and seventy of his [Ma Da's] bandits."[72] Instead of falling back to Mengting, Ma Da's band mounted a surprise attack on a small military encampment at Yangyi. There they overwhelmed the Qing troops left to defend the isolated outpost.[73]

The northwestern Hui never exceeded several hundred men whereas the Qing forces numbered more than one thousand.[74] After they put down the Lin'an Uprising in 1818, Qing fortunes changed dramatically; indicative of this is that in 1845 Yunnan officials hesitated to send an overwhelming military force to pursue and crush Ma Da; that, or they were no longer able to do so. Instead, local officials adopted an alternative strategy: they turned to the leaders of the local societies.

Apprehension (whether real or contrived—it is difficult to tell) over Ma Da's attacks quickly coalesced around fears of a "fifth column" of Ma Da supporters among Hui residents of Baoshan. Rumors began to swirl that several Hui from Ma Da's band had made their way into the city undetected and were collaborating with Mu Ruhe, the *ahong* (iman, or head religious leader) of the main mosque, to set a time and date for a joint attack against the Han from both inside and outside the city. On the agreed-upon date, once all was prepared, Mu Ruhe was to fire a shot from the top of the mosque as a signal for Ma Da to attack from outside the city wall.[75] In a series of hasty gatherings, local civil and military officials met with the local brotherhoods to devise a plan to exterminate the city's Hui populace.[76] No formal authorization for this from either the governor or the governor-general was ever requested (or at least recorded).

In the early hours of October 2, 1845, the local brotherhoods of the surrounding villages organized themselves into militias and marched into Baoshan under the pretext of protecting the city. There, over the next seventy-two hours, they meticulously carried out a massacre of the city's Hui population—men and women, young and old.[77] Local witnesses estimated that by the time the killing ended upwards of eight thousand Hui lay dead.[78]

The first memorial to the court from the newly appointed governor-general, He Changling, sent more than seven weeks after the massacre, was a version of events provided to him by local officials.[79] In it, these officials justified their actions as a response to rumors of a coming attack; they claimed they were simply taking precautions by allowing militia into the city and that when the Hui sounded their signal, they quickly subdued the revolt. They provided a vague account of the carnage, suggesting only that a few "people were killed, burned, or crushed."[80] He Changling summarized the events for the emperor and recommended that for their prescient and preemptive action, the local officials be considered for an imperial commendation.[81]

Then in December 1845, He sent another memorial, one that offered a dramatically different version of events. In this one he rebuked Western Intendant Luo for failing to verify the rumors of a Hui conspiracy before launching an attack on the city. Yet the governor-general continued to maintain that the attack had been justified; his contention was that Luo and the others had failed to distinguish between good and bad Hui.[82] In light of all this, he asked the court to rescind the commendations for Luo and the rest. Adhering to the administrative code, he then requested that he himself be punished as well for his errors in the matter.[83]

He granted that the incident had been mishandled but never admitted that a massacre had been carried out. The closest he came to this was when he stated that "last year Baoshan Han and Hui fought against each other [hudou]."[84] The court never thoroughly investigated official collusion in the massacre but did censure the governor-general for his lack of oversight and quickly transferred him to a lesser post.[85]

He's most glaring error in his handling of the massacre was to maintain the dogged belief that a Hui conspiracy existed. This, even though no evidence was ever produced to substantiate that Hui within the city had carried out violent acts or that Hui living in Baoshan had been in contact with those in surrounding areas. Nor does the historical record offer any information on the alleged key Hui conspirator, Mu Ruhe. Official reports never mention his name again, let alone whether he was dead, alive, or missing. Most critically, the rationale for allowing Han militias into the city rested entirely on the alleged threat that local Hui and the non-Yunnan Hui led by Ma Da were planning a synchronized attack on Baoshan. In later accounts there was no mention of any Hui attack on Baoshan by Ma Da; not only that, but the only concentration of Hui bandits was nearly thirty miles from Baoshan, and at the time these were being pursued by Qing troops and militia.[86]

CREATING A "PLACE FREE FROM SORROW":
EFFORTS TO RESTORE PEACE

Soon after the massacre, Hui proclamations appeared that offered a clearer version of the events. These openly accused local officials of collusion and called for revenge:

In the city there were more than eight thousand peaceful Hui residents—functionaries, soldiers, scholars, merchants—all peacefully fulfilling their role in society. . . . Local officials indulged in beautiful women, and coveted expensive items. Initially, they deceived us with posted declarations which read: If one Hui is killed, three [Han] will pay with their own lives. That was until early on the morning of October 2, when militia were loosed upon the city to commit wholesale slaughter. . . . If we Hui do not revenge the violence it will everywhere be repeated until every last

Hui is killed. . . . The fact that officials and soldiers aided the Han to exterminate the Hui, with dead piled as high as the mountain and blood as deep as the sea the suffering cannot have been in vain.[87]

Almost immediately on his arrival in 1846, the newly appointed governor-general, Li Xingyuan, expressed concern that the massacre and lack of any official investigation would "strike a chill into the hearts of the [average] Hui, while furnishing the pretext for wicked Hui to create disturbances."[88] Precisely as he feared, Hui reaction throughout western Yunnan was swift.[89]

In 1846 a Hui from northern Shaanxi Province, Huang Baba, led an abortive uprising in Mengting south of Baoshan.[90] A charismatic ahong who was "extremely well-versed in the Islamic scriptures, Huang attracted followers by promising to regain their Baoshan lands."[91] Later that same year in Yunzhou, Ma Guoxiang and another group of Hui carried out a series of raids against adjacent Han villages.[92] Official reports submitted to the emperor described these raids, accurately or not, as small and disorganized and as gaining little support from local Hui.[93] Prior to his departure, He Changling noted that local Hui in many areas of western Yunnan welcomed his efforts to block the influx of Shaanxi and Sichuan Hui into the region.[94] According to another account, a wandering Sichuan Hui who tried to incite fellow Hui to attack a nearby Han village was reported to local officials by the mosque ahongs.[95] Yet very often, cooperative acts such as these did little to garner aid from Qing officials.

All of the violent acts by Hui after the Baoshan Massacre were instigated by Hui from outside Yunnan. Meanwhile, the Muslim Yunnanese continued to rely on the Qing system to rectify the misconduct and barbarity of its own officials. In early 1846, four Hui traversed nearly the entire breadth of the empire at their own expense to file a grievance petition. This petition asked for an investigation of the Baoshan massacre as well as proper compensation for its victims.[96] As a direct result of this, the Daoguang emperor appointed a famous veteran of the Opium War, Lin Zexu, as the new governor-general. Lin was told to investigate the situation; the emperor warned him sternly that "it would not be enough to simply report that the case has already been dealt with, or dawdle and simply try to avoid responsibility." Lin had been handed the unenviable task of investigating the massacre even while restoring calm to western Yunnan.[97]

The new governor-general quickly began piecing together the sequence of events of the massacre. Just a preliminary investigation made it clear to him that He Changling had made drastic errors in his account. Lin offered the court a revised account of the massacre that placed the blame squarely on the Han brotherhoods and that revealed the calculating nature of the entire affair:

Han Chinese spread rumors that Hui rebels were scheming to enter Baoshan and kill all the Han, and that the rebels had secretly conspired with Hui inside the city to rise up simultaneously thereby delivering the city to the Hui. . . . As a result, on the second day of the ninth lunar month [October 2, 1845] the militia heads of Jinji, Banqiao and each village [shao] under the pretext of protecting themselves from the rebels, marched in a disorderly manner into the city, proclaimed they were there to save the city, and proceeded to slaughter all of the Hui within the city—regardless of age or sex. The [Baoshan] massacre resulted in the death of more than 4,000 Hui. The events all happened so quickly the military and civil officials in the city were unable to prevent them.[98]

Lin was the first to call the incident a massacre; that said, his version of events was imperfect at best.

Lin's account is suspect at several levels. His estimate of Hui killed understates that of most other accounts by nearly half. Local witnesses contended that well over four thousand Hui were slain; others suggested it was double that.[99] But Lin's biggest lapse was that he failed to mention the participation of local officials in the massacre. He even contended that the officials could not have prevented it. He probably knew this was far from true: the petition—supported by local rumors—had hinted that there had been official malfeasance. One member of the Han gentry stated that "Shen Jucheng [a prominent Incense Brotherhood leader] and the other [organizers] of the massacre originally believed that because [the massacre] was agreed upon by the officials within Baoshan, and certified by documents with the seals of the civil and military officials, as well as by a letter from all of the gentry in the county expressing the general support [of the plan], they were shielded from blame."[100]

Indeed, Lin had captured Shen and was holding him for his role in the bloodshed. When it became apparent to Shen and the other members of the Incense Brotherhoods who had been arrested that their former allies among the local officials were neither coming to their aid nor being arrested themselves, they committed suicide rather than face trial. Perhaps Lin was hesitating to investigate Qing officials because he believed that doing so would serve little purpose and would only further undermine the state's position. At the time, Lin was having to employ every available resource simply to wrest control of the Baoshan area from the Han brotherhoods.

The reassertion of state authority in the area after the Baoshan Massacre, unlike interventions by the government earlier in the century, was not welcomed by the local Han community. The power of the informal Han organizations over the area continued unchecked after the massacre of 1845. In the autumn of 1847, Lin ordered the arrest of nine prominent members of the Incense Brotherhood who were suspected of organizing the massacre. On January 5, 1848, under armed escort, these prisoners left Baoshan for the provincial capital, where they would face trial. On that same day's afternoon the convoy was passing a village stronghold of the local Incense Brotherhood when a horn sounded. On that signal, villagers streamed out to surround the escort and demand the release of their Incense brothers.[101]

The following day the leaders of the brotherhood, apparently to display their contempt for Qing authority, organized their private militias and once again made their way into Baoshan. On January 6, 1847, the Han brotherhoods carried out a second massacre of the the remaining Baoshan Hui.[102] In their efforts to wipe out the Hui, these roaming groups seemed indifferent to the lingering vestiges of the Qing state. The Han mob slew two Hui in the western intendant's residence and set fire to the district magistrate's yamen, where more than one hundred Muslim Yunnanese had sought refuge.[103]

Lin reacted quickly. Showing the mettle of a veteran official, he mobilized nearly ten thousand soldiers and personally led them to Baoshan. As word of Lin's approach spread, the resolve of those Han involved in the second massacre melted away and the principal leaders were meekly handed over to the local authorities. When Lin arrived in the city he found more than 329 prisoners awaiting trial.[104] He immediately ordered the summary execution of the nine Incense Society leaders; another 137 were sentenced to lesser punishment: flogging, followed by banishment to the northwestern frontier.[105]

Immediately after ending the lawlessness of the Incense Brotherhoods in Baoshan, Lin began addressing the grievances of the Baoshan Hui, who wanted their land returned and their property losses compensated. At the end of 1845, while still governor-general, He Changling had ordered that the lands of the Hui victims be rigorously protected and that absent owners be invited to return and reclaim them.[106] He was sympathetic to the Hui; however, competing claims of ownership and fears that Hui from outside the province would appropriate unclaimed lands discouraged him from resolving this matter during his tenure.[107]

When Lin arrived in Yunnan, he realized quickly that resolving land claims would be crucial to diffusing Hui discontent and creating some semblance of order.[108] However, from the beginning he felt that Hui estimates of deaths were excessively high and that many Hui were falsely claiming to be relatives of victims in the hope of benefiting from the government's compensation.[109] Perhaps this skepticism explains why he pursued an expedient but blatantly one-sided solution to the problem. Instead of seeking to return to the Hui the lands the Han had seized, he tried to implement a land-exchange program: the Baoshan Hui would be given land one hundred miles to the west along the upper Salween River.

Lin's description to the emperor of this area suggested that it was a fertile valley with "fruit trees and ripening grain," one that would offer the Hui a "place free from sorrow."[110] In fact, the upper Salween ran through a malarial zone of extreme western Yunnan. In effect, Lin was pursing a policy of ethnically based banishment. He hoped to send the Hui to a place where they would have little or no contact with Han Chinese, but his decision would have the unambiguous result of rewarding the Baoshan Han for their part in the massacre.

From the perspective of the Baoshan Hui, Lin's settlement left them doubly victimized. It would not only transfer their homes and lands to the Han but also cost them their economic well-being. The upper Salween Valley could be farmed, but it was of very poor quality compared to the fertile and highly coveted land of the Baoshan Valley.[111] Furthermore, Baoshan lay on one of the most lucrative trading routes between China and Southeast Asia, so the move would cost the Hui lucrative trading opportunities.[112] Lin himself acknowledged that the proposed region had proven unsuitable to earlier Han settlers; even so, he tried to pass it off to the Hui.[113] His policy of ethnic separation had been tried by others in the past, but rarely in a way that would have benefited the Han so one-sidedly.[114] Lin's policy of separation lacked even the facade of parity; it came across as a bald attempt to get rid of the Hui.

## Seeking the Proper Response: Government Perceptions of the Hui, 1845–1848

The three Yun-Gui governors-general who served from 1845 to 1849 in the wake of the Baoshan Massacre all contended that their policies for handling the Hui were impartial and accommodating. Indeed, the terminology each of these men employed was remarkably similar: He Changling advocated "maintaining justice and equality" (binggong chiping),[115] Li Xingyuan sought to "implement the law equitably" (zhifa chiping),[116] and Lin Zexu endeavored to "distinguish between good and bad, not between Han and Hui" (danfen liangyou, bulun Han Hui).[117] The tone of these policies was neutral, the manner in which they were implemented far less so.

All three programs reflected efforts to revitalize the baojia system of mutual surveillance. After the Baoshan massacre, the governors-general ordered all cattle protection associations (niucong) to disband and sought to strengthen the baojia household registration system so that it would be harder for non-Yunnanese to gain access to and taint local communities. Furthermore, He Changling advocated the reinstitution the xiangyue—public lectures on the Sacred Edicts, given to raise the community's moral tone.[118]

The problem with this approach was that the baojia system in Yunnan was in a lamentable state. One magistrate noted on his arrival in Yunnan in 1844 that the baojia placards were "no more than sheets of paper with fugitives and criminals able to hide without fear of being detected."[119] Even at its most effective, baojia was of little use as a preventive tool during times of discord; it was especially poor at responding to ethnic unrest.[120] In the first decades of the century, Bolin, Qingbao, and Ruan Yuan had adopted it in non-Han areas as a means of bolstering the existing ban on Han entering non-Han lands; then it had been only one of several proactive measures for thwarting future recurrences. It had not been seen as the primary solution.

The drawbacks of baojia and xiangyue can be gleaned from a close examination of the conflicts that arose after the Baoshan Massacre. In Baoshan in the late 1840s, baojia would have relied on the cooperation of the same community leaders who had instigated the Han–Hui violence. The ringleaders had included a Muslim ahong, a baojia unit leader (*jiazhang*), and several xiangyue leaders.[121] As Sow-Theng Leong found in his study of Hakka–Punti rivalries in southeastern China, baojia and xiangyue units tended to be split along ethnic lines; as a consequence, these institutions only bolstered community divisions and ethnic differences. Put simply, xiangyue often fostered ethnic conflict instead of dampening it.[122]

An even deeper problem plagued the three governors-general in their search for effective solutions to the violence. Permeating every level of Qing officialdom was an overriding concern with the Hui response to Han aggression, not the Han aggression itself. In their memorials, He Changling, Li Xingyuan, and Lin Zexu all acknowledged that the Han Chinese wanted to exterminate the Hui; yet they also insinuated repeatedly that were it not for the Hui there would be no Han Brotherhoods and thus—in a distinctly circular logic—no Han–Hui violence.[123] Li Xingyuan typified this attitude in his memorial to the emperor; he indicated that the first step in solving the problem lay in controlling the Hui: "In order to control the Hui, one must first control the bandits. If the bandits are not controlled, then the Hui cannot be controlled, and subsequently the Han Chinese especially cannot be controlled."[124] This made sense only if it was assumed that the Hui as a class were prone to violence, and Li clearly endorsed the centuries-old stereotype that they were: "The Hui display a strong sense of solidarity and their character is fierce. Year after year they harbor grudges and seek revenge. The Han Chinese are not strong enough to stop it."[125]

To suggest this only months after thousands of Hui had been massacred at the hands of Han Chinese—not once but twice—reveals the extraordinary extent to which anti-Hui biases had begun to saturate even the highest levels of Qing administration.

Over the next three decades, Lin Zexu's ethnically blind policy of "not discriminating between Han and Hui but between good and bad" would often be praised for its impartiality. Yet almost every time he voiced this policy he also intimated his own general distrust of the Muslim Yunnanese, qualifying his stance by playing on Hui stereotypes: "In Yunnan there is not a single location where there are no Hui, with law-abiding Hui few and wayward Hui numerous."[126]

Lin's bias is perhaps most visible in his efforts to adjudicate the backlog of cases from the broader Han–Hui violence that followed the massacre. In the department of Yaozhou, Lin estimated that the Han had suffered "eight times as many casualties as the Hui, . . . [and] lost nine times as many buildings"—an estimate that pushes the boundaries of plausibility, given the much larger Han population.[127] Whether Lin's numbers were accurate or not, in trying the cases of the more than 236 prisoners, he executed 138. Of these, no fewer than 101 were Hui.[128] Even if Lin was correct that the imbalance in death and damage merited the ethnic imbalance in his sentencing, the fact that the vast numbers of Han involved in the original Baoshan Massacre were never brought to justice, let alone executed, caused considerable resentment among the Hui.

Yet it would be unfair to suggest that this bias was Lin's alone. Unfortunately, Lin—like most late Qing officials—rarely explained how he arrived at his conclusions; thus we cannot today see the assumptions on which he based his legal decisions. However, with regard to one of the rare Han–Hui incidents to occur in eastern Yunnan, Lin suggested that he believed in harsher sentencing and that his bias against the Hui was legally upheld. In this particular case, which involved a Han attack on Hui miners, he ordered that the Han criminals be "immediately executed . . . in order to put the Hui community's hearts at ease." Yet when it came to dealing with the few Hui involved in retaliatory violence, he invoked a specific clause of the penal code to justify his sentence: "When three or more Hui are involved together in a criminal altercation, with at least one person using a weapon, regardless of who is the leader, [all] shall be sentenced to military service in the pestilential border areas of Yunnan, Guizhou, Guangxi or Guangzhou."[129]

This statute, created in the 1770s in response to rising suspicion that Muslims were involved in violence, reveals the customary belief among officials (and encoded in law) that the Hui deserved more severe punishment than other Qing subjects.[130] In his memorial Lin noted that although the Han and Hui were both to blame, "the Hui are particularly fierce so we should set an example for other Hui."[131] His invocation of the statute sent another clear message to the Muslim Yunnanese: in the eyes of the Qing, a Hui was more than a Chinese subject who happened to believe in the tenets of Islam.[132]

Despite the trials and executions, and despite other efforts to restore peace, the government never absolved the Hui of their alleged role as instigators of the Baoshan Massacre in particular and of the unrest in general.[133] Lin Zexu and Li Xingyuan, two of the empire's most respected administrators, had a propensity to characterize the Hui as a problematic people. This reflects a disturbing trend in policy and crisis management in Yunnan. The Daoguang emperor obviously encouraged this trend, since both Lin and Li received the title of Grand Guardian of the Heir Apparent (in 1847 and 1848 respectively) for their quick and competent handling of the Baoshan Massacre.[134]

## Conclusion

The departure of Lin Zexu in 1849 marks the end of a distinctively proactive period in Yunnanese administration. Each of the three governors-general had traveled to the sites of ethnic violence and left an indelible imprint on the province as a whole. They had attempted to satisfy many of the basic demands of the Baoshan Muslims who had petitioned the court. Lin in particular had crushed the widespread violence. Yet the emphasis on military solutions marked an ominous turn for Yunnan.

Ethnic violence in Yunnan had long been accompanied by strong political and moral overtones; these were mirrored in the policies of He Changling, Li Xingyuan, and Lin Zexu. In the Lin'an and Dao Shengwu conflicts, however, it was those Han who dared oppose the interests of the state who were labeled as traitors.[135] This perspective allowed the state to portray its crisis management as equitable and to represent its interventions as morally and politically correct. The same approach also allowed the Qing to circumvent the treacherous issue of ethnic bias by portraying those Han, by virtue of their attack on non-Han subjects, as anti-Qing. With the rise of anti-Hui violence, the actions of the three governors-general took on a decisively less neutral tenor.

It is commonly accepted that the Baoshan Massacre indicated a heightened antagonism toward the Hui at the local level. Yet the attitudes expressed and actions taken by the court in its responses to the violence reveal that anti-Hui bias was becoming a much broader phenomenon. In this new environment, Muslim Yunnanese subjects of the Qing received neither the special consideration extended to the non-Han nor the tacit benefits extended to the Han. The obvious consequence of this was a continuation of anti-Hui violence. Much less detected at the time was the accelerated erosion of Qing authority precisely *because* the government was willing to tolerate anti-Hui sentiment. Indeed, as informal local Han power structures and Qing officials posted to Yunnan increasingly became of one mind with regard to the menace of the Muslim Yunnanese, the likelihood of an even greater wave of anti-Hui violence grew apace.

# "All the Fish in the Pond": The Kunming Massacre and the Rise of the Panthay Rebellion

Governor-General Lin Zexu, in departing to serve in a new post in 1849, claimed that as a result of his efforts Yunnan would be secure for ten more years.[1] This was optimistic of him, given the uncertain times. During his two short years he had barely secured peace in Baoshan, let alone the whole of Yunnan. Lin was leaving Yunnan believing the Hui were at the root of the province's violence. All of his solutions to the unrest focused on the Hui and ignored the strong anti-Hui bias among the Han. Lin's actions had only alleviated the symptoms; the deeper problem of Han chauvinism was as potent as when he arrived.

The consequences of Lin's approach to the problems besetting Yunnan were most visible in Talang, a mining settlement in the south of the province where fighting had broken out between rival (and often illegal) gangs of miners. In the closing months of Lin's tenure, the acting prefect, Cui Shaozhong, arrested 112 bandits, including 46 non-Yunnanese (*wai fei*), 21 Lin'anese (*lin'an fei*), and 11 indigenous bandits (*yi fei*).[2] Despite the broad range of ethnic groups involved, Lin chose to differentiate this Talang violence from the anti-Hui hostilities occurring throughout Yunnan. In a memorial to the throne, he characterized the hostilities in Talang as largely a result of avarice and the rise in value of silver; nowhere did he refer to the interethnic animosities that were raging in the area.[3] Although anti-Hui violence persisted in all three regions of the province, nowhere in his appraisal of Talang did Lin allude to possible anti-Hui motives. By the time he left the province in the autumn of 1849, the court believed firmly that the problems in Yunnan had been resolved. Yet only months later, violence erupted again at the Talang mine.

The Talang mine was well known in the province for two things: its many deposits of silver and gold, and its miners, who spent their income "as if it was dirt."[4] This combination had fostered a class of idlers who "never panned for gold, [but] day and night went about gambling . . . with the strong losing but never paying and the weak winning but never collecting."[5]

The hostilities of late 1849 began when a Han Chinese gambled and lost a considerable sum to a Hui. Instead of paying his debt, the Han conspired with several compatriots to kill the Hui. Worried about their ability to handle the inevitable reprisals, the Talang Han traveled to Xizhuang, a village near Lin'an, to solicit further reinforcements and gain the support of the local gentry. There they made a tantalizing offer: easy wealth for those who joined them, with the added satisfaction of dealing a debilitating blow to the Hui. "If we were to drive the Hui from the mine," they contended, "then Lin'an would become a city of gold."[6]

The Xizhuang gentry offered their backing and organized a band of five hundred Han to march on the mine. The local magistrate at Talang, hearing rumors of their plot, notified his superiors and requested military reinforcements to fend off the impending attack. Several weeks and repeated entreaties later, support was still not forthcoming. With the Xizhuang toughs flowing into Talang, the remaining Han and Hui miners struck a hasty agreement, pledging to help one another defend their mines in the event of an attack.[7]

On October 14, 1850, the Xizhuang bands murdered a prominent Hui. The local Han, observing that they were not the main target of Han hostility, quickly withdrew their earlier offer of support and turned a blind eye to the ensuing bloodshed. Within several days, more than one hundred of their Hui neighbors were dead in what the local magistrate called the "largest case of murder and destruction the area had ever seen."[8] All Hui attempts to resist or retaliate were crushed. The Xizhuang bands remained in the area, looting the mines, terrorizing the remaining populace, and generally extracting everything of value from the mines—an amount the magistrate estimated at more than 100,000 taels.[9]

Worried about reports of escalating violence, provincial officials dispatched a small detachment of soldiers to the area. The Talang magistrate, frustrated at this small and belated show of support, lamented: "Earlier it was already clear the situation here was urgent . . . and [now] only ten soldiers were dispatched while the brigands can be counted by the thousands. It is just like throwing a glass of water on a burning cart of wood."[10]

It is unclear exactly why the higher officials did not respond more forcefully to the Talang incident. Two prominent Hui who survived the attack spent the next two years seeking retribution from all levels of the provincial government, to no avail.[11] In fact, no one was ever charged, arrested, or convicted; the offenders were left free to continue their violent ways. The disturbing absence of state authority in Talang and officials' reluctance to check the challenges to their prerogatives suggest that the state was losing its effectiveness in the absence of veteran officials like Lin Zexu.

Talang exemplified a problem that was growing throughout the province.

Between 1849 and 1855 five different governors-general had been appointed to Yunnan, two of whom never assumed office. The remaining three served an average of one year each. Yunnan's governors did only slightly better, averaging around twenty months each. The central court was shuffling its administrative personnel so rapidly in part because it was focusing more and more on a new threat: the Taiping Rebellion, which was already ravaging the lower Yangtze region. Given the increasingly desperate need for experienced officials to respond to the Taiping rebels, the court was quickly transferring Yunnan's top officials to Hunan, Hubei, and Zhejiang.[12]

The deterioration of government authority in Yunnan is corroborated by accounts from half a dozen French Catholic missionaries in the province at the time. These men had been in Yunnan since the late 1840s—longer than many of the officials themselves—and discussed the broader trends affecting Yunnan society. In the early 1850s they painted a bleak picture of the province, hinting at the ethnic tensions there and at the difficulty appointed officials were having in remaining neutral: "Yunnan is consumed by turmoil and confusion. The Muslims want to kill the officials, the Chinese want to kill the Muslims, and the officials want to kill the Muslims and the Chinese."[13]

In an analysis eerily reminiscent of the difficulties besetting Baoshan prior to the 1845 Massacre, another missionary contended that the root of the problem was the Han "from Sichuan and other provinces, with the Mandarins not having enough power to stop them."[14] Given their vocation—which was to proselytize—it is somewhat surprising that none of the missionaries in their reports back to France depicted the Hui as the principal antagonists in the violence.

Given the rising political aspirations of the Taiping to the east, the almost complete absence of any political agenda in Yunnan's violence is rather conspicuous. Father Chauveau, who lived in Yunnan in the early 1850s, was struck by the apparent differences: "[The Taiping Rebellion] in Guangxi is attempting to cleanse the political system; in Yunnan the question is of a different nature and is derived from, in what we would call in our modern scientific style, a social question. Each [of the ethnic] peoples is attempting to imprint their ideals on the society, with the Muslims, Chinese and natives each pulling from their own side."[15]

Despite this apparent lack of ideological motivation—or perhaps because of it—the extermination of the Muslim Yunnanese in the years after Lin's departure gradually became the primary objective of the Han Chinese.

## MINING INCIDENTS AND REPRISALS, 1854–1856

By 1854, broad areas of Yunnan verged on anarchy. In late April the same band of Han Chinese that had preyed on the Talang mine for several years marched unimpeded to the wealthy Shiyang mine in central Yunnan. During the fighting the Han militias that had been assigned to protect the mine joined the assailants. This combined force turned on the Hui, killing several hundred of them and burning all their dwellings and their mosque.[16] Bloody encounters like these took place mainly at mines. What fueled them was not economic rivalry so much as ethnic resentment.

In the months following the initial attack at Shiyang, skirmishes between Han and Hui bands escalated. Then in January 1855, Ma Rulong, a Hui from Lin'an prefecture whose brother had been among the first victims of the Han assault on Shiyang, led a group of Lin'an Hui in one last attempt to clear the mines of the Xizhuang bandits so that mining could be resumed.[17] By early February it had became apparent that the Hui could not work and defend themselves at the same time. Ma Rulong and his followers decided to block the entrances to their mines, divert the waterways, collect everything of value in the area, and return to Lin'an.[18] The Xizhuang band was now more than one thousand strong. When they found the Shiyang mines abandoned, with no miners remaining to extract the silver from the ore and few provisions available, they became enraged.

The band launched what would become a two-year campaign by methodically attacking six Hui villages in succession, looting and burning property and slaughtering all the Hui they encountered (see Map 6.1).[19] In May the Xizhuang band attacked the Malong mine, which was defended by an ethnically mixed group of miners. Although several years had passed since the Talang incident, the attackers' primary goal remained the extermination of the Hui. Just before launching their assault on Malong, the leaders called out to those defending the mine: "We only want to kill the Hui; it has nothing to do with Han and non-Han! Those of you who are able to kill the Hui and offer proof will be rewarded!"[20] By the time the killing was over, more than eighty Hui miners lay dead.

The campaign against Muslim Yunnanese continued through the summer of 1855. In July the Xizhuang band moved on to the town of Luochuan in Guangtong Department, where they pillaged thirteen Hui villages and massacred the inhabitants.[21] In all, they burned eleven mosques to the ground and murdered several thousand Hui.[22] In November the same band traveled to Zhennan Department, where it attacked eight villages, destroyed eight mosques, and killed more than one thousand Hui. The following February, they attacked Chuxiong, a transportation hub in central Yunnan, and massacred several thousand Hui in and around the city.[23] Over three years, then, the Xizhuang band alone cut a swath of destruction through three departments (Nan'an, Guangtong, Zhennan). By conservative estimates, more than eight thousand Hui were killed during this period. Most of the victims had been Hui villagers who died for no other reason than their ethnicity.[24]

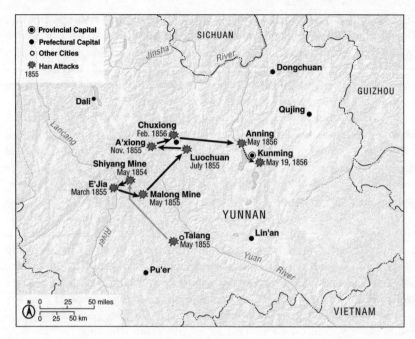

MAP 6.1. Han Attacks on Hui, 1854–1856

Word of the massacres spread throughout the province. The French missionaries kept one another informed of the violence. In the spring of 1856 Father Chauveau wrote to a fellow missionary: "The people here have suffered considerably because of all the small attacks, but the Muslims have suffered more than anyone. In some areas they were massacred to the last person, even women and children. In particular, a month ago, on the plain where I am, all who were Muslim were burned alive. Our Christians, grace to god, did not suffer."[25]

Around this time, another of Chauveau's colleagues, Father Leguilcher, who had been posted to a mission in western Yunnan near Dali, indicated that the attacks in his area were very often anti-Hui: "That which is certain is that under the directions of a low-ranking military official and sworn enemy of the Muslims several thousand Chinese profited from the celebrations of the Chinese New Year to organize a vast plot against the 'pilgrims of Mecca.'"[26]

These attacks were occurring in many parts of the province over a prolonged period of time, yet no level of government was taking steps to end the violence. The ranking official in Chuxiong Prefecture, the magistrate Cui Shaozhong, seems to have actually promoted the attacks, for the purpose of inflaming the hatred so as to encourage the Han to exterminate the Hui:

"[If] seeing that the Xizhuang side was strong, he then would help them kill Hui; if seeing the Hui were strong, he would then come to their 'aid' and help them kill the Lin'anese."[27]

It was Cui who had failed to send aid to quell the attacks at Talang several years earlier. This suggests that his anti-Hui views perhaps constituted support for the Xizhuang attacks.[28] Whatever his intentions, in the spring of 1856 new reports appeared in Kunming of the Chuxiong massacres. It was rumored that the Xizhuang band was on its way to Anning, several dozen miles from Kunming, to "kill all those Chuxiong Hui who had escaped."[29]

## The Kunming Massacre

In the spring of 1856, Yunnan's top provincial officials included the governor-general, Hengchun, the governor, Shuxing'a, the provincial judge, Qingsheng, and the newly promoted provincial treasurer, Sangchunrong. Hengchun, a Manchu, had served extensively in northern China in Shanxi and Shaanxi provinces before being appointed to Yunnan. In May 1856, however, he was away in Guizhou trying to quell the Miao Rebellion, which had begun the previous year.[30] In his absence, Shuxing'a was the ranking official in the provincial capital.

Shuxing'a was a Manchu and had served in the northwest. Unlike his superior, he had acquired an intense dislike of Muslims during his time in the northwest. According to one account, his antipathy had its roots in an 1853 incident. Ordered to lead a relief force to a town besieged by Muslim insurgents, he collapsed and fled in fear. The town fell to the rebels. "Angry and bitter [over the loss]," a mob composed of local Hui attacked him, "stripped him of all his clothes, and began to [carry out acts intended to] humiliate him."[31] Only the quick thinking of his servant, Chen Xi, who whisked him away to safety, kept Shuxing'a from what had all the ingredients of a horrible death. After this attack, Shuxing'a began to suffer from neurasthenia (*zhengchong*), an ailment characterized by heart palpitations, melancholia, fatigue, and other physical ailments.

In the years following this incident, Shuxing'a cultivated a deep hatred of all Muslim Chinese; he blamed them for his lingering sense of humiliation and for his deteriorating mental and physical health. On arriving in Yunnan he appointed his servant, Chen Xi, gatekeeper to the governor's yamen. Chen Xi quickly garnered considerable influence by restricting Shuxing'a's visitors to those who shared the governor's anti-Hui stance.[32]

As a consequence of Hengchun's absence in Guizhou and Shuxing'a's mental deterioration, the bulk of administrative duties devolved to the provincial judge, Qingsheng, and the provincial treasurer, Sangchunrong.

Little is known about Qingsheng; that said, his anti-Hui beliefs were apparent to most people. On one occasion he offered this chilling assessment: "The Hui bandits' hearts are evil. If we do not deal with them early on, then they will spread like a disease from the inside out."[33] Another source suggests that he used "extreme torture" when dealing with Muslim Yunnanese whom he considered criminal.[34] Sangchunrong's beliefs are even less clear. Like many young officials during the Daoguang reign, he began his career as a magistrate. He was appointed to the southern Yunnan district of Lin'an in 1844, and rose quickly from there until by 1855 he was Yunnan's provincial treasurer. His rapid rise illustrates yet another facet of 1850s Yunnan: the central court, distracted by the Taiping Rebellion and other matters, was increasingly promoting from within the province.

Still other factors would affect the coming conflict. By early 1856 the Kunming gentry were playing an increasingly influential role in tipping popular and official opinion against the Hui. Two members of the gentry, He Tongyun and Huang Cong, would be especially prominent in the events that were beginning to unfold in and around the provincial capital. Both these men had served high in the Qing bureaucracy and still had direct access to the court.

He Tongyun, a senior official in the revenue ministry and a native of Yunnan, had returned to the province in 1857 for the obligatory mourning period after the death of his father.[35] Little is known about his particular views; however, in the aftermath of the massacre he wrote several memorials to the throne that masked not only the depth of anti-Hui sentiment among the provincial elite but also the horrible atrocities being carried out under their instructions.

Huang Cong was born and raised in Kunming and had just retired there after many years as a high official in the war ministry. Now he quickly became a powerful individual in formal and informal Han Chinese circles, both in Kunming and throughout the province.[36] His previous high ministerial rank gave him considerable influence. It was said that he was "mistrustful of Hui and actively plotted ways to harm them."[37] He was to become a guiding force in the project of ridding Yunnan of what he referred to as "this despicable race."[38]

All seven men—Hengchun, Shuxing'a, Chen Xi, Qingsheng, Sangchunrong, He Tongyun, and Huang Cong—played critical roles facilitating the events that led to the Panthay Rebellion. The boundaries between officials and nonofficials, gentry and commoners, were becoming blurred as the anti-Hui atmosphere began to permeate Kunming as high as the most senior levels of governance.

In early 1856, several things happened that altered the nature of the violence that had been unfolding across Yunnan for several years—that changed that violence from largely unstructured actions to unequivocally premeditated acts. In the spring of 1856 the fighting that had begun in Talang and moved to Chuxiong now flared up near Kunming. The first skirmishes were in the village of Xiaobanqiao, about ten miles from the walled capital, between Xizhuang Han and a group of Hui. Shuxing'a, Huang Cong, and the anti-Hui faction quickly seized on this incident as a means to further their anti-Hui projects. Shuxing'a immediately began to portray this minor incident as a serious threat to the provincial capital.

Several days before the attack, a circular was "secretly transmitted to every prefecture, sub-prefecture, department, and district . . . within an eight hundred *li* radius [of the capital]." It ordered militias to form and kill the Hui.[39] Qingsheng then authorized an order allowing Han militia to "slay all [offenders] without being held accountable" (*gesha wulun*). Many interpreted this order as a government endorsement to massacre the Hui.[40]

The killing began on May 19, 1856, and continued for three days.[41] No Hui were spared. Eyewitnesses told Frenchman Émile Rocher: "The Muslims were massacred without pity. . . . The old and the young for whom escape was impossible did not find mercy before the butchers."[42] Women were raped and children were slain. According to one account, "a fetus [was left] still writhing and moving in the middle of the road."[43] The Muslim quarter was looted and the city's mosques were razed.[44] One report has it that the massacre ended only when Qingsheng's mother confronted her son and demanded that he halt the butchery of innocent people.[45] By the time the attacks stopped on May 21, 1856, at least eight thousand Hui lay dead.[46]

The slaughter of the Hui did not end there. The circular that authorized attacks on Muslim Yunnanese, and the government's apparent endorsement of the Kunming Massacre, spawned massacres throughout the province led by settler Han who needed little encouragement to act on their ethnic hatreds.[47] Over the next several months, uprisings erupted across the province "in places such as Chengjiang, Zhaotong, Lin'an and Qujing . . . with the attacks in Tengyue and Wuding being especially cold-blooded."[48] In the central Yunnan town of Wuding some two thousand Hui were massacred.[49] In western Yunnan, in the cities of Heqing, Jianchuan, and Lijiang, the slaughter was especially horrific.[50] When local officials attempted to prevent the violence, "the Han complained that pacifying the Hui was not Heaven's intent" and continued their efforts to exterminate the Hui.[51] As violence washed over the region, more and more Qing officials abandoned their policy of outwardly "punishing the bad and protecting the good" and began actively promoting "attacking the Hui in order to exterminate the Hui."[52]

Remarkably, Shuxing'a mentioned none of this to the emperor for many weeks. When he finally memorialized the throne on June 20, more than a month after the butchery in Kunming, his report contained no mention of a massacre. Taking a page from Baoshan, he instead cast the Han massacre of the Hui as a Hui conspiracy against the state. He wrote to the emperor that only his preventative measures, "resulting in the arrest of sixty-four Hui," had averted an imminent Hui attack.[53] In this entirely fabricated rendering, thirty Hui were said to have been carrying nitrate to make incendiary devices. Another fourteen had allegedly admitted to "plotting to act as a fifth column within the city by starting fires and then opening the city gates."[54] Shuxing'a went on to claim that several Hui had burned down their own mosques and committed suicide rather than be arrested—an act he presented as a clear indication of their guilt.[55] He concluded his memorial by assuring the emperor that government forces had killed "only seventy Hui" and thus maintained the peace.[56]

Shuxing'a's next memorial, a month after the first, was not nearly so sanguine. Clearly distraught over the forces he had unleashed, he began to suggest that the Hui "threat" was widespread in Yunnan. Yet he still sought to lay the blame on the Hui: "There is nowhere in Yunnan that there are not Hui. Though their numbers are not large, only ten or twenty percent of the Han, they make up for it in their strength. They are suspicious and fierce by nature. . . . Now throughout Lin'an and Dongchuan prefectures there are Hui bandits burning and looting villages."[57]

On August 31, Shuxing'a filed his third memorial in as many months. Only now did he finally allow that the violence had spread to almost every corner of the province. Yet he continued to imply that the Hui, dangerous and fierce, had been the cause of the violence from its inception.[58] In the six months left in his tenure, Shuxing'a never alluded to the massacre of any Hui in Yunnan. Whether he could admit it or not, by sanctioning the Kunming Massacre, he had ignited the Panthay Rebellion.

### THE PRETENSE OF CONTROL

It took more than half a year for the first official admission of any government culpability in the Kunming Massacre to surface. A memorial authored by Hengchun dated February 9, 1857, finally divulged that the provincial judge, Qingsheng, had issued a proclamation ordering militias to form with the right to slay any lawbreakers they encountered. His memorial continued: "But unlawful hanjian took advantage of this order to incite violence with Han killing many law-abiding Hui within the provincial capital."[59] In his rescript the emperor told Hengchun that while he should maintain the policy of "not distinguishing between Han and Hui and pacify them uniformly," the Hui should be suppressed.[60] Nowhere did the emperor call for any action to be taken against the Han for their role in inciting the violence.

Hengchun and the Qing court were approaching Yunnan's problems from sharply different directions. The emperor was clearly more concerned that yet another corner of his empire was falling into chaos. Instead of focusing on the growing evidence that several of his Qing officials had orchestrated a full-scale Hui massacre in the provincial capital, he advocated a strong military response against the rebelling Hui. Hengchun perceived Yunnan's problems quite differently. Believing that the Hui violence stemmed directly from the original massacre and the ongoing Han attacks, he sought to develop a strategy for minimizing acts that might further incite the Hui and for exercising control of the Han militias, whose attacks on Muslim Yunnanese communities were fueling the hostilities.

These strategies did not meet with the emperor's approval. "After half a year of dealing with the Hui rebels," the emperor admonished him, "there has not been the slightest progress."[61] Hengchun persevered, pointing out that further violence against the Hui was not the answer to Yunnan's current woes. "If the extermination of the Hui is the only purpose [of the Han]," he reasoned, "not only will the Hui never yield, but it will only further the Han's suffering."[62] Hengchun's assessment, by playing to the court's concern over the province's Han subjects, unintentionally offered the most unembellished account of the postmassacre situation. In the months following the Kunming Massacre, the Hui were not solely responsible for the escalating violence. In many areas of the province, Han were enthusiastically pursuing extermination campaigns against the them. Indeed, the Han hoped the rising violence would pressure the central court, in the name of stability, to sanction their anti-Hui crusade.

With little understanding of how the rebellion had started, the court vacillated: Should it pursue a strong military resolution to the violence, or should it attempt to negotiate a more peaceful resolution? This wavering is reflected in many early communications to Yunnan from the court, which offered little substantive guidance for provincial officials. The emperor's tone tended toward impractical platitudes: "There are good and bad Muslim Yunnanese. If you do not suppress the bad leaders not only will the Han suffer but the good Hui will also languish."[63]

The court was expressing an overriding concern for the Han, which it perceived as the true victims of the rebellion. But such a sentiment did not translate into any concrete plan of action for Hengchun. Nor did Beijing offer any substantial financial or military assistance.

Hengchun settled on a strategy of nonengagement. He was predisposed to a passive approach and assumed that if the military threat were removed, the violence would end. Yet this approach greatly underestimated just how strongly the Han, the Hui, and the non-Han had committed themselves to an extended conflict. Nor did it recognize that the main hostilities were not caused by his imperial troops, but rather by Han militias intent on purging Yunnan of the Hui—militias over which he had absolutely no control. As a consequence of his policy, in the spring of 1857 one prefecture after another fell into violent anarchy.

The court was still adamant that the Hui were the cause of the rebellion and quickly lost patience with Hengchun's wait-and-see approach. Official misgivings about the Hui had by now become rampant. Since the late eighteenth century, Hui insurgency in the northwest had grown into one of the imperial government's greatest concerns, and the court had become increasingly distrustful of the Hui.[64] In an insightful study about government treatment of Muslim violence, Jonathan Lipman points out that the Qing Board of Punishments "equated Muslims with the most violent, uncontrollable bandits within Chinese society and recommended severe penalties . . . when they violated the law."[65] As Lin Zexu's actions in 1849 indicate, although this bias against the Hui had its roots in the northwest, the prejudice had already been transferred to Yunnan.

By 1857 the court's engrained distrust of the Hui had combined with a deep impatience over the state of affairs in Yunnan. The court knew about Shuxing'a's mental instability and Hengchun's inaction and was deeply suspicious of their contradictory representations of the situation. It increasingly suspected that Hengchun's inaction was simply a stalling tactic on his part to conceal earlier Muslim Yunnanese offenses out of fear of being censured.

Reports from the war ministry official, He Tongyun, and the censor, Li Peihu—both in Yunnan at this time—fueled these suspicions. It is very likely that He Tongyun actively participated in the Kunming Massacre, yet the court considered him a neutral observer, since he had only just returned to Kunming to begin his obligatory three-year mourning period after the death of his father. In his account to the throne, He Tongyun painted the Hui as inherently violent and supported Shuxing'a's fabrication that Hui had attacked Kunming.[66] In a separate report, censor Li Peihu fueled the court's distrust of "pro-Hui" officials by placing the blame on local magistrates who "did not report the facts, but instead secretly meet with the Hui" and thus permitted Hui to gain the upper hand over law enforcement efforts by local and provincial officials.[67] These accusations—along with other reports—corroborated the court's view that Hengchun's indecisive and permissive behavior had allowed the Hui to loot and burn property and kill

Han without restraint.[68] The court felt that illicit actions such as these required a forceful five-point response.

The emperor's instructions to Yunnan officials, although decisive, reveal just how woefully ignorant of Yunnan affairs the court had become. First, he ordered the gentry in western Yunnan to form militias to augment the Qing military. Second, tusi militias were to be used in Yunzhou and Tengyue because they were "fast, mobile, and familiar with the area." Third, Hengchun was to seek the assistance of several retired officials now residing in Yunnan (such as He Tongyun, Li Peihu, and Huang Cong). Fourth, Hengchun was to enlist tusi like Zuo Daxiong, because he "is clear of right and wrong, good at fighting and the Hui are afraid of him."[69] Fifth, Zhang Liangji—who had been dismissed as governor of Shandong in 1854—was to return to service in Yunnan "because he had previously dealt with the Yongchang Hui [in 1845], and was familiar with the situation in Yunnan."[70]

The emperor's instructions revealed a profound misunderstanding of the situation in Yunnan. First, in many areas the gentry had already organized and fielded militias, which were attacking all Hui indiscriminately—not just those the state perceived as "rebels."[71] Second, it is clear that the emperor had interpreted the problem as primarily a Hui insurrection and did not wish to acknowledge that the Han were fomenting the violence through their ongoing efforts to eradicate Hui populations. Third, he either did not know or did not consider that many long-term Yunnanese—Han, non-Han, and Hui—did not side with the Han, who often treated them with contempt. In many areas where non-Han outnumbered Hui, the non-Han were not supportive of the Qing.

Finally, in bringing Zhang Liangji back to Yunnan, with the suggestion that his experience in Baoshan would be an asset, the emperor was showing a profound insensitivity to the suffering of the Hui over the preceding decade. Zhang Liangji had considerable administrative experience in Yunnan, having served as provincial judge, provincial treasurer, and governor; but in that province he was remembered primarily as Lin Zexu's front man in the land trade proposal that had been foisted on the Baoshan Hui after the 1845 Massacre.[72] From the perspective of the Yunnan Hui, the court's decision to bring back Zhang Liangji signaled that the Qing intended to end the current violence by siding with the Han, just like Lin Zexu had in Baoshan.[73]

This last point should not be taken lightly. Up to this point, every time the Han had launched organized attacks and carried out massacres on their communities, the Muslim Yunnanese had resisted the temptation to openly rebel. They had consistently appealed to Beijing for assistance, despite the open involvement of Qing officials in the attacks. The way many Muslim Yunnanese saw it, the government's actions after the Kunming Massacre indicated that they had again misplaced their trust. The court was so distracted by the Taiping Rebellion in the lower Yangtze and so ready to believe that the Muslim Yunnanese were the main instigators of the violence that it failed to notice that the events of 1856 were almost an exact repetition of the Hui massacres of 1839, 1845, and 1849, which local and provincial officials had attempted to conceal.

This time, however, the Yunnan Hui felt they had given the government enough chances. After the earlier massacres they had appealed repeatedly to higher authorities; after the Kunming Massacre no Yunnan Hui representative traveled to Beijing to plead for imperial intervention. If the court was aware of this, it showed no sign of it. Nor did the court ever order the provincial officials to discern between good and bad *Han*—only between "good and bad *Hui*." It was clear from the outset that the court was acting on the strongly held assumption that the Hui were at the root of the violence.

The Qing court was displeased with Hengchun's inaction in the spring of 1857, yet it was reluctant to remove him from his post as governor-general. Instead, in March 1857, the emperor chose the more expedient action of reprimanding him for his ineffectiveness and demoting him one rank. As a final warning, the emperor reproached him for "protecting the provincial capital while doing nothing else."[74] Thus shamed into action, Hengchun began launching his limited military forces against the insurgents.

For a time, military action seemed to improve the situation. Around the capital, government troops had retaken the small but strategically important towns of Yiliang, Haikou, and Yanglin; this allowed much-needed grain supplies to reach the capital. In the west there were reports of imperial victories in Zhennan and Yaozhou; in the east two important cities, Qujing and Dongchuan, were retaken.

But the situation was far from settled. In western and southern Yunnan, the largest urban centers—Dali, Lin'an, and Tengyue—were out of government control; in all three, the city authorities had fled with their official seals to Kunming.[75] To make matters worse, in early July 1857 the calm around Kunming was broken when a multiethnic force of several thousand rebels marched unexpectedly and unchallenged to the city walls. The rebel siege succeeded largely because Hengchun had dispatched his forces to other parts of the province, thinking that the area around the capital was secure from rebel attack. The siege underscored the extent to which wishful thinking had carried away those in charge.[76]

Hengchun had always hoped for a peaceful resolution and was utterly unprepared to withstand a rebel offensive. He had not stored any extra supplies within the capital's city walls or kept military forces in reserve to defend it. In addition to this failure of vision on his part, the recent string of minor government victories had lulled the civilian population into a false sense of security. In the months prior to the rebel attack, many residents had again begun working their land on the plain surrounding the city. Thus, when insurgent forces marched on the capital, Hengchun was forced to shut the city gates, leaving thousands of civilians defenseless before the advancing rebels. On July 21, 1857, he and Sangchunrong watched from the city walls as the rebels razed the suburbs of Kunming and killed the civilians they found.[77] Emotionally broken, militarily overwhelmed, and intellectually unable to resolve the situation, he and his wife hanged themselves.[78] Hengchun's death ended the last hope for a resolution that would be good for both the province and the empire.

## The Battle of Yaozhou: Qing Military Organization and Response

The Kunming Massacre of 1856 was the culmination of mounting state involvement in anti-Hui campaigns. Its aftermath did not, however, result in an entirely cohesive provincewide campaign against the Hui. Events during the summer and autumn of 1856 in the wake of the massacre reveal a clear pattern of provincial government sponsorship of anti-Hui attacks. Several key Qing officials posted in Yunnan worried about the newly forming Han militias. But these officials, much like Hengchun, tended to adopt passive and ultimately ineffectual strategies when confronted with violent acts by either Hui or Han.

If the situation was confused within the Qing bureaucracy, it was even more so among the populace. After the 1856 Massacre at Kunming, more and more Han embraced the project of exterminating the Hui. They were encouraged to do so by official circulars and the lack of official oversight. As Han attacks increased, Hui responses became far more organized and aggressive. To understand the profound consequences of official involvement in the early stages of the rebellion, it is crucial to look beyond the senior officials' motives and methods and consider the government's muddled early response to the rising violence.

In early June 1856, only weeks after the Kunming Massacre, one of the first organized outbreaks of Hui hostilities erupted in Yaozhou, an urban center midway between Dali and Chuxiong. In response, Governor Shuxing'a ordered the province's military commander, Wen Xiang, to lead several hundred soldiers from Dali to quell the uprising.[79] Wen Xiang, uncertain of the military opposition he would face, decided to mobilize nearly his entire garrison and leave behind a negligible defensive force. He also ordered the commander at Yongbei to lead reinforcements from the smaller garrisons at Heqing, Jianchuan, Lijiang, and Baoshan to rendezvous with him near Yaozhou. All of this left western Yunnan exposed.[80] Wen Xiang's choices would turn out to be among the most momentous of the entire first year of the rebellion.

Wen's reasons for leaving so few soldiers in the two main garrisons of western Yunnan were based on his past military experience in Yunnan as well as on certain assumptions he was making about the Hui rebels. The Qing military, especially in Yunnan, consistently relied on sheer numbers to overwhelm opposition and dissent. Some contend that besides this, Wen brought as many troops as he could so that he could help exterminate the Hui.[81] It is likely that Wen viewed Yaozhou and Chuxiong as strategically important supply centers and communication posts linking the grain-rich areas of western Yunnan with central Yunnan; thus a full and rapid show of force was required.[82] In addition, Wen did not know the exact size of the Hui forces at Yaozhou. He would have deduced that the Hui were numerous enough to capture and hold a large walled town with relative ease. He would also have been aware of the intermittent Han–Hui violence that had arisen in past years in the Yaozhou area. These assumptions would have led him to mount a force large enough to guarantee victory.

After arriving in Yaozhou in early August, Wen took almost a month to besiege the walled city. This was a common tactic during that era in that region; so far, most insurgencies had been isolated and easy to defeat in this way.[83] Just after achieving the encirclement, Wen received word of a Hui attack on Dali.[84] Unsure of the nature of the threat there, he was unwilling to lift his siege of Yaozhou and sent only a small force to help relieve the city.[85] On October 14, his tactics at Yaozhou bore fruit: the Hui leaders surrendered. Wen entered the city on October 26 and "pacified" the Hui.[86] His exhilaration was not to last; several days later he learned that Dali, a far more significant prize, had fallen into rebel hands.[87]

There are contradictory accounts of Wen's actions after the fall of Yaozhou. Official histories state that he executed some thirty Hui ringleaders; other accounts suggest that the top leaders escaped to join in the fighting at Dali.[88] An unofficial account by Li Yuzhen, a Han from Dali, indicates that Wen was so disgusted with the Han militias who had rushed to aid the Qing attack that he immediately ordered them to return to their homes. This order was not received well by the Han: "Wen Xiang, afraid the Lin'anese militia might become too arrogant and willful, allowed [the surrender of the Hui]. The gathered Lin'anese resentfully said: 'We exerted considerable effort and expense to arrive at this point. Now that we almost have them, you want to negotiate peace with them. This is exactly like encouraging the tiger's strength. If this comes to pass, do not come to us for help.'"[89]

The direct manner in which the Lin'an local militia challenged Wen Xiang, the highest military commander in Yunnan, indicates that pro-Hui officials were rapidly losing the support of the populace. It also highlights the increasingly forthright manner in which Han militants were challenging all who opposed their anti-Hui stance.

On December 5, 1856, Shuxing'a sent a memorial to the emperor conveying the basic sequence of events of the Yaozhou campaign. Eager to bear good news during a difficult time for the court, he greatly embellished his account of Wen Xiang's victory.[90] He stated that Wen's attack on the city had left two thousand rebels dead and that another four hundred had been killed the following day.[91] The "good" Hui of Yaozhou, together with the besieged Han, had chosen to surrender and had delivered one of the Hui rebels to the garrison as an indication of their honorable intentions. Wen relied on his military skills and the support of these Yaozhou residents to enter the city on October 26 and pacify the people. He captured four of the Hui leaders and took thirty-one more into custody. All of these rebels were put to death by slicing or decapitation.[92] The remaining Hui he released and allowed to return to their respective villages. So claimed Shuxing'a.

If the numbers in Shuxing'a's memorial were not an exaggeration, Wen might have been justified in remaining in Yaozhou. Yet no other document corroborates Shuxing'a's estimates. More to the point, if Wen's victory had been as clear as Shuxing'a suggested, why did Wen return to Kunming afterwards instead of continuing on to Dali, western Yunnan's most strategic military and commercial center, where his wife and children were prisoners of the Hui rebels? In fact, Wen did not venture out again from the walls of the provincial capital for several months, and only then because Hengchun ordered him to pacify the areas around Tonghai and Hexi to the south and east of Kunming.[93]

Shuxing'a's hyperbole aside, the Yaozhou campaign was of critical significance. Most contemporary accounts emphasize the strategic consequences of Wen's decisions: first, to empty the Dali garrison for his Yaozhou campaign; and second, to release a large number of the Hui he had captured after his victory there.[94] Yet to focus on these two elements omits perhaps the most significant aspect of 1856—the ongoing division of opinion among Qing officials regarding the increasingly active role of Han militias in the fighting.

The Han militias, including the ones present at Yaozhou, had been formed hastily throughout Yunnan in the wake of the Kunming Massacre and were intent on perpetuating the anti-Hui violence. They were often ill trained and poorly led and completely outside imperial control. An example was the militia formed by assistant brigade commander Zhang Zhengtai in the northwestern town of Heqing (near Lijiang) to carry out the order "exterminate the Hui." He had just returned the previous year from leading a group of Yunnan volunteers to fight the Taiping rebels in Anhui. Han throughout northwestern Yunnan flocked to his banner. His militia carried out successive massacres in Heqing, Lijiang, and Jianchuan, greatly increasing fears among Hui communities throughout western Yunnan.[95] His aggressive anti-Hui campaign—largely against Hui communities that had made no open signs of aggression themselves—intensified the very fears that Wen and other provincial officials were attempting to assuage.[96]

The conflicting strategies of Wen and Zhang attest to the divided and often heated differences among Qing officials as to how best to deal with the Hui. The prejudice of the government perspective is reflected in the fact that although many officials condemned Wen for his shortsightedness in releasing the Hui, none condemned the anti-Hui violence carried out under Qing auspices and by Qing officials throughout the province.[97]

Prior to the Kunming Massacre the atrocities committed by the Han in Baoshan and other locales had generally been confined to a single prefecture at any one time. In 1856 the widespread nature of Han attacks elicited an equally broad Hui response—one that caught both the aggressors and the Qing authorities off guard. Because the Panthay Rebellion did not emanate from an inherent Muslim desire for violence or from deep-seated anti-Manchu sentiment, the rebellion from its outset was notable for its lack of unity. Put another way, although the widespread attacks on the Muslim Yunnanese offered the Hui—and other non-Han groups—a *common* course of action, each rebel force gave precedence to its own specific goals.

In the months immediately after the Kunming Massacre, the Hui leaders in all three regions of Yunnan followed remarkably similar strategies: they emphasized their Islamic beliefs, sought non-Han support, and defended their core territories. At the same time, strong interregional tensions often thwarted hopes of unifying the various rebel centers. The complex cultural, ethnic, and regional divides among the various rebel groups would harden slowly until they came to define the framework of the rebellion.

## The Regional Roots of Resistance

As noted in earlier chapters, Yunnan's administrative structure mirrored the province's natural triadic division into eastern, western, and southern Yunnan. This influenced how the rebellion was perceived by the Muslim Yunnanese and how strategies were developed to address the violence. Memorials to the emperor reflected this division by habitually discussing the rebellion and its leaders in terms of regions.[98] Even when speaking in general terms of the disturbances, officials often invoked a three-region terminology to emphasize the widespread nature of the violence or to indicate its general location.[99] From the rebellion's outset in 1856, this regionalized perspective deeply affected its course—as the violence increased, as provincial officials responded, and as the rebel leaders came together.

None of the three regions escaped the fury unleashed across Yunnan by the Kunming Massacre of 1856. The Hui's vehement response stunned those Han communities whose actions had provoked it. The Muslim Yunnanese reaction was so swift and intense in large part because Ma Dexin—Yunnan's preeminent ahong—quickly communicated the news of the massacre to other Hui communities throughout Yunnan. In addition, word of the death and destruction falling on Hui in the province was quickly spread by refugees fleeing the largest of the early massacres: Kunming, Chuxiong, and Heqing.[100] Fueling this violent Hui reaction were the actions of Han communities as they continued to follow the directive giving local officials permission to attack the Hui.[101] The three regions reacted in unison but in qualitatively different ways. These early differences would have a dramatic impact on the rebellion's course.

### THE CONTEST FOR DALI

Dali had been the economic, political, and social nexus of western Yunnan as far back as the seventh century, when it was the capital of the Nanzhao and Dali kingdoms. The city was in the middle of an idyllic valley, at the center of broad, fertile plain sloping gently from the snowcapped Cangshan Mountains down to Erhai Lake. The valley narrowed to the north and south, forming defiles, which were guarded by two imposing fortresses. Properly defended, the valley could withstand even the most determined siege. In 1856 Qing officials noted that "if the rebels united, attacked, and occupied [Dali], it would be a disaster beyond words."[102]

By the end of May 1856, Hui communities in and around Dali had heard about the massacre in Kunming. From refugees of the attacks in and around Kunming and from proclamations, they also knew about the circulars calling for the formation of Han militias.[103] Their sense of foreboding was heightened by Wen Xiang's ambiguous intentions toward the Yaozhou Hui and by Heqing assistant brigade commander Zhang Zhengtai's campaign of extermination against Hui communities north of Dali.

When the violence broke out in August 1856 the civil officials stationed in Dali consisted of the western intendant, Lin Tingxi, the Dali prefect, Tang Dunpei, and the Taihe County magistrate, Mao Yucheng. Lin Tingxi and Tang Dunpei clashed over the correct course of action. According to one account, Tang pressed Lin to act aggressively: "allocating funds [for the defense of Dali], organizing the home garrison [lianyong], reorganizing the militia (mintuan), distributing weapons to the city soldiers, and quickly summoning Zhang Zhengtai to help defend the city and to consolidate the plan."[104]

In an intriguing example of how local officials in a single place could diverge in their perceptions of the Hui, Lin refused to request aid from Zhang precisely because he feared Zhang's rabid anti-Hui stance. Instead he pursued a more conciliatory approach, making public proclamations to the local Hui that the presence of the Han militias posed no great danger.[105] The fact that Han militias and Hui mobs were fighting pitched battles in the streets and that the markets had all been closed by his decree put the lie to his pretense of calm.

The Hui of Dali had little faith that the city's Qing officials would protect them. In Mianning, Baoshan, and Kunming, officials had pledged to protect the Hui only to aid the Han in their attacks. The Hui remembered this all too well and felt compelled to preempt what they fully expected would be an all-out Han attack on their community. Their fears were confirmed in late August, when local Han militias entered the city and took up positions at key intersections.[106]

On September 3 the Hui struck back, attacking and occupying the upper-pass fort at Shangguan to prevent Zhang Zhengtai and his forces from coming to the aid of the Han militias.[107] By September 6 there were armed skirmishes almost every day in the southern suburbs. Lin, in an attempt to prevent Han militias arming themselves with government weapons, ordered a seal to be placed on the regional commander's yamen, where the armory was located. On September 9, Hui groups in Dali, reinforced by Hui from neighboring villages, attacked the yamen and discovered the large cache of weapons.[108] Just before the armory fell, the assistant regional commander, Huai Tang'a, poisoned himself rather than face death at the hands the rebels.[109]

The following day, sensing that the Hui were quickly gaining the upper hand, the provincial commander and western intendant ordered the remaining troops and militias to form protective rings around their respective yamens. But it was too late: the day after that, September 11, a large contingent of Hui from Menghua (a city southeast of Dali), having heard about the fighting, traversed the mountain pass separating the two cities to reinforce the Hui in Dali.[110] Late that night, Hui rebels forced their way into the Lin's compound and killed him and his family. Early the next morning their severed heads appeared over the Hui-controlled West Gate.[111]

For the next seven days the city hung in the balance as the Hui pressed their advantage. The Han forces were slowly pressed back from their positions. In one last attempt to turn the tide, magistrate Mao Yucheng divided his remaining forces into two groups—one fighting toward the north, the other toward the south. He hoped one of these groups would draw the bulk of the Hui forces to itself, allowing the other to seize control of one of the Hui-controlled strongpoints at the city gates. Mao's sortie was a calculated gamble that failed disastrously. Neither of the two Han forces made it out of the city alive.[112] On September 16 the last top Qing official in the city, the prefect Tang Dunpei, slipped away with an armed escort, fleeing east for the provincial capital. Already over seventy and of frail health, Tang would never reach Kunming; he died several days later from physical and mental stress. In the final estimate "several tens of thousands" of Han and Hui perished in the battle for Dali.[113]

### A NEW BEGINNING

The battle for Dali constituted a sea change in Hui tactics: Hui from a number of localities had acted together in a way never seen during earlier outbreaks of violence in Mianning, Baoshan, and Chuxiong. After the Dali Hui started the fighting, Hui from other places had come to their aid in substantial numbers. Through this alliance, the Hui had been able to overcome the Han and Qing forces, which until now had used their superior numbers to overwhelm isolated Hui communities. But far more momentous than even this was the decision the Hui made, after gaining control of Dali, to form a political structure that would allow them to secure and extend their initial gains and establish an independent state.

The Hui military attacks in Dali, although well coordinated, had lacked a unified leadership. Throughout the battle, most Hui had fought in hometown groups. The result was serious fragmentation among the victors, with each group feeling it had been pivotal to the victory.[114] "Each [of the leaders] were proud of their own efforts, each unwilling to step down, but instead coveting the chance to become the leader and to achieve dominant command."[115] The day the Hui gathered to select a new leader, each candidate was given an opportunity to express why he should be chosen.

Accounts of this meeting state that most of these men emphasized their bravery and military prowess; only one, a man named Du Wenxiu, stressed the future importance of nonmilitary matters. "If you want to do great things," he asserted, "winning over people's hearts and minds is far more difficult than forcefully occupying their city."[116] Even more remarkable, given the ethnic tensions that must have been coursing through the Hui community, he argued that the uprising could not be limited solely to the Hui and must include the Han and non-Han because they "are numerous and the Hui few; it is particularly important that we include Han [in our plans]."[117]

In the end, Du Wenxiu was chosen as the new leader after several others shifted their support to him. Ostensibly, this was because all the competing groups had a high regard for him. It is also likely that he was perceived as a leader with broad support in western Yunnan who would not favor the interests of a single area.[118]

On October 23, 1856, on the Dali parade ground, Du Wenxiu was invested with the office of generalissimo (*zongtong bingma dayuanshuai*) and "Leader of All Muslims."[119] The imperial court would not ascertain his name until five years later.[120] Du was an inspired choice. Born in Baoshan in 1823, he was extremely intelligent, having earned his *xiucai* degree at the age of sixteen.[121] He was one of the three Hui who had traveled to Beijing to petition the imperial court for compensation after the Baoshan Massacre of 1845.[122] That petition had prompted the court to launch an investigation, but the resulting land swap (see chapter 5) had been far from satisfactory to Du, who never accepted the compromise. Having failed to secure a satisfactory settlement, he returned to western Yunnan, where he plied the region's trading routes for his family's caravan business. It seems that during these years he familiarized himself with Yunnan's economic, political, and multiethnic landscape.[123]

Du Wenxiu displayed a rare mixture of charisma, vision, and cosmopolitanism. His formal education in the Chinese classics had endowed him with a working fluency in classical Chinese as well as a familiarity with Chinese history, law, and bureaucracy. This did not make him unique among Yunnanese Hui. However, these attributes were coupled with a deft ability to challenge local and imperial authorities through officially recognized channels, and this is what distinguished him from both the ahongs and the militant Hui (many of whom were not Yunnanese). The Yunnan Hui had produced a number of individuals over the centuries who excelled at navigating the Chinese, Hui, and non-Han worlds of Yunnan; Du Wenxiu was a supreme example.

## Southern Rebels: Ma Rulong and Ma Dexin

Within narratives of the Panthay Rebellion, the insurrection in Dali is privileged to the exclusion of the disturbances in southern and eastern Yunnan. Most Chinese treatments refer to the rebellion as the "Du Wenxiu Uprising" and dismiss the strong and essential role played by Hui leaders in these other areas.[124] Although the Hui in southern and eastern Yunnan never captured a city of equivalent importance to Dali, they shaped the rebellion's course in fundamental ways. Specifically, rebel forces in southern and eastern Yunnan consistently posed the most direct threat to Kunming—the Qing's primary administrative presence in the province—and so bore the brunt of the Qing military pressure.

Initially, many of the uprisings in southern Yunnan paralleled what was occurring elsewhere in the province. However, they differed in three aspects from the fighting in Yunnan's other regions. First, much of the violence that had precipitated the rebellion, although it took place around Chuxiong and

Kunming, involved disproportionately large numbers of Lin'anese Han and Hui. This made the fighting in southern Yunnan especially fierce—a consequence of the running attacks that had been ongoing since the early 1850s. Second, Yunnan Hui and Yi partisans had attacked and secured several of western Yunnan's largest urban centers during the first several months of fighting; in contrast, the Hui of southern Yunnan never achieved unifying victories of this nature. As a consequence, the southern Hui leadership remained in a far more precarious position militarily and politically. At the same time, though, they were threatening the provincial capital, so from the perspective of the imperial provincial leadership, they were a powerful presence. Third, the Hui communities in southern Yunnan were far more dispersed. This gave rise to multiple centers of insurgency, each with an independent leader but all competing for a common vision. In the months immediately following the Kunming Massacre, Hui responses to that atrocity erupted in four distinct areas in southern Yunnan: Haikou, Chengjiang, Xinxing, and Lin'an (from north to south).[125] The violence was fiercest in Lin'an with sustained attacks and counterattacks between Han militia and the multiethnic rebel forces.

The fighting in Lin'an started after the May 19 massacre in Kunming. Relations between the Lin'an Han and Hui had been strained for many years. After the Hui heard about the proclamation encouraging the formation of Han militias, they circulated their own appeal asking the Han to end the killings.[126] In late June a Xizhuang Han militia entered the prefectural capital of Lin'an and slaughtered a large number of Hui within the city walls. After this they turned their attack to the surrounding Hui villages.[127] Despite their intensity these militia attacks failed to exterminate the Hui, and in the aftermath spawned a large number of independent Hui bands, each intent on leading the Hui response.

The largest of these early rebel groups was composed of Hui from Chengjiang, a city two days southeast of Kunming. This band stood out from the others mainly because of the prestige of its leader, Xu Yuanji, a prominent ahong with close ties with Yunnan's preeminent Muslim leader, Ma Dexin. Quite early in the fighting, Xu Yuanji called for the Hui of Chuxiong, Zhennan, and Chenggong, and other Hui from central Yunnan, to mount an attack on the Western Hills. This region was a strategically positioned ridge overlooking Dianchi Lake, within striking distance of the provincial capital. Xu's troops threatened Kunming in the summer of 1856, but Qing forces immediately dispersed them.[128] Even so, Xu's military skills and strong backing from Ma Dexin made him an important leader among the early insurrectionists.

Ma Dexin was Yunnan's most important Hui scholar and religious leader. He was born in 1794 in Dali and was sixty-four years old in 1856. His prominence was derived almost entirely from his impeccable Islamic credentials.[129] His family claimed to be descendants of Sayyid 'Ajall (which made them descendants of Muhammad) and had produced a long line of distinguished religious scholars. His early education was primarily Islamic in its orientation, although some who knew him suggest that he was quite conversant with the Chinese classics.[130] By seventeen he had attained the title of ahong and had left Yunnan to continue his Islamic studies in Shaanxi. After four years there he returned to Yunnan to teach in local religious schools (*madrasas*).

In December 1841, when he was forty-eight, he set out for Mecca.[131] After completing his pilgrimage he traveled widely in the Middle East, visiting Egypt, Istanbul, and Jerusalem before returning to Yunnan in early 1849 by way of Singapore and Guangzhou.[132] Soon after, he was invited to establish a madrasa in Huilong, which quickly became the most important Muslim educational center in southwest China. As Yunnan's preeminent religious leader, Ma Dexin was the only Hui whose prestige extended throughout the province; thus he emerged as a mediator between the competing Hui regional leaders.

The final southern Hui military leader to carve out a position right after the Kunming Massacre was Ma Rulong. He was the only Hui leader who had played an important role in the violence that led to the rebellion. Details of his life prior to the rebellion are sketchy. It is known that he was born and raised in a Hui village near Lin'an. In 1854 he organized a group of Lin'an Hui to avenge the murder of his brother by the Han at the Shiyang mine.[133] By the time the insurrection began he had already obtained a military licentiate (*wusheng*), and he claimed that an uncle of his had served as a brigade general for the Qing.[134] Several years earlier he had been working as an overseer (*kezhang*) while Han and Hui bands were fighting at the Shiyang mine, and he had led a band of local Hui to defend their fellow villagers.[135]

Ma Rulong and Ma Dexin seem to have been on familiar terms before the rebellion. According to one acquaintance, "Ma [Rulong] learned Arabic under the guidance of Ma Dexin, but as a student showed little disposition for his studies, and so his family allowed him to pursue his more natural preferences of physical exercise."[136] His lack of aptitude for formal studies did not diminish his faith. Louis de Carné, the French traveler, met Ma while traversing Yunnan in search of the source of the Mekong. It surprised him that beneath the man who "was covered with wounds, and [who] stripped off his clothes to show us his scars" there was a "fervent disciple of Muhammad."[137] In their first encounter, de Carné indicated that "as soon as Ma [Rulong] joined us, he began to question us about Medina and Mecca."[138] Postrebellion accounts would often downplay his role in the rebellion, yet while it was raging his unwavering adherence to Islamic principles and his strong ties to the Hui religious community would garner him much support among the Hui of southern and eastern Yunnan.

Ma Rulong enjoyed some military success in the uprising's early months but was unable to take Lin'an, the largest city in southern Yunnan. After several failed attempts, he established a sphere of control around Guanyi,[139] roughly halfway between Kunming and Lin'an. That region's harsh terrain offered a convenient and easily defended base for his operations.[140] Few documents survive from this early period, but it can be surmised that Ma's forces were the most multiethnic in the province.[141] Hengchun noted that "Qujiang Hui from Lin'an prefecture linked up with Hui and Yi from Chengjiang and other areas."[142]

In the spring of 1857, Xu Yuanji and Ma Rulong began, independently, to mount fresh offensives against the Qing forces. Xu Yuanji linked up with the Xinxing Hui and captured Chengjiang, Ningzhou, Chenggong, and Jiangchuan. Ma Rulong stormed Lin'an but once again failed to capture it. Recognizing the drawbacks of fighting independently, he approached Xu Yuanji and Ma Dexin with a proposal to combine their forces and attack Kunming.[143]

So it was that on June 13, 1857, Ma Rulong, "leading a force of Hui and non-Han (Hui-yi) several tens of thousands strong, suddenly attacked the provincial capital burning and looting the southern pass [area]. The city gates were closed abruptly because of the rebels' assault and killing. They attacked [the Kunming suburbs of] Dianchi and Panlongjia killing countless numbers in their attack."[144]

The siege lasted nearly a year and resulted in severe famine and countless deaths in the capital—including that of Hengchun, whose suicide was described in the opening pages of this study.[145] Xu Yuanji and Ma Rulong stopped all attempts by the Qing to break the siege but were unable to storm the battlements and seize the city.[146]

After Hengchun's suicide, the central court replaced him with Wu Zhenyu, Sichuan's governor-general. Soon after his arrival, Wu pursued a negotiated peace, promising the Hui their lands would be returned and that the Han most responsible for the massacre would be punished. In December 1857, in a memorial, he told the throne that a truce had been worked out and that the Hui would be returning to their home districts and occupations.[147] From Wu's reports of other incidents, however, it is clear that neither side had completely set aside its resentment. "On March 7th, disbanded [Han] militia formed roving bands declaring they had not been paid their salaries . . . [they] entered the capital and attacked several officials and killed four Hui."[148] Wu noted that they were paid and ordered to disperse. If Wu Zhenyu was able to buy off the Han, it is less clear how he placated the Hui.

Wu at first only hinted at how he had convinced the Hui to end the siege. Several months later, perhaps worried about how the court would react to his lenient approach, he reported that Ma Dexin had been granted the grade of fourth rank and officially recognized as the head of all Muslim Yunnanese and Yunnan's Muslim affairs.[149] Wu's memorials mention neither Ma Rulong nor Xu Yuanji. If he offered them offices, they were probably of low rank and insufficient to quench their thirst for distinction and wealth.[150] Perhaps the truce was enough incentive to convince both men to return to their respective bases, but it was not enough for them to give up their status as rebel leaders against the Qing.

The Hui rebels' failure to take Kunming would be a significant factor in the rebellion's outcome. It deprived them of a much-needed consolidating victory of the sort Du enjoyed when he captured Dali. It also seems that without a unifying victory, the eastern and southern rebel forces continued to resist forming a common army or strategy. Instead, in the wake of the failed siege, the leaders returned to their bases to strengthen their own positions.[151]

By early summer, Ma Rulong controlled about thirty-five small towns and county seats and had around five thousand men under his command.[152] Wellington Chan, in his study of Ma Rulong, is probably correct in asserting that "Ma's campaign to the south and southeast in 1858 must be looked upon as an attempt not only to replenish his supplies and gain more *yi* [non-Han] and other aboriginal followers, but also to bring the uncoordinated local bands of Moslem forces under his control."[153]

Although Ma Rulong would later gloss over this phase in his own account of the period, it is clear he had not yet achieved his personal aspirations, for he redoubled his efforts.[154] By June 1858 he had adopted the unambiguously seditious title of grand commander (*da yuan shuai*), established control over large areas of southern Yunnan, and attracted great numbers of soldiers to his cause.[155]

A growing consolidation of power among the most powerful of the southern rebels ushered in a period of harmonious relations.[156] Ma Dexin seems to have played a key role in these rapprochements. He acted as a mediator between regions; as a respected religious figure throughout Yunnan, he helped orient and validate the insurgency provincewide.[157] As a result of this new cooperation, by early 1859 the southern rebels had emerged again as a powerful military force.

Perhaps the Qing court hoped that the surrender of the Hui after the 1857–58 siege of Kunming would end the rebellion; if so, Hui rebel activities in eastern and southern Yunnan in 1859 dispelled such expectations. If anything, the situation was worse. There were more and more reports that the insurrection was no longer simply a "Hui rebellion" but included growing numbers of non-Han combatants. On January 1, 1859, Yunnan governor Zhang Liangji reported that the Qujiang rebels (almost certainly Ma Rulong's forces) had "linked up with Hui and yi bandits to the south of the capital and had occupied ten or more towns."[158] A short time later, another Hui force joined with Han forces to take the city of Anning to the west of Kunming.[159] In March the governor wrote that the Hui leader Ma Linghan had linked up with Tian Qingyu and Yang Zhenpeng and launched a surprise attack on Kunyang. Immediately after taking that city, Yang split off and attacked Haikou, occupying it on April 23. The sphere of rebel control was edging closer and closer to the walls of Kunming.[160]

The precise role Ma Rulong played in these various attacks is unclear. Whether he was merely biding his time in southern Yunnan or actively participating in these attacks is unknown. What *is* known is that he was competing with others on the informal rebel pecking order. In the spring of 1859 several events dramatically aided his quest for advancement. In March, Xinxing's ranking rebel leader, Ma Linghan, died from a wound received during the battle for Kunyang. Ma Rulong benefited from Ma Linghan's death and emerged as the ascendant rebel leader in the Lin'an and Pu'er prefectures. Through the latter half of 1859 and into early 1860, he attacked and "seized Tonghai, Kunyang, Anning, . . . Lufeng, and Guangtong."[161] By the end of the year, only the prefectural seat of Lin'an had eluded his control.[162] As 1859 came to an end, the territory under Ma's nominal power stretched from Simao and Ami in the south to Guangtong and Lufeng in the north—a vast sphere of influence that would have taken several days' march to cross.[163] Although he had failed to secure a major urban center, he now controlled a territory almost as large as that of the Dali regime and was the most important rebel leader in southern Yunnan.

## Eastern Yunnan: The Search for Order

In the summer following the Kunming Massacre, provincial officials were most concerned about events in eastern Yunnan.[164] That region had the richest mines in the province, which provided the financially desperate central government with much-needed income. Of even more significance for Qing officials in Kunming, all communications, military reinforcements, and vital supplies had to cross eastern Yunnan, either northeastward through Zhaotong to Sichuan or due east through Qujing to Guizhou. Early government assessments of the situation in eastern Yunnan tended to parallel those for the other two regions: they blamed the Hui for the violence. Typical is a memorial written to the emperor in September 1856:

The acting Dongchuan prefect, Wang Zhixu, in retaliation for violence caused by Hui at the nearby mines, burned and killed over one hundred villages outside of the

city. . . . While establishing peace, it resulted in an increase in the Hui bandits' potency. The previous Eastern Intendant Pan Jie went to considerable effort to give
them improper protection, and so the Hui grew even stronger. The Han of Dongchuan, Ludian, Zhanyi, Malong, Qujing, and Nanning are dangerously close to
being overwhelmed with the violence and killing.[165]

The strong anti-Hui bias of these officials is clear in this memorial's portrayal of the Han Chinese as victims and of officials who were trying to stop
the violence as collaborators. The reporting officials did not mention that the
attacks on the Hui had been sanctioned by provincial leaders; nor did they
mention that they were raising to positions of authority Han who were notorious among the Hui for the atrocities they had committed.[166] The most
flagrant of these appointments was that of military licentiate Huang Diankui, whose Lin'anese militias had taken part in the Chuxiong and Kunming
massacres.[167]

Given the importance of eastern Yunnan's mines, it is not surprising that
eastern Yunnan saw the bloodiest fighting in the months immediately following the Kunming Massacre. From the autumn of 1856 to the spring of
1857, there were small-scale Hui uprisings throughout the region.[168] Within
two months of the Kunming Massacre, Hui rebels had seized the communication hub of Yanglin, thus severing Kunming from interior China and
blocking vital grain shipments from outside the province. Shuxing'a sent out
Huang Diankui to retake Yanglin. In May 1856, Huang marched his government forces eastward toward Yanglin, quelling minor Hui hostilities
along the way. Approaching what seemed to be just another Hui-held village, he and his troops were lured into a marshy field. There they quickly
found themselves surrounded by Hui partisans, and the boggy ground made
a quick retreat impossible. In the bloody fighting that ensued, the Qing
forces were routed and Huang brutally killed. It was a major defeat for the
Qing.[169]

The capture of Yanglin and the defeat of Huang Diankui were firm proof
that the Hui of eastern Yunnan were as effective as their counterparts in the
other regions of the province. What they lacked was a prominent figure like
Ma Dexin or a key target like Dali to rally the Hui. As a consequence, eastern Yunnan, far more than the other two regions, was characterized by a
multitude of small insurgent groups that often overextended themselves and
that repeatedly found themselves facing numerically stronger government
forces. Yet they persevered. In the summer of 1857 two formidable leaders
emerged from these assorted groups: Ma Rong and Ma Liansheng.

Ma Rong was from Dongchuan. In the months following the Kunming
Massacre he established a sphere of control around the medium-sized town
of Xundian. Although he would never achieve the success of Xu Yuanji or
Ma Rulong, he was able to maintain a strong rebel presence in the region.

His erratic but steady raids on government outposts and transportation centers tied up the Qing's limited resources, which indirectly aided other Hui forces throughout the province.

Ma Liansheng was from the eastern Hui center of Ludian. Early in the rebellion he organized a band of Hui, who occupied a series of small towns directly north of eastern Yunnan's main administrative center, Qujing.[170] In early 1857 he finally captured the department seat of Zhanyi and declared himself "chief commander."[171] Having done so, he sent a representative to Dali deferring to the newly established leadership there. In return, the Dali regime conferred on him a seal of office and official rank. Ma's gesture was significant, given that he dominated the rebel leadership in his region. According to a later biography of Ma Liansheng, it was around this time that he claimed that nowhere in "the seven prefectures, [and all the] departments and counties in eastern Yunnan, is there anyone who dares to challenge me."[172] There is apparently some truth to this boast: by late 1858 Ma Rong and other prominent Hui rebels in eastern Yunnan had begun fighting under his banner. Ma Liansheng was undoubtedly the most powerful eastern Hui leader but was never able to establish a firm foothold in the region or a clear military organization. The Qing campaigns against his bases, first in Zhanyi and later in Xuanwei, were much better organized and equipped.

The insurrections that followed the Kunming Massacre were not limited to Yunnan. The best-documented indications of this involve Hui communities in several counties in western Guizhou Province, which had been the site of almost constant violence since the beginning of the Miao Rebellion in 1854. These communities joined the insurrection after the anti-Hui violence erupted in Yunnan. For example, Zhang Lingxiang, a Guizhou Hui, organized and secretly sent three hundred men from Pu'an subprefecture to Yunnan in 1856.[173] The following year, Hui in the western Guizhou towns of Xingyi and Zhenfeng carried out a series of strikes against government forces and outposts.

Clearly, in the months following the Kunming Massacre the Hui were uniting against those forces intent on exterminating them. That said, the rebellion would not have continued past its early outbreaks without the support of non-Han groups and—in many cases—Han Chinese sympathizers.

## Multiethnic Involvement

In 1858 a French missionary, Father Ponsot, wrote that "throughout this province, complete anarchy reigns. . . . Every province is left to itself, without any regular army, nor money with which to pay them, with brigands multiplying more and more."[174] The Catholic missionaries posted to Yunnan initially feared the religious enmity of the Hui rebels; soon, though, they realized they had "much more to fear from [the Han] brigands than the Muslims."[175] They shared this fear of Han bandits with much of the non-Han populace. Another Catholic missionary, Father Chauveau, suggested in a letter from that same period that "the *indigenes* have united with the Muslims in very large numbers because [they] prefer the yoke of the Muslims to the masses of Chinese bandits that the Mandarins have in their services."[176] In a comment that reminds us of the division between old-timers and newcomers, Ponsot noted that "the hordes [of brigands] to a large extent are comprised of Sichuanese."[177]

Yunnan's non-Han population, however, tended to perceive the Hui rebels as far more than the lesser of two evils. Over the years the Hui had worked to establish links with local indigenous communities. Now that Han militias and bandits were attacking them, they realized that they would need the support of these communities in order to survive.[178] After the Hui took Dali in western Yunnan, Du Wenxiu asserted that for their cause to succeed, it would have to attract a multiethnic following.[179] In the south, Ma Rulong, Xu Yuanji, and Ma Dexin were just as intent on forging alliances with both Han and non-Han.[180] This strategy succeeded: all the large non-Han ethnic groups seem to have participated in the rebellion in all three regions of the province. These groups included (but were not limited to) the Yi in northern Yunnan and the Zhuang and Dai in the south; the insurgents also garnered strong support from the Bai, Jingpo, and Tibetans.[181] Note well that the multiethnic rebel forces also included large numbers of Han—specifically, those whose families had settled in the province generations earlier and who, like the Hui, had adopted a more Yunnanese-centered perspective.[182]

At first, the top provincial officials played to the central court's perceptions that the non-Han were naive and easily duped. Thus in their memorials they declared that the Hui were "seducing the yi peoples" and tricking them into joining their rebel armies.[183] One such account even accused Ma Dexin of "changing the Hui character [in the circulars] to yi, and then showing it to the non-Han leaders who could read."[184] The same official went on to contend that at the beginning of the rebellion "Han, unable to see the advantages [of allying with the yi], happily massacred the yi."[185]

Notwithstanding the flawed assessments of many Qing officials and Han newcomers in 1856, ties between Hui and non-Han were nothing new. Dispatches dating back to the Baoshan incident indicate that local Qing officials were growing worried that the Hui and the indigenous groups might begin to forge alliances.[186] In the 1850s the emperor and high court officials were steering more and more of the empire's resources toward defeating the Taiping Rebellion; in this climate, they brushed aside the possibility of a multiethnic alliance in Yunnan as too preposterous to take seriously. As reflected in the emperor's five-point instruction to Hengchun, the Qing court had persuaded itself that the non-Han, if they involved themselves at all, would stay loyal to the government.[187] The swiftness with which Hui and other Yi elements banded together quickly punctured the court's optimism.[188]

By the autumn of 1856 it was being reported that Hui in southern Yunnan had "linked up with non-Han and occupied, burned and seized property."[189] Officials in western Yunnan were beginning to report that Hui and Yi were joining forces, with one such band "numbering more than 3,000."[190] And in eastern Yunnan—more than in the other two regions—the uprisings were gaining the strong support of non-Han. In and around Dongchuan in northeastern Yunnan, many Yi were flocking to the rebel banner; in the southeast, thousands of Zhuang were joining the Hui in numerous centers of resistance.[191] In neighboring Guizhou Province, the Miao had apparently allied themselves with the Hui.[192] In fact, there are no records of any substantial pro-Qing support anywhere in the province in the early months of the rebellion.

Some indigenous leaders became major forces in the rebellion, above and beyond their role as allies to the major Hui centers of insurrection. In the Ailao Mountains in the southwest, the Yi leader Li Wenxue had raised a multiethnic force several thousand strong by early June. By year's end he commanded more than ten thousand fighters and controlled territory in four counties.[193] According to eyewitness accounts, Li took the title "Grand Commander of the Yi" (yijia bingma dayuanshuai) and adopted a white flag with his surname and title.[194] Li Wenxue was relatively quick to accept an official title and lead his armies to fight under the auspices of the Dali regime. Even after the fall of Dali in 1872, the Ailao region would remain loyal to him and continue to fight under him.[195]

This early multiethnic involvement is important for two reasons. First, from the outset the multiethnic inhabitants of Yunnan never perceived the rebellion simply as a Hui-versus-Han conflict.[196] Second, even though the Yi had not been the specific targets of the Han violence, Yi resentment against Qing and Han inroads into their lands was strong. Past narratives of the rebellion, in an effort to lay blame on the Hui, have often perpetuated the false notion that the insurrection was predominantly a Han–Hui conflict. Ironically, it was only the Han who had such a singular focus for their aggression, and that focus was the Hui.[197] The non-Han fervently supported the rebellion, which suggests that in deciding to revolt against the Qing, they were comfortable crossing ethnic lines. Perhaps their motivation was as Du Wenxiu would later characterize it once the violence erupted: "All of the fish in the pond were affected [chiyu jieyang]."[198]

## Conclusion

Any meaningful analysis of the Panthay Rebellion must begin by considering the virulent nature of the Han attacks on the Hui populations in Kunming and the spontaneous and dispersed nature of the insurrection that followed. It is exceedingly difficult to understand why Qing officials and Han participants hated the Hui so much that they tried to eradicate them and thereby ignited the rebellion. It seems unbelievable that Qingsheng's proclamation "slay without being held accountable" could have been interpreted as "kill them one and all." But as Inga Clendinnen cautions in her eloquent study of the Holocaust: "Tone matters as well as text. It is necessary to understand how such extravagant sentences were spoken and such sentiments normalized."[199] In other words, in examining the days, weeks, and months immediately following the Kunming Massacre, one must not forget how formalized and engrained anti-Hui sentiment had become among certain segments of the new settler Han and—over time—among imperial officials appointed to Yunnan. These sentiments strongly influenced the central government's perceptions of events in the region—perceptions that dictated their directives to Yunnan officials.

The forces behind the large-scale and long-term violence that led to the massacres were quite complex. State and Han accounts—and histories of the rebellion ever since—contend that the massacres of the Hui were triggered by fears of Hui attacks on Han communities. Later investigations proved they were not: reports that the Hui were threatening Han communities were complete fabrications.[200] Tragic as it may seem, the Han were motivated mainly by an irrational and overwhelming resentment of the Hui, as evidenced in the Han Chinese determination "to rid Yunnan of this cursed race."[201] Such statements must not be treated as hyperbole. Even government sources suggest that by 1839 anti-Hui sentiment was commonplace among the newly arrived Han. By the 1850s, large segments of the population tacitly approved the Han attacks on the Hui. And local and provincial officials were willing to weave an elaborate web of falsehoods to prevent detection of these attacks. The violence that resulted from the widespread acceptance of this behavior far exceeded the more mundane multi-ethnic violence seen in feuds or short-term hostilities of the sort that occurred in the first decades of the nineteenth century.

Not until 1862, almost eight years after the Kunming Massacre, was the court finally informed—in a memorial from Yun-Gui governor-general Pan Duo—of the deep-rooted anti-Hui attitudes at play in the region and their corrupting effects on many of the state officials: "It first originated under Yongchang Prefect Luo Tianchi then continued under Governor-General Hengchun, Governor Shuxing'a, and Provincial Judge Qingsheng who all mistakenly listened to rumors and hearsay, and were deceived by 'demons and gods.'"[202]

But who were these "demons and gods" of which Pan spoke? They took many shapes and forms, including the Incense Brotherhoods, the local gentry, and in the case of the Kunming attack, Huang Cong, a retired official from the Board of War. However, the "demons and gods" cannot be explained by any single entity. More and more newly arrived Han and imperial officials had convinced themselves that the Hui needed to be eradicated. Han–Hui tensions became the axis around which local violence revolved, and state policy often unintentionally conformed to this bipolar perspective by accepting the Han–Hui division as a legitimate construct around which to organize pacification efforts. There was no single, mutually agreed upon rationale for the attacks, murders, and massacres other than to kill as many Hui as possible. Seen in this light, the source of the Panthay Rebellion lies less with the rebellious actions of the Hui, and more with fact that killing all Hui had come to be perceived as acceptable behavior and thus beyond questioning.

## CHAPTER 7

# Ambiguous Ambitions: Ma Rulong's Road to Power, 1860–1864

The early years of the Panthay Rebellion were extremely taxing on the Qing court and their representatives in Yunnan. The central court faced threats in all parts of the empire and had few resources to spare for the provincial officials who were trying to bring the province back under government control. In spite of this lack of central support, provincial Qing officials were able to mount several concerted attacks against the rebels in Dali. That city being the former western administrative center of the Qing in Yunnan, they considered the rebels who held it the biggest threat to Qing dominion in the region; thus Dali quickly became the focus of all the military campaigns.

Between 1856 and 1860 several campaigns were launched west out of Kunming for the purpose of retaking Dali. The first, led by the provincial commander, Wen Xiang, left the safety of Kunming in July 1857, almost a year after Wen's pyrrhic victory at Yaozhou. His troops succeeded in pushing the Dali forces back from Binchuan and Jianchuan into the security of the Dali Valley.[1] Then, in a strategic error that would be repeated several times by Qing forces during the rebellion, Wen overplayed his advantage by advancing too quickly toward his goal. His supply lines, which stretched from Kunming several hundred kilometers westward through many pro-Dali areas, were strained to the breaking point. As a consequence, he was forced to end his offensive and return to Kunming before he could launch a decisive blow against the city.

Wen Xiang's 1857 campaign points to a second recurring feature of the Panthay Rebellion. Although the various uprisings in the first years of the rebellion reflected strong regional divisions, these divisions did not preclude rebel forces from directly and indirectly helping one another in times of crisis. In the case of Wen's push toward Dali, this help took the form of the concurrent siege of Kunming (see chapter 6), led by Ma Rulong and Xu Yuanji, which made it difficult for Wen to maintain pressure on Dali. By year's end the Dali rebels had regained control of the major cities surrounding Dali, and the southern rebels were still besieging Kunming.[2]

The following year, 1858, Governor-General Wu Zhenyu's deteriorating health and imminent departure broke the stalemate between those officials pursuing a peaceful end to the rebellion and those who sought to resume their project to exterminate the Hui. During his year as Yun-Gui governor-general, Wu had asserted a balanced style of leadership. His request to be allowed to step down due to illness was accepted in December 1858.[3] In his place the emperor appointed Zhang Liangji. Zhang had served many years earlier as the Baoshan magistrate under Lin Zexu and had returned to Yunnan several months earlier as provincial governor. Xu Zhiming, a native of Guizhou, was then promoted to governor. With Wu Zhenyu's stabilizing influence gone, this new slate of officials quickly returned to the anti-Hui policies of 1856.

Zhang and Xu had recently been battling the Taiping armies in the east. Now in Yunnan, they concurred that a continuation of Wu's conciliatory approach would lead to a complete loss of Qing control over the province. The two men reinstituted a policy of suppression against all those who opposed government rule—but especially against the Hui. Throughout the spring of 1859, Zhang and Xu allowed the Han militias free reign to attack Hui communities, in effect breaking many of the promises Wu had made to Ma Dexin, Xu Yuanji, and Ma Rulong as conditions for ending the first siege of Kunming.[4]

To increase the pressure on the rebels at Dali, Zhang and Xu chose a young military officer, Zhu Kechang. A native of Yunnan, Zhu was a military licentiate and a decorated veteran of bandit suppression campaigns in neighboring Guangxi and Guizhou. As one of the more capable military leaders to emerge out of the 1857 siege of Kunming, he was the natural choice to lead the government's strongest offensive yet against the rebels in western Yunnan.[5]

In late February 1860, less than two months after Zhang assumed the office of governor-general, Zhu led his army westward from Kunming. Like Wen Xiang before him, his orders were to defeat Du Wenxiu and capture Dali; this would bring the rebellion to a quick and clear end.[6] At first, Zhu's military experience and knowledge of the region seemed to give the imperial forces the upper hand. In early March, Zhu routed Du's Pingnan armies in three consecutive encounters, killing more than two thousand rebels. Zhu then split his army into three smaller divisions and simultaneously attacked the districts of Yaozhou, Dayao, and Yunnan.[7] By April, all three objectives had been taken. Zhu now began preparing an advance on the cities that served as Dali's defensive perimeter.

Alarmed at how easily Zhu Kechang's troops were defeating all the rebel forces he launched at them, Du Wenxiu requested help from the province's religious leader, Ma Dexin; he also ordered his top general, Cai Fachun, to end his offensive in southwestern Yunnan in order to bring pressure on Zhu's flank.[8] While these requests were being sent out, the imperial forces occupied the small cities of Binchuan, Midu, and Hongyan—the last rebel garrisons protecting the Dali Valley itself. However, while Zhu and his forces were preparing a final push into the valley, the tide began to turn against them. Cai Fachun arrived with the most effective and battle-hardened of Dali's forces and swiftly worked his way north, retaking Midu and the Yunnan districts in quick succession. In Binchuan he caught Zhu's dwindling forces flatfooted and cut off their retreat. On September 9, the Dali troops swarmed the beleaguered imperial troops and killed Zhu.[9]

Zhu's defeat was a turning point in the rebellion. The Qing officials in Kunming did not know that Ma Dexin was also responding quickly and strongly to Du's request for aid.[10] At the rebels' most desperate moment since the founding of the Dali government, Ma Dexin reassured Du Wenxiu: "I have already secretly ordered my disciples [*mensheng*] Ma [Rulong] as the Grand Commander of Three Directions with Ma Rong as second in command . . . to launch a rearguard attack from their base in Yimen."[11] This clear signal from the most respected Islamic leader in the province seemed to signify that the regional divisions among the Hui leaders were finally ending.

With Ma Dexin's endorsement, Ma Rulong now commanded the largest single military force in Yunnan, imperial or rebel—an army of more than ten thousand Hui, non-Han, and Han. Ma Rulong quickly displayed a keen sense of strategy, playing on Zhang Liangji and Xu Zhiming's overriding concern for Kunming's (and their own) safety. He led his newly formed army out of its base south of Kunming and feigned an attack on the capital with a small vanguard force; meanwhile, the bulk of his army skirted the Kunming plain to the west. This prompted the Qing authorities to pull back their remaining forces to defend the capital. The rebels now had an open road to the east.[12] Ma Rulong continued to show his military acumen in a series of surprise attacks on the smaller towns of Anning and Lufeng. His rapid strike eastward, besides challenging imperial control in central Yunnan, disrupted supplies and communications between the provincial commanders and Zhu Kechang. After Kunming, Ma Rulong met no firm resistance until just outside Chuxiong, the largest urban center between Dali and Kunming [see Fig. 7.1].[13]

## THE BATTLE OF CHUXIONG

Chuxiong was a prefectural capital midway along the trunk road between Kunming and Dali. Because it was protected by massive city walls, Ma Rulong and his officers were compelled to adopt new tactics. Ma knew

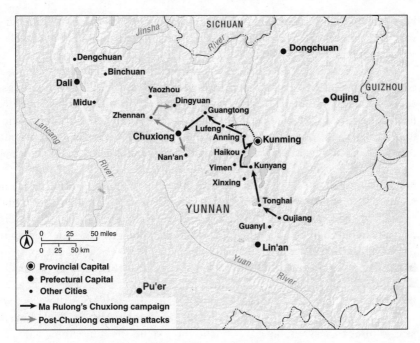

MAP 7.1. Ma Rulong's Chuxiong Campaign, 1859–1860

that a siege could tie up his troops for months; at the same time, he feared
the loss of life a frontal assault would surely bring. So he ordered his
soldiers—many of whom were miners—to build two tunnels under the wall
near the city's southwestern gate. Once the tunnels were completed, they
were packed with explosives. On June 11, 1860, Ma gave the order and
"there was a frightening blast and then, when the huge cloud of smoke and
dust had settled, there was an immense hole in the wall through which the
masses of Muslim [soldiers] flowed into the city."[14] All of the city's Qing
officials were caught and executed—all except one, who "escaped only by
dressing himself as a peasant" and who reported the devastating defeat to
his superiors in Kunming.[15]

Stirred by this victory, Ma Rulong dispatched two of his commanders,
Yang Zhenpeng and Li Fangyuan, to seize the neighboring towns of Nan'an,
Zhennan, and Dingyuan. All three fell with little resistance.[16] Until now, Ma
Rulong had never taken a city of any consequence, although large amounts
of territory had come under his control. The capture of Chuxiong changed
this. The successful two-month campaign catapulted Ma Rulong from
middle-rank rebel leader—one among many—to a commander second only
to Du Wenxiu himself in influence and military might. This campaign had

been launched as a desperate attempt to rescue Du Wenxiu; by the time it
was over, in every region of Yunnan, the momentum had shifted massively
to the Hui-lead rebel forces.

Yet this sudden success exposed a fundamental weakness in the regional
cooperation that had carried the insurgents to this point. Du Wenxiu assumed that Ma Rulong's obliging actions against the Qing in his time of
need amounted to an alliance, and he instructed his top general Cai Fachun
to offer Ma Rulong a position in the Dali government.[17] As Cai approached
the city, Ma Rulong, as if to acknowledge Dali's primacy, ordered his troops
to withdraw. He then handed the city over to the authority of Du Wenxiu.[18]
Yet paradoxically, Ma Rulong refused Du's offer of a position in the Dali
regime. Instead, he and Cai negotiated a division of Yunnan into two
spheres of rebel control, with Chuxiong as the dividing line: "The control
of the province will be divided with Ma Rulong subduing the area from the
provincial capital eastward [*shengyi yixia*] while Du Wenxiu would control
from Chuxiong westward [*Chuxiong yishang*]. After Yunnan is pacified,
then we will meet to carry out a unified expedition out of the province, and
then recover China, and expel the Manchu Qing dynasty."[19]

Why, after half a year of fighting to aid Du Wenxiu, did Ma Rulong re-
ject an offer to serve in his government and extend the multiethnic rule of
the Dali sultanate over Yunnan? There is no clear answer to this. There is
no indication that Ma Rulong wanted to sever relations with Du, and both
men seem to have respected Ma Dexin's role as Yunnan's spiritual leader.
Nor are there any suggestions of an acrimonious relationship between the
two leaders. Possibly, Ma Rulong wanted to consolidate his power in the
province. By the summer of 1860 he controlled a large area of southern Yunnan whereas only the northwestern edge of western Yunnan was under Du's
control. Eastern Yunnan was held by half a dozen other rebel groups. After
his recent victories, Ma Rulong was at the height of his power.[20]

So it is curious that he turned his back on the opportunity to unite the
insurgents—this, at a time when circumstances seemed so favorable to
handing the Qing a final defeat and thereby winning the entire province for
the Muslim Yunnanese.

Several factors perhaps counted heavily in Ma Rulong's decision. First
and foremost, Ma was a man ruled by his ego. Headstrong, aggressive, and
a strong believer in his own abilities, he may have yearned to deliver personally the final blow to Qing rule in Yunnan.[21] Perhaps he also reasoned
that if he captured Yunnan's greatest prize, Kunming, he would be able negotiate with Du Wenxiu from a position of strength. Du had been using the
title of sultan since his investiture as generalissimo but had carefully avoided
adopting a political title. Perhaps Ma was seeking to assume the position of

political head of state—something he might not achieve if he accepted prematurely a post in the Dali regime.

Du Wenxiu was nonplussed by Ma's rebuff. Ma was motivated by personal ambition, Du by the desire to provide a stable base for the Pingnan state. Du's military campaigns to secure the remaining cities in northwestern and southwestern Yunnan were progressing well, and he was reluctant to move eastward before western Yunnan was completely under Pingnan authority. At this juncture he also seems to have wanted to implement economic, social, and religious reforms in those areas already firmly under his control instead of forging ahead for territorial gains.[22] In the end, he did not understand Ma's rejection of his offer but was amenable to him applying continued military pressure on the Qing.

Neither Ma Rulong nor Du Wenxiu saw the decision to divide Yunnan into spheres of control as contravening the implied pact among all the Hui rebels for continuing the fight against the Qing. The agreement between Cai Fachun and Ma Rulong allowed for both sides to continue to fight to establish an Islamic state independent of imperial control. That was the common goal.

To almost everyone in Yunnan at the time, the fall of Kunming seemed inevitable. For many of Kunming's residents, the city's fall was not necessarily to be feared. The French missionaries would note in their accounts that Yunnan's rebel-controlled areas were often more stable than those outside rebel control: "The Hui rebels have already occupied a large number of towns . . . [but] for the moment at least, in this part [of the province] there are practically no more brigands."[23] This stability, his victory at Chuxiong, and his rising popularity in southern and eastern Yunnan allowed Ma Rulong to launch his plan to take Kunming. In the autumn of 1860, he returned to the walls of Kunming at the head of his army.

MA RULONG: AMBIGUOUS AMBITIONS

Dazed by Zhu Kechang's defeat (and death), by the loss of Chuxiong, and by the arrival of Ma Rulong's army outside the capital, the provincial authorities finally, four years after the Kunming Massacre, came face to face with the consequences of their anti-Hui extermination campaign. Governor-General Zhang Liangji was so "distressed and anxious, that he began to cough up blood" and handed over his seals of office to the provincial governor, Xu Zhiming.[24] With the rebel armies tightening their control of the area around Kunming, the provincial officials could see no alternative but to open negotiations with Ma Rulong and Ma Dexin.[25] The first official record of these discussions appears in a memorial dated January 17, 1861. Xu cast these negotiations as initiated by the desire of Ma Dexin, Xu Yuanji, and Ma Rulong to surrender. He vouched for the character and intentions of the Hui leaders, described Ma Dexin as the most respected Muslim leader in the province, and characterized Ma Rulong as "candid, upright and capable."[26] The next communication mentioning the talks, written two months later, was not nearly as flattering. In this memorial, Xu spun a very different story, suggesting that he had been hoodwinked by the rebel leaders' initial request for clemency but had discovered their ruse and decisively suppressed them: "The Hui bandits Ma Xian (known as Ma Rulong), and Xu Yuanji falsely asked for pacification and had secretly planned a surprise attack on the provincial capital. I ordered troops to fight and strengthened the defenses of the endangered city, restoring peace. Xu Yuanji was killed. Ma Xian escaped. . . . [but] was later burned to death."[27]

In such a situation it is difficult to determine exactly who was acting under false pretenses, but at the very least, Xu was playing with the truth when he suggested that Ma Rulong had been killed. Evidence that Xu's conduct in this affair was questionable came a month later, when Governor-General Zhang Liangji wrote to the emperor accusing Xu of "stirring up the wicked [Han] gentry, inciting the militia, then . . . pleading for help, stating that [under these circumstances] he could not pacify the Hui."[28] Zhang went on that Xu had plotted with Lin Ziqing, the ranking military official in Kunming, to lure the Hui into a trap, but they had caught only Xu Yuanji. Zhang, who had been granted a leave of absence due to illness, took this opportunity to disassociate himself from Xu's actions. In a series of memorials written over the next six months, he painted a scathing portrait of Xu Zhiming as a man with a "reckless personality who enjoyed killing Hui . . . had become covetous of wealth, and who was excessively lustful."[29]

Other officials and residents corroborated the governor-general's harsh assessment of Xu's anti-Hui stance. One account suggested that Xu was "predisposed towards killing [the Hui] and sought to block the Hui's opportunity to return to legitimacy [through pacification] by continuing to force them to rebel."[30] Xu himself hardly sought to hide his hatred of the Hui, brashly claiming in a memorial written soon after the failed surrender that "the disposition of the Hui is like that of a dog or a goat, the more one attempts to pacify them peacefully the more arrogant they become."[31]

Zhang also informed the emperor that Xu had orchestrated the assassination of the provincial judge, Deng Erheng. Deng had served in the province since the late 1840s. He rose through the ranks until, in 1860, with a dearth of officials willing to accept a posting in Yunnan, his career began to soar. Within a year he had been promoted to provincial judge, then provincial treasurer, then finally governor of Guizhou. In early 1861, before he could even leave to take up his duties there, he received orders to take up the office of Shaanxi governor.

According to Zhang and other individuals familiar with the situation, Xu Zhiming despised Deng Erheng. The reasons are unclear. One widely circulated explanation is that Deng, while serving as provincial judge, learned about Xu's libidinous excesses when a woman publicly accused him of raping her. Deng at first dismissed the woman's account; later, however, through unimpeachable sources, he learned that her report was entirely accurate. Xu grew increasingly fearful that after he left the province Deng would inform the imperial court of his deceitful behavior. So he secretly gave the order for Lin Ziqing to assassinate Deng while en route to his new post.[32]

After reading Zhang Liangji's accusations, the emperor realized that the situation demanded some form of intervention, although it was becoming increasingly difficult for the central government to effect any changes in the province. Xu's actions revealed just how little control the imperial court had over many of its officials there. Few officials dared accept a posting to the province, correctly sensing that the situation in Yunnan was likely to be dangerous both for one's career and for one's personal safety.

The lengths the court was forced to go to find officials willing to accept a post in Yunnan are exemplified in its efforts to find a replacement for Zhang Liangji. The emperor's first candidate, Liu Yuanjing, preferred to accept censure and demotion rather than accept the post of governor-general of Yunnan and Guizhou. The emperor's second choice, Fuji, postponed his departure for Yunnan indefinitely, offering a series of lame pretexts, until he was finally called to Beijing to answer for his insubordination.[33] Faced with no viable alternative, in December 1862 the emperor finally appointed Pan Duo, a seventy-year-old with an unexceptional record, as Yun-Gui governor-general.

If the situation in Yunnan seemed hopeless from faraway Beijing, it looked even worse to those actually living in Kunming. The harvest had been poor. The winter was especially harsh that year, and with the capital crowded with refugees from all over the province, the situation had became desperate. By December, hundreds were dying every day of starvation.[34] Just when it seemed that the situation could not possibly get any worse, the multiethnic armies led by Ma Rulong reappeared at the walls of Kunming, beginning the third siege the capital had endured since the rebellion had begun.[35]

## MA RULONG'S CHANGE OF HEART?

The impetus for this third siege lay with the actions of Lin Ziqing. Disappointed at the limited success of the ambush that had killed Xu Yuanji, he led a mixed force of Han militias and imperial troops on an offensive against Ma Dexin's home base at Chengjiang.[36] Incensed over Lin Ziqing's anti-Hui aggression, Ma Rulong raced north to cut off Lin's lines of supply

from Kunming. Ma then dealt a devastating blow to Lin's forces as they attempted to retreat back to the provincial capital. Enboldened by the ease
with which they carried out these maneuvers, Ma Rulong and Ma Dexin returned to the roles they had played in the Chuxiong campaign, and organized a rebel force—one that included the top Hui leaders of eastern and
southern Yunnan—for an all-out attack on the provincial capital.[37]

With the city's inhabitants starving and a horde of rebels camped outside
the city gates, Xu Zhiming had little choice but to negotiate with the rebels.
Unluckily for him, Ma Rulong having been deceived once was not so willing to enter into talks. Xu dispatched a series of envoys imploring the Hui
leaders to spare the city. Ma Rulong, fed up with the governor's tendency
to want peace only when convenient, angrily retorted: "Before when Ma
Chunlin came to negotiate a peace . . . Lin Ziqing ambushed Xu Yuanji, Ma
Shuangen, and Ma Minggong; and then attacked Chengjiang. I will not trust
these dog-officials again."[38] To demonstrate his loathing for Lin Ziqing, Ma
sent a courier into the city to post a public offer of "10,000 taels of silver
for anyone who could produce Lin Ziqing's head."[39] Yet this time, Ma made
no preparations to storm the city; clearly, he did want to negotiate a surrender with both Xu Zhiming and Lin Ziqing. But given the unmistakable
nature of the situation, who was actually doing the surrendering?

Wary of another of Xu's traps, the rebel leaders extended negotiations
over several weeks. Always, the imperial envoys were obliged to travel to
the rebel camp outside the city. At one point in the negotiations, Lin Ziqing
was "compelled to climb over the city wall using a rope in order to offer his
petition for peace."[40] All of this indicates that it was the Qing officials who
were desperate for a settlement.

When the siege ended on March 1, 1862, the arrival of Ma and his rebel
forces in the capital was more like an occupation than a capitulation: "[Ma]
Rulong led his party into the city, issuing a thousand demands to Xu Zhiming with none refused. Ma Rulong was given the office of Lin'an regional
commander, the Muslim religious leader Ma Dexin conferred with the title
of *beg* of the second rank, the rebel leaders in [Ma Rulong's army] . . .
received a variety of ranks."[41]

It was, however, the actions taken by Ma Rulong, Ma Dexin, and the
other rebel leaders on entering the city that left no doubt about who controlled the capital: "After outwardly submitting to the Chinese authorities
[the Hui] dominated the capital of the province, acting as if they were the
masters . . . when a Muslim passed on the street, no one dared quarrel over
the higher path."[42] The Hui also physically occupied many of the Han
households and yamens. There are indications that they also imposed many
of their ethnoreligious convictions on the Chinese populace. For example,
"street markets did not even dare to sell pork."[43]

There are other indications that Ma Dexin and Ma Rulong made only the pretense of capitulating in 1862. Even after taking up residence in the capital, Ma Rulong continued to issue proclamations bearing his seal of "Generalissimo of the Three Directions," hinting that he never fully intended to relinquish his authority as a rebel leader.[44] Moreover, those Hui who had remained within the city and not gone to fight were openly taunted by the Hui rebels as "fake Hui [jia Huizi]."[45] Ma Dexin accepted his promotion in rank as religious leader but refused to accept the civil title offered him, declaring that he did not want to be associated with the political dimension of the Qing regime.[46] These actions and the fact that Xu Zhiming granted the official titles to the rebels without consulting the emperor underscore the questionable validity of the "surrender."

When the imperial court finally received word of the conditions of surrender, it was highly skeptical of both Xu's motives and those of the rebels.[47] In particular, the high ranks of office granted to Ma Rulong and his cohorts troubled the court. Fearing that any lesser offer might jeopardize an already precarious position, the court acquiesced, but not without warning Xu Zhiming that his actions were being scrutinized.[48] In an edict addressed jointly to the newly appointed governor-general, Pan Duo, and the governor, Zhang Liangji (who had been ordered to return to Yunnan), the emperor stated that "for the time being [I] will permit these Hui to revert from their insurgency and be ruled under the loose-rein policy."[49] He also ordered Pan and Zhang to send him reports on the situation by secret means. Hoping to deprive the provincial clique of their military support, the emperor also suggested that Lin Ziqing be ordered on a mission that would take him out of Kunming into Sichuan.[50] Finally, the emperor sent an edict to Xu warning him that his transgressions were known to the court and that although the emperor was showing his mercy, further violations would not be tolerated and the "court could not be so forgiving and lenient."[51]

With the emperor against them and the rebels now masters of the city, the outlook for the core group of Han who had worked so hard to exterminate the Hui since 1856 was bleak. Émile Rocher captured their new mood: "What a humiliating finish for the mandarins who had, by their bad faith, even more than their remarkable oversight, ignited the insurrection and who were delighted [with their actions] right up until the last moment when they were overpowered."[52]

Huang Cong, the retired war ministry official who played such an instrumental role in coordinating the Kunming Massacre, committed suicide rather than submit to the domineering presence of the Hui.

Despite the court's own suspicions at the time and the distinctly ambiguous circumstances in which Ma Rulong and the other leaders surrendered, most postrebellion accounts of the surrender have taken Ma's actions at face value and declared him either a hero to the Qing for attempting to end the rebellion or, conversely, as a traitor to the Hui.[53] Yet as Taiwanese scholar Li Shoukong has pointed out, although Ma Rulong professed that his actions were in response to the treachery of local officials, he was not above using any pretext he could to enter the city.[54] Li asserts that Ma's decision in 1862 to accept Xu Zhiming's offer of capitulation was likely reached hastily and without any clear objective other than to gain access to the capital.[55] Supporting this thesis is the fact that accepting government terms for surrender as a means to enter a walled city was a ruse quite often employed by Hui rebels in the early years of the rebellion. It would surely have been a familiar tactic to Ma Rulong, given that such ruses had been employed on numerous occasions by southern and eastern Hui leaders.[56]

Having occupied the provincial capital Ma Rulong still was faced with the decision of which side to play against the other: Should he remain a rebel leader and join Du Wenxiu, or should he leverage his rebel status to bring piece and imperial control back to the Qing court? Perhaps Ma Rulong believed he had more time to establish himself as an important third power. If that was so, then he quite quickly would have realized his error, since a major factor in the court's acceptance of Ma Rulong's pacification, even though they questioned its authenticity, was the almost complete lack of Qing authority in the province. As noted earlier, the first two appointees to the office of governor-general had refused to enter the province. Without a high official to report on Xu Zhiming and curb his behavior, the court was powerless.

Then on November 2, 1862, roughly six months after Ma Rulong entered Kunming, the court's third appointment to the office of Yun-Gui governor-general, Pan Duo, finally entered the provincial capital.[57]

## Things Fall Apart: The Occupation of Kunming, 1863

The emperor eagerly awaited news from the first provincial-level official willing to enter the province in nearly three years. Contrary to what the court expected to hear, Pan Duo reported that the Muslim Yunnanese leaders and "the populace was all content [xise]."[58] Pan claimed that the Han gentry, in discussions with him, all praised Xu Zhiming's efforts to achieve peace with the rebel leaders. In light of this, he asked the court to delay any action with regard to Xu Zhiming, Ma Rulong, or any other of the newly appointed former rebels.[59]

Nor did the passage of time cause Pan Duo to change his opinion. Two months later, he was still reporting the positive results stemming from Ma Rulong's surrender: "Since the settlement of March of 1862, over ten months have already passed. Han and Hui in areas in and around the provincial capital and in eastern Yunnan, have returned to a routine and peaceful life. . . . I have been here for two months observing Ma Rulong. Since his acceptance of the terms of pacification, he has unreservedly had a complete change of heart [*sichu chengxin*]."[60]

In late 1862, Ma Rulong was given his first test of loyalty. He and a rising young Han military official named Cen Yuying were dispatched to Lin'an against Liang Shimei, a renegade magistrate of Lin'an in southern Yunnan. Enraged over the government's decision to accept Ma Rulong's surrender, he had severed all relations between the prefecture and the provincial government and was refusing to remit taxes and other remuneration to the capital—a serious offense in peacetime, but even more so given the Qing court's tenuous hold in the region. Yet the operation's target, the selection of Ma Rulong, and the timing of the campaign were based on more than political imperatives.

Ma Rulong was a native of Lin'an, so his intimate knowledge of the region made him a natural choice to lead the expedition. But it is equally likely that many officials in Kunming hoped the Hui would loosen their grip on the capital in his absence. Ma Rulong for his part did not accept the assignment out of altruistic motives for the Qing. Liang Shimei and Ma Rulong had been feuding since the outbreak of the rebellion, with Liang getting the better of Ma in each encounter. All of this was common knowledge, so rumors were flying regarding the actual motives of everyone involved. Some even conjectured that Pan Duo hoped Liang would defeat and perhaps even eliminate Ma Rulong.[61] Whatever his motives, in the winter of 1862 Ma Rulong set out southward toward Lin'an. The events his departure set in motion would have profound consequences; if indeed the Qing officials secretly hoped to rid themselves of Ma Rulong, they misjudged the part he played in controlling those rebels who had entered the capital with him.

Few sources are available to explain the actions of the rebels who ostensibly capitulated with Ma Rulong; even fewer are available to explain the actions of those Hui rebels who controlled many cities east of Kunming and into Guizhou. It was from both these quarters that the most serious threat to Qing control in the province arose since the beginning of the rebellion. In early March 1863, several weeks after Ma Rulong's departure, the Hui generals Ma Rong and Ma Liansheng stormed in from eastern Yunnan and seized control of Kunming.[62]

The leader of the insurrection, Ma Rong, had received the rank of assistant regional commander of Wuding after Ma Rulong's surrender in 1862.[63] Ma Rong's attack on Kunming suggests that he and many other rebels had no intention of passing their full support to the Qing. Indeed, Ma Rong's assassination of Pan Duo on March 4, 1863, left no doubt that many of Ma

Rulong's followers no longer trusted him to act in their broader interest to unify Yunnan under a rebel government.

The assassination of Pan Duo and the occupation of Kunming were glaring indications that the rebel leaders were attempting to transcend past regional divisions and unite under the Pingnan State's white banner. Hui accounts from this period drop the terminology of western, southern, and eastern Hui—a terminology encountered throughout the records of other periods of the rebellion. Instead they refer to themselves as Muslims (*jiaomen*) who for that brief moment see an opportunity to unite in opposition to the Qing.[64] Most striking is the single-minded goal of joining forces with Du Wenxiu. Clearly, they were beginning to understand that "the success or failure of the Muslims [in Yunnan] all rode on this one opportunity."[65]

On March 9, 1863, Ma Dexin accepted the office of governor-general and adopted the title "King-Who-Pacifies-the-South [*Pingnan Wang*]."[66] He occupied the governor-general's yamen, took possession of the official seals, and stopped using the Qing reign year when dating documents.[67] It seems that in accepting the position of governor-general he was not motivated solely by self-aggrandizement.[68] In imperial accounts, Ma Dexin's actions are described as motivated by "city elders (*qimin*) who . . . urged him to take over the office of Yun-Gui Governor-General."[69] However, his other actions do not reflect this. Given that the rebel leaders involved in the coup felt a strong allegiance toward Du, it is more probable that Ma Dexin hoped to hold the precarious alliance of rebel leaders together until control could be handed over to Du Wenxiu.[70]

From the first years of the rebellion, Ma Rong and Ma Liansheng had had strong ties with Du Wenxiu and the Dali regime. According to imperial accounts, the month before control of the capital was wrested away from Pan Duo, Du Wenxiu had conferred the titles of "General-Who-Pacifies-the-East [*pingdong dajiangjun*]" and "General-Who-Safeguards-the-North [*dingbei dajiangjun*]" respectively on Ma Rong and Ma Liansheng.[71] Their allegiance was hardly exceptional: many other local rebel leaders cooperated with Ma Rong and Ma Liansheng's plot by carrying out insurrections in districts that still lay outside rebel control. Xu Zhiming, in one of his last memorials to the throne, described the broad wave of support that rose with the news of Ma Rong's attack:

Rebel leader Du Wenxiu notified the various [rebel] groups to unite and attack in four columns, taking the opportunity to converge on the center of the province that was in disorder [due to Ma Rong's attack]. During this insurrection, the [rebels] rose up in revolt attacking simultaneously Fumin, Luoci, Wuding, Lufeng, Songming, Xundian, Luquan, and many other counties and districts. The bandits and rebels everywhere all responded [to Du's call] and throughout this period captured the cities. The acting Songming Department Magistrate, Zhang Hualong and the Lu-liang Department Magistrate, Song Gui were both killed. Also, the spreading disturbances affected the county and district seats of Lufeng, Guangtong, and Nan'an, as well as the three salt mines of Hei, Yuan and Yong.[72]

But before Du Wenxiu's Dali forces could reach Kunming, there was a surprising turn of events. Ma Rulong, having heard about Ma Rong's actions, returned from Lin'an, recaptured Kunming, and handed control of the city back to Qing officials and sympathizers.

### TRUE COLORS?

Ma Rong's conquest of Kunming rapidly and irrevocably changed the political landscape for the various rebel factions. Ma Rulong did not believe that Ma Dexin's motives for declaring himself king were entirely altruistic; he interpreted his actions as a plot to hand the province over to Du Wexin and recognize him as the new ruler of Yunnan.

The events leading up to Ma Rulong's return are murky. One account has it that Cen Yuying dispatched a "letter in a wax ball" to him, urging him to set aside his personal ambitions as a former rebel leader and return Kunming to imperial control.[73] Ma rushed back to Kunming with a small force and was met outside the city walls by several of his former officers, who rebuked him for abandoning his earlier goals and aiding the Qing: "If you only crave to be an official with no thought for your fellow Muslims, you should return to [your home in] Guanyi."[74]

Ma's sudden fall from grace among the eastern and southern Muslim Yunnanese was a consequence of two increasingly apparent realities. First, Du Wenxiu had assumed control of most of western Yunnan and over the past six years had established a viable alternative regime to that of the Qing. Second, many of the Hui who had surrendered with Ma Rulong had believed that their surrender was simply the most expedient means to take control of the province. If Ma Rulong was ambivalent about his role as a rebel—and perhaps he was—many of those who had surrendered with him clearly were not.[75] The rebels saw Ma Rulong as a defector because he had betrayed the anti-Qing cause, and this betrayal generated widespread resentment of his leadership.

Although their coup d'etat had been quick and efficient, the rebel forces within Kunming were not very large. Ma Rulong and Cen Yuying quickly realized this and merged the forces from their campaign on Lin'an with other local militias. On March 19, Ma and Cen launched a ferocious attack on two of the capital's massive city gates and stormed the city.[76] The ensuing battle lasted several days, with hand-to-hand combat in many districts.

After five or six days of street fighting, those loyal to the imperial cause gained the upper hand and restored order.[77] Ma Rong and Ma Liansheng fled east to their base in Xundian, where they continued their resistance.[78]

Immediately on entering the city, Ma Rulong proceeded to the governor-general's yamen, where he accosted Ma Dexin and ordered him to abandon his seals of office. Ma Rulong then placed him under what amounted to informal house arrest for the remainder of the rebellion.[79] He then began identifying those rebels who had assisted Ma Rong's coup. On discovering that many of his closest associates had "secretly received documents and seals [of office] from Du Wenxiu, Ma Rulong quickly investigated and had them summarily executed."[80]

## Rationalizing the Unknowable:
## Religious and Regional Divisions

Why did Ma Rulong, who had been a rebel leader just months earlier, turn against his fellow Hui and race back from Lin'an to help the Qing retake Kunming? Ma, who would later try to characterize himself as having wholeheartedly submitted to the Qing in 1862, destroyed his own rebel seals only after returning to Kunming in 1863.[81] Any attempt to uncover Ma Rulong's true sentiments inevitably encounters a multitude of contradictions, paradoxes, and ambiguities. But his actions do seem to have been influenced by several constants.

First, Ma Rulong's actions were driven mainly by a desire to remain autonomous from Du Wenxiu, whose influence was growing. It was because of this desire to stymie Du, rather than any strong loyalty to the Qing, that he never completely embraced his position as a Qing functionary during the critical fourteen months between his surrender and his counter-coup. This ambivalence came to an abrupt end when, in his absence, Ma Rong, Ma Dexin, and others acted to hand Kunming over to Du Wenxiu. He now had to choose: Would he acknowledge his rival's authority or that of the distant emperor? He cast his lot with the Qing.[82]

Ma Rulong's intense regional pride was an equally strong factor in his reluctance to join Du Wenxiu, the rebellion's principal leader. Regionalism was pervasive in Yunnan society and profoundly shaped the actions of both men. Ma's rebel title, "Generalissimo of the Three Regions," underscored his adherence to the view that Yunnan was a sum of its parts. Was it also an overt challenge to Du's more conventional project of a united and monolithic Yunnan? Regional faultlines ran across many of Yunnan's otherwise durable identities, and it is clear that Ma's regional sensibilities were especially sensitive. In particular, it seems that he felt that the south's role in the rebellion was insufficiently appreciated. In a letter to Du, written several months after he returned to Kunming in June 1863, Ma claimed that the Dali regime owed its very existence to the support of southern Yunnan: "On Zhu Kechang's campaign [westward], the [troops] at Yunzhou immediately responded. Tian Zhongxing flanked him, and those who were guarding Chuxiong fled. If it had not been for the Southern Yunnanese [Hui] forces attacking his rear, then there was nothing the western region [Hui] could have done, and there is no way you could not have known this."[83] It was Ma Rulong's regional pride—not a sense of loyalty to the Qing—that motivated him to rally to the aid of the imperial court.

Ma Rulong's reasons for capitulating in 1862, and for supporting the Qing cause in 1863, when examined carefully, do not reflect a predetermined plan thoughtfully pursued over time. Instead, both moves were reactions to events as they unfolded. After Ma delivered Kunming back to the Qing in 1863, his real motives would continue to be unclear to all but himself. One of his staunchest defenders, Governor-General Lao Chongguang, would later remark that although he felt Ma's loyalty to the Qing was beyond reproach, he "dare not think about what thoughts were hidden in the recesses of Ma's heart."[84]

### NEW TENSIONS OVER THE "OLD TEACHINGS"?

Despite the overwhelming evidence regarding Ma Rulong's personal motives, many analyses of the rebellion continue to hypothesize that sectarian differences among the Muslim Yunnanese heightened tensions between Ma Rulong and Du Wenxiu and their followers.[85] The question, generally speaking, is whether the Sufi-inspired teachings—referred pejoratively to as "new teachings" or *xinjiao*—had spread among those Muslim Yunnanese communities which practiced the Sunni Hanafite (referred to as "old teachings" or *laojiao*). And if they had, how widely?

This controversy over sectarian differences among the Yunnan Hui is part of a much broader debate on the effects of Sufism in Muslim Chinese communities in other parts of China during the Qing era. From the time Islam entered China in the seventh century until the late seventeenth century, almost every Muslim Chinese practiced the traditional Sunni, Hanafi Islam. By the nineteenth century these traditional Sunni groups were being referred to as *Gedimu* (transliterated from the Arabic term for old, *qadim*—or more colloquially as the "old teachings").[86] Most Gedimu communities centered on the village or neighborhood mosque. Besides being spiritual centers for the Muslim Chinese, these mosques served as the primary gathering points for contact with other Hui communities.[87]

During the seventeenth and eighteenth centuries, Muslim communities in many parts of China but especially in northwestern China formed two distinct Islamic communities: the Gedimu and the Naqshbandi. Two orders within the Naqshbandi flourished in China during the eighteenth and nineteenth centuries. The first, the Khufiyya order, was "permeated with an emphasis on a more active participation in society, the veneration of saints, the seeking of inspiration at tombs and the silent *dhikr* ('remembrance,' properly 'Khufiyya,' the 'silent' ones)."[88] The second, the Jahriyya order, advocated the "vocalization of the *dhikr*, wearing shoes at funerals, the length and cut of beards or mustaches," and disapproved of the veneration of Sufi saints.[89] By the late eighteenth century, tensions were beginning to increase between Jahriyya and Khufiyya in northwestern China.[90] For the purposes of this study, a key point is that as the violence escalated in the northwest, the Qing authorities began to blame the Jahriyya order for the growing social instability. The state proscribed the New Teachings and established heavy sentences for any Muslim involved in religious disputes.[91]

In contrast to the Gedimu communities, the Sufi orders of the Naqshbandi tradition were organized principally around Sufi "saints" and their *menhuan*, or saintly descent groups.[92] The finer points of Sufism are beyond the scope of this study; it should simply be noted that the introduction of this revivalist branch altered the traditional Islamic order in many parts of China. In Sufism, "the leaders of mosque throughout their [Sufi] order owed their allegiance to their *shaykh*, the founder of the order who appointed them."[93] The lineage-based menhuan could spread to noncontiguous areas much more quickly than the community-oriented networks of traditional Gedimu groups. This dimension of the Sufi orders meant that adherents could travel to other areas of China, even among other Gedimu communities, to compete for new converts.

Although these Sufi orders were flourishing in northwestern China by the beginning of the Panthay Rebellion, there is very little evidence that they had widespread appeal in Yunnan. It is true that there were Sufis in Yunnan and that Muslim Yunnanese Hui were exposed to Sufi beliefs; but it is difficult to ascertain with any precision the nature of the Muslim Yunnanese communities' pre-Rebellion contact with the new teachings. Several Chinese scholars have argued that the Jahriyya order arrived in Yunnan in the late eighteenth century with Ma Shunqing, son of Ma Xingyun, the order's founder. Ma Shunqing came there because of government persecution in the northwest.[94] Yet the evidence shows that after he arrived there was only minimal conversion to the Jahriyya order among the traditional Hui communities.

There is no question that there were religious tensions within Yunnan over the proper interpretation of Islamic beliefs; however, the religious frictions seem to have been largely within the mainstream dialogue, not between the larger orders. In the early Qing, Ma Zhu, a revered Muslim Yunnanese imam, devoted an entire chapter of his influential *Islamic Compass* to admonishing Yunnan Hui about the dangers of committing Islamic here-sies. In it he offered a cautionary tale about one heretical episode that had occurred in southwestern Yunnan in the seventeenth century.[95] Another in-stance of religious division is recorded immediately before the rebellion transpired in 1852 near Dali, when "Hui bandits named Ma Alue, and his daughter, called A-feng, were practicing heretical Islamic teachings. [She] was venerated and referred to by the term immortal [*xiangu*]."[96]

This narrative, which was included in the provincial gazetter, implies that the bandits incited religious divisions between "city Hui" (from Dali) and "heretical Hui." Yet nowhere in the narrative is any mention made of the proscribed New (Jahriyya) Teachings. This is a conspicuous omission, given that the overwhelming majority of officials posted to Yunnan in the late 1840s and the early years of the Panthay Rebellion had had extensive ex-perience with the bloody violence between practitioners of the New and Old Teachings in northwestern China. Considering the renewed violence in the northwest in the 1860s, few officials would have missed an opportunity to label any Yunnan Hui "bandits" as heretical; after all, this would have pro-vided a justification to suppress them. Yet nowhere in any government re-port or local gazetteer is there any hint that proscribed Sufi beliefs were being practiced in the region.[97]

Against this fragmentary proof that Jahriyya was taking root in Yunnan, there is considerable evidence that the vast majority of Muslim Yunnanese adhered to traditional Islamic beliefs. Du Wenxiu and Ma Rulong and many of the Hui rebel leaders had been students of Ma Dexin, a practitioner of traditional Gedimu teachings. Ma Dexin embraced a relatively conservative interpretation of Islam, one that emphasized a synthesis between Chinese culture and Islamic beliefs.[98] A primary obstacle to the theory that religious differences divided the Hui rebels is that Ma Dexin continued to instruct and communicate with both Du Wenxiu and Ma Rulong throughout the re-bellion.[99] Furthermore, Ma Rong, Ma Liansheng, and the other prominent leaders of eastern and southern Yunnan did not show any reluctance to es-tablish relations with Du Wenxiu before and during the occupation of Kun-ming in 1863. And among those Dali Hui who fled Yunnan after the rebel-lion ended in 1873, one might expect to find evidence of Jahriyya teachings. There is no such evidence.[100]

Du Wenxiu's religious beliefs are perhaps the most opaque. It is clear he was a devout Muslim who sought to promote Islam, but there is little in the records to suggest a religious inclination that deviated from that of most Muslim Yunnanese. Lin Changkuan, one of the strongest supporters of the view that Jahariyya teachings influenced the Pingnan government, contends that "the Dali regime was heavily colored by the New Teachings (Du Wen-xiu had many Jahriyya *ahongs*)."[101] Yet even though he is certain that the top Pingnan Hui shared those teachings, he also admits—tellingly—that "the evidence that Ma and Du split over the religious factional conflicts is not very convincing."[102]

There is, however, one tantalizing piece of evidence supporting religious differences, and it comes from the Frenchman Émile Rocher, who witnessed the end of the rebellion. In describing one clash he suggests that the siege of one rebel stronghold was prolonged due to "the fact that Ma Chenglin, although a Muslim, belonged to the New Teachings which had been established [in Yunnan] for some years; Ma Chenglin was considered as the head of this sect and Ma [Rulong] belonged to the Old Teachings. This created a certain enmity between them."[103] Rocher goes on to state that when Ma Chenglin was killed, his lieutenant Yang Jingping capitulated to Ma Rulong because he was "informed by different sentiments [than Ma Chenglin]." This suggests that although Yang and Ma Chenglin did not both embrace the New Teachings, they put aside their differences to fight the Qing together.[104]

To put it in somewhat different terms, there is clear evidence that an increasing variety of Islamic religious teachings did exist in Yunnan by the mid-nineteenth century. These disparate beliefs were held by the followers of Du Wenxiu as well as by those Hui who supported Ma Rulong. From events both prior to and during the rebellion, it is also clear that Hui from northwestern China were present in Yunnan. One source even suggests that Du Wenxiu was aided by "outsider Hui [waihui]."[105] However, the political and regional divisions between the Dali Hui and the other Hui leaders never seem to have been a function of religious differences. What seems far more likely is that the tolerance for ethnic, cultural, and linguistic differences that permeated the rebellion's leadership extended to religious differences as well.

## New Stratagems and Old Biases

With Ma Rulong's surrender in 1862 and his subsequent reoccupation of Kunming in 1863, the face of the rebellion was dramatically altered. The Qing court was beginning to realize that the situation in Yunnan was not a simple ethnic conflict between Han and Hui.[106] One of the earliest critiques of Qing policy came from Zhang Liangji, who wrote a series of memorials in 1862 offering one of the first accurate and pointed criticisms of the Qing court's policy toward Yunnan. Zhang expressly warned that among Han and Hui throughout Yunnan, "bad elements seem to be winning over the good, instead of the other way around."[107] In a remark notable for its sweeping indictment of the Han, Zhang stated "the Han definitely sought to force [the Hui] to rebel, it was [only] then that the Hui began to start to harbor thoughts of rebellion."[108] Zhang provided specific details and suggestions; however, it seems that his forceful indictment of the Han is what caused the court to reconsider using the pacified Hui to help end the rebellion.

In the wake of Pan Duo's assassination, in an effort to take advantage of Ma Rulong and Ma Dexin's professed desire to aid the Qing, the emperor instructed that a new policy of "using Hui to control Hui [yi Hui zhi Hui]" be implemented.[109] This new policy, which resembled a centuries-old strategy of "using barbarians to control barbarians [yi yi zhi yi]," sought to end the rebellion in a way that would not involve large infusions of money from the court, nor any expenditures of Qing personnel or military resources (which were sorely needed for the Taiping Rebellion). The shift in policy was rather half-hearted and even duplicitous, in that the emperor and many powerful officials doubted Ma Rulong's fealty to Beijing. The court's choice of this policy reveals an emerging pragmatism among central court officials to pursue policies that would require the barest allotment of court resources—even if it meant disregarding their own instincts.[110] The catalyst for this policy was the appointment of Governor-General Lao Chongguang, who had previously served as governor of Guizhou and who was thus perceived as conversant with the political, ethnic, and military terrain of southwestern China. Lao, a strong proponent of enlisting Ma Rulong to spearhead the Qing attack against Du Wenxiu, was appointed governor-general in June 1863.

Unlike many of the anti-Hui officials who preceded him, Lao sought to bring about more parity between the Han and the Hui with regard to how the state treated them.[111] Lao's stance was premised on the conviction—rare in Qing circles—that the Han were as much to blame for the rebellion as the Hui. Following this reasoning, he concluded that the court had two choices: the Qing could mount a massive military campaign with non-Yunnanese forces, a stratagem Lao knew the empire could hardly afford; or it could utilize Muslim Yunnanese leaders to help pacify the remaining rebels.[112] The court accepted Lao's strategy of procuring Hui support, even though this approach was still at odds with the position of many in the inner court, including the emperor. In accepting Lao's stance, the court also cashiered Xu Zhiming. The emperor remarked that "everything Xu Zhiming said and did all came from whatever the Hui told him to do"—a rather amazing declaration, given the many actions Xu carried out against the Hui.[113]

With Lao's appointment, Qing policy within Yunnan did turn more pragmatic. Many of Zhang Liangji's earlier proposals were significantly altered by Lao's approach. In one of his more colorful memorials, Lao lambasted a plan suggested by an official who had never ever been to Yunnan that had

proposed "six difficult and six easy steps [*liunan liuyi*]" to resolve the rebellion.[114] With typical aplomb, Lao dismissed the six difficulties as "self-
evident and the six easy steps, while appearing simple on the surface, in
practice difficult to implement."[115] In particular, he argued against the central premise of the report—namely, that the Hui were the greatest barrier to
peace. Lao contended that the greatest barrier was not the Hui but the ob-
sessively anti-Hui local Han gentry:

> Even if we began with ten thousand soldiers and divided them into three columns
> of three or four thousand each, how would this be enough since [we] could not avoid
> using the local militia? Unless we had a large military force to keep the local militia
> in control it would be a case of "the tail wagging the dog" (*weida budiao*). People
> such as Lin'an's Liang Shimei and Dongchuan's Yang Shencong all view themselves
> as the strongest, but are largely recalcitrant and overbearing, and if used incorrectly,
> likely would follow in the tracks of He Youbao and Lin Ziqing.[116]

Lao's dual policy—trust the Hui leaders, and be vigilant against anti-Hui
actions by the Han—ushered in a new period of tense peace in Yunnan, although the court would remain skeptical throughout.

Lao's sponsorship of Ma Rulong was one of several factors that helped
to make Ma's leadership more palatable to the Qing court in the months
after his capture of Kunming and Pan Duo's assassination. The first of these
was a report by Zhao Guang, president of the Board of Public Works and a
native of Yunnan. In it he informed the emperor that the local gentry felt
Ma Rulong and Cen Yuying had "fought as one . . . to defend the provincial capital."[117]

The second factor was grounded in Ma Rulong's realization that his only
real defense in the controversy over his motives was to act decisively against
the Hui rebels. To prove his loyalty, he set out on a campaign of many
months to capture Ma Rong, who had established a base in Xundian and
Qujing after fleeing Kunming.[118] In the autumn of 1864, Ma Rong was captured and brought to Kunming to be tried and executed. Émile Rocher, in a
graphic rendering of the event, recounted that Ma Rong was "brought
under guard to the capital. There he was displayed in an iron cage for a
month, when after the people were convinced of his identity, he was condemned to death by first having his legs severed and then being decapitated
with ten strokes of the saber."[119] Cen reportedly offered Ma Rong's severed
head to the Pan Duo's memorial tablet in the local Confucian temple.

Ma Rong's capture highlighted the effectiveness of using Ma Rulong to
pacify the Hui. By executing only the ringleaders, they could disarm a large
majority of common soldiers; this would greatly facilitate their pacification
efforts. At the same time, by allowing Ma Rulong to maintain a force largely
composed of Hui, they could avoid being accused of perpetuating the anti-
Hui policies of the earlier provincial officials.[120]

Notwithstanding Ma Rulong's successful pacification strategies, the court and other officials continued to express doubts about him. These stemmed not only from his being a former rebel and a Hui but also from reports detailing the chaotic administrative situation in Yunnan. Qing officials in Beijing and neighboring provinces were wondering more and more if Ma Rulong had saved them from losing the province to Du Wenxiu, only to establish his own seat of power there. At one point the Sichuan governor-general reported that Ma Rulong was in control of the provincial capital and that Cen Yuying had "secretly established his own clique," making any court-sponsored action difficult.[121] Indeed, no matter which way the court looked at it, by 1865 they were far more dependent on Cen Yuying and Ma Rulong than the other way around.

To understand the roots of the insurrection, it is crucial to look closely at its first phase, for it reveals the deep roots of religion, ethnicity, and regionalism in all regions of Yunnan. Past studies have assumed that Islam was the common denominator among the rebels and the basis of their ideology. Yet the rebellion never did solidify along religous lines, and many scholars have taken this as evidence of religious factionalism. Yet, although there seem to have been some sectarian differences among the Hui, religion was never the main cause of dissent among the various Hui leaders. Sectarian-based explanations ignore the fact that Du Wenxiu and Ma Rulong, although both Muslim leaders, at the same time were both quite clear that the Hui were, as a people, a minority among the Han and Yi.

Efforts to use religious differences to explain the breach between Ma Rulong and Du Wenxiu have often overlooked the roles played by the many non-Han allies. Ma Rulong may have been reluctant to join Du because he realized that his indigenous support rooted him to the south. He could not take Yi support for granted; their strength in numbers was an important source of his power. Had these groups turned against him, the result would have been devastating. Perhaps Ma even sensed that his non-Han allies were dissatisfied, for in November 1860 a French missionary noted that the Yi were not blindly following the Hui, as some of the Chinese documents suggest: "The *Lolo* . . . have also risen en masse against the Chinese who have vexed them for centuries. We were told that in these last few days the *Lolos* are now battling against the Muslims and maintain they too want to seize all of Yunnan!"[122]

Only in the early 1860s, nearly a decade after the rebellion began, did provincial officials begin to realize that the non-Han were a key element in the success the Hui were enjoying. The loss of Chuxiong and the obvious role the yi had played in that and in other Hui victories prompted the provincial authorities to begin rethinking the rebellion in terms of the Yunnan context: "Over the past several years throughout [the province] there have been disturbances that involved Hui linking up with *yi*. Within the province of Yunnan, the *yi* are the majority. . . . It is Hui who dare to cause these disturbances, completely reliant on their relations with the *yi* to become a force. [We] must first pacify the *yi*, and then the Hui will be isolated."[123] The problem with this strategy was that the government tended to err in thinking of the non-Han as a single monolithic entity.

We can fully understand the divided loyalties among the Hui only when we stop perceiving the "Muslim Chinese" as a static or monolithic body. That the Muslims did not respond to Han aggression in a uniform manner is consistent with the dynamic and multivocal nature of ethnic groups in general. Their actions must be understood in a local and regional context. Any effort to explain the Panthay Rebellion must address the issue of regionalism within the demographic context. The Muslim religious and ethnic identity was often the more visible of the three elements under discussion here (especially to the court); but it is the local and regional loyalties of the Hui that will allow a balanced understanding of the rebellion.

Ma Rulong, Ma Dexin, and the other rebel leaders of southern and eastern Yunnan figured prominently in the early years of the rebellion, but clearly, the Qing were most afraid of Du Wenxiu in western Yunnan. By 1863 his sphere of control extended from the highlands of Southeast Asia to the Tibetan borderlands. As the fall of Kunming in 1863 and the assassination of Pan Duo had demonstrated, Du's influence extended far beyond those areas of western Yunnan that were directly under his control. Although the rebellion was in its seventh year, the Dali sultanate was still shrouded in mystery for most Chinese. And as the court turned its attention westward, what they found startled even the battle-hardened central government.

## CHAPTER 8

# Rebellious Visions: Du Wenxiu and the Creation of the Dali Sultanate

## Defending the Yunnan World

For the Beijing court, Ma Rulong had been the face of the rebellion in the years following the Kunming Massacre. But for those experiencing the rebellion firsthand, the key political, ideological, and military leader of the rebels was Du Wenxiu. After he captured Dali and was selected as Generalissimo, Sultan, and Leader of all Muslims, Du guided the rise of the independent Dali sultanate in western Yunnan. Throughout his eighteen-year tenure, he worked to establish a style of government that reflected Yunnan's ethnic and religious diversity.

Du never saw the insurrection as simply a Han–Hui conflict. From the start, his regime promoted a political vision that reflected each of the region's three ethnic spheres (Han, Hui, Yi); it never sought retribution against Han who had attacked Yi. Thus the Dali state reflected a broad ethnic alliance, one based on anti-Qing rhetoric and on a desire to halt the reorientation of Yunnan that had been triggered by the recent Han migration. To this end, the Dali state often juxtaposed imagery from the Chinese, Islamic, and non-Han traditions; it also made a point of selecting civil and military officials from ethnically diverse backgrounds.

Except for Yakub Beg's insurrection in Xinjiang and the Taiping Rebellion in eastern China, the Panthay Rebellion was the only uprising in mid-nineteenth-century China that succeeded in establishing an independent government.[1] To achieve this end, Du Wenxiu and his fellow officials had to put in place an effective and popular system of rule that would attract support from all of Yunnan's diverse ethnic groups. But even before this, the fledging government had to deal with the military threats arising from the Kunming Massacre of 1856.

The Dali regime faced its strongest challenges in the first years of the rebellion as it struggled to establish solid political and military foundations. On October 11, 1856, less than a month after the rebels secured Dali, Zhang Zhengtai, the Heqing-Lijiang assistant brigade commander, attacked the city with his militia. Zhang had fought his way southward from Lijiang, slaughtering Hui communities at Heqing, Jianchuan, Langqiong, and Dengchuan, before arriving at Dali.[2] His inexperienced volunteers were organized well enough to massacre vulnerable Hui communities, but they were no match for the well-prepared and battle-hardened Hui veterans. Zhang was repulsed by Hui forces on all sides and forced to retreat north to his bases in the northwest.[3]

The following year the Dali forces faced the first formal challenge from the provincial capital. Hoping to crush the rebellion by striking at its core, Shuxing'a ordered Wen Xiang, the provincial military commander, to attack Dali from the east. This attack succeeded at first (see chapter 7) but was disrupted when Ma Rulong's first siege of Kunming broke Wen's supply lines. The following month, while the imperial forces were busy defending the capital, Dali troops marched north in an attempt to overpower Zhang Zhengtai and take Heqing and Lijiang. This attempt failed. Six months later, after a series of strategic errors, the Dali troops found themselves once again defending the northern pass of Shangguan.[4]

The Dali regime had survived these early challenges but had yet to make any strategically significant territorial gains. Its forces dominated much of western Yunnan, but there were still pockets of resistance controlled by Han militias intent on carrying out the 1856 call to exterminate the Hui. In the spring of 1859 the leader of one of the most dangerous of these pockets, the Han militia commander Dong Jialan, launched a surprise attack from neighboring Binchuan across Lake Erhai.[5] He landed with his troops below Dali and made his way to the city. Using explosives, he breeched the city's outer wall. His troops charged through the opening, catching the city's defenders by surprise, and pressed quickly toward the city center. After several hours, the attack's reinforcements failed to arrive and Dong and his vanguard were forced to retreat.[6] Enemy forces would not infiltrate the Dali plain again until the city fell fourteen years later.

Later that same spring the Dali regime's luck began to turn: two of the strongest threats to it were eliminated. Zhang Zhengtai, who controlled the wealthy northwestern towns of Lijiang and Heqing, had alienated many of his original supporters by assassinating opponents, practicing open extortion, and generally acting like a tyrant. In April 1859 a militia band several hundred strong and organized by the local gentry entered Heqing and assassinated Zhang.[7] On hearing this, many of his fighters dispersed, which effectively gutted the last major pro-Qing force in northwestern Yunnan. Soon after Zhang's death, Du Wenxiu captured Binchuan, killing the Han militia leader, Dong Jialan.[8] Thus within three months, the two men in western Yunnan most likely to threaten the Dali regime were dead.[9]

In the spring of 1860, the provincial government launched a three-pronged attack against Dali, which Ma Rulong deftly cut from the east, and Cai Fachun attacked in the west (see chapter 6). In early September, Cai Chunfa captured Binchuan (to the west of Dali), decimating the remaining Qing troops there and executing Zhu Kechang. It would be nearly a decade before Dali faced another direct military threat. By the end of 1860, a loose alliance among Ma Rulong, Ma Dexin, and Du Wenxiu controlled broad swathes of Yunnan; the imperial forces controlled only the city of Kunming and pockets of northeastern Yunnan. With provincial officials now concentrating on holding and expanding these areas, Du's military forces began to consolidate and establish functional control over much of western Yunnan.

Reassured by the victory over Zhu, Du turned his attention and troops northward. By mid-October, Pingnan armies were in control of northwestern Yunnan's three major urban centers: Jianchuan, Heqing, and Lijiang.[10] A year later, in 1861, key victories in the southwest consolidated the Dali regime's control of western Yunnan. From Tengyue in the southwest to Zhongdian in the north and Chuxiong in the east, Du Wenxiu was now indisputably the ranking political leader in the province. He and his fellow officials could now implement their political vision.

With the uprising now in its fifth year, many Yunnanese began to sense that a rebel victory was inevitable. French missionary Chauveau's evaluation of the situation was typical: "The Muslim victories are not solely in the west [xidao] but throughout the entire province . . . and the Muslim themselves do not hide the fact that their intentions are to conquer the whole of Yunnan and to establish an independent kingdom."[11]

As these events unfolded, the Qing court remained woefully uninformed about the Dali regime. The earliest detailed information Beijing received about it came in 1857 from the censor Li Peihu. His report was the first official communication to the emperor that the rebels "had established their own seditious state and appointed officials." But he then added incorrectly that "the head rebel who has now proclaimed himself king is the military licentiate Ma Mingkui."[12] It would be four more years before Du Wenxiu's full name appeared in a memorial to the emperor. Despite this early obscurity, Du Wenxiu was making great strides in forming a viable political alternative to the Qing in western Yunnan—an alternative based on the province's unique ethnic, cultural, and commercial context.

*Pingnan Government*

It is a challenge to present a coherent picture of Du Wenxiu's government, given that few documents survived Dali's fall in 1873. The records still extant—lists of officers, lists of regulations, a few personal accounts of imperial envoys who had been sent to Dali—convey more the ideal that informed Du's authority than the manner in which the laws and regulations were implemented. What is clear from those documents is that the sultanate was by and large a military government.

Du Wenxiu was the only ruler the independent state would ever know. For that entire period he held the Chinese title "Generalissimo of All Armed Forces and Calvary [*zongtong bingma dayuanshuai*]," rendered in Arabic as "Leader of All Muslims [*Qa'id jami' al-muslimin*]."[13] Both titles highlighted the role Du sought to play at the beginning of the rebellion. Less clear is whether he began to develop political aspirations as the rebellion ground on.

Details about the manner in which the regime's ideology and methods of governance manifested itself come from several European eyewitnesses who were either living in or traveling through rebel-occupied Yunnan at the height of the Dali regime's control. Most tantalizing is the consistency with which the different accounts indicate that Du adopted titles reflecting his de facto position as ruler of the Dali Sultanate. Thomas Cooper, after interviewing Dali rebels in the northwestern Yunnan town of Weixi, stated that Du Wenxiu "had been made Emperor" several years after the founding of the Dali regime.[14] In 1866, Father Fenouil, a Catholic missionary in Yunnan, asserted that "Du Wenxiu had now taken the title of the ancient kings of Dali."[15] Several years later his superior, Father Ponsot, referred to Du as the "king of the state [*roi d'etat*]."[16] Finally, Francis Garnier, the leader of the French Mekong Expedition, which traveled through Yunnan in 1868, noted in his memoirs that Du Wenxiu "took the title of king on the first day of the Chinese New Year (February 5, 1867)."[17] These European reports—each garnering their information from highly disparate sources—tell us consistently that Du had adopted some political titles, yet no document from the Dali government survives that explicitly uses the title of king.[18]

Some of the confusion may arise from the fact that they may have been attempting to render Du Wenxiu's Islamic title into Chinese.[19] Louis de Carné, a member of the Mekong Expedition, noted that "the Muslims call him Sulaiman while the Chinese append to his [Chinese] name the title *Yuanshuai* [Generalissimo]."[20]

The strongest confirmation that Du often used the official title Sulaiman is found on the seals of office given to the Dali Sultanate's civil and military officials. Typically, the official seals of the Dali regime were divided into two halves. Along one side of the seal the title of office was inscribed in Chinese. Along the other was—in highly stylized Arabic—Du's Islamic name, Sulaiman.[21] Du Wenxiu also used this title in an Arabic communication sent to England in 1872.[22] The prominent Muslim Yunnanese scholar Ma Lianyuan, who was fluent in both Arabic and Chinese, noted in his account of growing up in Yunnan that "in western Yunnan, Sulaiman, Du Wenxiu, became the ruler in Dali."[23]

Whatever his title, ultimate decision-making power was entirely in Du's hands. But he did not rule unaided. Helping him make decisions was an executive council of eight civil and ten military ministers. This council brought issues before Du Wenxiu, debated matters of state, and discussed military strategies. All official pronouncements, however, came from Du Wenxiu himself.

At the local level, the Dali regime retained the Qing administrative framework of prefectures, departments, and counties. However, these local governments were not headed by prefects or magistrates, as they would have been under the Qing; instead, the Dali administration drew its civil officials from the officer ranks at local military garrisons.[24] Other local officials were selected from among the local elites. Besides selecting civil officials, Du plotted out a network of military garrisons early in his reign, even for areas still under Qing administrative control such as eastern Yunnan.[25] Within a few years the regime had established a fully functioning network of military and civil officials numbering more than one thousand. Each office had its own seal, which was made of gold, silver, bronze, or wood depending on its ranking within the administration.[26]

Du Wenxiu's pledge to make the new government as multiethnic as possible would be honored as the Dali regime took shape. A list of ranking officers and officials from around 1867 tells us that more than twenty of these people were of indigenous origin; moreover, there was a ministry devoted entirely to non-Han affairs.[27] Among the more powerful of these officials was Li Wenxue (also called Li Zhengxue), an Yi from the Ailao Mountains south of Dali, who had supported the Dali regime from its early days. He was awarded the office of Commander of non-Han Affairs (*dasi fan*).[28] Members of the Bai, Yi, Dai, Hani, Lisu, and Manchu ethnic groups served as either civil or military officials, reflecting Du's stated intention to "spread the offices among the three cultures."[29]

Securing non-Han support was a key part of Du's strategy, yet it was his regime's capacity to introduce visible and meaningful change to the region that distinguished its rule from the Qing's and that secured the favor of the Yunnanese.[30] Du's strategy of pursuing non-Han allies was meant to sever the long-standing tributary ties between Beijing and many of Yunnan's ethnic groups. In 1863, Dali troops marched into Xishuangbanna and persuaded the local ruler to transfer his allegiance and resources to the Dali regime.[31] Along the Burmese border, the local headmen were paying a "tribute of five thousand bushels of rice to the Panthays" by the mid-1860s.[32] Captain Bowers, who accompanied a British team into southwestern Yunnan from Burma, noted in reference to those non-Chinese ethnic groups in the Southeast Asian highlands along the Yunnanese border that "all these tribes excepting the Singp'os and Paloungs, are subject to the Panthays, or give them such allegiance as they did their former rulers."[33]

Du Wenxiu's leadership and his regime's goals attracted support from beyond the former Qing boundaries of western Yunnan. A French official stationed in northern Indochina in the 1880s indicated that by 1863 "the Muslim Chinese that formed an independent state controlled from Dali by the Sultan Sulaiman, had sent to Xien-long, in the upper Mekong, a deputation of 250 individuals to secure the support of the Lao against the Chinese."[34] During the rebellion, Europeans reported that the Pingnan regime had won the allegiance of the innumerable small polities all along Yunnan's borders. One of these men indicated that except for one or two, "all these tribes . . . are subject to the Panthays, or give them such allegiance as they did their former rulers."[35]

The popularity of the Pingnan regime among the various ethnic groups in eastern Yunnan and western Guizhou indicates that there were equally strong links among far-flung Hui and non-Han communities in the two provinces. As noted earlier, the Yunnanese Hui had formed close military and political alliances with Yi, Zhuang, and other groups.[36] What is rarely acknowledged, however, is the presence of powerful Miao–Hui armies. By 1862, imperial officials in western Guizhou—especially in those counties bordering Yunnan—were expressing growing concern about how easily the various ethnic groups were linking together and taking formal control of all but one or two cities. According to one, imperial officials tried "to pacify the indigenous people, including the Miao and the Yi, but were ineffective [since] they had their own opinions on the state of affairs. . . . The Hui and the yi both are aiding [the Miao] and thus refuse to surrender . . . resulting in Xinyi alone remaining under imperial control."[37] Three days after this official wrote his memorial, Xinyi fell to the multiethnic rebels. For the next decade, many of the ethnically mixed regions of western Guizhou were aligned politically with the concerns and goals of the Dali regime.

As Dali's influence grew, there emerged a growing willingness among the Yi to join forces under the Hui. By 1857, Yi from southeast of Kunming had joined with the Hui to form an army of more than ten thousand men.[38] This support was vital to the Hui in the early years of the Pingnan regime. The Yi leader Li Wenxue and his army played a crucial role in the rise of the Dali sultanate as a political power. Such actions did not go unnoticed or unrewarded by the Hui leaders as they sought to forge their new state.

## MULTIPLE VISIONS: ISLAMIC, CHINESE,
## AND NON-HAN IMAGERY IN THE DALI SULTANATE

Central to the effort of establishing a viable government as the transformation of Dali into a symbolic center for the newly established Pingnan state. This center was to be imbued with a sense of imperial authority and legitimacy. Du selected terminology from the Islamic and Chinese traditions in creating the Pingnan state's symbolic structure. Symbols from a variety of traditions enabled Du to weave together a seamless mosaic of ideological justifications for the founding of the Pingnan State—a state that would fuse various political, religious, and ethnic symbols into a single coherent denunciation of the Qing court.[39]

Despite the presence of different symbolic traditions, the Pingnan ideology should not be interpreted as syncretic. Under the new government, all of Yunnan's various cultures retained their identities and continued to be free to articulate shifting local and regional experiences. The regime reorganized Islamic, indigenous, and Chinese forms into a new cultural system heavily colored by the transnational Yunnan context. Understanding this complex mix is fundamental to making any sense of the Panthay Rebellion. In this historical circumstance, Islamic influences coexisted with and sometimes dominated the nascent regime's efforts to establish an independent kingdom—never, though, to the exclusion of the other pan-ethnic and anti-Qing dimensions. The regime's very public interweaving of these traditions into visible signs of the Dali State reveals the leadership's commitment to inclusivity.

The Dali State, from its inception, saw indigenous support as vital, both politically and militarily. A Catholic priest stationed in Yunnan reported that "the indigenous people joined the Muslims because the marauding by the Chinese had, in their minds, rendered all of the [Chinese] odious."[40] Qing officials dismissed early reports of Yi animosity toward the state, and many administrators, such as Shuxing'a in a memorial the emperor, deluded themselves that the Hui were simply "seducing the yi peoples."[41] The swiftness with which the non-Han united behind the Hui in the months following the Kunming Massacre quickly disabused Qing officials of that idea.

In southern Yunnan, a local official reported that Hui "had linked up with non-Han [and] occupied and seized property."[42] In western Yunnan, Hui and Yi forces numbered "more than 3,000." Another government document stated that in the eastern part of province "the Muslims united with yi and Nong who all had old grudges against the Chinese."[43] This unity reflected the close ties that had been formed over centuries. The rapid crystallization of the Hui–Yi alliance highlights the fact that the Qing had allied themselves largely with a segment of the population who were out of touch with Yunnan's multiethnic culture. This group (primarily settler Han and anti-Hui officials) deluded themselves into believing the Hui were the aggressors and the Han the victims and as such that the non-Han populace would come to their aid.[44] Both assumptions proved to be tragically incorrect.

The Pingnan regime, far from marginalizing non-Han, made a point of incorporating them into its administration.[45] According to Chinese scholar Jing Dexin, members of the Bai, Yi, Dai, Hani, Lisu, and Manchu ethnic groups served as civil or military officials—a reflection of Du's stated intention to "spread the offices among the three cultures [Han, Hui, and Yi], since each has their own origins and behaves in their own way."[46]

Throughout his reign, Du Wenxiu displayed a genuine appreciation of the role played by non-Han in Yunnan society, both past and present. At one point, before an important military offensive, he alluded to the legacy of the Nanzhao Kingdom—a powerful state that along with Tibet had rivaled Tang China for supremacy in East Asia: "Even if we cannot realize far-reaching permanent victory, we can still achieve a smaller more remote success like that of the Nanzhao Kingdom which lasted eight hundred years."[47] By invoking the Nanzhao Kingdom, he was adroitly highlighting Yunnan's history of indigenous rule independent of Chinese control; at the same time he was emphasizing the importance of non-Han groups to the Pingnan State.[48]

The Pingnan state was clearly multiethnic, but it also had an undeniably strong Islamic hue. Within weeks of his investiture, Du ordered renovations to Dali's central mosque, which had been heavily damaged in the fighting. He followed this with a campaign of mosque construction and restoration that did not end until there were "five or six mosques" in Dali alone.[49] British visitors to Tengyue remarked that the Panthay official there paid a similar amount of attention to the city's main mosque; it was "under repair at present, [with] new wings having recently [been] added to it."[50] Given the multitude of demands on their time and resources, it is striking that top Pingnan officials paid so much attention to mosques.

Besides building and rebuilding mosques, Du established a hierarchy of religious offices charged with overseeing religious affairs. These offices evolved into one of the three administrative divisions of the government, the other two being civil and military.[51] In the early years of Du's rule the Pingnan leadership sought to revitalize Islamic learning and culture by establishing Islamic schools (*madrasas*), by printing the first Quran in China, and by encouraging the use of Arabic among educated Hui.[52]

The use of Arabic—always a key marker of Islam for the Hui in China—

became especially significant in the Pingnan state. The Pingnan bureaucracy and the Hui elite employed Arabic whenever possible. It is difficult to measure the degree to which Arabic displaced Chinese, but it is highly unlikely that, as some have suggested, Chinese language and Chinese characters were forbidden. Descriptions of the Pingnan yamen often mention both Arabic and Chinese calligraphy.[53] In Du Wenxiu's main hall "the walls were inlaid with marble and white marble slabs with quotations from the Quran, in gold, hung about the place."[54] That said, Arabic at the very least became the preferred language for external and diplomatic relations. The first British envoys seeking contact with the Dali regime found this out when they crossed into Pingnan territory from Burma and were presented with documents entirely in Arabic; they were compelled to wait several days until a Chinese translation could be obtained.[55]

This promotion of Arabic was only one dimension of the Pingnan State's efforts to position itself in the Islamic world. A powerful example of the Dali State embracing Arabic in order to further Islam is found in a proclamation carried to the Muslims of Lhasa by Hui caravaneers in the early 1860s.[56] Written in Arabic, the Tibet Proclamation casts the rebellion as a righteous response to treachery by idolaters. It employs Quranic and Islamic metaphors almost exclusively and carefully places the insurgency within an Islamic framework:

The cause of the dispute was that the Idolaters and their chiefs assembled together to kill the Muslims and began to insult their religion. . . . Having abandoned every hope of life, we fought with the Idolaters and God gave us the victory. . . . [The ruler's] name is Sadik, otherwise called Suleiman. He has now established Islamic Law. He administers justice according to the dictates of the Quran and their traditions. Since we have made him our Imam we have been by the decree of God, very victorious. . . . The Ministers and chiefs under our Imam are as single-hearted as Abu Bakr and as bold as Ali. No one can face them in battle. They are imperious to the Infidel but meek to the Muslim. The metropolis of Infidelity has become a city of Islam![57]

The Tibet Proclamation captures the new state's Islamic tone—a tone that without doubt was important to the Pingnan regime. Yet the Pingnan leaders never let their Muslim beliefs overwhelm the multiethnic character of their state. Indeed, attempts to characterize the Pingnan State as either Islamic or Chinese miss the point entirely. The state was Hui-led, and the Hui never saw being Chinese and being Muslim as mutually exclusive. The most obvious evidence of this inclusive identity was Du's own seal [Fig. 8.1]. On one side was his Chinese title, "Generalissimo [*zongtong bingma dayuanshuai*]," on the other his Islamic title, "Leader of all Muslims [*qa'id jami' al-muslimin*]." This Islamic title was included in every official chop distributed to the lower civil and military offices.[58]

FIGURE 8.1. Du Wenxiu's Seal

This inclusiveness permeated Dali's political culture, which consistently employed distinctly Chinese imperial symbols side by side with Islamic ones. In his efforts to transform Dali into the capital of a new state, Du co-opted Qing symbols while at the same time challenging their authority with imagery from the previous Ming dynasty and the contemporaneous Taiping rebels.[59] He selected these symbols with meticulous care, choosing ones that would resonate with all groups in Yunnan; he also made sure the seditious meanings of these symbols could not possibly be lost on the new state's subjects. Li Yuzhen, who interviewed long-term Dali residents in the late nineteenth century, noted that Du "set into action a series of building programs based on the Qing imperial institutions in Beijing, including [the construction of] an imperial Forbidden City—[with the walls] a kilometer in circumference. At both the upper and lower passes, he had 'Great Walls' built with only one entrance, which ran from high in the [Cangshan] mountains, and deep into [Erhai] Lake making the valley impenetrable."[60]

Although he adopted those symbols from the Chinese imperial court, Du highlighted the "foreign" nature of Manchu rule by borrowing titles and styles of dress (including his own imperial robes) from the Ming dynasty—the last "Chinese" dynasty to rule China.[61]

### SIGNS OF DISSENT

Historical descriptions of the era make careful note of the sultanate's broad range of political symbols deployed by Du. These symbols helped define and express the state's goals but do not convey which types of popular symbols were adopted by the residents of the newly established state. Among the population at large, perhaps the most common symbol of support for the Dali leaders and Pingnan rule was to cease shaving the forehead and pulling back the hair into a queue. Tonsure had been instituted by the Manchu Qing, who required it of all their Chinese subjects as a sign of submission to the new dynasty. Those who did not conform could be sentenced to death and often were. To grow out one's hair was a mark of support for Dali and an act of sedition against Manchu rule.[62]

Given the traitorous implications, it is not surprising that imperial sources regularly refer to the Dali rebels as "long-haired rebels [*changfa Huifei*]." Western observers, however, reveal to a much greater extent the degree to which Yunnanese living under rebel control adopted the practice.[63] Louis de Carné indicated that Du Wenxiu, "never one to overlook the details," had authorized his subjects "to wear the queue but under the condition that they did not shave their foreheads."[64] Thomas Cooper reported that in the Yunnan–Tibet border town of Weixi—which at the time of his visit was under Qing control—"there were a great many Mahomedans in town wearing their long hair, the Mahomedan badge, living in apparent indifference and security."[65] Cooper asked one Dali supporter "how it was that they lived in Imperial territory with long hair?"[66] The Hui "smiled a little scornfully, and observed that Mahomedan subjects had been well received in Weixi for [the] past two years [under Qing control], and there had been no restriction on the intercourse between Dali and Weixi."[67]

The Pingnan regime, keen to assert its distinctive political identity, issued an array of elaborate uniforms. As a British mission approached the Dali-controlled town of Tengyue in southwestern Yunnan, its leader, Edward Sladen, discerned a wide range of "Panthay officers of all grades and in full uniform."[68] On arriving in Tengyue he found the Panthay governor, Dasi Kong, wearing "a gray felt hat, somewhat resembling a helmet placed sideways, the front half of the rim being turned up and the back downwards. A gold rosette, set with large precious stones, formed a handsome ornament in front, and a blue silk top-knot fell down behind his back as a long tail. A richly figured, pale blue silk coat reaching to the ankles, and overlapping on the right side, completed his costume."[69] Sketches published by another member of the Sladen expedition reveal that many of the soldiers tucked their long queues into elaborate turbans.

The uniforms seem to have quickly become potent symbols of the state. Before leaving Burma, Sladen had sent two non-Han Karen escorts ahead to contact the Dali regime. Several weeks later, with the expedition nearing the Yunnan border, the Karen escorts returned bearing letters but dressed in clothes so different from their original outfits that Sladen almost did not recognize them: "The two men were got up most gorgeously in blue jackets and Mahomedan skull-caps, richly braided with silver and gold, and below the former they wore yellow silk coats reaching below the knee, and, suspended from the upper button-hole of their jackets, one had a pink and the other a blue, square piece of cloth, like a pocket handkerchief, with an embroidered square at the attached corner."[70]

The Dali representatives had dressed the two messengers in clothing that would facilitate their return through a precarious border area—an indication of how familiar and respected their government's official uniforms now were among the general populace. The acceptance of the rebels' long hair and attire—both within and outside the Dali regime's direct sphere of control—tells us that the rebel government was growing in stature in the neighboring regions. It also strongly suggests that the Dali government was seeking to put behind it the conflicts that had ignited the rebellion. Instead, it sought to emphasize the strong multiethnic dimension and vision for the newly founded state.

### TRADING ON THE MARGINS

The caravan trade had long been vital to western Yunnan's economy, and it loomed large in Du Wenxiu's vision of his new state. Initially, trade between western Yunnan and its partners suffered as a result of the rebellion. No clear military front had been established between the imperial and rebel forces, and many towns traded hands four and five times before finally coming under Dali control. By the early 1860s, with territorial boundaries becoming more stable, the Dali government had taken measures to encourage the resumption of trade.

The Dali regime promoted trade by promising to protect those traders who crossed into Dali-controlled territory. To this end, it instructed its local magistrates "to indemnify traders for any robberies that might be committed on them in his territory."[71] In other words, any goods lost through theft were to be reimbursed by local officials and the inhabitants of the area. This would encourage the local people to safeguard all caravans. The same officials were to post guards at the main passes linking Yunnan to the neighboring regions and offer free lodging to traders.[72]

Implementing this program at a time of fluctuating borders must have been a sisyphean task. Yet European eyewitnesses suggest that the government succeeded very well in its efforts to promote the caravan trade. Thomas Cooper wrote that local people attributed the considerable level of trade to Du Wenxiu's efforts to foster "trade as much as possible, both by the imposition of light duties and a rigorous administration of justice."[73] He added that the traders he encountered all "lauded the security of the White banner [Dali-controlled] territory."[74] Indeed, among the Yunnanese, the Dali-controlled areas had a reputation for being far safer and less corrupt than areas under imperial control. Han and non-Han traders told John Anderson that "in all cases [the Panthay] officers protected the passage of merchants, and dealt much more justly by them than the [imperial] mandarins had been accustomed to do[ing]."[75]

Nor were the Dali laws relating to caravans mere idle guidelines. During their six weeks in Tengyue, the Sladen mission witnessed sixteen public executions of those who had broken the caravan laws. These were carried out with a pageantry that astonished them: "The criminal was led to the outskirts of the bazaar by a small escort, with music and banners flying, and, with his hands tied behind his back, was made to kneel by the side of the road. The executioner chopped off the head usually at one blow; the body was buried on the spot, and the ghastly head hung up by the gate of the town."[76] Clearly, this was not arbitrary violence, and it indicates how far the Dali Kingdom was willing to go to revive Yunnan's cross-border trade. It was their belief that prosperity would follow stability.[77]

To help restore the cross-border trade, Du Wenxiu himself established a trading company in Burma.[78] He also opened two cotton-trading bureaus in Ava, one of them supervised by his younger sister.[79] In Tengyue, the Sladen mission noted the results of these efforts. Anderson, who was the mission's doctor, described the bazaar there as having stalls and shops selling a wide assortment of dry goods, jade, and gold, both for domestic consumption and for trade with Burma.[80]

The government imposed light duties—far less inflated than in the past—on goods that crossed its borders, and it collected them uniformly. The first official contact a French expedition had with the regime on its way to Dali was a "customs post established on the left bank of the river collecting the duty on the commercial caravans who were traveling towards Dali."[81] Francis Garnier, a member of this expedition, spoke with several Dali officials and learned that in trade with Tibet, "the traders pay at Weixi a duty of one-tenth tael per pack-animal."[82]

Salt wells were also vital to Dali's economy.[83] In an agreement with Ma Rulong after he seized Chuxiong in 1860, the Dali government assumed control of three of the five main salt works in Yunnan. In 1864, Jia Hongzhao memorialized that the Baiyanjing and Heiyanjing salt wells "were all under the control of western Yunnan [Hui] forces and were completely monopolized by the Hui rebels."[84] The Qing made efforts to reclaim these wells, but given the substantial revenue earned from them, the Dali government went to considerable effort and expense to retain control.[85] The Dali government also invested in improvements to the existing wells, such as one in Qiaohou north of Dali, which was among the most productive of all during the rebellion.[86]

Du Wenxiu's pragmatic approach allowed Dali to stabilize itself relatively quickly and to extend that stability throughout the territory it controlled. Contrast this with conditions in eastern Yunnan and in neighboring Guizhou, where the Miao Rebellion was still raging. Indeed, life under the sultanate offered greater protection from bandits and rogue officials than those areas of Yunnan under nominal imperial control.[87] In general, first-hand accounts of the Pingnan State point to an overwhelming concern for political and commercial stability.[88]

## Divided We Stand: Reconfiguring Notions of Hui-ness

Despite all the progress the Dali Sultanate had made in its first years, it was forced to reappraise its goals and strategies after Ma Rulong abruptly surrendered to the Qing in 1862 and returned Kunming to imperial control the following year. Ma Rulong's decision to aid the Qing rattled the Pingnan regime and the Qing as well. Obviously, Ma's decision was going to impede Dali's aspirations to control Yunnan completely. Less obvious was the emperor's concern over Ma's abrupt display of loyalty to the Qing. The emperor's advisors were split, with one group advocating that the court continue to follow the recently implemented policy of using Hui to control Hui. They argued that because few resources were available, the emperor had little choice but to use the tools available to him within Yunnan.

A second group cautioned that to allow Ma Rulong and officials who had risen through the ranks only after the rebellion started (and who were thus untrustworthy) to fight the rebellion for the Qing would be taking a huge risk. In their view, this policy would reduce Yunnan to a pulp and "Cen [Yuying] and Ma [Rulong] would become the tail that wagged the dog."[89]

What neither side realized was that Ma Rulong held far less power than both his supporters and detractors imagined. In casting his lot with the Qing, Ma Rulong was gambling that he would be able to negotiate with Du Wenxiu and bring the conflict to a peaceful end. Yet to accomplish this he needed the resources and backing of the Qing.

Those in Beijing who hoped to implement "using-Hui-to-control-Hui" favored such a strategy. This scenario perhaps seemed plausible to a court that had few feasible alternatives, but few understood that for every action Ma Rulong took to demonstrate his loyalty to the Qing, he was undermining his standing among the Yunnan Hui. In foiling Ma Rong's 1863 coup attempt, he had made himself look more reliable to the Qing court, but he had also undercut his position among those whose help he needed desperately to convince Du Wenxiu to accept the Qing court's conditions of surrender.

At another level, Ma Rulong's defection to the Qing only made the situation worse for the court. The Panthay Rebellion up until 1863 had never been wholly unified. As so clearly illustrated during the 1860 Chuxiong campaign, the rebel forces despite their common opposition to the Qing remained divided. Ma Rulong's capitulation fundamentally changed this. Faced with the prospect of Ma Rulong aiding the Qing, his hitherto supporters immediately recognized the need to rally under the Pingnan banner and recognize Du Wenxiu's leadership if they hoped to prevent Yunnan from falling back under Qing dominion.

Even without firm Qing support, Ma Rulong did succeed in opening lines of communication between the Pingnan regime and provincial representatives stationed in Kunming. By August 1862, only months after Ma Rulong entered Kunming, Governor Xu Zhiming could report to the emperor that "Ma Dexin's niece and her daughter came from Dali to visit . . . in order to see the positive results of peace."[90] This was the first of many documented cases of Hui traveling between Dali and Kunming in an effort to bring about a negotiated peace. These missions marked a new phase of relations between Dali and Kunming and indicated, far more clearly than before, just what was fueling the rebellion and blocking a peaceful resolution.

In 1863, only months after Pan Duo's assassination, Ma Rulong dispatched his first mission to persuade Du Wenxiu to surrender. To seek a settlement, he sent to Dali a team of ten respected Hui headed by Ma Futu.[91] At first the negotiations were ineffectual, with each side attempting to convince the other that they alone were the true protectors of the faith in Yunnan.[92] Realizing the futility of further debate, Ma Futu admonished Du that his "actions were self-seeking and thus harmful to Muslims (jiaomen), so I will take my leave."[93]

On the eve of Ma Futu's scheduled departure, when all hope of a resolution seemed lost, a massive earthquake rocked Dali. The Chinese had long seen earthquakes as physical manifestations of Heaven's displeasure over worldly transgressions. Du and his top advisors feared that the earthquake represented just that. Their confidence shaken, several of Du's officials hurried over to Ma Futu's lodgings and implored him to stay another two days. He agreed, and was quickly escorted to an audience with Du, who proposed that the two of them sign three pacts. The first outlined the terms of his surrender to the Qing court; the second indicated in detail how the deeply divided regions of Yunnan would be reunited; the third proposed a marriage agreement between the children of Du Wenxiu and Ma Futu.[94] The following day, Ma Futu set out for Kunming with the agreements in hand and Du's promise that if they were satisfactory to Ma Rulong, he would travel to Kunming to surrender.

Du and his council began to regret their decision almost immediately. They wavered for several days and then slowly regained their composure as well as their determination to fight on.[95] Du composed a message to Ma Futu stating that he would abide by the agreements only if Ma Rulong would first accept a post in the Dali government—an option Du knew Ma Rulong could not accept and that would effectively abrogate the agreements. If Ma Rulong failed to agree to Du's condition, the emissaries were to return the signed agreements by messenger. Ma refused Du's demand and returned the agreements. His displeasure was evident in his ominous warning to Du that "even good medicine cannot cure a difficult disease. Western Yunnan will sooner or later be defeated."[96]

Less than a year later, Yang Zhenpeng, a Hui general who had only recently gone over to the Qing, arrived in Dali asking for an audience with Du Wenxiu. It is unclear why he traveled to Dali, on whose orders, and what his intentions were; the accounts of his visit are tangled and often contradictory. His detractors suggest that after helping capture Yaozhou for the imperial forces, Yang spent his days in drink and lascivious activities. It is alleged that during this time he hatched a plot to assassinate Du.[97] He recruited two Hui officers, who were to travel separately to Dali. They agreed to rendezvous with Yang on February 1, 1864, in order to assassinate Du.[98]

On the appointed day, Yang was able to procure an audience with Du. During that meeting his accomplices tried to force their way into the inner court. Du's guards immediately locked the palace's massive doors, thwarting the attack.[99] The two attackers realized their plot had failed and attempted to flee Dali, but the sentinels guarding the lower pass had been alerted and caught them. They were marched back to Dali and brought before Du, who quickly ordered them executed.[100] Yang Zhenpeng pleaded ignorance of the entire affair. Many Pingnan officials doubted this; even so, he was pardoned by Du.

Around this time, in 1864, Ma Dexin traveled to Dali to make a last formal attempt to negotiate with Du Wenxiu.[101] This would be the only documented occasion during the rebellion that the two met face to face. Ma was sympathetic to Du's cause; even so, he tried to convince Du that by continuing the rebellion he was doing the Qing's bidding. If the fighting continued, Hui would simply be killing Hui. "We should have the [Qing] government fall into a Hui plan," Ma argued, "[and] not let the Hui fall into the government's [plan]."[102] Other accounts indicate that Ma also warned Du that as soon as the Qing court defeated the Taipings (which by 1864 was practically assured), they would begin diverting money, troops, and weaponry into Yunnan, making a Pingnan victory impossible. Despite Ma's foresight—this is precisely what would happen—Du refused to change his position and instead beseeched Ma to accept a position in Dali, one far "more splendid than that which he held in Kunming."[103] The negotiations ended in the spring of 1864 with Ma returning to Kunming empty-handed.[104]

## BRIDGING THE MUSLIM–HUI DIVIDE

The chasm between the two groups of Hui rebels, as evidenced by these failed negotiations and by Ma Rulong's earlier refusal to join Du's government, indicates that the imperial court was mistaken to view the Hui as a static or monolithic body and as synonymous with Islam. That the Hui did not respond to Han aggression in a uniform or unified manner is consistent with the multiethnic dynamic of Yunnan in general and of the Yunnan Hui in particular. The rift between Ma Rulong and Du Wenxiu is visible not only in the three missions to Dali just described but also in letters the two leaders exchanged over more than five years. These letters vividly illustrate how the Hui in southwestern China perceived their ethnoreligious identity at the time. With regard to other areas of the Muslim world, Dale Eickelman and James Piscatori have suggested that being a Muslim is often less significant than *how* that role is configured in relation to other customs, identities, and shared "imaginings."[105] Ma Rulong, Du Wenxiu, and other Hui expressed themselves with a self-awareness that was narrowly religious but at the same time, and far more broadly, ethnoreligious.

Han chroniclers of the rebellion era consistently used several terms to identify the Hui, which were sharply different from the ones the Hui applied to themselves. Throughout the nineteenth century, Qing government documents employed four terms when referring to the Yunnan Hui: Huimin, Huiren, Huizhong, and Huizi. Each contained the Hui ideogram in combination with a second ideogram that indicated "people" or "group of people." The four resulting compound characters had subtle differences; even so, Qing officials and the Han elite used them interchangeably.

As noted in chapter 3, Yunnan Hui tended to refer to themselves as either Muslims (*mumin*) or Hui. Although being Hui meant also being Muslim, the relationship between "Muslim-ness" and other identities (such as local, regional, and occupational) allowed for shifting notions of what it meant to be Hui. The two terms were not synonymous although they did overlap to a degree: Hui were almost certainly Muslims, yet the term mumin had a more restricted meaning. Moreover, neither the Hui loyal to the Pingnan regime nor those allied with the Qing government seemed to have considered their actions inconsistent with their identity as Muslims, Hui, or Chinese. They were able to differentiate between these complementary identities. A good illustration of this relates to how Du Wenxiu and Ma Rulong used the terms Huimin, Huijiao, and mumin in their correspondence between 1862 and 1868.

After Ma Rulong's mysterious decision to capitulate to Qing forces in 1862, he and Du vied for the position of leader of the Yunnan Hui. A recurring point of contention in the correspondence between the two leaders—one that persisted for the remaining ten years of the rebellion—related to the tension each felt between being a Hui leader and being a Muslim leader. A mumin was part of "one Muslim family"; yet at the same time, a Huimin, Huijiao, or Hui was part of the three peoples (Han, Hui, Yi) that constituted the world of Yunnan. It is difficult to assign meanings to these terms one-and-a-half centuries later: Did this terminology indicate a nested relationship between the two identities or a bifurcated one? A close reading of the documents from this period of unprecedented Hui ascendancy offers a rare glimpse of what this relationship was. In their letters to each other during the rebellion, Du Wenxiu and Ma Rulong seem to have employed mumin when the context was relations between Muslims; in contrast, they more often invoked the terms Hui, Huimin, and Huijiao when writing about the Hui as an ethnic group. Nor was this usage limited to Ma Rulong and Du Wenxiu. In 1862, one year before accepting a commission under Du, Ma Liansheng adopted the title of "Leader of Eastern Yunnan's *san jiao* Military Affairs" (*zongtong yidong sanjiao junfu*).[106]

A few months after defecting to the Qing, Ma Rulong wrote to Du Wenxiu to persuade him to end his resistance. He began this letter by justifying his actions:

Looking back at all the past dynasties, the Qing has treated its people [min] benevolently. . . . The violence [against the Hui] in Yunnan, was clearly not at the court's instigation. Just think, if the Hui [Huimin] of each province can have peace, why would [the court] want to wipe out only those of Yunnan? It was all because the [local] officials were not honorable, [instead] stirring up problems and reporting it as Han–Hui violence. Local officials have now clarified that the uprising was a result of Han massacring Hui [han mie hui] so the court has decreed that a strategy of peaceful resolution be followed and all officials are now peacefully complying.[107]

Ma was portraying the earlier conflicts and rebellion in ethnic terms as Han versus Hui. Yet having just defected to the Qing, he could hardly emphasize his ethnic allegiance as a Hui in this letter. So instead, in the next paragraph, he repeatedly used the term mumin in an effort to highlight the religious beliefs he shared with Du: "Given that all Muslims [mumin] are one family and that now two-thirds of Yunnan has negotiated peace the one [Muslim] family is the most important point. . . . Peace is really for the good of Muslims [Mumin] as a whole, with absolutely no desire to harm the intentions of the Western Yunnan [Muslims]."[108]

What is striking about this letter, aside from Ma's considerable bravado, is his effort to tack back and forth: he discusses the Hui in religious terms, and then he discusses them in ethnic terms, always distinguishing between the two identities, never conflating them. In the above extracts Ma carefully uses the term Hui when describing the Muslim Yunnanese as the victims of the early violence; yet in the second part of the letter he exclusively employs the term mumin. He deftly broaches this division between an ethnic Hui identity and a religious Muslim identity when explaining to Du why the Hui have thus far succeeded in their rebellion: "The reason we, the Hui, are winning all our battles is that we as mumin soldiers[109] are not fighting for [personal] reputation and money, but for Islam [jiaomen], therefore, God [zhenzhu] is protecting us."[110]

Ma Rulong's letter points to a disconnect between the terms Hui (Huimin) and Muslim (mumin), with the former referring to a group of distinct people and the latter to a community of believers. It is likely that in using mumin, Ma was hoping to persuade Du as a fellow Muslim to join him in a common action. Yet he employed Huimin when describing objectively the treatment of the Hui as an ethnic group at the hands of the Qing government.

Du Wenxiu replied less than a week after receiving Ma's letter. He categorically refuted each of Ma's appeals and amplified the rigid distinction between Huimin and mumin. In a direct rejoinder to Ma's plea for the two of them to act as "one Muslim family," he wrote: "[Obviously] all Muslims [mumin] under Heaven are one family, so why do we need to differentiate between different groups [within Islam]? Now [the Pingnan regime] is setting up the posts of governor, general, officers, commanders, etc., and although they are outwardly only titles, inwardly they are supporting all believers [jiaomen] so friends and families near and far all happily follow."[111]

Du then indicated that although he and Ma were part of one family as fellow Muslims, Ma's defection to the Qing was the reason why the Yunnan Hui were divided. To summarize, the correspondence between Ma and Du indicates clearly that both men distinguished between mumin and Huimin; this in turn sheds light on an important aspect of Hui identity in late imperial Yunnan. It does not, however, fully explain the ambiguity of the terminology they used—terminology that is still used today.

An example of this ambiguity relates to the term *Huijiao*. The Hui rarely use this term among themselves to refer to Islam. During his fieldwork among Muslim Chinese communities in the 1980s, Gladney "rarely heard Hui refer to themselves as Hui *jiao tu* [Hui religion disciples] and only occasionally as *Hui jiao*."[112] This parallels what we see in Hui documents written during the rebellion—again, Huijiao rarely appears. The question is, "Why not?" Part of the answer is that for the Yunnan Hui the term had a highly specific meaning. It did not simply refer to their religious beliefs; instead, it pointed to something entirely different from Islam—to a broader set of ethnic markers, traditions, and occupational tendencies that defined what it meant to be Hui.

Several years after this initial exchange of letters, during the peak of the Pingnan offensive in 1868, Ma Rulong wrote a letter to a senior Pingnan official in which he elucidated the distinction between being Hui and being Muslim. Besides restating his earlier arguments, he rather disingenuously called on the common religious beliefs of the Yunnan Hui past and present, hoping to persuade the Pingnan regime to give up its resistance:

Our ancestors were all subjects of the Qing, how could our generation try and change it? Would that not lead us to adopting a position of no loyalty or filial duty? More to the point, the Hui [huizhong] of every province are already obeying [the Qing], so that even if the whole of Yunnan were to rebel we are simply putting ourselves on the outside [of the Qing]. How could that hurt the court? What good will that achieve for my kind (wo jiao)? . . . That the religion of my fellow Hui [wo Hui zhijiao] have become more known since the Qing . . . we cannot say that the court is not treating our kind [wojiao] graciously.[113]

Throughout his appeal, Ma repeatedly invokes terms such as coreligionists (tongjiao), Muslims (mumin), and Hui people (Huizhong, Huimin). Especially revealing is Ma's use of wojiao and "the religion of my fellow Hui [wo Hui zhijiao]." Clearly, Ma was seeking to distinguish "my kind [wojiao]"— a phrase that in the traditional context would undoubtedly be translated as Islam—from "the religion of my fellow Hui [wo Hui zhijiao]." This somewhat clumsy turn of phrase is also significant in that grammatically speaking, it upholds the distinction between being Hui and being Muslim while indicating the strong links between the two. Finally, Ma, several paragraphs later, reinforces this ethnoreligious division when he chides the Pingnan Hui by stating: "How can I not know that the Hui of Western Yunnan are [part of] the Muslim family [mumin yijia]?"[114]

Untangling Du Wenxiu's and Ma Rulong's usage of the terms mumin and Hui may on the surface appear overly complicated. There are, however, several reasons why Hui probably does not simply refer to a Chinese subset within the larger global Muslim community. If Hui were simply Han Chinese who practiced Islam, one would expect this to be self-evident. At the very least, it hardly seems to merit Ma's sharp reply to Du that he obviously knew that the Hui of western Yunnan were part of the Muslim family (mumin yijia).[115]

Plainly stated, the Panthay Rebellion either exposed or accentuated the gap between being Hui and being Muslim—a gap that Ma Rulong tried desperately to paper over in order to bring about the surrender of Du and his Pingnan regime. This in turn raises a quite different question: If Ma Rulong and (as we will see) Du Wenxiu did not mean Islam when they used the term Huijiao, what did they mean?

Present in all of the letters examined above is the Chinese term jiao. Often glossed as "religion" in modern Chinese and as "teachings" in the early modern era, it was apparently employed in the multiethnic context of nineteenth-century Yunnan as shorthand for the broad cultural customs of a particular ethnic group.[116] During the rebellion, jiao assumed a meaning closer to what today might be referred to as "culture." This meaning of jiao appeared most unambiguously in the commonly used term *san jiao*, which served as an abbreviated or alternative way to denote Yunnan's "three cultures."

Within Yunnan the use of jiao in conjunction with an ethnonym tended to be employed, not pejoratively in distinguishing one group's beliefs from those of others, but rather as an open acknowledgment of the salient cultural and ethnic aspects of each ethnic grouping present in Yunnan. This meaning is most visible in the phrase san jiao, which was often used in China proper to denote the three main religions of the Han Chinese—Confucianism, Buddhism, and Daoism. In Yunnan it served as a formulaic reference denoting the "three cultures" (e.g., Han, Hui, Yi) of the region. Indeed, it seems that the term san jiao was applied along ethnic lines denoting all of the ethnic groups in Yunnan in the same manner that *sanyi*, or the three regions, referred to all of Yunnan.

Ma Rulong and Du Wenxiu both employed the term san jiao in their correspondence in an attempt to situate their actions as Hui within Yunnan's broader ethnic context and to justify their decisions as serving the interests of all Yunnanese regardless of their ethnicity. In his 1868 letter to Du, in emphasizing his desire for peace, Ma used san jiao when rationalizing his surrender to the Qing: "In 1862, I saw the peoples of the three cultures [san jiao] suffering great misery and killing [one another] and was afraid it would offend God. So I led the South and Eastern Hui [Huijiao] into the provincial capital to be pacified."[117]

Du, in his *Declaration of War*, a document posted throughout the Pingnan State in 1867, eloquently employed san jiao to promote the regime's multiethnic agenda in its battle against the Qing: "Ponder for a moment that in Yunnan province, the three cultures [san jiao] of the Han, Hui and yi [were peacefully] coexisting for [the past] one thousand years. . . . [But] ever since the Manchu Qing dynasty was founded my people have been mistreated for two hundred years."[118]

Du's formulation explicitly designated the groups constituting the "three cultures" as Han, Hui, and Yi while implying that these three groups—which formed the san jiao—represented a distinctive Yunnanese culture. In this context, it makes no sense to interpret san jiao as the "three religions"; when understood in the triadic ethnic formulation of Yunnan society, the term becomes far more intelligible.[119]

## LINES IN THE SAND

The debate between Du Wenxiu and Ma Rulong and the terms they employed highlight the complex formation of religious, ethnic, and political consciousness in China's late imperial period. Various labels did overlap and were often used to refer to the same people; furthermore, these terms were often referents for quite distinct identities. In any analysis of nineteenth-century Yunnan, an awareness of these distinctions is critical. With regard to the Hui, the Han Chinese often employed terms in ways that erased all distinctions among religious, ethnic, and regional identities. To equate the Han's refusal to differentiate these identities with an absence of Hui ethnic identity is to perpetuate that Han bias today.

These conflicting conceptions of ethnicity and religion were not simply a war of words. For the Dali regime to sustain itself as a political entity outside Qing authority, it would require more than a carefully constructed ideology. Du Wenxiu, his multiethnic followers, and the Dali Sultanate itself were always aware that their fate would depend in large part on events outside their independent realm. After the Taiping Rebellion was defeated they realized they could no longer sit back in western Yunnan and let other powers decide their fate. By now, Ma Rulong and Du Wenxiu knew that one was bound to vanquish the other. But who would it be?

## CHAPTER 9

# Ethereal Deeds: The Struggle to Reclaim Yunnan, 1867–1873

## The Pinnacle of Success:
## The Pingnan State, 1867–1869

In the spring of 1867, Du Wenxiu, the leader and commander-in-chief of the multiethnic Dali Kingdom, launched his troops from the city of Dali in a massive assault on Kunming, the last major imperial stronghold in Yunnan Province. Five columns of troops spread out from north to south and attacked along an eastward trajectory with devastating effectiveness, capturing all towns they encountered. For nearly ten years, Dali had been the political, cultural, and commercial center of the Hui-led insurgency against the Qing dynasty. Over that time the rebels had slowly strengthened their control over much of eastern and southern Yunnan. Just over six months after opening their initial campaign in the east, Du's generals surrounded Kunming, trapping the bulk of the imperial army and leaving only a few of the province's easternmost prefectures under imperial control. For the next two years Du and his multiethnic allies were the undisputed masters of Yunnan.

In the spring and summer of 1867, with the Dali regime at the height of its power, Du Wenxiu issued three public decrees. The first was his *Proclamation from the Headquarters of the Generalissimo* (*shuaifu bugao*), which appealed for popular support for the sultanate's eastward campaign; the second was his *Declaration of War* (*shishi wen*); and the third and last was his *Summons to Arms* (*xingshi xiwen*). These three documents expressed clearly and emphatically the regime's ideological, military, and political objectives as well as its vision for an independent Yunnan.

All three decrees were crafted to raise broad support for the kingdom's final push to control the entire province and offered a forceful critique of Manchu rule in Yunnan. Instead of casting the rebellion as the expression of a specific ideology or religious creed, Du Wenxiu highlighted the erosion of moral righteousness under the Qing. Adopting the tone of a reluctant rebel, he justified the rebellion by detailing the Qing's many deviations from the proper role of Chinese emperors:

There is a saying that it takes a civil administration to keep the peace, and the military to stabilize the country. When the Five Emperors depended upon rituals and music to rule, the Three Kings had to fight to pacify all the land under Heaven. All men act in accordance with their conscience. The reason for this expedition is to chastise the Manchus who took our land for more than 200 years treating the people [*renmin*] as horses and ox, regarded life as expendable like the trees and grasses, injured my brothers, and tormented the Hui.[1]

Du's statement denotes a marked shift from the regime's earlier hope to free all of China from Qing rule. His declarations of 1867 reveal a hope to "achieve a smaller more remote success like that of the Nanzhao" and control only Yunnan.[2]

Du's change in goals likely stemmed from the Qing's recent victories over Hong Xiuquan and the Taiping rebels. He now felt compelled to frame his proclamations in specifically Yunnanese terms. More consistent with his statements early in the rebellion, he also underscored the province's panethnic nature. Thus in his *Summon to Arms* he portrayed the Qing as fomenting strife between ethnic groups:

Generalissimo Du of the foot-soldiers and cavalry is leading an expedition in five routes to recover of the whole realm of Dian [Yunnan] to expel cruelty and to alleviate the good and lawful. . . . In the province of Dian-nan [Yunnan], the Hui, the Han, and the non-Han have been living among one another for over a thousand years. Friendly towards each other, helping one another in times of need, how could there be divisions between [us]? But since the Manchus usurped the throne for more than two hundred years, our people have been maltreated.[3]

French explorer Louis de Carné intuited Dali's revised territorial aspirations when he noted that peace could be secured if the Qing "would accept Yunnan, as the boundaries to the independent kingdom which [Du] aspires to establish."[4]

The proclamations emanating from Dali reflected more than simply pro-Yunnan and anti-Qing sentiments. They underscore just how deft Du Wenxiu was at promoting his vision of an independent and multiethnic Yunnan. In his *Declaration of War*, he noted: "The army has three purposes: first we must root out the Manchus, then conciliate the Han and, thirdly, weed out the wicked [collaborators]."[5] In his decrees, Du consistently emphasized the central fact of Yunnan's multiethnic population and that ethnic tolerance would be a cornerstone of his regime.

Du was aware of the danger that the rebellion might be perceived as simply a Han-versus-Hui conflict, so in his proclamations he carefully articulated a message that would attract all Yunnanese. The clearest example of this was his *Summons to Arms*, in which he reminded the Yunnanese of the events that had provoked the rebellion and were making it drag on:

When the Shiyang Mine Incident erupted "all of the fish in the pond were affected."[6] Those who were strong turned violent and oppressive, those who were weak could find nary a mouse hole in which to hide. . . . Incompetent officials, exhausting all of their ruses, concocted policy on the fly. [They] acted in opposition to the correct principles; perversely, the murderer of a vice general [*xiezhen*] was promoted as vice general, and the murderer of a military commissioner was promoted as military commissioner. Learned men withdrew and incompetents conspired. At first they helped Han massacre Hui, now they helped Hui massacre Han; then they helped Han kill Han, now they help Hui kill Hui.[7]

In other words, the conflict affected all Yunnanese, pitting good against evil and preying on the divisions between and within ethnic groups. To not fight would to be to succumb willingly to that evil; to fight would be to secure peace in the name of all that Yunnan represented.

This was the message of a reluctant warrior. In his *Declaration of War*, Du Wenxiu as generalissimo portrayed the final campaign as one against the imperialist forces, not against the Yunnanese themselves: "We are facing the other side with spear and lance only because of their opposition. . . . When we achieve victory in our attack there must be no looting, no coveting others' wealth and property, and no mistreatment of women."[8]

Together the three proclamations present a confident and determined government that was clear in its political and ideological stance. Under Du Wenxiu, it had survived militarily, it had founded a government with broad and strong popular support, and it was determined to build an independent Yunnan.

## The Dali Sultanate's Final Offensive: 1867–1868

Dali's military offensive of May 1867 was an all-out attack on eastern and southern Yunnan. It is unclear why Du and his council chose this moment to launch the campaign. Earlier in the year, Ma Rulong and his fellow Hui officer Yang Zhenpeng had led Qing forces west toward Dali. Perhaps Du had waited for the imperial forces to be drawn out of their defensive positions in and around Kunming. Perhaps the imperial offensive coincided with plans already laid by Dali's generals. Or perhaps it was—as some suggest—that news of Governor-General Lao Chongguang's sudden death in late February had reached Dali.[9] What *is* clear is that by early July 1867, Du's armies, "several tens of thousands of soldiers," were crushing all the imperial forces in their path.[10]

The westward offensive met little sustained resistance at first. Each of Du's sixteen top generals had been assigned objectives in a coordinated

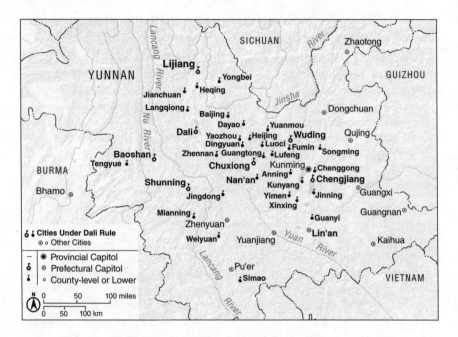

MAP 9.1. Cities under Dali or Hui Control, 1867–1868

main thrust toward central Yunnan. Together, they overwhelmed the Qing outposts. Seeking not to repeat the mistakes of Qing attacks on Dali, the sultanate went to great lengths to avoid overextending its supply lines. Instead of relying entirely on caravans from Dali, its armies employed artisans at designated cities along the route to make gunpowder and other items essential to the offensive.[11]

Dali's strategy also hoped to coax those Hui officers under Ma Rulong to shift their allegiance to Dali. According to Émile Rocher: "Emissaries from the sultan of Dali took letters to officials in districts [under imperial control] where Hui were in command, exhorting them to join the ranks under his banner, which would in the near future be floating over all the province. Seduced by this vision which assured them power, as well as by the fact they were of the same religion, many among them joined the rebels."[12]

This strategy bore fruit almost immediately. Only days after the campaign began, two key Hui commanders, He Guoan and Yang Xianzhi, surrendered the western Yunnan city of Dayao to the rebels and joined its eastward campaign.[13] A steady string of defections followed as the armies advanced eastward.

As the main column of the Dali forces approached Kunming, the rate of defections escalated dramatically. The first to go over to Du's side were Ma Rulong's close associates, Yang Zhenpeng and Tian Qingyu. By covertly signaling their intentions in advance, the Pingnan army easily captured Jinning and Chenggong without a battle.[14] Only six months after leaving Dali, rebel forces began to pour onto the plain surrounding Kunming (see Map 9.1). As they took up their positions, three more Hui officials took advantage of Ma Rulong's absence from Kunming to join Du Wenxiu's forces. Du bestowed on each the title of general (*dasi*) and pressed the assault on Kunming.

CHERISHING AN AUDIENCE FROM AFAR

By the spring of 1868 the Dali regime and its non-Han allies controlled cities from the Tibetan border to Tengyue on the Burmese border and from Pu'er in the south to Xundian in the northeast—more than thirty county or prefectural seats in all. His troops now surrounded the provincial capital and had defeated every major imperial force in the province.

Around this time, two groups of Europeans, one French and the other British, were traveling through rebel-controlled Yunnan. The French Mekong Expedition, led by Francis Garnier[15] and Louis de Carné, entered Yunnan from the south in the autumn of 1867 and eventually reached Dali by way of southern Sichuan. The British group under Colonel Edward Sladen entered Yunnan from Burma in May 1868 and spent several weeks in the southwestern town of Tengyue, which the Panthays controlled. Neither group knew about the other's presence and objectives. Both met and talked to top officials from the Dali regime and were later able to offer extraordinary insights into the goals and achievements of the twelve-year sultanate.

The two expeditions were organized under distinctly different auspices but had similar goals. The leaders of both sought most of all to learn more about a regime that had carved out an independent kingdom and fended off Qing attacks for more than a decade. Throughout their travels in Yunnan in 1867 and 1868, they observed a mature state at the height of its powers. Yet both expeditions were driven by more than innocent curiosity. They also wanted to evaluate the commercial potential of Yunnan and to ascertain Dali's position vis-à-vis the growing European presence on Yunnan's southern border. Finally, each group hoped to travel to Dali and meet Du Wenxiu, who remained a mystery in the West.

In contrast, the Europeans posed little mystery to Du Wenxiu and his officials, who seem to have been well informed about the growing European presence in Southeast Asia. Du had been sending trading missions to Burma, so his regime would surely have been aware that France and Britain were a growing presence in the region. There is also evidence that the Dali regime was in contact with a number of Southeast Asians, attracting individuals with technical, religious, and linguistic expertise.[16] Even more intriguing is that the sultanate may have employed European military advisors. Many members of the two expeditions reported rumors that five, fourteen, or sixteen "Europeans" were employed by the Dali court.[17] These rumors are difficult to assess; the foreigners may not have been Europeans at all but, as French explorer Garnier suggests, "probably Burmans or Hindoos, for their skin was nearly black," or even Malays.[18] That said, it is not inconceivable that Europeans, Indians, and Southeast Asians traveled to the Dali Kingdom since Italians, French, Irish, British, Filipinos, and Indians had at various points aided the Taipings.[19] If Europeans did ever serve the sultanate, their secret remained well kept.

Whether or not the Dali court knew why the European missions were on its territory, Du Wenxiu realized they might be powerful allies against the Qing. Du's attentiveness to the regime's international position is rarely acknowledged, yet it was evident in the different receptions the two expeditions enjoyed. Even before arriving in Yunnan, the British expedition had requested and received permission from the sultanate to travel to Dali. The French expedition had stumbled into the province in search of the source of the Mekong and was completely unaware of the rebellion; as a consequence, Du treated its members with far more suspicion.

The French Mekong Expedition was the first of the two European missions to enter Yunnan in 1867. On arriving in Kunming in late December 1867, its leaders met Ma Rulong and Ma Dexin and received assistance from French missionaries residing in the capital.[20] After resting for several weeks they asked permission to travel to Dali. Because of Du's military offensive, this was denied them (and derided as extremely foolhardy). They did, however, procure a letter of introduction, in Arabic and Chinese, from Ma Dexin. With this, they decided to attempt the journey without authorization. To evade Dali's offensive in central Yunnan, they were compelled to travel north through Dongchuan, then west along the upper Yangtze before dropping south toward Dali.

On the basis of Ma Dexin's letter, the French were graciously welcomed by all local Panthay officials along their route. In perhaps the most bizarre twist of their journey, they met another French Catholic missionary in a remote village a day's journey from Dali. Father Leguilcher had been living clandestinely in Dali-controlled territory since the beginning of the rebellion. After listening to their plan (and fearing for their safety), he agreed to escort them to the city and act as their translator.[21] On February 29, 1868, the French explorers, led by Leguilcher, arrived at the fortifications of Shangguan, which sealed the upper pass leading to the Dali plain. After deliberating for a full forty-eight hours over how to receive the rather sudden visitors, Du Wenxiu and his council gave the French permission to proceed down the valley to Dali.[22]

Early in the morning of March 2, 1868, they passed through Dali's massive city gate and were escorted to Du Wenxiu's residence. As word spread, a growing throng of people began to press around the Europeans, intent on getting a look at them. In the confusion, a guard snatched the hat from the head of one of the French soldiers so that Du, who was watching from above, could better see his face. The Frenchman, unsure and angered, "punished this insolence with a blow that bloodied the face of the aggressor."[23] To prevent further incidents, Du ordered the Frenchmen to be quickly escorted to lodgings just outside the city walls.

Soon after they settled in, a member of Du's council visited the French to ask them why they were in Dali. On being told they wanted an audience with the sultan, he informed them that audiences with Du Wenxiu followed specific ceremonial rules. Above all, every individual coming before Du was required to "genuflect three times before the Sultan"; also, no one would be allowed to carry a firearm.[24] The French officers refused to perform the *koutou* before any foreign sovereign. The official agreed that in lieu of performing the *koutou* they would only have to show Du the same respect they would offer their own sovereign; however, they still had to pledge not to bring firearms with them.

The following morning, the officials returned and told them that Du Wenxiu wished to see only Father Leguilcher. Leaving his companions behind, the Catholic priest was escorted to an audience hall, where two imposing cannons were permanently trained on the main doorways, primed and loaded to prevent any attempt on Du's life. As he entered, he found the sultan waiting for him. Throughout the three-hour audience, the priest remained standing. Du peppered him with questions: How long had the priest lived on territory controlled by Dali? What was the mission of the French explorers? What authority did they have from their own government to travel to Dali? When Leguilcher told him he had lived in Yunnan for more than fourteen years, Du displayed his characteristic aplomb by informing the priest: "Then you are my subject." Clearly, he took this declaration quite seriously, since he followed it with an offer for Leguilcher to remain in western Yunnan and assume a post in the Pingnan government.

Du also displayed a startling awareness of and tolerance toward Leguilcher's Christian beliefs. At one point he informed Leguilcher: "I have read your religious works and I have found nothing inappropriate." Du then informed him that "Muslims and Christians are brothers."[25]

The sultan was less pleased with the missionary's role in helping the French expedition reach Dali. Displaying a nuanced understanding of Yunnan's geopolitical importance, Du berated the missionary for "introducing into Dali people of their sort . . . who come to map the roads, measure the distances and sketch the countryside with the intention of occupying it."[26] Obviously concerned about the French expedition's territorial interests in Yunnan, he ordered Leguilcher to "tell them that they can help themselves to all the territory along the Lancangjiang [Mekong] River but that they are obliged to stop at the borders of my kingdom."[27] As the audience concluded, he ordered the priest to "take the French to the edge of my state, and tell them to never come back."[28] The following day the French were escorted to the upper pass. From there, under cover of night, they began their journey back to Qing-controlled Yunnan.

Based largely on this one incident, Du Wenxiu has been portrayed as having had minimal understanding of or desire for relations with France and Britain. He has been represented as starkly antiforeign. In perhaps the best-known analysis of Du's foreign policy, Chinese scholar Tian Rukang concluded that "Du resisted foreign intervention in the Muslim rebellion and expelled foreign expeditions from rebel-held territory."[29] Yet this seems not to have been the case.

Thomas Cooper, who was in Yunnan in 1868 at the same time as the French, offered perhaps the most commonly given reason why Du Wenxiu gave the French an unfriendly reception. He posits that a monetary loan arranged by Garnier and de Carné while they were in Kunming had disastrous consequences for them when they arrived in Dali. In return for the funds, which they desperately needed, Ma Rulong asked them to send him a shipment of arms when they returned to Shanghai. It seems that this deal was not made in secret. When Cooper was in Weixi, a Hui merchant told him that "news of this proposal had at once been sent to the Emperor Du Wenxiu and Lieutenant Garnier was doomed but for the timely help of the missionaries."[30] Du was far better informed of their actions than the French realized at the time.

By the French explorers' own accounts, Du Wenxiu seems to have probed their intentions quite carefully. Once they arrived in Dali, one of the first questions Du's officials asked them was whether they had been "expressly sent by their sovereign to Dali."[31] To this they replied—perhaps too candidly—that when they left Indochina neither they nor their government had any knowledge of the rebellion, so how could they have been sent to meet with Du? The French assumed this was an innocent question; in fact, Du had already been in contact with Sladen's mission from Bhamô and was likely asking himself what opportunities the French might offer his regime—and what threats they might pose.[32]

The above scenario would be entirely speculative except that Father Leguilcher's superior in Kunming, when writing to the mission's directors in Paris several months later, mentioned that Du encouraged him to "return [to Dali] since we have also learned of an English commission which is making its way to Dali from Ava, Bhamo, etc."[33] If this is true, Du was acutely aware of events far beyond Yunnan and was carefully considering possible contacts with Western governments.

Sladen's mission experienced a far different reception. Having arranged their visit the previous year, on May 23, 1868, they were greeted at the Dali–Burma border by a multiethnic escort of "Panthay and Kakheyn [Karen] guards."[34] The following day they were guided to Tengyue, an important entrepôt, where the governor extended them an official welcome. During their visit the "governor stated that the Sultan had been pleased to hear of our intended visit to Tengyue"; however, because he could not guarantee their safety on the roads, they would not be allowed to continue to Dali.[35]

For the next six weeks, however, the British were free "to come and go as we liked."[36] In stark contrast to the cool reception the French had received in Dali, the local hosts treated the British—and their Indian soldiers, many of whom were Muslims—as honored guests. Despite the open friendliness displayed by both sides, very little actually came of Sladen's mission. The British never did obtain a commercial treaty, but they did come to an understanding with the governor over "the duties which should be levied on future caravans, and received letters expressive of the desire of the Panthay sultan's government to enter into friendly relations with our government and foster mutual trade."[37] In turn, the British supplied the governor with "two seals, wherewith to authenticate his future letters."[38]

Although its specific accomplishments were minimal, the mission laid the groundwork for future relations and left both sides content and hopeful. On their return, the mission's ranking officers, Sladen and Anderson, submitted reports which proposed that British authorities begin promoting trade with Dali. Just over a year after their return, on November 30, 1869, an assistant political agent was assigned the task of protecting those British merchants who were interested in trade with Dali.[39] The Sladen mission could not have known that even as its members walked through Tengyue's city gates to begin their return journey to Burma, Dali's military fortunes in eastern Yunnan were beginning to turn for the worse.

THE TURNING TIDE

In the spring of 1867, Ma Rulong's situation in Kunming remained bleak. Ma had staked his future on a Qing intervention in Yunnan that had yet to materialize. Two years earlier, in December 1865, an imperial censor had warned the court that "the only official in Yunnan's provincial capital was Ma Rulong. Cen Yuying was far away in Qujing. The Governor-General and Governor have not been in Yunnan for a long time."[40]

This of course was an understatement. In 1860, after Zhang Liangji was ordered to Beijing to be investigated, the only governor or governor-general who dared enter the province and take up his post in Kunming had been Governor-General Pan Duo. As if to confirm the fears of those who had refused to enter the province before him, Pan was assassinated only four months after arriving there. His death capped an amazing run of ineptitude, bad luck, and corruption among the province's top imperial representatives. Mary Wright's laconic summary of the pathetic performance of Yunnan's officials during the rebellion: "Among the governors-general and governors of the period, one was murdered, one was a suicide, one lost his mind, one refused to enter the province to take up his duties, and several had to be recalled for gross incompetence."[41] Except for Pan Duo's brief residence, between 1860 and 1866 no one occupied the governor-general's yamen in Kunming. The same was true for the office of governor: between 1863 and 1868, all appointees either refused to enter the province or were ordered to fight the Miao rebels in neighboring Guizhou (see Tables 9.1 and 9.2).

Ma Rulong's position improved slightly on March 21, 1866, when Governor-General Lao Chongguang finally entered Kunming. He had been appointed immediately after Pan Duo's death four years earlier but had refused to enter the province for nearly three years, only doing so when the court threatened him with dismissal. Lao and Ma quickly developed a constructive working relationship and began organizing a campaign against western Yunnan. Then, less than a year later, just as the campaign was set to begin its march westward, Lao suddenly fell ill. He died four days later, on February 21, 1867.[42]

With the loss of his key imperial patron, Ma Rulong and those Hui who had accepted Qing offices several years earlier once again came under suspicion from both the court and those anti-Hui elements still prevalent in Yunnan and neighboring provinces. Rumors spread that Lao had been murdered as part of a plot to keep the province under Hui control. Other reports suggested that the Hui "who could not pardon him for their humiliation at his hands . . . poisoned him."[43] These accounts were almost certainly the product of lingering bias and fertile imaginations.

There is little evidence that Lao was murdered. In response to rumors about poisoning, one commentator pointed out: "We should remember the important positions that many Muslims occupied [under Qing governance] and the good relations their leaders had with the viceroy [Lao] making it difficult to conceive of any interests that would [have made them] want him dead."[44] Such logic, however, was no impediment those who continued to suspect the motives of Ma Rulong and other Hui.

In all likelihood, Lao's death was no mystery; it was only bad timing. According to Father Fenouil, who met with the governor-general the evening

## TABLE 9.1
### Tenures of Office: Yun-Gui Governor-General

| Name | Tenure of office | Period in Kunming (months) | Reasons for leaving office |
|---|---|---|---|
| Hengchun | 1855 (January)–1857 (July) | 13 | Suicide |
| Wu Zhenyu | 1857 (August)–1859 (January) | 17 | Poor health |
| Zhang Liangji | 1859 (January)–1860 (November) | 20 | Called to Beijing |
| Liu Yuanjing | 1860 (November)–1861 (August) | 0 | Dismissed (refused to enter province) |
| Fuji | 1861 (August)–1861 (December) | 0 | Dismissed (refused to enter province) |
| Pan Duo | 1861 (December)–1863 (March 4) | 4 | Assassinated |
| Lao Chongguang | 1863 (June)–1867 (March) | 11 | Died in office |
| Zhang Kaisong | 1867 (May)–1868 (March) | 0 | Dismissed (refused to enter province) |
| Liu Yuezhao | 1868 (March)–1873 (October) | 48 | Dismissed |

SOURCE: Guo Tingyi, *Jindai Zhongguo Shishi Rizhi*, and Wei Hsiumei, *Qingchao Zhiguanbiao*

## TABLE 9.2
### Tenures of Office: Yunnan Governors

| Name | Tenure of office | Period in Kunming (months) | Reasons for leaving office |
|---|---|---|---|
| Shuxing'a | 1855 (January)–1857 (July) | 30 | Called to Beijing (died en route) |
| Sang Chunrong | 1857 (July)–1858 (July) | 12 | Called to Beijing |
| Zhang Liangji | 1858 (July)–1858 (July) | 0 | Never assumed office because of illness |
| Xu Zhiming | 1858 (July)–1863 (April) | 57 | Dismissed |
| Jia Hongzhao | 1863 (April)–1864 (September) | 0 | Dismissed (refused to enter province) |
| Lin Hongnian | 1864 (September)–1866 (March) | 0 | Dismissed (refused to enter province) |
| Liu Yuezhao | 1866 (March)–1868 (March) | 0 | In Guizhou fighting Miao rebels. |
| Ceng Yuying | 1868 (March)–1876 (April) | (Often on military campaigns) | Promoted to acting Gov. Gen. in 1873 |

SOURCE: Guo Tingyi, *Jindai Zhongguo Shishi Rizhi*, and Wei Hsiumei, *Qingchao Zhiguanbiao*

before his death, Lao had been unable to talk. When queried about his illness, he had "placed his hand underneath his heart indicating that was the area of his pain."[45] This led the missionary to suspect a stroke or heart attack as the cause of death. Even so, the campaign to remove Ma Rulong from his position began almost at once.

On March 10, word of Lao's death reached Governor Liu Yuezhao, who was more than twenty days distant in Guizhou. Although he lacked any firsthand knowledge of the circumstances of Lao's death and had never even entered Yunnan, he immediately dispatched a memorial maligning Ma Rulong.[46] In his memorial he criticized Ma and the other pacified Hui. Reverting to hackneyed stereotypes, he told the court that "the Hui disposition is outwardly loyal but inwardly plotting evil intentions."[47] Yet he also asked to remain in Guizhou, arguing that situation there was more urgent than the one in Yunnan.[48]

The emperor's rescript suggests he was predisposed to Liu's anti-Hui stance. In it he expressed concern that the provincial capital had no ranking official now that Lao was dead. Thus it was vital "that the [newly appointed] Yun-Gui Governor-General enter the capital."[49] On this front, however, the court made little headway. The replacement for Lao, an official named Zhang Kaisong, made excuses for more than half a year not to enter the province before finally being dismissed.[50]

In the interval, Ma Rulong was not aiding his own cause. In late July the court received reports that Ma's army was in full retreat. In his first foray westward, he had encountered the full force of Du Wenxiu's offensive; not only that, but his troops were dying from the plague in large numbers.[51] By early October all imperial forces in western Yunnan were either under attack or in retreat from Du's offensive. By December 1867 Kunming itself was within striking distance of the Dali armies.[52] Within months it had become extremely unlikely that Ma could lead the projected western campaign. He had lost Lao Chongguang, his primary imperial supporter, and the Hui officers on whom his military future depended were deserting in ever increasing numbers.

Individually, Ma Rulong remained resolutely loyal to the Qing. There are no indications whatsoever that he contemplated joining Du Wenxiu's government. In his communications from the period, he praised recent Qing admissions of past wrongs and chastised those Hui who had turned their backs on the court's generous offer of clemency. By now he also realized that because he continued to resist, most Hui leaders would forever consider him a betrayer of his people.

Ma Rulong's growing isolation from the Hui did not go unnoticed by the Qing. In memorials dating back to 1864, imperial officials noted that his own troops were growing increasing hostile toward him and suggested that even Ma Dexin had opposed Ma Rulong's acceptance of the policy of "using Hui to fight other Hui."[53] Ma Rulong replied to these charges by describing Du Wenxiu's crimes as far worse, "adhering neither to state laws [guofa] nor the teachings of the Qur'an [jingdian]."[54] By ardently promoting the Qing and bolstering his position vis-à-vis the court, he was undermining whatever leverage he had among his fellow Hui.

As Ma Rulong lost support among the Hui, his usefulness to the empire declined. The Qing now saw him as an increasingly isolated leader of troops whose loyalty was questionable, so they began looking for other ways to counter the grave threat posed by Du Wenxiu.[55] By the winter of 1867, Ma Rulong had no chance left of leading the Qing to victory. He would continue to play a vital role, but never again would the court be tempted by his strategy of "using Hui to defeat the Hui." Instead, the court would turn to another man, who had been rising rapidly through the military and civil ranks. His name: Cen Yuying.

## THE RISE OF CEN YUYING

Cen Yuying was a native of neighboring Guangxi Province. In the wake of Taiping uprisings in 1850, he had formed a militia and quelled several minor insurrections around his hometown, Xilin. His victories were sufficiently worthy that the governor-general recommended he be assigned to the post of assistant magistrate.[56] Soon after the Panthay Rebellion broke out in 1856, Cen led his militia into Yunnan to help the Qing put down the unrest there. He participated in the first imperial campaign on Dali in 1857—for which he received a commendation from the throne—but it was not until 1859 that his military prowess began to have an impact on the imperial army's operations in Yunnan.[57]

Having returned to his home county in 1858 to recruit more men, he reentered Yunnan in 1859 reinvigorated and heading a formidable militia of several thousand men. In their first engagement, his troops overpowered a group of Hui insurgents occupying the county seat of Yiliang, twenty miles east of Kunming.[58] After capturing the city and executing the rebel leader, Cen was rewarded with the office of acting magistrate of Yiliang. The following year he joined forces with the acting provincial military commander, Lin Ziqing, in a successful attack on the departmental seat of Lunan, a day's march south of Yiliang.

These two quick victories at a time of imperial defeats earned Cen the praise of Governor Xu Zhiming, who in 1861 promoted him to acting prefect of Chengjiang, a wealthy prefecture southwest of Kunming. Cen's rapid rise continued when at Xu's behest he helped orchestrate Ma Rulong's final surrender to the Qing in 1862. Soon after that he was appointed acting provincial judge. Thus in less than three years he had made himself a key figure in the imperial's government's desperate efforts to retain control of the province.

The following year Cen sealed his high reputation both in the province and in the court by reacting quickly to Pan Duo's assassination. Joining forces with Ma Rulong, he took Kunming back from the rebels and crushed what had been the most serious threat to Qing authority up to that point in the rebellion.[59] Although they had retaken Kunming together, Cen Yuying and Ma Rulong would have a strained relationship for the rest of the rebellion. Neither man ever openly expressed his sentiments, but it is telling that they only rarely based their operations in the same city. Ma Rulong remained in Kunming; Cen based himself in the eastern Yunnan city of Qujing. It is probable that like many other Han residents of Yunnan, Cen questioned the imperial court's strategy of allowing a Hui to dominate the province's political and military affairs.[60]

The situation had not changed three years later, in 1866, when Lao Chongguang entered the province as governor-general. This is not to suggest that Cen suffered in the eyes of the court or fellow officials because of his frosty demeanor toward Ma Rulong. In his memorials to the throne, Lao spoke highly of Cen's military accomplishments and strategies for the future. Yet Lao's evaluation of the situation made it clear that he believed Ma Rulong, not Cen, would be key to ending the rebellion in Yunnan.[61] Lao was basing his strategy on the belief that sending an imperial force led by a Han Chinese would only exacerbate ethnic tensions and that Ma, as a Hui, would be in a stronger position to persuade Du Wenxiu and his generals to surrender.

A few months after arriving in Kunming, Lao Chongguang wrote to the throne announcing a new military strategy for Yunnan and Guizhou: Ma Rulong would lead the campaign against western Yunnan, and Cen Yuying would be sent to suppress the Miao rebels in neighboring Guizhou.[62] These two campaigns would set the course for the remaining career of each man, although neither could have known it at the time.

In April 1866, Cen led five thousand of his best troops out of his base at Qujing, northward toward Zhenxiong, in the notoriously unstable area where the borders of Sichuan, Guizhou, and Yunnan all touch. Over the next several months, Cen crushed the new uprising. He then crossed into Guizhou Province.[63]

For more than a decade, Miao rebel activity in northwestern Guizhou had been centered around two towns, Zhugongjing and Haimugu. Repeated efforts to take these towns from the rebels had failed.[64] Cen perceived the main problem of the past pacification efforts in Guizhou as suffering from there being "more than one authority, so that the armies [in the past] did not know whose orders to follow."[65] Cen confidently added that "by leading a Yunnan Army [*dianjun*], I will need less than 120 days wipe out the [rebel] camp."[66]

Cen launched his campaign against the Miao strongholds in March 1867, employing a broad array of tactics, including night attacks and ruses, and sometimes motivating his men by joining the fighting.[67] One after another, the rebel strongholds fell to his army. In early June, only four days after his self-imposed time limit, he captured the last rebel garrison. Yet he had little time to savor his victories: he received word of Du Wenxiu's victories in western Yunnan and immediately returned to that province.[68]

### THE FINAL SIEGE OF KUNMING

While Cen was returning from the wilds of northwestern Guizhou, the situation in Kunming became desperate. By the time the French Mekong expedition arrived in the capital in December 1867, the city was already destitute. "The misery is substantial in Kunming," Carné reported. "There is a considerable number of beggars dirty and gaunt, dressed, even with the cold, in only a few tatters of felt who wander the streets."[69] Du's troops still had not reached Kunming when the French left two weeks later; even so, they had been told that "at any moment Kunming could be taken."[70]

Perhaps Cen Yuying was still nursing his resentment of Ma Rulong, for he made slow progress toward Kunming even though an attack was imminent.[71] By July 1867 he was back at his base in Qujing. Six months later he still had not arrived in Kunming, citing the need to protect eastern Yunnan from further violence. Then in early 1868 the Dali armies began to close in on Kunming from all sides. In the north, Dali General Yang Rong took Fumin; in the west, General Liu Cheng drove the Qing defenders onto the plains of Kunming; in the south, a multipronged attack captured Yimen, Kunyang, and Chengjiang.[72]

In early March 1868 the Dali armies began to close in on Kunming itself, systematically looting and burning every village and small town within a three- to five-mile radius of the capital. By mid-March, Du's commanders had completely surrounded the city. Only one minor road leading east from Kunming allowed intermittent contact between Cen and officials inside the capital. Conditions in the city deteriorated from bad to worse: food was in short supply, diseases were spreading, and Hui were deserting to the Dali army.

In a memorial to the emperor (written from a safe distance—he was presently at the Yunnan–Guizhou border), Governor Liu Yuezhao described the plight of Kunming's defenders: "As of right now, the rebels threaten every prefecture and district near and around the capital. The capital itself is already completely besieged, and because we have run out of food and pay rations [for the troops]."[73] The French missionary Fenouil, who was actually residing in the city, wrote to a friend that "the war continues to ravage the capital and the area all around it; the plague holds sway, and the famine begins . . . [and] the Red Banner [Imperial army] is in retreat while the Muslims make new progress every day."[74]

At its peak, the Hui controlled more than thirty county and prefectural capitals, including Xundian and Songming to the east of Kunming (see Map 9.1).[75] It is estimated that Du Wenxiu had mobilized all eighteen of his generals and was leading between 200,000 to 250,000 soldiers, almost all of whom were involved in the siege of Kunming.[76]

To make matters worse for Ma Rulong and his imperial allies, Du was succeeding well at convincing Hui officials, so vital to the city's defense, to defect to him. According to Ma's close associate, Ma Futu, Ma had 15,000 troops who were personally loyal to him.[77] Yet numerous other sources indicate that many of Ma's Hui leaders were beginning to defect as well as plotting his fall. In mid-March, hoping to inspire mass defections, four of Ma's closest associates devised a plan to assassinate Ma. The plot was foiled at the last moment. Had it succeeded, the city would have been handed over to the rebels.[78] Émile Rocher suggests that when this plot came to light more than forty Hui were killed by Ma in a purge of Hui officials whose loyalties were suspect. Ma had the four leaders taken into custody and summarily beheaded. Their heads were displayed along the city walls as a warning to others.[79]

Reports from these days suggest that the executions did much to soothe the general public's growing angst regarding Ma Rulong's loyalty. Father Fenouil wrote to a colleague that Ma seemed truly loyal to the Qing and was executing those Hui who tried to revolt against him.[80] If Fenouil and other residents of Kunming felt more confident about Ma Rulong, the court and other provincial officials did not. They were sure the time had come to try new tactics. Sensing this shift, Cen Yuying made his move to break the siege of Kunming.

## FIGHTING AGAINST THE TIDE

Strongly motivating the court's search for a new solution at this juncture was the fact that by the end of 1867 neither Yun-Gui governor-general Zhang Kaisong nor Yunnan governor Liu Yuezhao had shown any intention of entering Yunnan. To remedy this, the emperor cashiered Zhang and promoted Liu to governor-general. Cen Yuying was appointed governor.

Cen was already in Yunnan when he received his promotion, which made him the first Yunnan governor to actually be in the province since Xu Zhiming's recall to Beijing five years earlier. The promotion and renewed pressure from the emperor prompted Liu to move into the northeastern corner of Yunnan, but he would not enter Kunming for nearly another eighteen months. Chongshi, an imperial official in Sichuan, wrote a scathing report on Liu's behavior suggesting that "after [his] promotion he became arrogant and conceited, making no plans. His memorials exaggerated the situation making it appear far better than it was and saying he had achieved military victories, [when in fact] the provincial capital was under siege and the rebels had the upper hand."[81]

Cen's promotion and the court's reluctance to push Liu any further indicated a decisive shift in the court's handling of the rebellion. By appointing an individual whose experience was based almost entirely on his military prowess in the far corner of the empire, the imperial court was acknowledging the ineffectiveness of court-appointed officials. If the court was hoping to finally see some results, instead of the inaction that had typified Cen's predecessors, they did not have to wait long.

In March 1868, less than a month after the Dali army encircled Kunming, Cen Yuying launched an ambitious plan to free the provincial capital and central Yunnan. He divided his army—now well over ten thousand strong—into three smaller forces. The first of these marched due east toward Kunming by way of Yanglin and Dabanqiao in order to strengthen the tenuous supply lines to the capital. The second, led by the brightest and most ruthless of Cen's young military officials, Yang Yuke, made a carefully executed sweep to the north, by way of Dongchuan, to the Sichuan border town of Huili. From there, Yang's force would be able to circle back on the Dali troops occupying the strategically important towns of Yuanmou and Dingyuan, to the north of Kunming.[82] Cen Yuying led the third prong of the attack along a more southern trajectory toward the capital by way of Chenggong.[83]

All three prongs of the attack achieved their objectives with surprising speed. Yang dashed north, winning successive victories at Yuanmou, Wuding, and Luquan.[84] On May 18, 1868, his group took the last Hui-controlled town along the vital northern supply route, allowing vital supplies to flow freely to Kunming.[85] Cen followed these victories with a strong thrust to the southeast that broke through the Dali lines and opened communication and supply routes to Yiliang and Chenggong to the east.[86] On November 19, 1868, Cen took up residence in the governor's yamen in Kunming (his superior, Governor-General Liu Yuezhao, would not enter the capital for another eleven months).[87]

Not all of these victories were permanent. In the twelve months following the successful campaigns of Yang and Cen, the two sides traded control over half a dozen towns. In January 1869 a French missionary wrote that the two armies "take and retake the towns [and] in the meanwhile everyone suffers."[88] But by forcing Du Wenxiu's generals to respond to attacks in areas away from Kunming, Cen was weakening Du's massive offensive and permanently breaking the siege of Kunming, which had been the main objective of the rebel forces. As provincial judge Song Tingchun suggested in a memorial to the emperor that spring: "At present the main body of the Western rebel's forces are all committed to the attack on the capital. Because their supplies are in short supply and their soldier's pay due, maintaining such a high level of pressure on the capital will be difficult, and for the long term impossible."[89]

The Dali forces faced other woes besides military ones. With the coming of spring, plague and other diseases began to thin out the ranks and dramatically reduce the rebels' fighting readiness. Among the victims was Du Wenxiu's best general, Ma Guochun.[90] Simply stated, the Dali forces were beginning to lose a war of attrition against the Qing, who were now bringing their considerable reserves to the field.

### THE LAST BATTLES, 1869–1874

The failure of Dali's eastern offensive did not lead to a collapse in popular support or political stature. Over much of the next three years, Du's military commanders retained control of profitable trade routes and mines. Several important cities, such as Chuxiong, Lijiang, and Chengjiang, changed hands no fewer than three times after 1868. That said, in the final years of the rebellion, the Dali forces won few victories and were in almost constant retreat.

By 1869 most of central Yunnan had been cleared of Dali forces. Cen Yuying, Yang Yuke, Ma Rulong, and other imperial generals now slowly began to push west. Yang attacked along a northern course toward Dali, retaking the lucrative salt wells at Baiyanjing and Heiyanjing as well as the district seats of Yuanmou and Dayao. He bypassed Dali, which was heavily defended, and continued north to Langqiong and Dengchuan.[91] Cen pushed west along the trunk road between Kunming and Dali, taking Guangtong, Chuxiong, Nan'an, Midu, Dingyuan, Lufeng, Xinxing, and Binchuan in the last six months of 1869.[92] Ma Rulong drove south into his former sphere of influence, battling not only the rebels but also recalcitrant Han Chinese.

In many respects, these victories were less a reflection of improved military tactics and more a result of the Qing court finally being able to support its officials in Yunnan. Up until 1869, the rebellion had been fought mainly with resources available in the province. There had been minimal outside leadership or, for that matter, interference. Now, however, the court in Beijing was beginning to regain its political and economic equilibrium. More to the point, the Taiping Rebellion was finally over, so the court could turn its attention to the Panthay Rebellion and begin applying its financial, military, and political resources to ending that conflict.

A telling indication of this shift was the dramatic rise in funds available to the provincial leadership. Between 1862 and 1866, Yunnan had received a total of 134,000 *liang* in additional court-ordered funds from other provinces.[93] In contrast, in 1868 alone the province received 220,000 *liang*. This rate remained steady until 1872, when it increased to an average of almost 800,000 *liang*.[94] In addition, Cen Yuying implemented a system whereby the payments—mainly from other provinces—were made monthly through those provinces' respective trading firms (*shanghao*) in Chongqing. This system simplified the payment procedure in a single stroke, ensured higher rates of payment, and normalized the schedule for depositing revenues in the provincial coffers.[95]

Cen's successful campaign against Dali was based on several other critical factors. In particular, he developed a more dependable fighting force. In March 1869 he wrote to the emperor that to attack Dali with the largest possible number of soldiers was not always the most efficient use of the province's fiscal and military resources: "The total number of professional soldiers and militia number over 80,000, but they are not competent. I intend to cull out the top 60,000 to use in my attack against the rebels. To do this I must select the 60,000 who are the strongest, not those who are old or weak."[96]

Cen grouped these soldiers into three armies and sent them on a three-pronged attack through southern Yunnan, central Yunnan, and northern Yunnan. He assigned the bulk of his soldiers to the central army and appointed his most trusted and successful officer, Yang Yuke, to lead this force.

Furthermore, the provincial leaders were clearly aware of the dramatic advantages to be gained from applying the latest military tactics and technologies.[97] Both sides of the rebellion understood the benefits of European rifles and cannons.[98] Governor Lin Hongnian, as early as 1865, memorialized the emperor requesting foreign rifles and for "thirty or forty soldiers to come to Yunnan and train the forces here [to fight Dali]."[99] Du Wenxiu is said to have looked toward Burma for arms. According to Émile Rocher: "The Muslims, more experimental than the Chinese in the art of war, have gotten from Burma through caravans a large quantity of firearms . . . of all kinds and origins. These arms have for some time been surpassed in Europe, and were sold by the English to the Burmese who in turn sold them to the rebels."[100]

It seems that Ma Rulong was better supplied than either the imperial forces or the rebels. Louis de Carné recorded that "the courts of his palace were full of piles of lances; the corridors, of sacks of balls, buck-shot and long-barreled muskets. His armory, which he made us visit afterwards, still more astonished us; for it was well stocked with European arms—double-barreled guns, breech-loaders, rifled carbines, revolvers, and pistols of all kinds. . . . He maintains, at Shanghai and Canton, agents who supply him with what he wants."[101]

The last years of the rebellion tended to be fought less along fast-moving fronts, where firearms might have played a major part, than in extended sieges of walled cities. During these sieges, "five or six pieces of artillery with several gunners who knew how to use them" were employed with some success.[102]

Several accounts indicate that Cen borrowed the expertise of several Europeans—including Rocher, who traveled to Yunnan to cast three or four cannons.[103] Yet there is little evidence that this increased firepower gave the imperial forces much of an upper hand. Indeed, most European accounts suggest that cannons were given too little to do too late in the affair.[104] They were sometimes useful when a siege had dragged on for many months, but they were unwieldy and difficult to transport over Yunnan's mountainous terrain; thus they were employed only sparingly.[105]

At least as important as additional funds and improved firepower was Cen Yuying's effort to win back the hearts of the Yunnanese. As governor, he understood the importance of reestablishing a semblance of security and peace over the retaken areas. He reviewed all previous local appointments, restored those officials he considered reliable, removed those found to be incompetent, and appointed promising young ones. He arranged exemptions from land taxes in districts impoverished by war, disease, and natural disasters. Revenue-producing mines and salt wells were quickly repaired and reopened.

Most revealing of Cen's commitment to reestablish normalcy was that he personally oversaw the provincial civil examinations in Kunming in 1870—the first to take place since 1856.[106] Military examinations resumed the following year. This tells us he was astute in his assessment of the situation in Yunnan. He understood that if he was going to end the rebellion, he would have to offer the Yunnanese a peaceful alternative to fighting. After sixteen years of rebellion, Cen's strategy of normalization was an attractive one to the Yunnanese, who were tired of the fighting and the suffering.

For Cen the turning point came in 1871, when the imperial troops passed through Yaozhou. In a memorial to the emperor, he wrote: "To the east of Yaozhou lies Dingyuan, to its north Dayao, to its south it borders Zhennan. Since 1856, the rebels have occupied [Yaozhou], and imperial soldiers have been unable to defeat them." After the city fell in the spring of 1870, the imperial forces enjoyed a string of rapid victories, capturing cities throughout the province.

By June 1871, Cen's forces had reoccupied thirty-two cities that had been under Pingnan control.[107] Qing forces now converged on Dali, attacking in quick succession the district seats of Yongping and Yunnan (forty and thirty-five miles from Dali respectively). The last administrative seat before Dali, Zhaozhou, fell to the Qing in the spring of 1872.[108] Now all that lay between them and Du's capital were the upper and lower passes into the Dali Valley.

## The Sultan's Last Stand

Du Wenxiu had heavily fortified the two narrow defiles at the northern and southern ends of the Dali Valley.[109] Yang Yuke realized that a frontal assault on the passes would be suicide and that a siege would take too much time. So instead, he disguised several of his soldiers as salt merchants and had them enter the city to link up with Han sympathizers as a fifth column.[110] He ordered another battalion to approach the southern fort from the rear. This required them to climb down the face of the Cangshan Mountains, which rose sharply from behind the fort.

On June 12, 1872, Yang gave the signal for his forces to advance. At their approach, Han partisans raised a red flag over the inner fort and took it without firing a shot. Two days later, after Yang had reinforced his position, the residents of Dali could see the red flag of the imperial forces flying over the position. The Dali Sultanate, after more than fifteen years of independence, was approaching its end.[111] The rebel troops did not give up without a fight. It would take the imperial forces almost six more months of fierce combat to work their way up the plain and assault the heavily defended city of Dali.[112]

By late December, Qing troops released from other campaigns were streaming into the valley and Du's council was frantically debating how to end the rebellion. Their greatest concern was to prevent Yang Yuke's troops from inflicting retribution on the surrendering populace—something they commonly did.[113] On December 25, 1872, Du, surrounded by his top advisers and generals, held his final council. With Dali surrounded by more than ten thousand imperial soldiers, Du's top general, Yang Rong, advised him to surrender. Yang told him that fighting to the bitter end would only bring further hardships on the common people, with little honor to Du Wenxiu. After long deliberation with his council, Du stood up and ended the debate: "What you have said is true. If this generalissimo [Du] decides to fight to the death, then truly not even a chicken or dog will be left alive. If this generalissimo leaves the city, then I can save the old and the young."[114] When his council agreed, Du told them: "Very well then, tomorrow morning I will leave the city."[115]

济滇师著

FIGURE 9.1. Woodcut of Du Wenxiu's Execution

The following morning, as the sun rose over the Cangshan Mountains, Du Wenxiu donned his ceremonial robes, bid farewell to his family and advisers, and entered his yellow sedan chair. His subjects crowded the lanes to pay their last respects to the man who had ruled them for the past seventeen years. As he reached the Southern Gate he stopped and expressed his gratitude for their emotional display of grief.[116] Then he swallowed a fatal dose of opium and ordered his sedan chair to take him to the Qing encampment outside the city. When he arrived at Yang Yuke's camp, semiconscious, his last request was to "spare the people [*shao sharen*]."[117] He was dead by the time he was delivered to the Qing commander.[118]

Not to be deprived the satisfaction of killing him, Yang "rushed him out in front of the army and decapitated him. He gathered [Du's] head, his seal, clothing and ceremonial headdress as evidence for [later] corroboration."[119]

Du's sacrifice was in vain; it did not satisfy the Qing forces' desire to destroy the last vestiges of the Pingnan regime (see Figure 9.1).[120]

Cen Yuying was still thirty miles from Dali when Du surrendered. Now he rushed to the scene of his decapitation.[121] There, instead of launching an all-out attack on Dali, he acted as though Du's sacrifice had quenched the imperial army's desire for revenge. He accepted the surrender of the generals who had escorted Du to Yang Yuke's camp and even offered them Qing offices. He posted notices prohibiting his soldiers from killing or looting for three days. In a seemingly conciliatory gesture, he also "ordered all who submitted to shave their heads and deliver their weapons of war."[122] These measures lulled the populace into a false sense of security and allowed the Qing to position their troops for a final attack on Dali. Three days after Du's surrender, Cen invited Du's top generals to a banquet. After they were seated, Cen gave a signal and "seventeen heads rolled on the ground."[123] The following day the massacre began. It would last three days.[124]

The people of Dali fought ferociously until the end. The line between fighting to the death and a final Qing massacre was a thin one. One imperial official would recall that "the road . . . was ankle deep in blood. . . . Neither man, woman nor child who was Muslim was spared."[125] Cen's own estimate of the numbers slaughtered—a conservative one—was ten thousand.[126] Four thousand of the dead were said to have been women, children, and the elderly. Hundreds drowned trying to escape by swimming across Erhai Lake. Others attempted to flee through the narrow passes at either end of the valley. All were chased down and slain by Qing troops.[127] The soldiers were ordered to cut the ears from the dead and deposit them at Yang Yuke's headquarters. In the end there would be more than ten thousand pairs of these grisly trophies, filling twenty-four huge baskets. These, and Du Wenxiu's head, were sent to Beijing as mute proof that the Pingnan regime had been drowned in its own blood.[128]

With Du's death and the massacre of thousands of Hui in Dali, the rebellion, for all intents and purposes, was over. The remaining centers of rebel resistance—the walled towns of Shunning, Yunzhou, and Tengyue—were all retaken between March and June 1873. The last rebel stronghold—Wusuo, an insignificant outpost southwest of Tengyue—fell to the Qing on May 4, 1874.

Yet for the Hui, the terror did not end even then. After the slaughter, those women and children who had been spared or found still alive were sold off to imperial soldiers and officials to serve as servants or concubines.[129] Other survivors had their land, homes, and other property confiscated. Those who had lived in Dali were no longer allowed to even enter the city. A European resident of postrebellion Dali suggests that this prohibition did not last: "Very soon after this date, the people began to return to the city, and re-established themselves."[130] But for the next three decades, a sign forbidding traitorous Hui to enter Dali hung over the city's main gate. In the face of the last Qing suppression campaigns and renewed intolerance for Hui, many Muslim Yunnanese moved into the highland regions of Burma and Thailand. There they established communities that survive to this day as a living legacy of the Panthay Rebellion.[131]

## CHAPTER 10

# Epilogue: The Aftermath of Rebellion

The static, two-dimensional, and—for the imperial court—convenient portrayal of the Panthay Rebellion as simply a "Muslim rebellion" has endured until the present day. It was the last of the mid-nineteenth-century rebellions in China to be suppressed, and this narrative of the rebellion meshed nicely with the court's efforts to portray itself as a powerful government that was not morally bankrupt. It is notable that representations of the Yunnan Hui in Western and Chinese scholarship have barely changed since the Hui were assigned an ethnic classification separate from the Han and the Yi in the nineteenth century.

Few earlier or present-day accounts of the rebellion refer to the increasingly violent Han massacres of the Hui in 1839, 1845, and 1856. Nor do these accounts, which are rooted in Han–Hui dualism, point out that the Dali regime had strong multiethnic support. Because these biased accounts have been perpetuated, the Yunnan Hui are still reified today, just as they were 150 years ago, and the interactive nature of Yunnan society continues to be ignored. The schema does tell us how the Han Chinese and the Qing framed the rebellion; but it does little to shed light on how the Hui and other ethnic groups living in Yunnan (including some Han) perceived the rebellion and why they resisted the violence against them so strongly and for so many decades. Nor does this incomplete historical record show how the diverse groups making up the Dali State constructed a new political framework reflecting their multiethnic perspective.

The Panthay Rebellion devastated Yunnan. In a memorial to the throne, Governor-General Cen Yuying estimated that "the total population of the province was not fifty percent of what it had been prior to the rebellion."[1] If that is accurate, and if James Lee's estimate of ten million people for Yunnan's population before the rebellion is correct, fewer than five million people remained in the province in 1874.[2] However, the dramatic drop in population cannot be attributed entirely to the rebellion itself. As French explorer Louis de Carné suggested, it was the rebellion together with "epidemics, a scarcity of goods, and emigration that had reduced . . . the population of Yunnan by nearly half."[3]

Western Yunnan was hit especially hard by the rebellion. The city of Chuxiong, which changed hands at least six times during the rebellion, was said to have lost 90 percent of its original population by the time it was retaken by the Qing in 1869.[4] Baoshan had been one of the largest and wealthiest cities in western Yunnan; it emerged from the rebellion with "barely ten to twenty percent of its former population remaining."[5] Jingdong in southwestern Yunnan went from a registered population of more than five hundred households to fewer than fifty. When the Scottish traveler Archibald Colquhoun visited there a decade later, he found a city of "half-ruined outer walls, yamens, gateways and buildings of various sorts."[6]

It is often overlooked how many Hui fled to highland Southeast Asia—to northern Burma, Laos, and Thailand—in the mid-nineteenth century. Local accounts of this population movement talk of a Ho (or Haw) invasion. Given the likelihood that Hui should be included in this broad ethnic category, it is fair to suggest that many former Pingnan rebels fled south to escape the Qing armies.

With the withdrawal of the Pingnan regime, Chinese imperial oversight returned quickly. In a fascinating description of the return of Chinese influence, one European reported that "these excellent Shans . . . were troubled in mind by a Proclamation just issued by the Governor-General Cen, ordering them, or, rather their wives and daughters to adopt the Chinese dress. They were of the opinion, they said, that everyone should be allowed to follow his own culture ("jiao"), theirs was that women should dress in tunics and skirts, not sacks and trousers."[7]

In this book I have contended that the Pingnan regime tolerated other ethnic groups or at the very least benignly neglected them; I have also highlighted the role that culture (*jiao*) played in the Yunnanese world view. The defeat of the Dali-centered rebel movement marked the beginning of renewed efforts by the imperial government to control its border regions and influence the cultures of those who lived in those regions.

In its aftermath, the Panthay Rebellion (like the Pingnan regime itself) affected an area much broader than what had fallen under its direct control. In his study of border history, violence, and myth, Proschan posits that the highlands of Southeast Asia were overwhelmed in the mid-nineteenth century by a southward-moving wave of Chinese irregular troops known as the Yellow, Red, or Black Flags (the banners under which the different groups massed). Furthermore, "during the course of their penetration, the Ho were allied from time to time with local Tai-Lao groups (including most notably, the Tai chief of the Sip Song Chau Tai, Cam-Houm or Deo Van Tri) and, most importantly from our perspective, with the Kmhmu."[8] Significantly,

Proschan's data indicate that most of these outbreaks of violence occurred in the years immediately after the Panthay Rebellion—many years after the end of the Taiping Rebellion, which many have long considered the catalyst. A French official traveling through the region several years later suggested that "throughout the era [of the rebellion] . . . Tongkin [northern Vietnam] served as a refuge for the defeated and troubled almost without interruption."[9] In what is likely a reflection of their involvement, there are Muslim Chinese settlements throughout this same region to the present day. This is not to suggest that former Taiping rebels were not involved; rather, I am suggesting that the Pingnan regime's emphasis on Southeast Asia led to this population movement in the years after its fall.

Whichever ethnic group dominated these "Chinese" groups from the north, within Yunnan no single group suffered more than the Muslim Yunnanese after the rebellion ended. When the rebellion began, around one million Hui lived in the province; by 1874, only a small fraction remained. Yunnan's Hui population still has not recovered to its prerebellion level. Because they led most of the rebel activities, they died during the final campaigns far out of proportion to their numbers. Thousands of Hui were slaughtered as the Qing armies moved westward, taking one rebel city after the next.

Quite often, besieged populations preferred death to capture. In early 1873 the residents of Menghua, a day south of Dali, unable to find ways to continue resistance and intent on depriving their enemies of the satisfaction of killing them, committed mass suicide. According to one account: "They assembled all the precious objects [of the city] into one group of houses and lit it on fire. When the flames were almost out, poison was distributed to the women, children and elderly, and when the men who had been manning the defenses against the imperial forces were all but alone, they lit the city on fire and only then opened the city gates to their assailants."[10] Almost certainly, actions like these were a response to the practice of Qing armies (except that of Ma Rulong) to promise to spare those Hui who surrendered only to slaughter them after they laid down their arms.

The Qing forces commonly treated any Hui who survived—usually women and children—as part of the spoils. The French adventurer Jean Dupuis traveled throughout the province in the years immediately after the fall of Dali. "I see still even now in Kunming," he noted, "soldiers in possession of vast sums [of money] followed by the [captured] women and children who they sell here."[11]

In cities where Hui did survive, Qing officials often forbade them to rebuild their mosques. A traveler to Yunnan more than twenty years after the rebellion's end discovered in the southwestern city of Tengyue that "the Muslims were not authorized to rebuild a mosque that would allow them to freely pray to God. They had succeeded, a little clandestinely, in a private home to carry out their Friday prayers and, in this same home, slaughter, according to the proper rites, the cows and sheep."[12] In Dali, two of the four surviving mosques had been converted into Buddhist temples; the other two remained closed.[13]

Anti-Hui attitudes, reminiscent of those prevalent in prerebellion Yunnan, were common in all public and private interactions between Hui and Han. Nothing was more indicative of the renewed official acceptance of anti-Hui bias than the actions of Cen Yuying in the years after the rebellion. A task made much easier when the emperor promoted him to governor-general as an acknowledgment of his actions during the rebellion. For his greatest act of revenge, he waited until Ma Rulong had been promoted to a new post outside Yunnan; then, in April 1874 he ordered an investigation into the recent activities of Ma Dexin, the most revered Muslim leader in the province. Charging Ma Dexin and his associates with attempting to foment unrest, the investigating official had three prominent local Hui killed immediately and Ma Dexin arrested. "I then sent Yunnan Prefect Mao Qinglin [to bring Ma Dexin back to the capital]," Cen wrote in a memorial to the emperor, "but when they reached Anjiang village Ma Dexin went on a hunger strike and was near death. So I ordered that he be summarily executed."[14] Few Hui in the province were deceived by Cen's words; they knew full well that if such a prominent Hui leader could be openly assassinated, there was little hope for those Hui who hoped to begin life anew.

As a result of Qing brutality and official bias, many Muslim Yunnanese simply moved away, establishing communities in the highlands of Burma and Thailand.[15] In these new settlements they continued to participate in cross-border trade and to practice their religious beliefs without fear of retribution. Not all of these groups sought peace, however; some seem to have been active as bandits along Yunnan's southern frontier.[16]

There was no official discussion of the rebellion and no effort to address the reasons for it so as to prevent a recurrence. When the rebellion ended, Cen Yuying focused on returning Yunnan to stability and normalcy. He requested—and was granted—a suspension of taxes, an increase in permanent scholarships for holders of military and civil degrees, and a permanent increase in the provincial degree quota.[17] This last point was particularly significant for Yunnan's elite. The rebellion had prevented provincial exams from being held in 1858, 1861, 1864, and 1867 (besides putting a stop to special exams in 1859 and 1862), and those exam quotas now needed to be made up. It had also resulted in a diminished pool of qualified degree candidates. It would be many years before Yunnan again began producing enough scholars to fill the higher quotas that had been granted.

In his attempts to restore order, Cen barely acknowledged the rebellion's causes. His focus on Yunnan's immediate needs at the end of the rebellion is understandable, yet it can be argued that this lack of reflection by Cen and other Han officials contributed to the myth that the Muslim Yunnanese were the main instigators of the Panthay Rebellion. Absent from Cen's actions are investigations in response to calls for reform by provincial officials such as Wu Zhenyu, Sang Chunrong, and Lao Chongguang. Thus, ironically, the seventeen-year-long Panthay Rebellion had been quelled by officials who had far more in common with those who began the anti-Hui violence than with those few individuals who attempted to stop it. This generation of officials depicted the rebellion as almost entirely a result of Hui violence against the Qing.

This lack of reflection on the rebellion's causes is also rooted in the fact that in the years immediately following the rebellion, new and urgent challenges from British and French interests were demanding the full attention of provincial leaders and the Qing court. In the south, the French were beginning to examine the possibility of opening the Red River to trade with Yunnan. In the west, the British were renewing their efforts to restore commerce between Burma and China. While Cen Yuying tried to meet these challenges, unresolved issues between Yunnan's non-Han and Hui populations continued to fester, disrupting any sense of normalcy.

Cen's dismissive attitude toward the enduring unrest among the non-Han led to Yunnan's first major diplomatic incident: in early 1875, British interpreter Augustus Margary was killed by remnant non-Han rebels while trying to help the Browne Expedition cross from Burma into Yunnan. The ensuing diplomatic fray ended with the Qing court agreeing to a new set of concessions and the payment of a large indemnity.[18]

An often overlooked dimension of the rebellion is the complex impact it had on Yunnan's multiethnic population. Both the Qing court and the new provincial elite well realized that the Hui's many non-Han allies had played a pivotal role in the Panthay Rebellion. Throughout the rebellion, local and provincial officials reported on this multiethnic involvement.[19] The Qing government tended to conceptualize the non-Han as monolithic entity, like the non-Han category (yi) itself, and this points to a fundamental flaw in the court's interpretation of the rebellion. Like the Hui, the non-Han were highly fractured along regional and ethnic lines, to the point that ethnic groups sometimes fought both the Chinese and the Hui.[20] What held the alliance together was that most of the groups involved were unified in their opposition to the Qing and new Han immigrants.

The Yi's general support of the Hui rebels is what had given the rebellion its potency. Initially this Yi support had been specifically against local Han and local authorities, with the range of any given ethnic group largely restricted to one area. One can make the case that Ma Rulong's range of operations was delimited in the same manner. It is worth noting here that the indigenous ethnic groups' resistance to the Qing presence—whether in the form of new Han immigrants, increased taxes or banditry, or problems relating to tusi governance and baojia policies—did not end with the defeat of Du Wenxiu.

Indeed, even after the rebellion ended, Yunnan continued to be wracked by many of the same problems that had plagued the region prior to 1856. Relations between Han and the various other ethnic groups were still contentious, and violence continued to break out. In the summer of 1875, Father Ponsot wrote about a new rebellion among a non-Han group in southwestern Yunnan, which "no longer under Muslim rule sought to revolt and liberate themselves from Chinese authority."[21] In another incident along Yunnan's border with Vietnam, insurgent groups composed of former rebels and non-Han bandits grabbed control of commerce along the Red River and created a zone of authority that imperial troops dared not enter.[22] The sustained presence of non-Hui resistance—well after the rebellion was supposedly suppressed—contradicts the claims of Cen Yuying and others that the rebellion had been entirely a Han–Hui affair. Rather, the Panthay Rebellion in many ways was the final battle in a centuries-long process to formally and firmly orient Yunnan toward central China.

The violence perpetrated under the rubric "Panthay Rebellion" requires more than the superficial rendering that too often has been given by historians. To focus solely on the Muslim Yunnanese insurrection is to overlook the impact of the Han aggression that did so much to ignite this conflict. Those groups who found an initial source of unity in the face of Han aggression gave the rebellion its form. Yet these groups, even though they were linked by opposition to economic exploitation and religious discrimination and by a yearning for ethnic survival, lacked a long-term unifying force strong enough to overcome their diversity. In the end, the government was able to crush the multiethnic resistance, but it never did answer for itself the complex question of how to sustain imperial rule in an ethnically complex region. Only by understanding the many ethnic, religious, and political actions that precipitated the Panthay Rebellion can we begin to see that it was more—much more—than simply a conflict between Han and Hui.

# Chinese Characters

ahong 阿訇

baba 八把
Bai 白
Baiyang (chang) 白羊（廠）
Baiyi 擺夷
banmeng 版猛
baojia 保甲
Bo Lin 伯林
bonong 播弄

Cai Fachun 蔡發春
Cangshan 蒼山
Cen Yuying 岑毓英
changfa Huifei 長發回匪
chiyu jieyang 池魚皆殃
Chuxiong 楚雄
Chuxiong yishang 楚雄以上

Dai 傣
Dali 大理
Danfen liangyou, bulun hanhui 但分
   良誘，不論漢回
Dao Shengwu 刀繩武
Daoguang 道光
daojia tu 道家徒
daojiao tu 道教徒
Dasi 大司
Dasi Fan 大司番
Dasi Kong 大司空
dayuan shuai 大元帥
daye 大爺
dian 點
Dian jun 滇軍
Dingbei Dajiangjun 定北大將軍
donglao shanhuang 洞老山荒

Du Wenxiu 杜文秀
duichang 對唱
Dulong 獨龍

Erhai 洱海

fansi 蕃司
fei 匪
fojiao tu 佛教
Fuji 福吉

gaitu guiliu 改土歸流
Gao Laowu 高老五
Gao Luoyi 高羅依
gedimu 格底目
gelao hui 哥老會
gesha wulun 格殺勿論
Guiliang 桂良
Guzong 古宗

han 悍
Han 漢
Han mie Hui 漢滅回
Hani 哈尼
Hanjian 漢奸
Hanjiao 漢教
He Changling 賀長齡
He Guoan 合國安
He Tongyun 何彤雲
He Youbao 何有保
Hengchun 恆春
Hong Xiuquan 洪秀全
hudou 互鬥
Huai Tang'a 懷唐阿
Huang Cong 黃琮
Huang Diankui 黃殿魁

Hui 回
Huijiao tu 回教徒
huiguan 會館
Huihe 回紇
Huihu 回胡
Huihui 回回
Huihui cun 回回村
Huihui ying 回回營
Huihui zhai 回回寨
Huijiao 回教
Huimin 回民
Huiren 回人
Hui-yi 回夷
Huizhong 回眾
Huizi 回子
Huizu 回族

Jia Hongzhao 賈洪詔
jia Huizi 椵回子
jiang nei 江內
jiao 教
jiaofei 狡匪
jiaomen 教門
jiazhang 甲長
Jingpo 景頗
Jinsha Jiang 金沙江
jinshi 進士

kezhang 課長
kuangguan 礦官
Kunming 昆明

Lancang Jiang 瀾滄江
Lao Chongguang 勞崇光
lao jiao 老教
Lei Wenmei 雷文枚
li 里
Li Peihu 李培祜
Li Wenxue 李文學
Li Xingyuan 李興源
Li Yuzhen 李玉振
Li Zhengrong 李崢鎔
liang 兩

lianyou 練勇
Lijiang 麗江
Lin Tingxi 林廷禧
Lin Zexu 林則徐
Lin Ziqing 林自清
Lin'an 臨安
Lin'an fei 林安匪
ling chi 凌遲
Lisu 栗傈
liu nan liu yi 六難六易
Liu Yuezhao 劉嶽詔
luo yi 玀夷
Luoluo 玀玀
luoma hui 騾馬會

Ma Chunlin 馬春林
Ma Da 馬大
Ma Dexin 馬德新
Ma Futu 馬負圖
Ma Guoxiang 馬國祥
Ma Liansheng 馬聯陞
Ma Minggong 馬明公
Ma Mingkui 馬名魁
Ma Rong 馬榮
Ma Rulong 馬如龍
Ma Shuang'en 馬雙恩
Ma Wenzhao 馬文昭
Ma Xian 馬獻
Ma Xingyun 馬行雲
Ma Zhu 馬注
mafou 馬伕
Manzi 蠻子
Mao Qinglin 毛慶麟
Meng Hui 蒙回
mensheng 門生
Mianning 緬寧
Miao 苗
Miaojiao 苗教
Miaozi 苗子
min 民
Ming 明
Minjia 民家
mintuan 民團

minzu 民族
Mu Ruhe 馬汝和
Mumin 穆民
Mumin yijia 穆民一家

Nanzhao 南詔
neidi 內地
niu cong 牛叢
Nongren 儂人
Nu jiang 怒江

Pan Duo 潘鐸
panbo 盤剝
Pingdong Dajiangjun 平東大將軍
Pingnan Guo 平南國
Pingnan Wang 平南王

Qiang 強
qimin 鰭民
Qin Xianzhong 秦賢中
Qing 清
Qingbao 慶保
Qingsheng 清盛
qiyi 起義
quanzi pang 犬字旁
Qujing 曲靖

renmin 人民
Ruilin 瑞麟
rujia tu 儒家徒

san jiao 三教
Sangchunrong 桑春榮
Sanyi 三迤
Sanyue jie 三月街
shanghao 商號
shao sharen 少殺人
Shen Jucheng 沈聚成
shengyi yixia 省議以下
Shengyu ting 聖御庭
shichu chengxin 實出誠心
shishi wen 誓師文
shuaifu bugao 帥府布告

Shuxing'a 舒興阿
shuyi 鼠疫
siji ruchun 四季如春
Song Gui 嵩貴

Tai 泰
taizi shaobao 太子少保
Tang Dunpei 唐惇培
Tian Zhongxing 田仲興
tiandi hui 天地會
tu 徒
tufei 土匪
tumu 土目
tushe 土舍
tusi 土司

wai fei 外匪
wai Hui 外回
wai yi 外夷
Wan Lingui 万林桂
Wang Jianping 王健平
Wang Zhixu 汪之旭
weida budiao 尾大不掉
Wen Xiang 文詳
wo Hui zhijiao 我回之教
wo Huizu 我回族
wo jiao 我教
Woni 窩泥
wu juren 武舉人
Wu Sangui 吳三貴
wu xiucai 武秀才
Wu Zhenyu 吳振棫
wusheng 武生

xiang 響
xiangba hui 香把會
xiangu 仙姑
xiangyue 鄉約
xicheng 洗城
xidao 西道
xidou 喜鬥
xiedou 械鬥
xiezhen 協鎮

xinjiao 新教
xingshi xiwen 興師檄文
xise 喜色
xiucai 秀才
Xiyi 悉宜
Xu Yuanji 徐元吉

Yang Rong 楊榮
Yang Xianzhi 楊先芝
Yang Yaodou 楊耀斗
Yang Yuke 楊玉科
Yang Zhenpeng 楊振鵬
yaopai 腰牌
yeren 野人
Yeyi 野夷
yi 夷
Yi 彝
yi Hui zhi Hui 以回制回
yi jian 夷奸
yi jiang 夷疆
yi yi zhi yi 以夷制夷
yifei 夷匪
Yijia bingma dayuanshuai 彝家兵馬
   大元帥
Yilibu 伊里布
Yongli 永厲
Yongzheng 雍正
youfei 遊匪
yu Hanren wuyi 与漢人無異
Yuan 元
yuanshuai 元帥

yuchun 愚蠢
Yunnan 雲南

Zang Hui 藏回
Zhang Fuguo 張福國
Zhang Hualong 張化龍
Zhang Jingyi 張景沂
Zhang Liangji 張亮基
Zhang Lingxiang 張齡象
Zhang Xunzheng 張循徵
Zhang Zhengtai 張正泰
Zhang Zhixue 張志學
Zhang Zihong 張子洪
zhanggu 掌故
zhangqi 瘴氣
Zhao Guang 趙光
Zhao Shizhi 趙士志
zhaobi 照壁
Zheng He 鄭和
zhengchong 症忡
Zhenzhu 真主
Zhongren 狆人
Zhu Di 朱棣
Zhu Kechang 褚克昌
Zhu Zhanchun 朱占春
zhuandian 轉點
Zhuang 壯
Zhuji Jie 豬集街
zongjiao 宗教
zongtong bingma dayuanshuai 總統
   兵馬大元帥

# Abbreviated References

DBX      *Dianxi bianluan xiaoshi* [A brief narrative of western Yunnan disturbances]. 1939. In *Huimin qiyi* [Hui rebellions], edited by Bai Shouyi. Shanghai: Zhongguo shenzhou guoguang chubanshe. 81–96.

DCZZ      *Dengchuan zhouzhi* [Gazetteer of Dengchuan department]. 1855. Compiled by Hou Yunjin.

DSDJ      Ma Guanzheng. "Dianyuan shisinian dahuo ji" [A record of the fourteen years of tragedy in Yunnan]. In HMQY, I:291–301.

DSSW      Li Yuzhen. "Dianshi shuwen" [A description of the Yunnan affair]. In YHQS, 184–228.

DWQL      *Du Wenxiu Qiyi Lunji* [Collected essays on the Du Wenxiu uprising], edited by Gao Fayuan. Kunming: Yunnan Daxue Chubanshe, 1993.

DWTZM      *Du Wenxiu tongshu zhiguanti minglu* [List of officials under Du Wenxiu's command]. c. 1867. In *Huimin qiyi* [Hui rebellions], edited by Bai Shouyi. Shanghai: Zhongguo shenzhou guoguang chubanshe. 183–92.

DXG      *Dali xianzhigao* [Revised gazetteer of Dali district]. 1915. Compiled by Zhou Zonglin.

HMQY      Bai Shouyi, ed. *Huimin qiyi* [Hui rebellions]. 1953. 4 vols. Shanghai: Zhongguo shenzhou guoguang chushanbe.

LGY      Li Xingyuan. *Li wengong gong zouyi* [The memorials of Li Xingyuan]. Taibei: Wenhai Chubanshe, 1974 (1865).

LLXZ      *Longling xianzhi* [Gazetteer of Longling district]. 1917. Compiled by Zhang Jian'an. Taibei: Cheng wen chu ban she, 1975 (1917).

MEP      Société des missions-étrangères de Paris [Paris society of foreign missions]. Archives of the Société des missions-étrangères de Paris. Paris.

MFS      Ma Futu. "Ma Futu siji" [Private account of Ma Futu]. In HMQY, II:365–408.

QPHF     *Qinding pingding Huifei fanglüe* [Imperially commissioned record of the campaign to pacify the Hui rebels]. 1896. Compiled by Yixin. Taibei: Wenhai Chubanshe, 1972 (1896).

QSL      *Qing shilu you guan Yunnan shiliao* [Historical materials on Vietnam, Burma, Thailand, and Laos excerpted from the Qing veritable records]. 5 vols. 1984–86. Compiled by the Yunnan Provincial History Institute. Kunming: Yunnan renmin chubanshe.

QSXMS   Cheng Xiayu. *Qing shengxun xinan minzu shiliao* [Materials found concerning the ethnic minorities in the southwest in precepts issued by Qing emperors]. 1988. Chengdu: Sichuan chubanshe.

TNZJ     "Talang Nan'an zhengkuang ji" [A record of the Talang, Nan'an, mining incident]. In HMQY, I:249–62.

WDSL    Ma Shengfeng. "Wuding shilue" [An account of the Wuding incident]. In HMQY, II:15–42.

XWZZ    *Xuanwei zhouzhi* [Gazetteer of Xuanwei department]. 1844. Compiled by Liu Beilin. Taibei: Chengwen chubanshe, 1967(1934).

XYH     Xu Yuanhua. "Xiantong Ye Hupian" [The unofficial account of the Xianfeng-Tongzhi rebellion in Yunnan]. In HMQY, 1:279–290. Shanghai: Zhongguo shenzhou guogang chubanshe, 1953.

XYTG    *Xu Yunnan tongzhigao* [Revised comprehensive gazetteer of Yunnan]. 1901. Compiled by Wang Wenshao. Taibei: Wenhai chubanshe 1966 (1901).

YBY     Li Yuanbing. "Yongchangfu baoshanxian Han-Hui hudou ji Du Wenxiu shixing geming zhi yuanqi [The Han–Hui conflict in Baoshan district of Yongchang prefecture and the reasons for Du Wenxiu's revolution]." 1931. In HMQY, I:5–9.

YCFZ    *Yongchang fuzhi* [Gazetteer of Yongchang prefecture]. 1886. Compiled by Liu Yuke.

YGZ     *Lin wenzhong gong zhengshu* [The memorials of Lin Zexu]. 1935. Shanghai: Shangwu yinshukuan.

YHSLD     Yunnansheng bianjizu [Yunnan editorial board]. *Yunnan
          Huizu shehui lishi diaocha* [Investigations of Yunnanese Hui
          society and history]. 4 vols. 1985–88. Kunming: Yunnan
          minzu chubanshe.

YMJW      *Yuanmou jiwen* [Yuanmou chronicles]. 1930. In HMQY II,
          213–16.

YNXZ      *Yunnan xianzhi* [Gazetteer of Yunnan district]. 1890. Comp.
          Huang Bingkun. Taibei: Chengwen Chubanshe, 1967 (1890).

YHQS      Jing Dexin, ed. *Yunnan Huimin qiyi shiliao* [Historical
          records on the Muslim uprising]. Kunming: Yunnan minzu
          chubanshe, 1986.

# Notes

CHAPTER I

1. Many documents describe Hengchun standing on the city wall overseeing the defense of the city. The most important of these are QPHF; Luo Qirui, *Yunnan zhanggu*, 610; Pourais, *La Chine*, 78.

2. QPHF, 5:7a; Pourais, *La Chine*, 79, 81.

3. QPHF, 5:7a.

4. Ibid., 5:8b–9a.

5. Ibid., 5:7a.

6. Ibid., 5:8b–9a.

7. Pourais, *La Chine*, 78; Luo, *Yunnan zhanggu*, 610.

8. QPHF, 3:12a–b. An imperial censor informed the court—incorrectly, it would turn out—that Ma Mingkui, a Hui *jinshi* degree holder, had been named king; see 3:16a.

9. Ibid., 3:16b.

10. Ibid., 3:17a; Wang Jianping, *Concord and Conflict*, 259. Shuxing'a had more than a decade of experience in a variety of posts in the northwest.

11. QPHF, 1:11b. Shuxing'a actually suggested that the Hui "make up less than ten or twenty percent of the Han."

12. Ibid., 6:18b–19a; Rocher, *La Province chinoise de Yün-nan*, II:36.

13. QPHF, 6:13b.

14. Zhang Tao, "Dianluan jilue," 266. This tragic change in meaning is achieved relatively easily since the two phrases differ only with the omission of a tree radical from *ge*, making it *ge*—the first character in the gesha wulun order. A leap that could also have been made easily when the commands were transmitted verbally.

15. QPHF, 5:21b.

16. Ibid., 5:21a, 6:21a–b, 14:16b; YHLSD, I:99–100; HMQY, I:297.

17. QPHF, 3:17a–14b.

18. Ibid., 4:2b–3a

19. Ibid., 4:2b–3a.

20. Ibid., 3:18a, 4:3a.

21. Luo, *Yunnan zhanggu*, 610.

22. Ibid.

23. QPHF, 5:7a; Luo, *Yunnan Zhanggu*, 610.

24. QPHF, 1:11b.

25. Ibid., 4:3a, 4:8b; YGZ, 6:11a.

26. QPHF, 4:3b.

27. Ibid., 5:2b–4b. Shuxing'a makes a similar comment; see Ibid., 5:5a.

28. Ibid., 5:6b–7b; Ma Guanzheng, "Dianyuan shisinian dahuo ji," I:296; Pourais, *La Chine*, 78.

29. QPHF, 5b:9a.

30. Ibid., 5:9a–b; XYTG, 81:14b–15a.

31. QPHF, 5:9a–b; Luo, *Yunnan zhanggu*, 610.

32. YGZ, 7:13b–14b.

33. YBY, I:5–9; Jing Dexin, *Du Wenxiu qiyi*, 35; QPHF, 14:16b.

34. Rocher, *La Province chinoise*, II:36; QPHF, 6:18b–19a, 8:3b–4a.

35. Lee, "Food Supply and Population Growth," 729.

36. See Armijo, "Narratives Engendering Survival," 298–99, who compares the attitudes of these new Han immigrants to "white settlers throughout much of the world . . . [who] felt entitled to the resources of 'their' state, regardless of whether or not 'others' were already in possession of them."

37. For examples of this, see Daniels, "Environmental Degradation," 7–13; Giersch, "'A Motley Throng,'" 76–81.

38. Atwill, "Trading Places."

39. Armijo-Hussein, "Sayyid 'Ajall[dı] Shams Al-Din," 88–94.

40. HMQY, II:216; XYTG, 4:10b.

41. DCZZ, 4:3b.

42. DXG, 34:43b; Pillsbury, "Pig and Policy," 154–57.

43. Gladney, *Muslim Chinese*, 21–26.

44. T'ien, *Moslem Rebellion in China*; Wang Jianping, *Concord and Conflict*, 1996; Lin Changkuan, "Chinese Muslims of Yunnan," 1991; Jing Dexin, *Du Wenxiu qiyi*, 1991; DXG, 1915; Henri d'Ollone, *Recherches*; Israeli, "Islam in the Chinese Context," 79–94; Qiu Shusen, *Zhongguo Huizu*, 576–90.

45. Sow-Theng, *Migration and Ethnicity*.

46. Rawski, *The Last Emperors*, 5; Crossley, "Thinking about Ethnicity," 7–8.

47. Elliot, *The Manchu Way*, 17.

48. Bai Shouyi, *Minzu zongjiao lunji*; Deng Baohua and Wang Huaide, *Yisilanjiao shi*; Lipman, *Familiar Strangers*; Gladney, *Muslim Chinese*.

49. QPHF, 3:12a, 4:4a–5b, 4:15b–16a, 5:3b–6b.

50. Ibid., 5:6b–7b.

51. Wang Shuhuai, *Xiantong Yunnan Huimin shibian*, 346.

52. As is so often the case, the strongest proponents of this perspective are encountered in textbooks on Chinese history. See for example Hsü, *The Rise of Modern China*, 254–55; Fairbank, Reischauer, and Craig, *East Asia*, 474–75; and especially Wright, *The Last Stand of Chinese Conservatism*, 113–15. Almost inevitably these accounts invoke Han–Hui competition over dwindling mineral resources as the primary catalyst.

53. Dillion, *China's Muslim Hui Community*, 58–59; Israeli, "Islam in the Chinese Context," 79–94; Wang Jianping, *Concord and Conflict*, 249.

54. For examples of this see Wang Shuhuai, *Xiantong Yunnan Huimin shibian*, as well as HMQY for Bai Shouyi's collection of documents relating to the rebellion. This fixation is equally apparent in QPHF, an imperially sponsored collection of imperial documents relating to the rebellion.

55. The best-known work is *Du Wenxiu qiyi* by Jing Dexin.

56. In fact, many works, such as Bai Shouyi's HMQY and the official Qing work, QPHF, lumped them together as Muslim rebellions; this reflected an assumption of Muslim unity that transcended ethnic and geographic boundaries. For a ground-breaking look at the Muslim rebellion in Kashgar led by Ya'qub Beg see Kim Hodong, *Holy War in China*.

57. One of the key disseminators of the term was Major E.B. Sladen, who traveled to Yunnan in 1868. An extract from his writings was presented to the Royal Geographic Society and then printed in *Proceedings of the Royal Geographical Society*, 357–62.

58. Anderson, *Report*, 150. For a fuller discussion of the term see Lin Changkuan, "The Etymological History of Panthay," 353; Chan, "The 'Panthay Embassy' to Britain, 1872," 116n15.

59. Gill, *The River of Golden Sand*, 303.

CHAPTER 2

1. *Sanguo yenyi*, 722–24.

2. Davenport, "Report," 24; Benedict, "Bubonic Plague in Nineteenth Century China," 109.

3. Reid, *Southeast Asia in the Age of Commerce*, 53; Forbes, "The Cin-Ho (Yunnanese Chinese) Caravan Trade," 21–23.

4. For an outstanding example of the intermediary role of these groups see Pasquet, "Image et réalité du système tributaire," 147–56.

5. *Puer fuzhi gao*, 17:3a, in Cui Jingming and Lu Ren, "Yuan, Ming, Qing shiqi," 41.

6. See Hosie, *Three Years in Western China*, 95; Litton, *Report*, 5.

7. Chinese terms and place names have been altered to conform to their standard pinyin renderings for the sake of continuity and in order to avoid confusion for readers who are unfamiliar with other, nonstandard renderings of geographic place names commonly employed in the nineteenth century. Colquhoun, *Across Chrysê*, 263. For a similar reference see Clarke, *Kwiechow and Yün-nan Provinces*, 70–71.

8. Tambiah, *Culture, Thought, and Social Action*, 260.

9. Tooker, "Putting the Mandala in its Place," 324.

10. *Yunnan Tongzhi*, 30:40b.

11. I thank Rebecca Wiener for suggesting this metaphor to describe Yunnan's ridge-and-valley topography.

12. Bourne, "Report," 10.

13. Baber, "Report," 8.

14. Ibid., 11.

15. Fitzgerald, *The Tower of Five Glories*, 190–91.

16. Yan Zhongping, *Qingdai Yunnan tongzheng kao*, 9; Sun, "The Transportation of Yunnan Copper," 141.

17. Hosie, *Three Years in Western China*, 140.

18. National Geographic correspondent and Naxi scholar Joseph Rock traveled across such bridges well into the 1930s.

19. Margary, *Notes*, 44.

20. S.T. Wang, *The Margary Affair*.

21. See Desgodins, *Le Thibet*, 345. Mules were usually preferable to horses; only the poor used donkeys.

22. Wang Mingda and Zhang Shilu, *Mabang wenhua*, 113; Hill, *Merchants and Migrants*, 49.

23. Baber, "Mr. Grosvenor's Mission," 12. See also Gill, *The River of Golden Sand*, II:314. For an example of a Tibetan caravan see Hosie, "Report," 26. For an example of a Hui caravan see Rocher, *La Province chinoise du Yün-nan*, I:81.

24. Rocher, *La Province chinoise du Yün-nan*, I:20.

25. *Dianzhi*, 68.

26. Spencer, "Kueichou," 167.

27. Sun, "The Copper of Yunnan," 122–23.

28. Bourne, "Report," 10.

29. Hill, *Merchants and Migrants*, 40; Van Spengen, "The Geo-History of Long-Distance Trade in Tibet," 26. *Guzong* was the local Chinese term for Tibetan.

30. QSL, 5:678–79; Forbes, "The 'Cin-Ho' Muslims of North Thailand," 178.

31. Wu Xingnan, "Qingday qianqi de Yunnan," 75.

32. Dubernard and Desgodins, "Les Sauvages Lyssous," 63–64.

33. XYTG, 50:9a–11b; Chiang, "The Salt Trade in Ch'ing China," 204.

34. XYTG, 50:1a–9a; 13b–14a. Catholic missionary Desgodins also describes salt wells along the banks of the Lancang River near the Tibetan border; see Desgodins, *Le Thibet*, 343.

35. *Zhang Yunsui Memorials*, in Wu Xingnan, "Qingdai qianqi de Yunnan," 75.

36. XYTG, 52:4b–5a. One sign of the state's increasing efforts to maintain its monopoly was the modification to the certificate system used to verify the taxes paid on salt at customs houses across the province. Originally one certificate could cover the loads on several animals; this proved so difficult to monitor that the policy had to be changed to one certificate per animal.

37. Zelin, "The Rise and Fall of the Fu-Rong Salt-Yard Elite," in Esherick and Rankin, *Chinese Local Elites*, 84.

38. Gervais-Courtellemont, *Voyage*, 234. Hosie also mentions the difference in the color between the darker Sichuan salt and the lighter Yunnan salt; see "Report," I:66.

39. Li 1831:4b, in Mueggler, *The Age of Wild Ghosts*, 173.

40. XYTG, 50:11b–12a. It is interesting to note that the emperor's rescript ordered the salt well "to be closed and bandits who privately open the well to be punished so as not to re-establish old practices [of selling salt]." This plan seemed unlikely to succeed since the officials could not even control the salt production and trade when it was open and ostensibly under their control.

41. XYTG, 50:11b–12a; Wang Song, *Daoguang Yunnan zhichao*, 115–16; for other instances see XYTG, 50:1a–b. This was likely a perennial problem; British customs inspectors in the early years of the twentieth century also report that "much of the salt was carried out of Yunnan to Laos and the British Shan States." See *China, Maritime Customs Decennial Reports* (1906), 494, cited in Hill, *Merchants and Migrants*, 44.

42. Davenport, "Report," 22. For an account of the revived nature of the fair see Gervais-Courtellemont, *Voyage*, 234.

43. Li Gui, *Yunnan jindai jingjishi*, 139; Cui Jingming and Lu Ren, "Yuan, Ming, Qing," 42. A variety of systems existed that dictated the number of days between markets; thus the Tonghai County "7–*Jie*" markets were held on the seventh, seventeenth, and twenty-seventh days of the lunar month, and the yi markets rotated according to the twelve-animal cycle. See Li Gui, *Yunnan jindai jinjishi*, 137.

44. Many scholars have asserted that Japan stopped exporting copper to China in the early eighteenth century. In fact, Japan in 1715 did not end its exports, but only reduced them sharply by 40 to 50 percent. See Hall, "Notes on Early Ch'ing Copper Trade with Japan," 427–61. For a more in-depth discussion of the Yunnan's role in the Qing's copper supply see Yan Zhongping, *Qingdai Yunnan tongzheng kao*, 3–9.

45. Sun, "Ch'ing Government and the Mineral Industries Before 1800," 841.

46. Ibid., 9.

47. XYTG, 44:6b; YHSLD, I:50. It seems that the primary administrative difference between the Yunnan mines and mines in other parts of the empire was that the Hui were a prominent presence in the former, but not the latter.

48. The Hui were never—at least in Yunnan—broken down by province into smaller work teams. This is likely because few non-Yunnanese Hui came to work as miners.

49. Hua Li, "Qingdai baojia zhidu jianlun," 96–97.

50. Yan Zhongping, *Qingdai Yunnan tongzheng kao*, 27. In theory, the team bosses were under the "mine overseer" (*kezhang*); in practice, the team bosses reported directly to the mine supervisor, although it is possible that at some mines the mine supervisor and the mine overseer were one and the same person.

51. Rocher, *La Province chinoise du Yün-nan*, II:222–24.

52. YTZG, 160:inter alia.

53. MEP, 539:220.

54. For a brief overview of the yi (and Yi) see Harrell, *Ways of Being Ethnic in Southwest China*, 174–75.

55. The term *yi* was also employed to categorize non-Chinese peoples as less civilized barbarians. In Yunnan it seems to have been used more to indicate an ethnic Other; however, it retained sinocentric undertones of Han superiority, in the sense that this Other shared a certain degree of barbarian-ness. That the Hui were not part of this oppositional paradigm reflects in part the marginal position the Muslim Yunnanese held.

56. My use of the term "non-Han" is not intended to perpetuate this disparaging connotation. Rather, because the term was often used indiscriminently to refer to any Yunnan ethnic group, and in order to not overstep my interpretive boundaries in relation to the historical texts in question, I use the term "non-Han" as the most accurate English translation for ethnic groups identified as *yi*.

57. When referring to the Hui, "Muslim Yunnanese" is preferable to "Yunnanese Muslims." The latter overemphasizes the religious element of their identity. As will be discussed later, they are more than simply Muslims who live in Yunnan.

58. XYTG, 3:20a, 160:1a–5b;

59. Ibid., 161:4a.

60. Lee, "Food Supply and Population Growth," 15. In his thorough study of the demographic evolution of southwest China, Lee suggests caution, noting that "at least half of the population did not register."

61. Chen Bisheng, *Dianbian sanyi*, 39. Colquhoun, in *Across Chrysê*, II:196, makes a similar statement. For intermarriage see Rocher, *La Province chinoise*, I:19.

62. For a sampling of such "aberrant" behavior see "Yunnan sheng li shi yan jiu suo bian[d2]," QSL, V:307, 310, 563, 573.

63. *Chuxiong xianzhi*, [d3]2:28a.

64. Lee, "Food Supply and Population Growth," 23.

65. Gladney, "The New Central Asians and Turkey," 14. For a similar argument in published form see Gladney, "Nations Transgressing Nation-States," in Atabaki and O'Kane, *Post-Soviet Central Asia*, 301–23.

66. Lee, "Food Supply and Population Growth," 738–42.

67. QSXMS, 178.

68. Rowe, "Education and Empire," in Elman and Woodside, eds., *Education and Society in Late Imperial China*, 420.

69. Lee, "Food Supply and Population Growth"; Giersch, "'A Motley Throng,'" 74; Lu Ren, *Bian qian yu*, 136–42.

70. Lee, "The Legacy of Immigration in Southwest China," 303; You Zhong, *Yunnan minzu shi*, 359. See also Lee, "Food Supply and Population Growth," 729, where the author notes that in the nineteenth century "the size of the [unregistered] non-Han eludes us."

71. Sun, "The Board of Revenue in Nineteenth-Century China," 202; Taeuber and Wang, "Population Reports in the Ch'ing Dynasty," 406; Ho Ping-ti, *Studies on the Population of China*, 51–52. All three point out the omission, underreported nature, and unsatisfactory process of population registration in the nineteenth century. One concrete illustration that the court realized that underreporting was taking place is that in 1819 the emperor called on the Yun-Gui governor-general, Bai Ling, to erect a system by which to clarify the population counts in areas under tusi control; QSXMS, 177.

72. Yang Xifu, *Sizhitang wenji*, 6:5a; *Anshun fuzhi*, 2:1a, cited in Lee, "Food Supply and Population Growth," 727. As Philip Kuhn notes in *Soulstealers*: "We have no reliable way of gauging the numbers of proportion of displaced persons in the Prosperous Age"—a fact far more true in Yunnan than in the lower Yangtze valley, which Kahn was studying. See Kuhn, *Soulstealers*, 42.

73. QPHF, 9:19b.

74. Ibid., 19:18a–b; see also *Yunnan Tongzhi gao*, 30:1a.

75. Depuis, "Voyage," 43; MEP, 439:133.

76. D'Ollone, "Les musulmans du Yun-nan," 214. See also Rocher, *La Province chinoise*, I:138–39.

77. Clarke, *The Province of Yunnan*, 39. See also Gill, *The River of Golden Sand*, 302. A British traveler to Kunming in 1887 even remarks on the "strong differences from the Chinese type" of the residents. See Bourne, "Report," 11.

78. *Yunnan sheng dangan shiliao congbian*, 323–70.

79. See Davenport, "Report," 17; Gervais-Courtellemont, *Voyage*, 93.

80. Wien, *China's March toward the Tropics*.

81. MEP, 539:133; Rocher, *La Province chinoise*, II:12.

82. Harrell, "Ethnicity, Local Interests, and the State," 521.

83. Harrell offers a compelling discussion of why this is so in his book-length study of the Yi, *Ways of Being Ethnic in Southwest China*, 174–78.

84. Hosie, *Three Years in Western China*, 107.

85. Davies, *Yün-nan*, 390.

86. Rocher, *La Province chinoise*, II:10. Some foreigners incorrectly thought that the difference between black and white Yi was one of acculturation.

87. Jenks, *Insurgency and Social Disorder in Guizhou*, 33.

88. In this instance I have retained the disparaging Qing-era ethnonym of *Yeren* because the modern classification of *Jingpo* likely refers to a much smaller subsection of people than that referred to by the term Yeren.

89. Dessaint, *Au Sud des nuages*, 28.

90. Launay, *Histoire de la mission du Thibet*, 210.

91. XYTG, 3:16b–17b, 19a–b; QSL, II:144–45; Sladen, *Proceedings*, 357–62.

92. Rocher, *La Province chinoise*, II:21–22; see also Fitzgerald, *The Tower of Five Glories*.

93. *Zhaozhou zhi*, in You Zhong, *Yunnan minzu shi*, 530. For a similar statement see *Dianyi tushou*, in Song Guangyu, ed., *Huanan bianjiang minzu tulu*, 71; Mackerras, "Aspects of Bai Culture," in particular 51–57.

94. *Zhaozhou zhi*, in You Zhong, *Yunnan minzu shi*, 530.

95. Lee, "The Legacy of Immigration," 303; Van Spengen, "The Geo-History," 26.

96. Most Tai refer to themselves as "Tai" (or a cognate), whereas Dai is the Chinese ethnonym given to them by the People's Republic of China. See Wijeyewardene, "Thailand and the Tai," in Wijeyewardene, ed., *Ethnic Groups across National Boundaries*, 48. Hsieh Shichung suggests that Dai was the suggestion of Tai members from Xishuangbanna, who wanted "to adopt a word with the sound *dai*." See Hsieh Shichung, "On the Dynamics of Tai/Dai-Lue Ethnicity," in Harrell, ed., *Cultural Encounters*, 319.

97. Wyatt, *Thailand*, 6.

98. Wang Zhusheng, *The Jingpo Kachin*, 60–61.

99. The name Sipsong Panna refers to the "twelve panna," which were ruled by lords. Hsieh Shichung, "On the Dynamics of Tai/Dai-Lue Ethnicity," 314.

100. Wang Wenguang, *Zhongguo gudai de minzu shibie*, 306.

101. *Lin'an fuzhi*, in Wang Wenguang, *Zhongguo gudai de minzu shibie*, 307.

102. You Zhong, *Yunnan minzu shi*, 538.

CHAPTER 3

1. Yao Jide, "Xi'nan xichou gudao yu," 186; Fan Jianhua, "Xi'nan gudao yu Han," 73.

2. Backus, *The Nan-chao Kingdom*; Forbes, "The Cin-Ho Caravan Trade," 4.

3. Both Joseph Fletcher and Dru Gladney have described the successive movements of Islamic ideas and Muslim peoples into China as "tides." For an overview of these see Gladney, *Muslim Chinese*, 36–63.

4. Rossabi, "The Muslims in the Early Yuan Dynasty," 288; Yang Zhaojun, *Yunnan Huizu shi*, 29.

5. Armijo-Hussein, "Sayyid 'Ajall Shams Al-Din," 194.

6. Rossabi, "The Muslims in the Early Yuan Dynasty," 290. Rossabi's comment is not meant to imply that Sayyid 'Ajall's Islamic influence was contrary to the wishes of the central court. In fact, Sayyid 'Ajall remained in near constant contact with the imperial court and Qubilai approved of his policies in Yunnan and, in Rossabi's words, "did not urge the creation of a Muslim state that might seek independence from Yuan China."

7. For a compelling introduction to Sayyid 'Ajall's administration in Yunnan see Armijo-Hussein, "Sayyid 'Ajall Shams Al-Din," chs. IV–V.

8. It is difficult to arrive at an exact number. The popular belief is that he constructed twelve mosques; however, Ming-era sources suggest that only two were actually built under his auspices. See Bai Shouyi, "Diannan Conghua," 635.

9. Sayyid 'Ajall's exalted status continues. Today, every year at the end of Ramadan, Muslim Yunnanese commemorate his accomplishments by holding special prayers at his tomb several miles outside Kunming. Armijo, "Narratives Engendering Survival," 311–12.

10. Wade, "The Zheng He Voyages," 3–5.

11. YCFZ, 28:17a–18b; XWZZ, 8:59a–b; YNXZ, 7:11b–12b; LLXZ, 9:8a–b; TYTZ 1887, 4:1b, 4b.

12. Israeli, "Muslims in China," 321.

13. Wang Jianping, *Concord and Conflict*, 241.

14. Lipman, *Familiar Strangers*, xxiii; see also Gillette, *Between Mecca and Beijing*, 11–13.

15. Bodde, *Chinese Thought, Society, and Science*, 148–9.

16. Armijo-Hussein, "Sayyid 'Ajall Shams Al-Din"; Schwartz, "Some Notes of the Mongols of Yunnan," 101–18. An example of such assimilation is that many Mongol troops settled throughout Yunnan in the thirteenth and fourteenth centuries; today, however, they are represented by only eight thousand Mongols, who are concentrated in Tonghai County in central Yunnan.

17. Ma Weiliang, *Yunnan Huizu lishi*," 101–6. For an insightful modern example of how the Hui have employed their Muslim identity and culture to bolster their identity against assimiliation, see Gillette, *Between Mecca and Beijing*.

18. Gladney, *Muslim Chinese*, 26.

19. Ibid., 323.

20. Allès, *Musulmans de Chine*, 289.

21. Bai Shouyi, "Guanyu Huizushi de jige wenti," 192. In a 1984 essay, Bai Shouyi further clarified this issue by stating that those "who believe that Hui [*Huizu*] are Muslims, and Muslims are Hui [*Huizu*] are simply incorrect. . . . We must not say that all those who believe in the Islamic faith are all Hui, this is absolutely untrue." See Bai Shouyi, "Guanyu Huizushi gongzuo de jige yijian," 226.

22. Chan, "The 'Panthay Embassy' to Britain, 1872," 100–17.

23. Allès, *Musulmans de Chine*, 29.

24. Gladney, *Muslim Chinese*, 20.

25. Ibid., 19; Lipman, *Familiar Strangers*, xxiii; Gillette, *Between Mecca and Beijing*, 11–13; Allès, *Musulmans de Chine*, 29.

26. Ma Zhu, *Qingzhen zhinan*, 1041.

27. Luo Wenbin, *Pingqian jilue*, 3:10a, 4:8a, 10:21b; *Qingshi liezhuan*, 44:49a.

28. QPHF, 6:12a; Du Wenxiu, "Shuaifu Bugao," 123; Ma Rulong, "Fu dasiheng yang rong deng shu," 142; see also Li Yuzhen, "Dianshi shu wen," 193; DXG 9:14b. Within Chinese studies, many scholars have discussed the origins of ethnicity in the Chinese context, but most begin their examination at the turn of the century when Dr. Sun Yat-sen promoted the idea of "five peoples of China" (*wuzu gonghe*)— referring to Han, Manchu, Mongolian, Tibetan, and "Muslim" peoples—in order to forward his discussion of Chinese nationalism. Sun's usage of *wuzu* was almost certainly based on the Japanese term *minzoku*. The ideograph of *zu* in the People's Republic today is inextricably intertwined with the term *minzu* or "nationality." Here it likely has a less reified meaning, yet it does seem to offer a distinct impression of an awareness that "Hui" are an ethnic category. Only rarely employed in the nineteenth century, its appearance in Yunnan can perhaps be traced to links between the Pingnan regime and that of the Taipings, who are also recorded as using the term as applied to other ethnicities. See Crossley, "Thinking About Ethnicity," 1990, 10n13.

29. Du Wenxiu, "Shuaifu bugao," II:123.

30. Proschan, "Peoples of the Gourd," 1000.

31. Ibid., 1027.

32. Harrell, ed., *Cultural Encounters*, 28.

33. Ibid.

34. *Menghua xianzhi*, 16:1b; *Zhaotong xianzhi*, 10:3b; You Zhong, *Yunnan minzu shi*, 278; Yang Zhaojun, *Yunnan Huizu shi*, 62.

35. For an extensive listing of such villages see Jing Dexin, *Du Wenxiu qiyi*, 2–3. See *Maguan xianzhi*, 1:1a–18b, for a prime example of this. Each village is categorized by its name, distance from county seat, and ethnicity of the people who live there. For specific examples of Hui-dominated villages see an essay written in 1856 by Ma Enpu in *Dali xianzhigao* [Revised gazetteer of Dali county] (1915), 24:42a–b.

36. Zhang Chaoyu, ed., *Kunmingshi dimingzhi*, 125, 228. Huihuiying, in Gongcheng County, was settled during the Ming.

37. Wu Qianjiu, "Yunnan Huizu de lishi yu xiankuan," 140. In "Les musulmans," 325, Cordier translates an article that perpetuates this view from the Yunnan newspaper *Guanghe tianbao*, May 13, 1912. For a fuller discussion of Han stereotypes of Hui see Lin Changkuan, *Chinese Muslims of Yunnan*, 161.

38. Zhang Chaoyu, *Kunmingshi dimingzhi*, 304. The street today retains a vestige of this name in that it is a homophone of the past name but now means Pearl Street. For a reproduction see insert in Li Xiaoyou, ed., *Kunming fengwuzhi*, 1 (map no. 4).

39. *Yuanmou jiwen*, in HMQY, 217; XYTG, 4:10b.

40. DCZZ, 4:3b; QPHF, 4:2a, 3:14a; DXG, 24:42b.

41. Ma Weiliang has written extensively on this topic. His articles on Hui relations with other non-Han groups have been collected in Ma Weiliang, *Yunnan Huizu lishi yu wenhua yanjiu*, 101–209.

42. Gladney, *Muslim Chinese*, 32–33.

43. Gervais-Courtellemont, *Voyage*, 36.

44. Hanna, "The Panthays of Yunnan," 70.

45. Cao Kun, "Tengyue duluan jishi," in HMQY, II:219; see also XYTG, 4:10b; DXG, 24:42b. A more recent example of a positive perception of the Hui in an otherwise generally negative opinion is the popular belief among Han that Hui restaurants are cleaner than Han ones.

46. Cao Kun, "Tengyue duluan jishi," in HMQY, II:211. Gervais-Courtellemont, *Voyage*, 147–48; Ma Weiliang, "Qingdai chuzhongqi Yunnan Huizu de kuangyeye," 31.

47. *Yunnan yejin shi*, 23, in Ma Weiliang, "Qingdai chu-zhongqi Yunnan Huizu de kuangyeye," 32.

48. *Yongsheng xianzhigao*, in Ma Weiliang, "Qingdai chuzhongqi Yunnan Huizu de kuangyeye," 34; Rocher in his work on the province also mentions Muslims owning mines prior to the rebellion, but these then ended up in the hands of Han Chinese. See Rocher, *La Province chinoise*, II:251; there are strong indications that many Hui operated salt wells as well. See Yang Zhaojun, *Yunnan Huizu shi*, 90.

49. Rocher, *La Province chinoise*, II:31.

50. DXG, 24:42b.

51. The use of typical Hui surnames can only offer a general figure, since sometimes Han and indigenous peoples took up these names as well. In Yunnan the most common surnames for Hui are Ma, Na, Sai, or Sha. See XYTG, 101:1a–17b.

52. XYTG, 101:1a–17b.

53. Ma Weiliang, *Yunnan Huizu lishi yu wenhua yanjiu*, 229–36.

54. Davies, *Yün-nan*, 67.

55. Alice Wei, "The Moslem Rebellion in Yunnan," 8.

56. Le May, *An Asian Arcady*, 188; Forbes, "The 'Cin-ho,'" 13, 26.

57. Forbes, "The 'Cin-ho,'" 17.

58. Thongchai, *Siam Mapped*, 97–99.

59. Wang Zhusheng, *The Jingpo*, 74–75.

60. Thongchai, *Siam Mapped*, 5; Leach, *Political Systems of Highland Burma*; Moerman, "Ethnic Identification in a Complex Civilization," 1215–25; Barth, "Introduction," in *Ethnic Groups and Boundaries*.

61. QPHF, 9:19b; QPHF, 19:18a–b; see also *Yunnan Tongzhi*, 30:1a. Lee's estimate of Yunnan's mid-nineteenth century, although still only an educated guess, is the best estimate based on available data; see Lee "Food Supply and Population Growth," 729.

62. Eickelman and Piscatori, *Muslim Travellers*, iv.

CHAPTER 4

1. Struve, *The Southern Ming*, 168–78.

2. *Daqing shizong xianhuangdi shilu*, 64:20b–21a, in Herman, "Empire in the Southwest," 47.

3. *Huangchao jingshi wenbian*, in Wu Xinfu, "Shilun qingchao," 18.

4. Ni Tui, *Yunnan shilue*, in You Zhong, *Yunnan minzu shi*, 519.

5. XYTG, 77:1a.

6. Herman, "Empire in the Southwest," 69.

7. MEP, 539:219.

8. For an example of one evaluation that reflects the state's consternation and strategy see *Dao-Xian-Tong-Guang sichao zouyi*, I:72.

9. XYTG, 20:20a–b, 42:13a, 15a, 20b–24b.

10. *Kuangwu dang*, VI:3202, in Qiu Lijuan, *Qingdai Yunnan tongkuang de jingying*, 151.

11. Kuhn, *Soulstealers*, 47.

12. For a nuanced description of frontier complexities see Giersch, "'A Motley Throng'," 67–94. Pasquet offers a brilliant exposition of the competing claims over the region and the influence of the mines in "Entre Chine et Birmanie," 41–68.

13. QSL, II:193.

14. Ibid., II:199.

15. Ibid., II:201.

16. Kwong, "The T'i-Yung Dichotomy," 264. See also Palmer, "The Surface-Subsoil Form of Divided Ownership," 48.

17. Yen Ching-Hwang, "Ch'ing Changing Images of the Overseas Chinese," 268.

18. XYTG, 3:20a

19. QSL, II:219. A declaration so self-evident leads one to wonder which acts were in fact permitted by the local officials.

20. Ibid., II:146.

21. XYTG, 3:20a.

22. QSL, II:213.

23. Although evidence pointing to this phenomena is scarce, it was apparent enough for French explorer Francis Garnier to note it. See Garnier, *Voyage*, 518.

24. Leong, *Migration and Ethnicity in Chinese History*, 21.

25. *Xuxiu jianshui xianzhi*, 4:1b–2a; QSL, II:148–49.

26. For a brief and sometimes inaccurate summary of this uprising see You Zhong, *Yunnan minzu shi*, 567–68. The primary sources offer a more complex picture: *Xuxiu jianshui xianzhi*, 4:2a–3b; XYTG, 19b–23b; QSL, 150–52; QSXMS, 176–77.

27. *Xuxiu jianshui xianzhi*, 4:2a.

28. QSL, II:148.

29. *Xuxiu jianshui xianzhi*, 4:2a–3a. *Jiangnei*, or within the river, is a geographical referent demarcating the areas more heavily inhabited (by Han Chinese). The river boundary was primarily the Yuan River (although in western Yunnan the same term referred to the Lancang River), with *jiangwai* referring to the areas to the southwest of the rivers. It was also often a shorthand term implying beyond the pale, or non-Han lands.

30. XYTG, 3:19b–20a.

31. Ibid.

32. Ibid., 3:20a.

33. QSL, III:127–28.

34. XYTG, 3:22a.

35. Schoppa, "Local Self-Government in Zhejiang," 516; Rowe, "Ancestral Rites and Political Authority," 294–96.

36. XYTG, 3:23a.
37. Ibid., 3:23b.
38. Ibid.
39. Ibid., 3:23a. This is eminently clear, given the fact that he promoted "the cutting of trees in the mountainous areas" because forests facilitated the hiding of villainous elements.
40. The geographic distinction is an important one, for although the disturbances of 1800 to 1806 were substantial, they were clearly more oriented against the government than against the Chinese migrants. See XYTG, 3:4a–b; QSXMS, 215–19; QSL, II:203–14; Launay, *Histoire de la mission du Thibet*, I:222.
41. QSL, II:214–32.
42. QSXMS, 229.
43. Huang, *Code, Custom, and Legal Practice in China*, 72.
44. QSL, II:213–15.
45. QSXMS, 234, dated June 24, 1821; QSL, II:228, dated July 20, 1821. *Dian* land transactions were a traditional system of mortgaging property whereby one could in theory buy the land back. However, Qingbao noted that aside from many tusi selling their official estates (*guanzhuang*) to Han settlers, there were also illicit sales by *tumu* and *bashi* (native leaders under the tusi), as well as sales by non-Han tenants. From Qingbao's comments (quoted below) it seems that primary landholding rights in non-Han areas could be sold to Han; what remains unclear is whether Qingbao was fully attentive to land transaction issues pertaining to rents. For a discussion of issues concerning tribal land rights see Shepherd, *Statecraft and Political Economy*, 248–56.
46. XYTG, 3:26a; Qin Bao, *Zougao*, 10 (no pagination), quoted by Daniels, "Environmental Degradation, Forest Protection and Ethno-history in Yunnan." I am indebted to Daniels for making available the full text of his article, which is in large part a synopsis of Fusaji, "Sindai Unnan yakihatamin no hanran," 276–288.
47. QSL, II:230. The military commander in question was replaced as a result of his inaction.
48. Daniels, "Environmental Degradation," 11. I am grateful to Christian Daniels for providing me with a copy of this article.
49. *Dayao xianzhi*, 6:3b–4a.
50. In Daniels, "Environmental Degradation," 10. Translation is Daniels.
51. QSL, II:228.
52. Ibid.
53. Ibid., 230. Qingbao had recommended that the latter two officials be degraded three ranks, but the emperor, expressing leniency, only degraded them two.
54. *Ruan Yuan nianpu*, 181.
55. XYTG, 3:32b–33a, *Ruan Yuan nianpu*, 180–86.
56. XYTG, 42:23b–24a.
57. *Ruan Yuan nianpu*, 183.
58. XYTG, 3:33a.
59. *Ruan Yuan nianpu*, 183.
60. Hsieh Shi-Chung, *Ethnic-Political Adaptation and Ethnic Change*, 309.
61. *Dao-Xian-Tong-Guang sichao zouyi*, I:72. The memorial is dated 1822.

62. XYTG, 3:28b–29a.

63. Yi Duanshan, "Zhiji cha liumin zhuoyi changcheng qin," in Fang Guoyu, ed., *Yunnan shiliao congkan*, IX:13.

CHAPTER 5

1. *Yingxuetang chaolu*, in YHQS, 1–61.

2. Ibid., 11. Twelve Hui were killed in the first melee; then, later on, six who were hiding were "ordered executed" by the *kezhang*, for a total of eighteen. Jing Dexin points out correctly that the actual document distorts the facts slightly by stating in summary that the Hunanese and the Hui "indiscriminately killed each other." From Hunanese admissions, it is obvious that most of the violence was carried out by the Hunanese.

3. Ibid., 12.

4. XYTG, 43:30a–31b; YHQS, 10.

5. *Diannan kuangchang tulue*, 13, in Jing Dexin, *Du Wenxiu qiyi*, 23.

6. YHQS, 10; for non-Han involvement see also XYTG, 43:20a–b.

7. XYTG, 44:22a.

8. YHQS, 48.

9. Ibid., 54; *Yunnan tongzhi*, 106:26; XYTG, 81:1a; *Xuxiu Shunning fuzhi*, 17:2. All state that ninety-nine Hui were killed. More than seventy bodies were uncovered, but the final report submitted by Wu Yanchen, the provincial treasurer, and Shi Pu, the provincial judge, stated that an accurate number of the dead (*shangbi*) was ninety.

10. YHQS, 18. Xu in his testimony goes on to say that the "rumor" was even put into writing and delivered anonymously to the Buddhist temple, which served as the center of the Hunanese community.

11. The Hunanese team boss, Xia Xiushan, led the attack and was found responsible for the deaths of at least one family. He was ordered put to death by slicing and beheading (*lingchi*). Lu Zhengfa was not found to be directly linked to any deaths; he received one hundred strokes, which would kill any but the strongest man, as well as banishment.

12. YHQS, 2–5.

13. Ibid., 5–9.

14. Ibid., 34.

15. For a sampling see XYTG, 81:1a–9b; *Xuxiu Shunning fuzhi* (1905), 17:9a–21a; *Xuxiu Malong xianzhi*, (1917), 1:25a–28b; *Yunnan xianzhi*, (1890), 7:11b–12b; DXG, 9:14a. For the three main published works on the rebellion see Wang Shuhuai, *Xian-Tong Yunnan Huimin shibian*, 49–53; Jing Dexin, *Du Wenxiu qiyi*, 22–33; Wang Jianping, *Concord and Conflict*, 248–52.

16. DXG, 9:14a.

17. XYTG, 79:4b.

18. Gui Liang, "Chiti Ma Wenzhao," in HMQY, I:72.

19. These and the following details are contained in ibid., I:72–75. See also Wang Shuhuai, *Xiantong Yunnan Huimin shibian*, 52–53.

20. "Mianning Huimin Kouhun Gao," in HMQY, I:85–86. The mosque is described as three stories tall and topped by a minaret.

21. Gui Liang, "Chiti Ma Wenzhao," in HMQY, I:85. Often, these were referred to as screen walls and built opposite entrances to temples or yamens.

22. Ibid., I:73. The term describing Yang and Zhao is ambiguous. In one source they are described as evil gentry (*e-jin*), but likely they were *xiucai*.

23. The term *waqf* in Chinese is *wogefu*.

24. Gui Liang, "Chiti Ma Wenzhao," in HMQY, I:73. In "Mianning Huimin kouhun gao" it is suggested that local non-Han also were brought in by the henchmen to fight the Hui; HMQY, I:85.

25. Gui Liang, "Chiti Ma Wenzhao," in HMQY, I:73–74; "Mianning Huimin kouhun gao," HMQY, I:85–86.

26. Gui Liang, "Chiti Ma Wenzhao," in HMQY, I:74; "Mianning Huimin kouhun gao," in HMQY, I:85–86.

27. QSL, I:234.

28. "Chiti Ma Wenzhao," in HMQY, I:76; "Mianning Huimin kouhun gao," HMQY, I:86.

29. QSL, II:233. Document dated May 13, 1840.

30. Ibid. Document dated May 21, 1840.

31. Lamley, "Lineage Feuding in Southern Fujian and Eastern Guangdong," 31–32.

32. "Chiti Ma Wenzhao," in HMQY, I:76.

33. YHSLD, I:126.

34. Numerous sources refer to this incident but disagree as to where it took place. Li Yuanbing suggests it occurred in Banqiao village while rice was being planted; see Li Yuanbing, "Yongchangfu baoshanxian Han-Hui," in HMQY, I:5. Another account suggests it transpired during the annual temple fair, which was held on stage at the Beiyue Temple. That would link it with the later fighting that occurred during the Five Sacred Mountain God festivities and suggests the territorialism typical of communal feuding.

35. YHSLD, I:126.

36. For an instance of Hui using songs as a medium to insult Han, see He Changling, *Naian zouyi*, 11:19b.

37. Ibid., 12:55a.

38. Two years earlier, in 1843, on the occasion of a Buddhist pilgrimage, an attack by one Hui on a Buddhist pilgrim was so harmful that the Hui was executed. See Li Yuanbing, "Yongchangfu baoshanxian," in HMQY, I:4.

39. Ibid., in HMQY, I:3. Although it is not stated, the procession described was likely a symbolic demarcation of *religious* territory and thus even more contentious to the Hui as it passed in front of their mosque.

40. Ibid., in HMQY, I:3–4. The symbolic importance of these temples as symbols of the Han might be further reinforced by the fact that each of the five temples was burned to the ground by Hui soldiers during the Panthay Rebellion. See *Yongchang fuzhi*, 1886, 26:4b.

41. Ibid., in HMQY, I:4–5.

42. YGZ, 1:15b, 3:7a.

43. He Changling, *Naian zouyi*, 11:28a; Zhang Mingqi, "Xian-Tong bianluan jingli ji," in YHQS, 82–83.

44. From the descriptions in extant documents these groups reflect David Own-by's assertion that these *hui* secret societies "often existed alongside or in between traditional institutions allowing their members to achieve various ends, ranging from mutual aid to criminal entrepreneurship to, on occasion, rebellion." See Ownby, "Introduction," 36. See also Murray and Qin, *Tiandihui*, 231–35, which indicates occasional Tiandihui uprisings in Yunnan.

45. Li Yuanbing, "Yongchangfu baoshanxian," in HMQY, I:3.

46. He Changling, *Naian zouyi*, 11:28b–29a.

47. Literally the phrase is "if one person has a problem, then everyone will help" (*yiren youshi dajia bangzhu*).

48. He Changling, *Naian zouyi*, 11:28b–29a; Li Shoukong, "Wanqing Yunnan Huibian shimo," 430–31.

49. Li Yuanbing, "Yongchangfu baoshanxian," in HMQY, I:3; Li Shoukong, "Wanqing Yunnan Huibian shimo," 430–31.

50. Li Yuanbing, "Yongchangfu baoshanxian," in HMQY, I:3. Dian Murray found only three incidences of Tiandihui in eastern Yunnanese towns that bordered Guizhou and Guangxi provinces, where the Tiandihui were far more prevalent. Murray, *The Origins of the Tiandihui*, 78–79.

51. YGZ, 3:7a.

52. Han Pengri, "Yixi Han-Hui shilue," in HMQY, I:178.

53. For an excellent overview see He Huiqing, "Yunnan Du Wenxiu," 13.

54. Li Yuanbing, "Yongchangfu baoshanxian," in HMQY, I:3. Li Yuanbing suggests that the escort could number upwards of five hundred men!

55. Han Pengri, "Yixi Han-Hui shilue," in HMQY, I:178–79.

56. He Changling, *Naian zouyi*, 11:28b.

57. Ibid., 11:39b.

58. Ibid., 12:28a–b; YGZ, 3:7a.

59. Sheng Yuhua, "Yongchang Hanhui hudou anjielue," in YHQS, 63.

60. YGZ, 3:7a.

61. Ibid., 3:2b. Regarding a later incident, Lin estimated that the Incense Brotherhoods in the seven villages (*qi shao*) "are not less than several hundred thousand." See YGZ, 3:5b. He Changling also accuses them in 1833 of burying a man alive; see YGZ, 1:16a.

62. He Changling, *Naian zouyi*, 11:35a; also Sheng Yuhua, "Yongchang Han-Hui hudou anjielue," in YHQS, 63. The Chinese character in these men's names (*sha'an*) almost certainly indicates they were from the northern province of Sha'anxi.

63. He Changling, *Naian zouyi*, 11:35a.

64. Even He Changling cannot seem to get the story straight. In his first account he has Ma Da fighting with the Han (*Naian zouyi*, 11:29a). Then several days later he omits any mention of a fight (Ibid., 11:35a).

65. Ibid., 11:35a–b.

66. Li Bingyuan, "Yongchangfu baoshanxian," in HMQY, I:4–5.

67. He Changling, *Naian zouyi*, 11:35b; Sheng Yuhua, "Yongchang Hanhui hudou anjielue," in YHQS, 64.

68. He Changling, *Naian zouyi*, 11:36b; YGZ, 1:4a–b. The largest group of Yunnan Hui came from Yunzhou.

69. Sheng Yuhua, "Yongchang Hanhui hudou anjielue," in YHQS, 64.

70. He Changling, *Naian zouyi*, 11:36b, 11:46b, 12:56b.

71. Ibid., 11:37a–38a.

72. Ibid., 11:38a.

73. YGZ, 1:17b. One Han Chinese memoir suggests that the whole garrison was put to death, but it seems unlikely that such a defeat would have escaped Lin Zexu's thorough examination of the cause of the massacre. See Sheng Yuhua, "Yongchang Hanhui hudou anjielue," in YHQS, 66.

74. He Changling, *Naian zouyi*, 11:37a–b; Jing Dexin, *Du Wenxiu qiyi*, 36.

75. *Gongzhongdang*, DG 25/12/10, 19:412–415. He Changling offers several versions. In one account, Ma Da and Mu Ruhe actually met. It bears mentioning that when He Changling later interrogated and sentenced the Hui, there was no mention of a plot. Nor does the name "Mu Ruhe" *ever* again appear.

76. He Changling, *Naian zouyi*, 11:13a–14b; YGZ, 7:13b–14b.

77. YGZ, 7:13b–14b.

78. HMQY, I:5–9; QPHF, 14:16b.

79. He Changling, *Naian zouyi*, 11:32a.

80. Ibid., 11:40a.

81. Ibid., 11:13a–4b. See also HMQY, I:4–5.

82. He Changling, *Naian zouyi*, 12:11b. He Changling cast his criticism quite softly, stating that "Luo did not prepare well nor did he carry out the attack appropriately."

83. Ibid., 12:12b.

84. Ibid.

85. Ibid., 12:11a–14b.

86. Regarding the position of Ma Da and Qing troops see ibid., 11:16a. It should be remembered that the attack was supposed to occur the same night as the massacre; thus it does not seem logical that the Hui inside the city would have proceeded with their attack when no Hui force materialized to attack from the outside; ibid., 11:13a. For further discussion of the inconsistencies of Luo's account see Jing Dexin, *Du Wenxiu qiyi*, 36–37.

87. Anonymous, "Proclamation of the Hui of Yongchang," in HMQY, I:91–92. The language in this document clearly juxtaposes the Hui's long history in Yunnan as upright citizens with the clear complicity of the officials in killing Hui, and not just in Baoshan. Significantly, this document also lists the other incidents at Xiyi, Baiyang Mine, Yunzhou, and Mianning.

88. LGY, 13:74a.

89. Ibid., 14:27b, 13.11b; *Gongzhongdang*, DG:9503. For an instance where both Han and Hui parties were from outside Yunnan, see LGY, 3:11b–12a.

90. *Xuxiu Shunning fuzhi*, 1905, 17a–18b.

91. He Changling, *Naian zouyi*, 12:25b–26a.

92. LGY, 14:11a–12b.

93. Ibid., 14:11b; He Changling, *Naian zouyi*, 12:26b. This is also reinforced by the predominance of non-Yunnanese Hui in the bands described here.

94. Ibid., 11:46b.

95. Ibid., 11:26a.

96. Li Bingyuan, "Yongchangfu baoshanxian," in HMQY, I:6.

97. YGZ, 1:11b.

98. Ibid., 7:13b–14b.

99. Wu Qian suggests that at least eight thousand died in the organized geno-
cide; see "Yongchang Huimin xiwen," in HMQY, I:91. Li Yuanbing states that "over
1,300 Hui were killed by the first night and altogether over 8,000 died"; Li Yuanbing, "Yongchangfu Baoshanxian Han-Hui hudou ji," HMQY, I:5–9. The petition
eventually carried to Beijing by Hui seeking official resolution of the affair, also
judged the number of deaths to be eight thousand. Finally, Zhang Mingle in his account of the massacre in *Xiantong bianluan jingli ji* states that the number of dead
"was no few than eight to nine thousand"; in Jing, *Du Wenxiu qiyi*, 35. Yun-Gui
Governor-General Pan Duo, in 1862, estimated the number of deaths at eight thousand, see QPHF, 14:16b.

100. Zhang Mingqi, *Xiantong bianluan jingli ji*, in YHQS, 84.

101. YGZ, 3:5b.

102. Ibid., 5:4a. A later account suggests that the escorting officials escaped back
to Baoshan, sounded the alarm to close the gates, and attempted to hide the Hui in
various official *yamens* for their safety.

103. Ibid., 3:5b–6a; 5:5b.

104. Ibid., 5:1b. Lin's move to suppress the Han uprising was complicated by
the fact that on his way there he encountered an unrelated conflict in Midu.

105. A rather ironic punishment, given that Lin himself had served time in the
same area; YGZ, 5:9a–11b, 6:23a–b. In his final tally, Lin notes that he executed a
total of twenty-six; this indicates that in the following months other leaders must
have been caught and brought before him; YGZ, 7:12a–13b.

106. He Changling, *Naian zouyi*, 12:5a–b. Such postings were a response to the
fact that magistrates from neighboring areas reported several hundred Hui fleeing
into their districts.

107. He Changling, *Naian zouyi*, 12:6a–7b.

108. YGZ, 4:8b–9a. Lin specifically bemoaned the fact that suddenly all Hui
were claiming to belong to families aggrieved during the massacre; He Changling,
*Naian zouyi*, 30b–31a. Many of the Hui arrested stated they revolted in part to get
Hui lands out of Han control.

109. YGZ, 4:8b–9a.

110. Ibid., 10:21b.

111. Lee, "The Southwest," in Will and Wong, *Nourish the People*, 443.

112. YGZ, 10:22a–b. Although never forced to move, the Hui were not offered
other compensation. Whether as a result of Lin's program or local coercion, a local
official noted in 1855 that "most of rich land in Baoshan had been Hui, but the Hui
had been driven out and the rich lands given over to the Han"; QPHF, 1:2a.

113. YGZ, 10:22a–b.

114. QSL, II:228. Qing Bao never simply conceded the ill-begotten land to the
Han interlopers; rather, he ordered local officials to sort out the ownership with an
eye to punishing those Han who had obtained the land illegally.

115. *Naian zouyi*, 12:39a.

116. YGZ, 1:2a; LGY, 14:28b.

117. YGZ, 6:11a; LGY, 1:11b.

118. He Changling, *Naian zouyi*, 11:25b, 11:34a, 12:39a–b. The adoption of the *xiangyue* lectures in these particular instances seems to have provided the perfect context for not resolving the differences but instead expanding on them; often many of these lecturers were leaders of the violence; see LGY, 14:11b.

119. *Guangtong Xianzhi*, 80:16a; in Kung-chuan Hsiao, *Rural China*, 73. This sentiment was noted even earlier, in 1836; see Fang Guoyu, Xu Wende, Mu Qin, eds. *Yunnan shiliao congkan*, 9:13–14.

120. Rowe, *Saving the World*, 388. Rowe notes that "official rhetoric to the contrary, the system atrophied rather quickly on its implementation under the Qing."

121. LGY, 14:11b.

122. Leong, *Migration and Ethnicity in Chinese History*, 51 (see also 72).

123. YGZ, 3:7b; LGY, 4:28a.

124. Ibid., 14:27a.

125. Ibid., 14:26b. An almost identical phrase is attributed to the acting Baoshan District magistrate, who stated: "The Hui character is fierce and they come to the aid of one another. The Han dare not challenge them, but their hatred [towards the Hui] has amassed over many decades"; see Han Pengri, "Yixi Han-Hui shilue," in HMQY, I:178.

126. YGZ, 4:8b.

127. Ibid., 2:12a–b, 15b.

128. Ibid., 8:5a–8a. It should be noted that Lin requested and received permission to carry out immediate summary executions (*jiudi zhengfa*) to avoid the onerous and dangerous task of transporting the prisoners to Kunming for trial. Also, Bai Shouyi makes a critical editorial error in *Huimin qiyi* I:240, mistakenly transcribing the original document by substituting Hui for Han.

129. YGZ, 2:8b, 9b–10a.

130. Lipman, *Familiar Strangers*, 100.

131. YGZ, 2:15b.

132. These classes of statutes were from one to several grades heavier than those meted out to non-Muslims for the same offenses. See Lipman, *Familiar Strangers*, 100.

133. He Changling, *Naian zouyi*, 11:30a–31a.

134. For Li, see Hummel, *Eminent Chinese of the Ch'ing Period*, I:458. For a more complete citation see LGY, 13:71a–b; for Lin see Hummel, *Eminent Chinese*, I:513 or, for the complete citation, QSL, III:418. Lin was posthumously granted the title of Grand Mentor of the Heir Apparent; see QSL, III:496.

135. XYTG, 3:32b–33a; *Ruan Yuan nianpu*, 1995, 180–86.

CHAPTER 6

1. Li Yuzhen, DSSW, in YHQS, 189; Alice Wei, "Moslem Rebellion in Yunnan," 66.

2. YGZ, 10:16b–17b. In one of the rare reappearances of the term, Lin accuses two Han of hanjianism (YGZ, 10:6a) for linking up with bandits from outside Yunnan. The non-Han, although prominent in Lin's version of events, will vanish

from any subsequent reports—a small indication of the blinkered nature of the sources.

3. YGZ, 10:17b.

4. TNZJ, in HMQY, I:251.

5. Ibid.

6. Ibid., I:252.

7. Ibid.

8. Ibid.

9. Ibid., I:253.

10. Ibid., I:252.

11. Ibid., I:253.

12. See Wei Hsiu-mei, II:559; 650 for a listing of officials posted to Yunnan and their length of tenures.

13. MEP, 539:614 (April 3, 1852).

14. Ibid., 539:817 (August 1, 1855). Fifteen years later, Garnier, while traveling through the province as a member of the French Mekong Expedition, also noted a valley in western Yunnan where there were especially large numbers of Sichuanese immigrants. He recorded that "it is only the Chinese, who have recently immigrated from Sichuan who can claim in Yunnan a racial purity. . . . This antagonism between the old and the new Chinese singularly favors the Muslim Rebellion"; see Garnier, *Voyage*, 518.

15. MEP, 541:194 (July 8, 1854).

16. TNZJ, 254; Rocher, *La Province chinoise*, II:35.

17. Rocher, *La Province chinoise*, II:33–34.

18. TNZJ, 257–58. Neither the Hui nor the Hui bands established a permanent presence at Xizhuang; rather, the attacks occurred over an extended period of time, with interim periods of relative calm when one or the other bands returned to their own hometowns.

19. TNZJ, 258.

20. Ibid., 259; See also DSDJ, 293–94.

21. Anonymous, "Diannan zaji" in HMQY, II:247.

22. Li Shoukong, "Wanqing Yunnan Huibian shimo," 458.

23. *Chuxiong xianzhi*, 1910, 6:7b; DNZ, in HMQY, II:247; XYTG, 81:10a. One source suggests that five thousand Hui were killed; see Yao Huating, "Chuxiong binchen kangbian shilue," in HMQY, II:3–4.

24. There is little hard evidence to support assertions of any substantive countermeasures by the Hui. See QPHF, 1:6a–b.

25. MEP, 539:885 (April 28, 1856).

26. MEP, 541:241 (February 24, 1856).

27. The seesaw nature of the miners coming and going from the mining site facilitated Cui's strategy; QPHF, 2:1b; DSDJ, 293.

28. YGZ, 10:17b. Later officials acknowledged Cui's highly opportunistic style, which further aggravated the already unstable situation; see QPHF, 19:18a. After being promoted to the post of Dongchuang prefect Cui was eventually censured for his behavior by Governor-General Hengchun but allowed to remain in office (*gezhi liuren*). See QPHF, 4:9a.

29. *Yunnan tongzhi*, 107:7, in Jing Dexin, *Du Wenxiu qiyi*, 1991, 57; QPHF, 7b–8a.

30. QPHF, 1:12b, 16a.

31. Ibid., 3:16b.

32. Ibid., 3:17a.

33. Zhang Zhongfu, "Luyun jishi gao," in HMQY, II:426.

34. *Wenzong shilu*, 196:12a, in Wang Shuhuai, *Xiantong Yunnan huimin shibian*, 103.

35. Wei Hsiu-mei, *Qing jizhi guangbiao*, II:97.

36. In many secondary sources his name was often mistakenly written as Huang Zhong or Huang Cong. For his official career see Wei, *Qing jizhi guangbiao*, 105.

37. QPHF, 6:18b–19a; Rocher, *La Province chinoise*, II:37.

38. QPHF, 6:18b–19a; Rocher, *La Province chinoise*, II:37.

39. It is unclear who ordered this although it was likely either Shuxing'a or Huang Cong. QPHF, 2:6a, 5:13b–14a, 6:19a–20a, 8:4a; DSDJ, in HMQY, I:294; DXG, 9:17a; Rocher, *La Province chinoise*, II:36–37.

40. QPHF, 4:2b; "Dianhui jiluan," in YHQS, 272; "Dianluan jilue," in HMQY, I:266.

41. Bai Shouyi, ed., *Huizu renwuzhi*, 6. The massacre is still remembered today in Kunming, with the local ahongs fixing June 14 (the day the massacre was believed to have occurred) as "Remembrance Day [*wangren jie*]." For a description see *Yunnan yisilan wenhua lunwen yiji*, 304. Father Chauveau suggests it was the Islamic New Year; however, although it was Ramadan, the fasting did not end until June 4, 1856.

42. Rocher, *La Province chinoise*, II:39.

43. DSDJ, 294.

44. Cordier, "Les Mosques du Yunnanfu," 153.

45. DSDJ, 294.

46. Governor-General Pan Duo suggests two to three thousand; QPHF, 14:16b. One witness states that nearly twenty thousand were killed; see Wang Dingchen, "Qing xiantongjian Yunnan Huibian jiwen," in HMQY, II:300. A year after the event Wu Zhenyu suggested the number was "several thousand"; QPHF, 5:21a. Many secondary accounts misquote Wu's estimate by substituting the word "households" for people; see Jing Dexin, *Du Wenxiu qiyi*, 1991, 64; and Bai Shaoyi, *Huizu Renwu (Jindai)*, 6. Sangchunrong when taking office glossed completely over the Kunming Massacre and insinuated that the violence moved directly from the Shiyang mining incident to the provincewide disturbances; QPHF, 5:15a. A turn-of-the-century Western account states that fourteen thousand died in the massacre. The registered population of Kunming was 430,825. XYTG, 35:4b–5a.

47. Garnier, *Voyage*, 455.

48. QPHF, 12:10.

49. WDSL, in HMQY, II:29.

50. Zhao Qing, "Bianyuan jiaoyuan lu," in HMQY, I:45.

51. QPHF, 12:10; see also WDSL, 26.

52. QPHF, 6:18b–19a. See QPHF, 8:3b–4a, for his censure by the court for his involvement in forming illegal Han militias to attack the Hui. Rocher states that he

committed suicide in 1860 when Ma Rulong and Ma Dexin were given offices in exchange for their surrender, and Huang realized his anti-Muslim campaign could not succeed. See Rocher, *La Province chinoise*, I:67.

53. QPHF, 1:7a–9b.

54. Ibid., 1:8b. As in Baoshan, one must ask the question: For whom were the gates to be opened?

55. Ibid., 1:8b–9a.

56. Ibid., 1:9a–b. A variation of this story appears in a Han account justifying the massacre and providing evidence of a Hui plot for rebellion in Kunming; see Anonymous, "Dian-Hui jiluan," in YHQS, 271–74.

57. QPHF, 1:11a–b.

58. Ibid., 2:1b–2a. In this description the officials were accused of protecting the pernicious Hui activity and the Han were cast as the victims. This was presented by the officials as the primary catalyst for the Kunming Massacre.

59. Ibid., 4:2b. Note how the usage of hanjian here still intimates a linking of Han with some non-Han force.

60. Ibid., 4:2b.

61. Ibid., 3:17b–18a. This edict was in reaction to censor Li Peihu's detailing of the military defeats and lack of leadership.

62. Ibid., 4:2b–3a.

63. Ibid., 3:18a.

64. Lipman, *Familiar Strangers*, 100–3.

65. Lipman, "Sufism in the Chinese Courts," in de Jong and Radtke, *Islamic Mysticism Contested*, 567.

66. QPHF, 2:1a–2b. He Tongyun went as far as to suggest that the Chuxiong magistrate Cui Zhaozhong enlisted five hundred Hui to fight the Han.

67. QSL, II:313; QPHF, 2:13b. The court interpreted these events and set a court of action largely on the basis of his assessment. Either he had influence with the court or the latter saw few alternatives. See QSL, II:306–307, for the full rescript on He's comments.

68. QPHF, 2:14a. Li is technically correct, since Shuxing'a did become ineffectual after the massacre. Yet it was Shuxing'a's earlier actions that had incited the Hui to rebel.

69. Ibid., 2:15a.

70. Ibid., 2:16a–b. These directives follow the recommendations He Tongyun made several months earlier; 2:32b–3b. See 5:14b for the emperor's award to Zhang Liangji of the fifth-grade button of rank to wear before the latter headed to Yunnan to help Wu Zhenyu fight the Hui.

71. Wang Shulin, "Dianxi Huiluan jilue," in YHQS, 233; *Heqing zhouzhi*, 19:3a–4b.

72. Zhang served as Baoshan magistrate from 1846 to 1847, as provincial judge from 1849 to 1850, and as provincial treasurer for four months in 1850. He was promoted to governor in 1850 and served for just under two years, until June 1852. See Wei Hsiu-mei, *Qing jizhi guangbiao*, II:154.

73. YGZ, 10:24a–25a. Lin includes a copy of Zhang's proposal and comments in his memorial.

74. QPHF, 4:3b–4a.

75. Ibid., 4:10a–11b.

76. Ibid., 5:6b.

77. DSDJ, 296; QPHF, 5:7a; Pourais, *La Chine*, 78.

78. QPHF, 5:9a–b; XYTG, 81:14b–15a. Rocher mistakenly places Hengchun's death immediately after the Kunming Massacre, and more erroneously, as a reaction to it. Another version has it that Hengchun's wife, humiliated by her husband's inability to govern effectively, hanged herself first; then Hengchun, distraught and also humiliated, hanged himself. This same description notes that he died in a room called the "Hengchun Room"—a word play on the Chinese word for "room," *ting*, and the resting place for a coffin prior to burial, also *ting*. There is a long history of anecdotes about persons dying in conditions linked to their names. For this informal account of Hengchun's death see Luo Qirui, *Yunnan zhanggu*, 610.

79. DXG, 9:17a; XYTG, 81:3a, 11a; QPHF, 1:7a; 1:13b. It is interesting that according to early reports, non-Han were also active in western Yunnan. This memorial (dated August 31, 1856) was the first to express concern over the possibility of Hui and non-Han linking together to create even greater disturbances.

80. DXZ, 9:16b; QPHF, 1:7a; XYTG, 81:11a; Jing Dexin, *Du Wenxiu qiyi*, 79. As we will see, the Heqing forces never arrived; they were occupied with their own anti-Hui campaigns in northwestern Yunnan. Censor Li Peifu states that only three hundred soldiers were under Wen's personal command in Dali.

81. DSSW, 192.

82. For a discussion of grain storage in Yunnan during the eighteenth and nineteenth centuries see Lee, "The Southwest," 443.

83. XYTG, 81:13a; QPHF, 2:8a–9b; 3:6b. There is considerable disagreement over the timing of the siege and surrender. Official Qing sources all agree on the October date, but Li Yuzhen suggests it occurred in August; see DSSW, 192.

84. QPHF, 2:11a. The first memorial containing this information is dated October 17, 1856—almost two months *after* Dali was taken by the Hui forces.

85. "Xianfeng bingchen jiluan luxu," in YHQS, 176. Wen also ordered the Heqing–Lijiang regional commander, Fu Sheng, to advance on Dali with five hundred soldiers.

86. QPHF, 3:6b–7a.

87. DSSW, 194–95. To be fair, the force he did send arrived too late to aid in the city's defense.

88. Regarding sources of Hui leaders executed, see *Yunnan tongzhi*, 107:7, in Jing Dexin, *Du Wenxiu qiyi*, 73–74. Regarding the Hui survivors who made their way to Dali, see DXG, 9:17a.

89. DSSW, 193. The Dali gazetteer also suggests this, but pointedly implies that Wen distrusted the Han militias as much as he did the Hui. Also, it is unclear whether this Linanese militia is the same that had terrorized the region the previous year; DXG, 9:17a.

90. QPHF, 3:6a–b.

91. Ibid. Shuxing'a's figures are almost certainly a gross exaggeration. See censor Li Peihu's estimate, which indicated that only "a little over a hundred Hui" were involved in actively occupying Yaozhou; QPHF, 2:15a. Shuxing'a himself initially put the numbers at three hundred Hui; QPHF, 1:5a.

92. Ibid., 3:7a.

93. Ibid., 4:5a–b.

94. DXZ, 9:17a; DSSW, 193; Alice Wei, "The Moslem Rebellion in Yunnan," 88–90.

95. DSSW, 193.

96. Wang Shulin, *Dianxi Huiluan jilue*, in YHQS, 233. French explorer Louis Carné, who traveled to Kunming in late 1867, suggests that Zheng was involved in killing Muslims and alludes to the widespread organization of the killing: "He [Zheng] resolved, in concert with the Lijiang *mandarin* and another Chinese leader to organize a mass massacre of the Muslims throughout Yunnan all on the same day." See Carné, "Expedition du Mekong," VIII:658.

97. For examples of this bias see Li Yuzhen, "Dianshi shuwen," 192–94; DXG, 9:16b–18a; Wang Shulin, "Dianxi Huiluan jilue," 233–34.

98. QPHF, 2:13b–14a. Obviously, officials spoke of "Hui rebels," but this was usually in the abstract. When the talk was of a specific event or trend, the terminology employed typically used the regional designation. The divisions also appear in privately funded works on the rebellion. See also DSSW, 192.

99. QPHF, 2:14a; 6:15b.

100. Zhao Qing, "Bianyuan jieyuan ji," in HMQY, I:45.

101. DXG, 9:16b; "Bianyuan jiaoyuan lu," in HMQY, I:50.

102. QPHF, 2:14b. Li's reference to Dali as a shield reflected its location on the main route to Lijiang in the northwest and to Baoshan in the east, as well as the fact that it was prominently situated in relation to Chuxiong and Jinghong.

103. Zhao Qing, "Bianyuan jieyuan ji," in HMQY, I:45; DXG, 9:16b.

104. DSSW, 194. For a discussion of the term *lianyong*, see Brunnert and Hagelstrom, *Present Day Political Organization of China*, 341.

105. DXG, 9:17b–18b, for a discussion of the Qing officials' lack of leadership.

106. DXG, 9:17b–18b; DSSW, 193. Alice Wei suggests that the released Muslims from Yaozhou were the catalyst for the Hui uprising in Dali; this seems doubtful, though, since the siege in Yaozhou was raised a month after Dali was captured. See Wei, "The Moslem Rebellion in Yunnan," 90.

107. DSSW, 193. There are some discrepancies among sources with regard to the date the Hui launched their attack. For consistency I have adhered to the dates used in the Dali Gazetteer unless otherwise indicated. The difference is usually only one or two days.

108. "Xianfeng bingzhen jiluan liji," in YQHS, 176; DXG, 9:17b.

109. DXG, 9:17b.

110. Li Shoukong, "Wanqing Yunnan Huibian shimo," 466–67.

111. QPHF, 3:15b.

112. DSSW, 194; DXG, 18a–b.

113. XYTG, 81:11b; DSSW, 193–4; DXG, 9:17a–18b.

114. DSSW, 193–94; DXZ, 9:19b–20a.

115. DXZ, 9:20a.

116. Ibid., 9:20a.

117. Ibid., 9:20a; He Huiqing, "Yunnan Du Wenxiu jianguo shibanian shimo," nos. 12, 13 (663). Other indigenous groups played a prominent role in his later proclamations; in particular, in his *Summons to Arms* he stated emphatically that

"in Yunnan, the Han, Hui and *yi* have been living peacefully together for more than a thousand years." See "Xingshi xiwen" in HMQY, II:131.

118. One anonymous account asserts that the nominal head of the Menghua Hui, Lan Jinxi—a Hui from Shaanxi—refused after the victory to share with others the goods seized by his group. Du and his close friend Ma Jinbao approached and asked him to share his spoils with the group. An argument ensued that seemingly ended with Lan agreeing. However, the next day, a crowd of people, angry over Lan's behavior, killed Lan and presented his head to Du. If this did indeed happen, it removed a key rival of Du. Yet in the Dali Gazetteer, Lan's name is still listed as a top official. See "Dianxi bianluan xiaoshi," in HMQY, II:89–90.

119. There are many accounts of this. Besides the sources listed below see "Du Wenxiu Becomes Commander," in Luckert and Li Shujiang, *Mythology and Folklore of the Hui*, 265–68.

120. The earliest memorial that mentions Du as the head of the rebellion appears on July 21, 1861; see QPHF, 10:26a. Peculiarly, though, the term "Du rebels" is employed much earlier, in late 1857; see ibid., 6:17a.

121. See "Dianxi bianluan xiaoshi," in HMQY, II:90. Some suggest that Du passed the exam in 1848—highly unlikely, since he had not yet returned from Beijing following the Baoshan Massacre (see Tsai Yuanlin, "Confucian Orthodoxy vs. Muslim Resistance," 322). One source even suggests that he was born in 1827 and passed the exam when he was twelve, in 1839. For other sources indicating that Du was a *xiucai*, see YHSLD, I:121; Alice Wei, "The Moslem Rebellion in Yunnan," 100.

122. Bai Shouyi, *Huizu renwuzhi (Qingdai)*, 4.

123. Alice Wei, "The Moslem Rebellion of Yunnan," 62; "Dianxi bianluan xiaoshi," in HMQY, II:84. Numerous sources indicate that Du was the son of a Burmese caravan trader. This is repeated by the French explorer Louis de Carné, "Exploration du Mékong," 86:658.

124. Jing Dexin's *Du Wenxiu qiyi* is typical of this approach.

125. "Dianhui jiluan," in YHQS, 272.

126. "Jianshui Huimin xiwen," in HMQY, II:55–56. The appeal includes an affirmation of the Hui's historical presence in Yunnan since the Yuan Dynasty, directly refers to Huang Cong's plot, and beseeches the upright Han to quell those Han intent on killing the Hui.

127. XYTG, 81:12a; Ma Rulong, "Fudasi yang rong deng Shuxing'a," in HMQY, II:140.

128. XYTG, 81:11b.

129. There is some confusion over Ma's year of birth. Rocher states that he was born in 1793 while Wang Xuhuai suggests 1794; see YHQS, 115fn4. Zhang Liangji in 1863 mentions Ma was seventy; thus, depending on his birthday, he was born in 1793 or 1794; see QPHF, 12:11b.

130. Rocher, *La Province chinoise*, II:46–47. Even if schooled in Chinese until seventeen as Rocher suggests, it seems that Ma Dexin was more comfortable writing in Arabic; almost all his writings were first written in Arabic and then translated by his disciple, Ma Anli. Not until he was forty did he formally began to study Confucianism; see Lin Changkuan, "Three Eminent 'Ulama' of Yunnan," 105.

131. A translation of Ma's *Record of a Pilgrimage* can be found in Deveria,

*Origine de L'islamisme en Chine*, 32. Rocher erroneously suggests that Ma began his journey in 1839; see Rocher, *La Province chinoise*, II:47.

132. Ma's Islamic erudition benefited considerably from the eight years he spent in the Middle East, where he collected valuable Islamic texts and had numerous intellectual encounters. For an accessible overview see Lin, "Three Eminent 'Ulama' of Yunnan," 105; Rocher, *La Province chinoise*, II:46–48.

133. TNZJ, 257–58.

134. Ma Futu, "Ma Futu siji," in HMQY, II:367; Wellington Chan, "Ma Julung," 88.

135. Rocher, *La Province chinoise*, II:49; "Qixi shilue," in HMQY, II:45–46.

136. Rocher, *La Province chinoise*, II:49.

137. Carné, "Exploration," 904.

138. Carné, *Travels*, 272–73.

139. XYTG, 81:12a.

140. *Jianshui xianzhi*, 4:3b–4a; *Yunnan tongzhi*, 107, in Jing Dexin, *Du Wenxiu qiyi*, 90.

141. TNZJ, 256; Rocher, *La Province chinoise*, II:51; QPHF, 5:3a–4a, 8:18a, 9:1a–2b. When Ma Rulong finally accepted the "pacification and settlement" (*anfu*) agreement from the Qing, his strong ties to the indigenous communities would be reflected in the fact that numerous *yi* leaders under his leadership surrendered with him. See XYTG, 82:1a.

142. QPHF, 5:6b–7a.

143. QSL, II:317; "Dianhui jiluan," in YHQS, 273.

144. XYTG, 81:14b.

145. "Dianhui jiluan," in YHQS, 274; DSSW, 199; DSDJ, 296.

146. *Xuxiu jianshui xianzhi*, 4:4b.

147. QPHF, 7:6a–b.

148. Ibid., 7:6a.

149. Ibid., 12:22a; XYTG, 81:17a.

150. XYTG, 81:17a. It also notes that Ma Linghan refused to submit.

151. Li Shoukong, "Ma Rulong xiangqing shi yanjiu"; *Dalu zazhi* 20, nos. 1, 15.

152. "Diannan zaoji," in HMQY, II:257.

153. Chan, "Ma Ju-long," 92.

154. Ma Rulong, "Fu dasi yang rong dengshu," in HMQY, II:140.

155. That Ma Rulong adopted the title of generalissimo is not debated, only the timing. See "Dianhui jiluan," in YHQS, 276, 278; Xu Yuanhua, "Xianfeng yehuo bian," in HMQY, I:283; DSSW, 206; DSDJ, 297.

156. For examples see XYTG, 81:16a–21b; Rocher, *La Province chinoise*, II:55.

157. Ma Dexin often gave conflicting signals as to what his real motives were, but for examples of his actions, see XYTG, 81:18b; He Huiqing, "Yunnan Du Wenxiu jianguo," 14:16–17. In particular, note XYTG, 81:17b, where it is remarked that Ma Dexin "makes a secret compact" with Yang Zhenpeng—who later will link up with Ma Rulong.

158. QPHF, 7:31a.

159. Ibid., 9:6a.

160. Ibid., 8:11b–12a.

161. Rocher, *La Province chinoise*, II:63; *Chuxiong xianzhi*, 6:11a. There is considerable confusion among accounts as to which route Ma Rulong took to Chuxiong. A Dali gazetteer suggests that Ma also attacked Yimen and Xinxing on his way to Chuxiong. See DXG, 9:23a; see also Li Shoukong, "Wanqing Yunnan Huibian shimo," 476.

162. DSSW, 204.

163. XYTG, 81:19a–b; "Dianluan jilue," in YHQS, 274–75; *Xuxiu jianshui xianzhi*, 4:5a.

164. QPHF, 1:11b, 15a–16a.

165. Ibid., 2:1b–3a. He also blames these eastern officials for causing Chuxiong prefect Cui Shaozhong's behavior—and also protecting the Hui!

166. QPHF, 6:19b.

167. XYTG, 81:10b; Xu Yuanhua, "Xiantong Ye Hupian," in Bai Shouyi, HMQY, I:281. Huang Diankui is often identified as the leader of the Han band that skirmished with Hui in Anning just before the Kunming Massacre.

168. *Xuanwei xianzhigao*, 1:11b–12b; QPHF, 3:1a–2b.

169. Jing Dexin, *Du Wenxiu qiyi*, 98.

170. Miao Yongling, *Ma Liansheng zhuanlüe*, in YHQS, 352.

171. *Zhanyi zhouzhi*, in Na Lanzhen, "Ma Liansheng qiyi," in DWQL, 245.

172. Miao Yongling, *Ma Liansheng* zhuanlüe, in YHQS, 353.

173. Jenks, *Insurgency and Social Disorder in Guizhou*, 132–36.

174. MEP, 539:951.

175. Ibid., 951.

176. Ibid., 979.

177. Ibid., 951.

178. QPHF, 9:1a–2b, 7:27b.

179. See He Huiqing, "Yunnan Du Wenxiu jianguo," 12:9–12 and 13:34–36.

180. QPHF, 9:4a–7b.

181. For a sampling of non-Han participation see QPHF, 1:7a–8a, 2:11a, 3:4b, 3:12a, 4:4a–5b, 4:13b–16b. See also Ma Weiliang, *Yunnan Huizu lishi*, 84–87.

182. QPHF, 2:23a.

183. Ibid., 2:23b, 1:13b.

184. Ibid., 19:18b–19a.

185. Ibid., 19:19a.

186. *Gongzhongdang daoguang*, 8202; YHSLD, I:166.

187. *Naian zouyi*, 11:12a. There is some indication that they did. For one indication that Hani joined Imperial troops in their fight against Hui see Garnier, *Voyage*, I:432.

188. QPHF, 2:16b–19a.

189. Ibid., 4:4a. It is difficult to tell whether the somewhat delayed non-Han support is more a lack of early awareness on the part of the officials, or simply a lack of initial interest by the non-Han.

190. For an example with both these terms see QPHF, 4:24b.

191. See ibid., 2:33a; 3:4a–5a.

192. *Ping qian jilue*, 3:10a.

193. DSSW, 220.

194. For complete discussion of Li's flag and title see Ye Tong, *Dali Huizushi yu*, 69–70.

195. Zhang Qingfen, "Jiantan shijiu shiji," in DWQL, 197–98.

196. DXG, 9:20a; DSSW, 198; and MEP, 541:579 (September 12, 1863) offer just a sampling of the Hui's broad multiethnic alliance, which included Han from the outset. In stark contrast, many of the Han would until the bitter end refuse to recognize Hui who wanted to fight with the Qing; see QPHF, 18:16a, 20:2a; "Dian-luan jilue," in HMQY, I:270.

197. Alice Wei, "The Moslem Rebellion in Yunnan," 85, 113; Wang Jianping, *Concord and Conflict*, 248.

198. Du Wenxiu, "Xingshi xiwen," in HMQY, II:131. Meaning that although the Hui were the targets, everyone was affected by the violence.

199. Clendinnen, *Reading the Holocaust*, 93.

200. YGZ, 7:13b–14b; Li Shoukong, "Xianfeng liunian Yunnan Shengcheng," *Dalu zazhi*, 20(6), 174–77.

201. Rocher, *La Province chinoise du Yün-nan*, II:37.

202. QPHF, 14:16a. Note how strongly Pan Duo emphasizes that the rebellion was not a direct result of the mining violence—a point that would have been well taken by many past studies of this event.

## CHAPTER 7

1. DWG, 9:21a; "Dianluan jilue," in YHQS, 199; QPHF, 4:20b. For a detailed village-by-village account, see Heng's memorial dated April 28, 1857, in QPHF, 4:22a–25a. Alternatively, some sources suggest that the Dali forces tricked Wen Xiang into believing that his most able commander, He Ziqing, was dealing with the Hui so as to double-cross Wen; this led to He's dismissal. See He Huiqing, "Yunnan Du Wenxiu jianguo shibian shimo," no. 14, 36.

2. QPHF, 4:20b; 4:22a–25a.

3. *Qingshi liezhuan*, 48:45a.

4. DSDJ, 297.

5. *Qingshi liezhuan*, 44:49a.

6. Ibid., 44:49a; DSDJ, 296; Jing Dexin, *Du Wenxiu qiyi*, 125.

7. QPHF, 9:9b; He Huiqing, "Yunnan Du Wenxiu jianguo shibianian shimo," no. 14, 36–37. The numerous placenames that employed Yunnan can be somewhat confusing. Within the province of Yunnan, the Kunming was known as Yunnanfu, the prefecture surrounding the capital of Kunming was referred to as Yunnan prefecture, and, finally, there existed a district near Dali with the name of Yunnan.

8. *Qingshi liezhuan*, 44:49a–b; Li Shoukong, "Wanqing Yunnan Huibian shimo," 475–76.

9. DXG, 9: 24a; QSL, II, 105; DSDJ, 297; *Qingshi liezhuan* 44:49b; Jing Dexin, *Du Wenxiu qiyi*, 346. Alice Wei mistakenly places Zhu's death in 1859; see "The Moslem Rebellion," 112. For the final imperial account see QPHF, 9:9b, 10:15b–16a.

10. *Qingshi liezhuan,* 44:49b.

11. Li Yuzhen, DSYL, 206–7; He Huiqing, "Yunnan Du Wenxiu jianguo," 36–37; XYTG, 81:35a; DXG, 9:23a.

12. For the extent of this ploy see Zhang Tao, "Dianluan jilue," 268.

13. Some accounts suggest that Ma's original intent was to attack Kunming; despite this, it seems quite unlikely. For examples of this confusion see Bai Shouyi, *Huizu Renwu (Qingdai),* 67–68; He Huiqing, "Yunnan Du Wenxiu jianguo," no. 14, 38. He Huiqing dates the event in 1858—a mistake Wei replicates, having Ma Rulong's first siege of Kunming end in June 1858—and then claims that Zhu Kechang's campaign westward occurred the following year. See Alice Wei, "The Moslem Rebellion in Yunnan," 109–11; QPHF, 9:10a.

14. Rocher, *La Province chinoise,* II:63; for the government account see QPHF, 9:10b–11a. Note that Rocher mistakenly places the battle of Chuxiong in the year 1859.

15. Rocher, *La Province chinoise,* II:63.

16. *Chuxiong xianzhi,* 6:17b–18a; Li Shoukong, "Wanqing Yunnan Huibian shimo," 476.

17. XYTG, 81:28a.

18. Rocher goes so far as to say that when Ma Rulong saw the white banner of Du's army, he retired from the city and removed his troops, thus handing the city over to Du. See *La Province chinoise,* 64.

19. "Diannan zaji," 265. This is purportedly a firsthand narrative account of the rebellion, so it is unclear whether the author (unknown) inserted the standard anti-Manchu slogan at the end himself or whether this was an actual goal of the agreement. A similar account, "Dianhui jiluan," does not include this last sentence. See "Dianhui jiluan," 277. With regard to the division of Yunnan, this quotation—although somewhat ambiguous in English—stipulates clearly that in a local context the spheres of influence of both leaders were to be the halves of the province where their powerbases already existed. For a clear delineation of Du Wenxiu controlling western Yunnan (*yixi yidai*) and Ma Rulong the eastern and southern regions (*yidongnan yidai*), see "Dianhui jiluan," in YHQS, 275.

20. As Wellington Chan points out, perhaps one of the clearest indications of Ma's dramatic ascent is the number of Hui leaders who followed him when he surrendered to the Qing; see Chan, "Ma Ju-long," 99. Though the assumed goal of such a surrender and their ties with Ma Rulong are later brought under doubt when many of them later defect to Du Wenxiu.

21. Louis De Carné suggested several years later that Ma Rulong was in fact jealous of Du's stature in 1860. See "Exploration of the Mekong," VIII:652 (April 1, 1870).

22. "Dianxi Huiluan jilue," in YHQS, 237.

23. MEP, 541:287.

24. QPHF, 9:27a. Zhang Liangji confirms that Xu came to his residence but argues that Xu implored him to not allow them to surrender; see QPFH, 10:5a.

25. For an account partial to the Hui see DSSW, 209; for the imperial account see QPHF, 9:26a–27a.

26. QPHF, 9:27b–28a.

27. Ibid., 10:1a; 9:27a.

28. Ibid., 10:5a. Zhang suggests he was incapacitated.

29. Ibid., 10:9b. The emperor obviously believed Zhang Liangji's assessment since he related the details at a later date; see 10:14b.

30. "Diannan zaji," in HMQY, II:265; QSL, II:331.

31. QPHF, 10:10a.

32. Ibid., 11:1a–b; Luo, "*Yunnan zhanggu*," 610–11.

33. Ibid., 11:6a, 17a–18b.

34. For a description of the winter see MEP, 541:424. Regarding the conditions inside the city see Rocher, *La Province chinoise*, II:70.

35. QPHF, 13:18a–b.

36. Ibid., 10:17a; Chan, "Ma Ju-Lung," 97.

37. Rocher, *La Province chinoise*, II:69–70. Note that Rocher gives the incorrect date.

38. "Diannan zaji," in HMQY, II:265.

39. DSDJ, 297.

40. QPHF, 13:10a, 15:1a.

41. Zhang Tao, "Dianluan jilue," in HMQY, I:269. Rocher indicates that Ma Dexin was offered the post of intendant but refused it.

42. Pourais, *La Chine*, 39. The presence of Catholic missionaries did not seem to bother Ma Rulong or Ma Dexin. An amazing test of this tolerance is reported by Pourais, who recounts that when a dozen Hui soldiers asked him what he thought about Muhammad, he replied that "Mohammad is in Hell and all who follow his religion will come to the same end." Although enraged, the Muslims did not harm the missionary. See ibid. The Hui in other areas of China had a long and cordial relationship with Christian missionaries, even assisting some of the early ones, acknowledging their mutual belief in God. But as Armijo-Hussein pointed out to me (personal correspondence, February 2004), this did not stop missionaries from later concentrating their efforts on proselytizing among the Hui.

43. QPHF, 15:2a; Zhang Tao, "Dianluan jilue," in HMQY, I:269. In an interesting aside, Carné suggested that the dominant position of the Hui extended beyond Kunming into any area where Hui predominated: "the villages are for the most part inhabited by Mussulmans, who although still in subjection to the emperor, spread around them such terror that the frightened Chinese dared not rear their pigs except in secret, and even refused to sell us any." See Carné, *Travels*, 282.

44. QPHF, 15:2a; Zhang Tao, "Dianluan jilue," 269.

45. Zhang Tao, "Dianluan jilue," 269.

46. Rocher, *La Province chinoise*, II:70.

47. QPHF, 13:10a, 13:12a–b.

48. Ibid., 13:12b.

49. Ibid., 13:10b.

50. Ibid., 14:4b–5a.

51. Ibid., 17:23a.

52. Rocher, *La Province chinoise*, II:70.

53. Alice Wei, "Moslem Rebellion in Yunnan," 114; Chan, "Ma Ju-lung," 99–100. A similar perspective is offered by Tsai Yuan-lin: "Finally, when [Ma] saw it

was getting to be too much for him, he stopped fighting and accepted the peace terms of the provincial officials." See Tsai Yuan-lin, "Confucian Orthodoxy vs. Muslim Resistance," 335.

54. Ma Rulong, "Shaoyu dianyuan shenmin," in HMQY, II:71.

55. Li Shoukong, "Ma Rulong xiangqing zhi yanjiu," 15.

56. *Xuxiu Songming zhouzi*, 3:1a–5a; for a later attempt at this ploy see QPHF, 8:2b.

57. QPHF, 17:12b.

58. Ibid., 17:12b–13a.

59. Ibid., 17:23a. Instead, the emperor sent an edict to Xu Zhiming warning him that his transgressions were known to the court and that although the emperor was showing his mercy, further violations would not be tolerated and the "court could not be so forgiving and lenient."

60. Ibid., 18:9a–9b.

61. Ibid., 20:2a, 18:16a; Zhang Tao, "Dianluan jilue," in HMQY, I:270. Many sources acknowledged Ma's long hatred of Liang. See Cordier, "Les musulmans," 205; Carné, "Exploration du Mékong," 901. For an account suggesting that Pan had secretly supported Liang in his battles against Ma Rulong, hoping that Liang could defeat Ma, see Zhang Tao, "Dianluan jilue," in HMQY, I:270. By this point Ma had also been granted the title of Lin[an]-Yuan[jiang] Regional Commander, in addition to He[qing]-Li[jiang] Regional Commander; see QPHF, 16:10a–b, 19:9a.

62. QPHF, 18:21b; Cen Yuying, "Cen xiangqing gong nianpu," 2:2a; Chan, "Ma Ju-long," 102; Rocher, *La Province chinoise*, II:77–78. The sources regarding the sequence of Pan's arrival in Kunming and Ma's departure are contradictory. In Cen Yuying's "Cen xiangqing gong nianpu," it is indicated that Pan entered Qujing in October and only came to the capital after Ma's departure; Cen Yuying, "Cen Xiangqing gong nianpu," 2:10b–11a. For a complete account of Liang's activities see *Xuxiu jianshui xianzhi*, 5:4a–9a.

63. Cen Yuying, "Cen xiangqing gong nianpu," 2:11b.

64. "Ma Futu shiji," in HMQY, II:373.

65. Ibid.

66. YTZG, 82:3a. Some later accounts suggest that Ma Dexin resisted calls to take any office but acquiesced when officials indicated that only he could "save the provincial capital from the bandits"; see "Ma Fuchu xiansheng shilue" [Biography of Ma Fuchu], in Lin Xinghua and Feng Jinyuan, eds., *Zhongguo yisilan jiao*, 711.

67. QPHF, 20:13b, 50:2b; XYTG, 82:3a; Rocher, *La Province chinoise*, II:46. Ma Dexin only used the traditional twelve-stems system of dating; see Zhang Tao, "Dianluan jilue," in HMQY, I:272.

68. He Huiqing, "Yunnan Du Wenxiu jianguo," (14)38, (15)32; "Ma Fuqu xiansheng shilue," in Li Xinghua and Feng Jinyuan, eds., *Zhongguo yisilanjiao shi*, 590.

69. QPHF, 20:3b; Rocher, *La Province chinoise*, II:78–79; QPHF, 20:4a–b. Another curious side note: in a list of Dali officials Cen Yuying is listed as a counselor, or aide de camp (*canmo*), but the long annotation next to his name indicates that "during the occupation of the provincial capital by Ma Rong selected Ma Dexin as governor-general. Yunnan Governor Xu Zhiming and Cen listed their names and

affixed their fingerprints alongside as proof of the election." "Du Wenxiu tongshu," in HMQY, II:183.

70. In an interesting twist, one account claims that Cen Yuying advised Ma Dexin *not* to take the title of king or emperor because Du Wenxiu would contest; rather he should simply adopt the title of governor-general. Zhang Tao, "Dianluan jilue," HMQY, I:271—72.

71. YTZG, 82:2a, 20:4a–b.

72. QPHF, 19:7b–8a.

73. Zhao Fan, *Cen Xiangqin gong xude jiefu tu*, plate 8; For a nonimperial account see DSDJ, 300.

74. Ma Futu, "Ma Futu shiji," in HMQY, II:374.

75. QPHF, 20:5b–6a; XYTG, 82:2b; QPHF, 24:5.

76. QPHF, 18:16b–17a, 21b–22a. For a similar account see Li Yuzhen, "Dianshi shuwen," 214–15. For similar versions see Zhao Fan, *Cen Xiangqin gong xude jiefu tu*, plate 7; Carné, "Expedition," VII:901. In fact, the court had been notified several weeks earlier by the Sichuan governor-general QPHF, 18:11a–b.

77. Rocher, *La Province chinoise*, II:79.

78. QPHF, 19:14a–b.

79. Rocher, *La Province chinoise*, II:79; Carné, "Expedition," 901.

80. QPHF, 19:10a–b.

81. Zhang Tao, "Dianluan jilue," HMQY, I:271–72.

82. Wellington Chan suggests a similar explanation: that Ma Rulong's behavior "stemmed from a desire to eliminate all possible rivals, not to ingratiate himself to the court in Peking." However, Ma Rulong's behavior to Ma Dexin was much more one of strong protection, not rapid eradication. Chan, "Ma Ju-long," 103.

83. "Zhi Du Wenxiushu," in HMQY, II:100.

84. QPHF, 20:6b.

85. Lin Changkuan, *Zhongguo Huijiao*, 112–13; Ma Tong, *Zhongguo yisilan jiaopai*, 126–28. For an introduction to Sufism in China see Fletcher's groundbreaking work on the topic "A History of the Naqshbandiyya in China," in B. Manz, ed., *Studies on Chinese and Islamic Inner Asia* (London: Variorum, 1995), 1–46. For a discussion of the misuse of xinjiao and laojiao see Gladney, *Dislocating China*, 127–28.

86. The terminology of "old" and "new" teachings was a highly referential terminology that often depended on the community involved and the latest "new" teachings. However, it was the dominant terminology of the period, and for our purposes reflects the basic divisions.

87. As Ma Tong suggests, it is important to remember that Islam in China had at least three different communities of thought (Gedimu, Yihewani, and the Hanxue), which should be considered separately from the study of the *menhuan* orders (such as Jahriyya and Khufiyya). See Ma Tong, *Zhongguo*.

88. Gladney, *Muslim Chinese*, 48.

89. Lipman, *Familiar Strangers*, 103.

90. Ibid., 88.

91. Ma Tong, *Zhongguo*, 126–28.

92. For an clear overview in English see Gladney, *Muslim Chinese*, 41–45. As

Lipman has indicated, the term *menhuan* is likely derived from *menhu*, "great family" or "official family." For a more historical discussion of the emphasis on saintly lineages from the founders of the Sufi order, see Lipman, *Familiar Strangers*, 70.

93. Gladney, *Muslim Chinese*, 41.

94. Ma Tong, *Zhongguo*, 126–28; Bai Shouyi, *Huizu renwuzhi*, (*Qingdai*), 27.

95. Ma Zhu, *Qingzhen zhinan*, 997–1001. It is not entirely clear what type of heresy Ma Zhu is referring to, since he seems—like the Confucian officials of the day—primarily worried about Daoist-like transgressions.

96. XYTG, 81:9a. Xian'gu is a Daoist reference to one of the Eight Immortals of Daoism, who was a woman.

97. The following officials all had considerable experience dealing with Muslim violence in one or more of the provinces: Lin Zexu, Wu Zhenyu, Shuxing'a, Pan Duo, Hengchun.

98. See the forewords written by several of Ma Dexin's students in their translation of Ma's *Sidian Yaohui*, in which these concerns are explicitly addressed. For an explanation in English see Lin Changkuan, "Three Eminent Chinese 'Ulama' of Yunnan," 108.

99. XYTG, 81:17b; He Huiqing, "Yunnan Du Wenxiu jianguo," no. 14, 36–37; Li Shoukong, "Wanqing Yunnan Huibian shimo," 474–75.

100. Archives d'outre mer 31AF (11 Octobre 1889). M. Challemel Lacour in his report to the Ministry of Foreign Affairs indicates that the Muslims of Yunnan "practice an Islam that adheres to the Sunni Hanefite rituals."

101. Lin Changkuan, *Zhongguo Huijiao*, 112.

102. Lin Changkuan, "Chinese Muslims of Yunnan," 226.

103. Rocher, *La Province chinoise*, II:160.

104. Despite the familiarity of several Yunnan officials with Islamic sectarianism in northwest China, none ever mentioned it as a factor in the fighting. See Chan, "Ma Ju-long," 117n99.

105. Zhao Qing in "Bianyuan jieyuan lu" notes suggestively that Du was aided by "outsider Hui" (*waihui*). This does not specifically name their religious leanings; it does, however, reveal that the Muslim Yunnanese in western Yunnan had much more contact with Hui from northwestern China than did their counterparts in other parts of the province; see HMQY, I:51.

106. QPHF, 12:15a; HMQY, II:355.

107. QPHF, 12:9a.

108. Ibid., 12:10a.

109. Ibid., 19:10a.

110. Ibid., 20:8a.

111. Chan, "Ma Ju-Long," 103.

112. QPHF, 20:1a–2b, 20:7a–8b, 21:19a–22b.

113. Ibid., 20:8a.

114. Ibid., 20:7a.

115. Like many of the officials with grandiose ideas on how to end the rebellion, Fu Sheng never entered the province but chose instead to remain in Sichuan near the Yunnan–Sichuan border to file his reports—an offense for which he was dismissed on January 24, 1864. See QPHF, 23a–b; XYHS, 199. Luo mainly wanted an end to

the rebellion at the smallest cost and the greatest benefit to Sichuan. A perspective seen in QPHF, 21:20a–21b.

116. QPHF, 20:8a.

117. Ibid., 22:5a–6b.

118. Ma Futu, "Ma Futu shiji," in HMQY, II:376–77; for Cen's role see Zhao Fan, *Cen xiangqin gong*, plates 8–9.

119. Rocher, *La Province chinoise*, II:80.

120. QPHF, 20:6a; DSSW, 214. In fact it was Ma Rulong's strategy to execute only the rebel leaders while pacifying the common soldiers that greatly facilitated his success. See QPHF, 24:6a–7b.

121. QPHF, 23:2b.

122. MEP, 539:1230. The term "Lolo" in Chinese was often a broad term to indicate those ethnic groups in the mountainous areas of Yunnan.

123. QPHF, 9:19b.

CHAPTER 8

1. See Kim Hodong, *Holy War in China*.

2. Zhao Qing, "Bianyuan jieyuan," in HMQY, I:51–52.

3. Anonymous, "Heqing Jiwen," in HMQY, II:209; DXZ, 9:19a–b. For an extremely detailed (if exaggerated) account of Zheng's activities in this early period, and the contention that it was "a sudden rain storm" that caused his troops (which numbered "50–60 thousand") to retreat, see *Heqing zhouzhi*, 19:3a–4b.

4. DXG, 9:14a–b; XYTG, 81:14a; *Langqiong xianzhilue* 11:47b–48a. The sources rarely agree on the order, dates, and officers involved in the battles for the population centers around Dali. The above particulars should not be taken as entirely accurate but rather as generally indicating the temporary nature of military victories during this time.

5. DXG, 9:21a–b; "Dianshi shuwen," in YQHS, 203–4; Ma Yuan, "Du Wenxiu yu baiqi," in YHSLD, IV:55. There is some disagreement whether the militia actually crossed Erhai. Some state that a fierce storm on the day of the attack prevented this. See He Huiqing, "Yunnan Du Wenxiu jianguo shibanian shimo," no. 14, 16.

6. "Dianshi shuwen," YQHS, 204. The attack had been planned as a two-pronged assault, but the other forces never materialized.

7. QPHF, 8:15a; "Dianshi shuwen," YQHS, 204–5. For a detailed account see *Heqing zhouzhi*, 19:7a–b. Accounts vary as to who masterminded his assassination, but likely it was Heqing magistrate Wu Shumei; see DXG, 9:22a. His death was recounted to French explorers on their travels through the province several years later; see Carné, *Travels*, 299.

8. DXG, 9:11a–b.

9. *Heqing zhouzhi*, 19:7b; Jing Dexin, *Du Wenxiu qiyi*, 109.

10. QPHF, 12:3a–4b.

11. MEP, 539:1229.

12. QPHF, 3:15a–16a. Li Peihu divulged not only the newly established Pingnan Guo but also all of the other losses, as well as Shuxing'a's inaction (owing to his mental condition), which bordered on dereliction of duty.

13. I want to thank Zvi Ben-dor for his efforts to help me understand the complex dimension of Du's Arabic title. Also for his suggestion that the title appears to be a clever variation of the "Amir al Mu'minin" title used by the first caliph, Abu Bakr, and later Islamic rulers.

14. Cooper, *Travels*, 350.

15. MEP, 541:870 (June 12, 1866). It is unclear what title this might be, as Fenouil romanizes this term as "kin tche," which might possibly be the Nanzhao term "ji jia wang."

16. MEP, 542:30 (September 6, 1868); 542:60 (July 10, 1869)

17. Garnier, *Voyage*, 456.

18. The most explicit articulation of Du's unwillingness to adopt a political title comes from the Dali envoy to Great Britain, Liu Daoheng, who indicated in a discussion with Walter E. King that "his father [Du Wenxiu] was styled commander in chief [*dayuanshuai*] *only*" (emphasis in original). See British Library, India Office, LPS/5/594/178a.

19. Anderson, *Report*; Carné, "Exploration"; Gill, *The River of Golden Sand*; Garnier, *Voyage*; d'Ollone, *Recherches sur les musulmans chinois*.

20. Carné, "Exploration du Mékong," 658. Anderson made a similar claim; however, it is evident that he had read Carné's account so it is not clear whether he was basing his statement on his own evidence. See Anderson, *Report*, 149. The most strenuous attack is in Tian Rukang, "New Light on the Yün-nan Rebellion," 30. See also Jing Dexin, *Du Wenxiu qiyi*, 264–67.

21. For reproductions of these seals see *Yunnan shaoshu minzu guanyin ji*, 59–86. I thank the head of Yunnan University's history department, Lu Ren, and the staff of the Yunnan Provincial Museum for helping me view the original seals. See Baber, *British Parliamentary Papers*, 845.

22. British Library, India Office, LPS/5/594/157a.

23. Ma Lianyuan, "Bianyu dazaxue xu," in Li Xinghua and Feng Jinyuan eds., *Zhongguo yisilan jiashi*, 593.

24. Alice Wei, "The Moslem Rebellion in Yunnan," 187.

25. "Dianshi shuwen," in YHQS, 196; DXZ, 9:20b.

26. He Huiqing, "Yunnan Du Wenxiu jianguo," nos. 13, 15; *Heqing zhouzhi*, 19:4b. He Huiqing indicates, for example, that after Meghua was defeated, eighty-six chops were recovered. On a research trip to that county in 1998, I happened on a Hui family from a long line of ahongs who showed me one of the only chops remaining in private hands—evidence of the rebellion's enduring potency among Hui even today.

27. DWTZM, 183–200; Alice Wei, "The Moslem Rebellion in Yunnan," 213–15; Yegar, "The Panthay," 75.

28. DWTZM, 189; DSSW, 219

29. Ma Weiliang, *Yunnan Huizu lishi yu*, 82; Du Wenxiu, *Guanli junzhen tiaoli*, 118; Jing Dexin, *Du Wenxiu qiyi*, 173–5.

30. MEP, 541:580 (September 12, 1863).

31. Archives d'outre mer, 31AF (11 Octobre 1889); Garnier, *Voyage*, I:487.

32. Anderson, *Mandalay to Momien*, 175.

33. Bowers, *Bhamô Expedition*, 110.

34. *Archives d'outre mer*, 31:B11 (11 octobre 1889).

35. Bowers, *Bhamô Expedition*, 110.

36. In HMQY, I:313.

37. *Pingqian jilue*, 9:19a.

38. Ma Shaoxiong and Zhao Rusong, "Du Wenxiu qiyi," in Yunnansheng Bianjizu, eds., *Yunnan weishan yizu*, 113.

39. Du Wexin, "Shishi wen," 127.

40. MEP, 539:943 (December 24, 1857).

41. QPHF, 2:23b.

42. Ibid., 4:5b.

43. Ibid., 24:4b; Cordier, *Les musulmans du Yunnan*, 191–92.

44. QPHF, 2:11a–12b, 23a, 19:18a–19a.

45. DWTZM, 183–92; Yegar, "The Panthay," 75.

46. Jing Dexin, *Du Wenxiu qiyi*, 173–75; Du Wenxiu, "Guanli junzhen tiaoli," 118.

47. Du Wenxiu, "Fu Yang zhenpeng shu," 106.

48. Ma Chaolin, "Ruijishugao zhaiyao dishisan ben," 187.

49. Yang Zhaojun, *Yunnan Huizu shi*, 148; YHSLD, I:213. It is unclear exactly how many mosques existed within Dali prior to the rebellion, nor is it clear if the informant is speaking of the entire Dali valley or just the walled city of Dali.

50. Bowers, *Bhamô Expedition*, 70.

51. Bai Shouyi, *Huizu rewuzhi (Jindai)*, 9; Tian Rukang, "Youguan Du Wenxiu duiwai," *Lishi yanjiu* 4 (1963), 146.

52. Du Wenxiu, *Guan junzhen tiaoli*, 117; He Huiqing, "Yunnan Du Wenxiu jianguo," 15; Bai Shouyi, *Huizu rewuzhi (Jindai)*, 13. The original woodblocks used to print the Quran were said to have been preserved by an imam living in Eryuan. For a more indepth description about the printing and history see Lin Changkuan, "Chinese Muslims of Yunnan," 284–85.

53. Bowers, *Bhamô Expedition*, 70.

54. Clarke, *Kwiechow and Yun-nan Provinces*.

55. He Huiqing, "Yunnan Du Wenxiu," 15; Anderson, *Mandalay to Momien*, 94; Chan, "Ma Rulong," 115; YHSLD, I:112.

56. Garnier, *Voyage*, I:565; see also Jest, "Kha-che and Gya-Kha-che," 8–11.

57. Garnier, *Voyage*, I:565.

58. For reproductions of these seals see *Yunnan shashu minzu*, 59–86. These and other seals from the Dali state are in the Yunnan Provincial Museum.

59. DXZ, 9:20b; Zhao Qing, "Bianyuan jieyuan lu," 52.

60. Li Yuzhen, "Dianshi shuwen," 196.

61. DXZ, 9:20; He Huiqing, "Yunnan Du Wenxiu," 15.

62. For an eloquent discussion of the symbolic significance of tonsure see Kuhn, *Soulstealers*, 56–58.

63. QPHF, 21:11a–12a. Variations in reference to the long hair include Ma Futu's use of the term *fafei* in "Ma Futu Shiji," in HMQY, I:373; and *yixi fani* (western hair-rebels), in QPHF, 44:36b.

64. Carné, "Exploration du Mékong," 674.

65. Cooper, *Travels*, 330. The French explorers also commented often on the

manner in which many Pingnan subjects wore their hair long and unbraided; Carné, *Travels*, 317, 319.

66. Cooper, *Travels*, 332.

67. Ibid.

68. Sladen, "Exploration via the Irrawaddy and Bhamo," 361. Carné also remarked that on meeting their first "mussulman functionary ... the sultan, who was not unmindful of details, has already occupied himself about his subjects' costume"; see Carné, *Travels*, 317. A Pingnan reference to uniforms appears in the list of regulations: "soldiers who steal and sell food, hay, or uniforms will be executed." See "Guanli Junzheng Tiaoli," in HMQY, II:119.

69. Anderson, *Report*, 315.

70. Ibid., 256.

71. Carné, *Travels*, 319–20. Rocher also mentions that "the Dali government offered sufficient security, and the [exchange of] contraband became well established." See Rocher, *La Province chinoise*, II:68.

72. YHSLD, I:111; Lin Changkuan, *Chinese Muslims of Yunnan*, 277; Rocher, *La Province chinoise*, II:69.

73. Cooper, *Travels*, 330.

74. Ibid., 330.

75. Anderson, *Report*, 152.

76. Anderson, *Mandalay to Momien*, 243. Anderson later learned that the criminal, in this instance, had been found "in the bazaar selling stolen goods."

77. *Cen Xiangqing gong zougao* 9:28, in DWQL, 109; see also "Du Wenxiu qiyi yu Dian-Mian maoyi," in ibid., 108–10.

78. Rocher, *La Province chinoise*, II:69.

79. "Du Wenxiu de mianhua dian," in YHSLD, I:136–37.

80. Anderson, *Mandalay to Momien*, 199–204.

81. Garnier, *Voyage*, 507.

82. Ibid., 522; YHSLD, I:111.

83. Generally speaking there were three centers of salt production: Guantong county north of Chuxiong; Zhennan county east of Chuxiong; and several wells in Pu'er prefecture. See XYTG, 50:9a–11b; Rocher, *La Province chinoise*, II:107.

84. QPHF, 20:25a. This assessment is supported by Sichuan governor-general Luo Bingzhang; ibid., 20:20a.

85. Ibid., 20:24b–25a; YHSD, I:122.

86. Ma Shaoxiong and Zhao Rusong, "Du Wenxiu zhengquan shiqi," in YHSLD, II:103–4.

87. Anderson, *Mandalay to Momien*, 244–45.

88. *Cen Xiangqing gong zougao*, 9:28, in Gao Fayuan, *Du Wenxiu qiyi lunji*, 109.

89. QPHF, 23:4a.

90. Ibid., 16:2a.

91. Alice Wei, "Moslem Rebellion in Yunnan," 135–36. Ma Futu was a cousin and close advisor to Ma Rulong. There is confusion over the sequence (and even the existence) of many of the missions to Dali, which suggests that these were carried out in semisecrecy and not publicly well known; QPHF, 20:14a.

92. Ma Futu, "Ma Futu shiji," in HMQY, II:375.

93. Ibid., 375.

94. Ibid., 375; Li Shoukong, "Wanqing Yunnan Huibian shimo," 93.

95. Ma Futu, "Ma Futu shiji," in HMQY, II:376.

96. Ibid.

97. DSSW, 216.

98. Ibid., 216. There are varied accounts about how Yang arrived in Dali and his mission as emissary from Ma Rulong. Rocher suggests that Yang was captured and brought to Dali as a prisoner. Few dispute that he was actually in Dali at the time. See Rocher, *La Province chinoise*, II:81–82; Cen Yuying, *Cen xiangqing gong nianpu*, 2:5a.

99. DSSW, 216; DXG, 9:27a.

100. Ibid., 216; DXG, 9:27a.

101. DSSW, 217. It may have been known that Yang was a prisoner, as Rocher suggests. Quite suggestive of this line of argument is that the Yaozhou Gazetteer records that Ma Dexin passed through Yaozhou on his way to Dali in January 1864, a month before the putative attack on Du; see *Yaozhou Zhi*, 1885, 4:24b.

102. DSSW, 217.

103. Rocher, *La Province chinoise du Yün-nan*, II:83.

104. Ibid.; DSSW, 217; DXZ, 9:27a. The one discrepancy is in the Dali Gazetteer, which states that Ma Dexin and Du did agree to divide Yunnan into spheres of influence; however, it states that Cen Yuying and Ma Rulong "were not informed of this agreement." Such an agreement, if one ever existed, more likely stemmed from the original Chuxiong agreement between Cai Fachun and Ma Rulong.

105. Eickelman and Piscatori, *Muslim Travellers*, 21.

106. Miao Yongling, "Ma Liansheng Zhuanlüe," in YHQS, 353.

107. Ma Rulong, "Zhi Du Wenxiu," in HMQY, II:99.

108. Ibid.

109. The word *mumin* here clearly modifies the word "soldiers" in a manner reminiscent of the famous line "Onward, Christian soldiers." Note how this strengthens the Muslim dimension of Hui identity but also indicates clearly their discrete nature with respect to each other.

110. Ma Rulong, "Zhi Du Wenxiu," in HMQY, II:99.

111. Du Wenxiu, "Fu Yang zhenpeng su," in HMQY, II:106.

112. Gladney, *Muslim Chinese*, 20, 98; Allès, *Les Musulmans de Chine*, 29. Gladney remarks on a Hui colleague correcting another Hui who spoke of *Huijiao*: "Hui believe in Islam [*yisilin jiao*] not their own Hui religion [*Huijiao*]."

113. Ma Rulong, "Fu dasiheng," in HMQY, II:139.

114. Ibid., 140.

115. Of course, none of the above negates the fact that most Hui were Muslims. What I am suggesting is that by the nineteenth century, Islam was not the sole defining factor among the Hui. Although Islam never ceased to be a meaningful part of their identity, Yunnan Hui identity was rooted in a broader ethnoreligious spectrum of identities.

116. The modern Chinese compound for religion, "zongjiao" is a twentieth-century neologism that was most likely borrowed from Japan and that was promulgated most fervently in the years after the 1911 revolution (see Bodde, *Chinese*

*Thought, Society, and Science*, 149). Debates between Zhang Binlin, Kang Youwei, and other revolutionaries at the turn of the nineteenth century demonstrate that there was far from a consensus on whether Confucianism was a learning (*xue*), a way (*dao*), a religion (*jiao*), or simply a doctrine (Shimada 1990, 102). This suggests that up to that point there was little tangible idea of religion in the organized and institutionalized form as it exists in the West. In the nineteenth century, jiao was most likely better understood as "teachings" than as "religion." The context in Yunnan seems quite different—although perhaps not as unique as one might first assume, since the term *Hanjiao* was in common use throughout China, and I have found references in neighboring Guizhou to *Miaojiao*. See Ling Ti'an, *Xian-Tong Guizhou junshi shi*, 5:1b.

117. Ma Rulong, "Fu dasiheng," in HMQY, II:140.
118. Du Wenxiu, "Xingshi Xiwen, in HMQY, II:131.
119. Du Wenxiu, "Guanli junzhen tiaoli," in HMQY, II:118.

CHAPTER 9

1. Du Wenxiu, "Shuaifu bugao," in HMQY, II:123.
2. Du Wenxiu, "Fu Yang zhenpeng shu," in HMQY, I:106.
3. "Xingshi xiwen," in HMQY, II:131.
4. Carné, *Travels*, 292.
5. Du Wenxiu, "Shishi wen," in HMQY, II:127.
6. Meaning that although the Hui were the targets, everyone was affected by the violence.
7. Du Wenxiu, "Xingshi xiwen," in HMQY, II:131.
8. "Shishi Wen," in HMQY, II:127.
9. QPHF, 28:18a; Zhang Tao, "Dianluan jilue," in HMQY, I:274.
10. QPHF, 30:10a; Ma Futu, "Ma Futu siji," in HMQY, II:383; see also Wang Dingan, "Pingdian pian," in YHQS, 257–58.
11. Rocher, *La Province chinoise*, II:110.
12. Ibid., II:108.
13. XYTG, 82:17a–b. For an official albeit colored explanation see QPHF, 33:9b–10a.
14. There are slight discrepancies between the sources, but the final outcome is the same in every case. Cen Yuying, "Cen xiangqing gong nianpu," 2:17a; QPHF, 33:5b–6a; Li Shoukong, "Wanqing Yunnan Huibian shimo," 498.
15. Technically, the expedition was led by Doudart de Lagrée; however, due to illness he was left with the expedition's doctor outside Dongchuan in northeastern Yunnan. There he died. Garnier replaced him as ranking officer.
16. Garnier, *Voyage d'exploration*, 585; Cooper, *Travels*, 324. The terminology employed by the two French explorers is vague. Garnier is the more precise of the two and distinguishes between Europeans and Malays; Carné speaks of Burmans, Hindoos, and Europeans. Such conjecture might well be dismissed out of hand except that Cooper describes rumors suggesting these Europeans served "as teachers of the Koran"—hardly a likely activity for most nineteenth-century Europeans. See Cooper, *Travels*, 331.

17. Carné says he heard there were fourteen "Europeans"; Garnier says there were sixteen Europeans and four Malays; Cooper maintains there were five Europeans. See Carné, *Travels*, 324; Garnier, *Voyage*, 580; Cooper, *Travels*, 331.

18. Carné, "Exploration," 680; Garnier, *Voyage*, 580.

19. Spence, *God's Chinese Son*, 238–39.

20. Garnier, *Voyage*, 459.

21. Ibid., 510.

22. Clarke, *The Province of Yunnan*, 50.

23. Garnier, *Voyage*, 512; Gervais-Courtellement, *Voyage*, 206, writes that as Leguilcher told him the story several decades later, Du Wenxiu had been standing in a central tower and had ordered one of his men to remove the men's hats so as to better see their faces.

24. Garnier, *Voyage*, 512.

25. Ibid., 513.

26. Carné, "Exploration," 681.

27. Garnier, *Voyage*, 513.

28. MEP, 542:23 (August 2, 1868).

29. Tian Rukang, "New Light on the Yün-nan Rebellion," 49.

30. Cooper, *Travels*, 443–44.

31. Garnier, *Voyage*, 513.

32. Anderson indicates that by February 19 they had sent letters by messenger describing their purpose and that they had the full support of Panthay leaders in Yunnan. The messengers (those whose clothes were described earlier) returned from Tengyue on March 9 while the mission was still at Ponsee, several days' march north from Bhamô. Thus it is plausible that the messengers had reached Tengyue and that word had reached Du of the British and their intentions. Indeed, Anderson reports that on arrival in Tengyue, the Panthay governor there stated that "the Sultan had been pleased to hear of our intended visit to [Tengyue]." See Anderson, *Report*, 231; and *Mandalay to Momien*, 195.

33. MEP, 542:30.

34. Anderson, *Mandalay to Momien*, 178.

35. Ibid., 195.

36. Ibid., 196.

37. Ibid., 246.

38. Ibid., 246.

39. Lin Changkuan, "Chinese Muslims of Yunnan," 337.

40. QPHF, 26:20b–21a.

41. Wright, *The Last Stand of Chinese Conservatism*, 114.

42. QPHF, 28:18a; Rocher, *La Province chinoise*, II:103. Yunnan governor Liu Yuezhao simply describes him as "dying of an illness"; see 28:18b. Alice Wei mistakenly reports this date as January 9, 1867; see Alice Wei, "Moslem Rebellion in Yunnan," 142. Wei Hsiu-mei makes a rare mistake in stating Lao's death as April 2, 1867; see Wei Hsiu-mei, *Qingji zhiguan biao*, II:560; 71. Lao was sixty-five when he died.

43. Pourais, *La Chine*, 72. Rather strangely, it is Western writers who have kept the myth alive that Lao met his end in suspicious circumstances. See Broomhall, *Islam in China*, 138.

44. Rocher, *La Province chinoise*, II:103.

45. MEP, 541:955 (April 13, 1867).

46. QPHF, 28:23a.

47. Ibid., 28:18b.

48. Cen Yuying, "Cen xiangqing gong nianpu," 2:16a; QPHF, 29:15b–16a.

49. QPHF, 28:19b; 24a.

50. Ibid., 30:18a, 32:5a–6b. The court was not amused by Zhang's delaying tactics, although almost fifteen years later, he was again assigned to Yunnan, this time as governor. He died there in 1886.

51. QPHF, 29:16b; Wang Dingan, "Pingdian pian," in YHQS, 257–58; Cen Yuying, "Cen xiangqing gong nianpu," 2:16b.

52. QPHF, 30:1a–2a, 21b–22b. Cen himself had positioned troops at strategic points in eastern Yunnan so as to prevent their spread in that region of the province.

53. Ibid., 21:17a.

54. Ibid..

55. Ibid., 21:18a.

56. "Cen xiangqin gong zougao," in Fang Guoyu, *Yunnan shiliao congkan*, IX: 161–62. The governor at that time was Lao Chongguang.

57. Ibid., 163.

58. Ibid., 163–64.

59. Hummel's description of Cen's early career, although factually generally accurate, should be used with caution because several dates are in error. See Hummel, *Eminent Chinese of the Ch'ing Period*, 742–43.

60. Many local Yunnan officials refused to recognize Ma Rulong's role and broke off communications with the provincial level of government. The most famous (and successful) of these was Liang Shimei. Carné described him as "loathing Muslims, [both] those who remained faithful to the emperor and those who revolted. . . . What is for sure is that he refuses to obey the governor-general"; Carné, "Expedition," 892.

61. For a representative sample of Lao's comments on Cen see QPHF, 27:22a–25b. For a similar comparison for his comments on Ma Rulong see QPHF, 28:9a–12a.

62. "Cen xiangqin gong zougao," in Fang Guoyu, *Yunnan shiliao congkan*, 164.

63. QPHF, 28:1a.

64. Jenks, *Insurgency and Social Disorder*, 149.

65. Alice Wei, "The Moslem Rebellion in Yunnan," 145; "Cen xiangqin gong zougao," in Fang Guoyu, *Yunnan shiliao congkan*,IX:164.

66. "Cen xiangqin gong zougao," in Fang Guoyu, *Yunnan shiliao congkan*, IX:164.

67. "Cen xiangqin gong zougao," in Fang Guoyu, *Yunnan shiliao congkan*, IX:165.

68. By 1868 the worst of the fighting in Guizhou had ended, although sporadic fighting continued there for another five years. Jenks, *Insurgency and Social Disorder*, 153–54.

69. Carné, "Exploration du Mékong," 909.

70. Ibid., 903.

71. QPHF, 29:16a.

72. Jing Dexin, *Du Wenxiu qiyi*, 146.

73. QPHF, 33:2b.

74. MEP, 542:16.

75. QPHF, 43:1a, 44:1a, 33:5a–6b; XYTG, 82:20a–b.

76. MFS, 383.

77. Ibid.; also QPHF, 32:12b–14a, 17a.

78. QPHF, 33:6b, 10a. See Cen Yuying, "Cen xiangqing gong nianpu," 2:17b–18a; DXG, 9:29b.

79. Rocher, *La Province chinoise*, II:109.

80. MEP, 542, 16–17 (August 2, 1868).

81. QPHF, 34:7a.

82. Ibid., 33:17a.

83. Ibid.; for a synopsis of Cen's maneuvers see Jing Dexin, *Du Wenxiu qiyi* 148–49.

84. DSSW, 221–22.

85. QPHF, 33:13b–14a, 18a; DXG, 921b; Cen Yuying, "Cen xiangqing gong nianpu," 2:18b.

86. QPHF, 33:18a–b.

87. Cen Yuying, "Cen xiangqing gong nianpu," 3:5a; QPHF, 39:18a, 38:13a–17b.

88. MEP, 542:40 (January 2, 1869).

89. QPHF, 33:9a.

90. Rocher, *La Province chinoise*, II:114.

91. DSSW, 225; XYTG, 82:25–b.

92. Cen Yuying, "Cen xiangqing gong nianpu," 3:5b–6b.

93. QPHF, 31:5a–b, 36:21. For a general overview see XYHS, 246–50.

94. Liu Yuezhao, *Dian-Qian zouyi*, 9:15a–16a, 9:19a–20b, 9:44b.

95. QPHF, 39:19a–20b.

96. Ibid., 36:28a.

97. Dali did have its own more traditional armory. Zhao Qing listed six craftsmen (all Han), each of whom specialized in firearms, explosives (gunpowder), rockets, fortifications, or seal carving. See Zhao Qing, "Bianyuan jieyuan lu" in HMQY, I:63.

98. Zhao Qing, "Bianyuan jieyuan lu," in HMQY, I:63; QPHF, 26:23b; and Carné, *Travels*, 273 all substantiate this fact.

99. QPHF, 26:23b. The emperor's rescript was favorable, but several years passed with no action.

100. Rocher, *La Province chinoise*, II:110–11. Rocher notes that the guns had diverse origins, including Germany and England, with many of the guns engraved "*Fabrique de Châtellerault, 1830.*" Rocher's comments are substantiated in an interview with Yang Fanxiu conducted in 1958; see YHSD, I:111n.

101. Carné, *Travels*, 273. It is curious that Ma Rulong's stockpile was so large. The arrival of the French coincided with his return from the failed westward campaign of 1867; one would have expected him to put the guns to use against the surging Pingnan forces.

102. Rocher, *La Province chinoise du Yün-nan*, II:140.

103. MEP, 542:72–73 (September 13, 1870); Anderson, *Mandalay to Momien*, 339.

104. Archives d'outre mer, 24:A60 (n.d.). In particular, it seems that Dupuis and Légier (besides Rocher) were the key Europeans in Yunnan.

105. Baber, "Report," II:141–43.

106. All degree quotas missed during the rebellion were made up; others were granted by the emperor for the suffering caused by the rebellion and the people's contribution toward ending the rebellion; see Cen Yuying, *Cen xiangqin gong yiji*, 4:45a–b, 5:18a.

107. QPHF, 42:23b–24a. Chenggong, Puning, Fumin, Songming, Yimen, Anning, Luoci, Lufeng, Kunyang, Xundian, Wuding, Luquan, Yuanmou, Chuxiong, Guangtong, Nan'an Dingyuan, Dayao, Yaozhou, Zhennan, Binchuan, Yunlong, Dengchuan, Langqiong, Heqing, Lijiang, Jianchuan, Yongbei, Mianning, Weiyuan, Xinxing, Chengjiang.

108. QPHF, 44:24b; DSSW, 227; XYTG, 82:39a–b.

109. Rocher, *La Province chinoise*, II:164–65; QPHF, 45:13b.

110. QPHF, 45:15a.

111. Rocher, *La Province chinoise*, II:168–69.

112. QPHF, 45:17a.

113. Ibid., 46:22b; Rocher, *La Province chinoise*, II:178–79; Gervais-Courtellemont, *Voyage*, 187.

114. "Dianxi bianluan xiaoshi," in HMQY, II:94–95.

115. Ibid., II:95. Rocher's account offers a strikingly similar portrayal of Du's final discussion with the council; Rocher, *La Province chinoise*, II:179.

116. Rocher, *La Province chinoise*, II:183. Rocher suggests that he even answered questions.

117. Colquhoun, *Across Chrysê*, I:263. This was verified by an interview Colquhoun had with a former officer of Yang Yuke and has entered the mythology surrounding Du's death. Luckert and Li, *Mythology and Folklore*, 277–78.

118. Accounts differ regarding precisely when Du took the poison and what type of poison he used. For an excellent overview see Jing Dexin, *Du Wenxiu qiyi*, 315–29. Dupuis suggests that he poisoned himself with "sheets of gold"; Dupuis, *L'Ouverture du fleuve Rouge*, 76. Another popular version is that he swallowed the gall bladder of a peacock; for the complete account see Luckert and Li, *Mythology and Folklore*, 274–78.

119. QPHF, 47:3a.

120. "Sanchao jilue," in YHQS, 385; Rocher, *La Province chinoise*, II:184; MEP, 542:192.

121. QPHF, 47:3a.

122. Clarke, *Kweichow and Yunnan*, 59.

123. Rocher, *La Province chinoise*, II:185. The Dali Gazetteer, although not so graphic, suggests this deception; DXG, 8.

124. QPHF, 47:3b.

125. Colquhoun, *Across Chrysê*, 243.

126. QPHF, 47:5b. One official whom Baber later interviewed said there could not have been this many dead "because it would have stunk more"; Baber, *British Parliamentary Papers*, 6.

127. QPHF, 47:6a–7b.

128. MEP, 542:193 (September 23, 1873); Rocher, *La Province chinoise*, II:186. Amazingly, four of Du's children survived this mass slaughter. They ranged in age from three to thirteen. Two of the sons died, one from smallpox and the other from being given the wrong prescription. His two daughters were imprisoned in Kunming. See QPHF, 47:8a–b; Alice Wei, "The Moslem Rebellion in Yunnan," 166–67.

129. Dupuis, *L'ouverture du fleuve rouge au commerce et les Les Événements du Tonkin, 1872–1873*, 75–77; Broomhall, *Islam in China*, 144; Armijo, "Narratives Engendering Survival," 301.

130. Clarke, *Kwiechow and Yun-nan Provinces*, 61.

131. These Muslim Yunnanese communities were well documented by Western travelers in the early part of this century, as well as by several anthropological studies in more recent years. These people still perceive themselves as descendents of Yunnan; many residents of Thai and Burmese hilltowns claim descent from "Dali Guo" or the Dali regime.

CHAPTER 10

1. Cen Yuying, *Cen xiangqin gong yiji*, 11:8a–b. Wang Shuhuai agrees with this estimate but admits that such figures are at best approximations. See *Xiantong Yunnan Huimin shibian*, 315.

2. Lee, "Food Supply and Population Growth," 729. Dupuis, a French adventurer, traveled to Yunnan many times in the 1870s and confirms this estimate, suggesting that "five to six million individuals" died during the rebellion. Dupuis, "Les Evenements du Tonkin," 77.

3. Carné, "Exploration," 677.

4. *Chuxiong xianzhi*, 1910, 4:4.

5. XYTG, 81:28b. Other cities affected on a similar scale included Jingdong, Yuanjiang, and Tengyue.

6. Colquhoun, *Across Chrysê*, 137–38.

7. Bourne, "Report."

8. Proschan, "Cheuang in Kmhmu Folklore, History, and Memory," 180. I am grateful to Professor Proschan for making this insightful article available to me.

9. Archives d'outre mer, 24:A60(2) (17 January, 1880).

10. Rocher, *La Province chinoise*, 188.

11. Dupuis, "Les Evenements du Tonkin," 76.

12. Gervais-Courtellement, *Voyage*, 180. Twenty-eight years after the event, the residents of Xiaguan were also prevented from building a new mosque.

13. Ibid., 201, 203.

14. QPHF, 50:3a.

15. Hill, *Merchants and Migrants*, 15–16; Scott and Hardiman, *Gazetteer of Upper Burma and the Shan States*, 740.

16. Hill, *Merchants and Migrants*, 71–73; Forbes, "The Yunnanese ("Ho") Muslims of North Thailand," 91–93.

17. Chao Fan, *Cen xiangqin gong yiji*, 4:4:45a–b, 5:18a.

18. S.T. Wang, *The Margary Affair*, 114–26.

19. QPHF, 9:19b.

20. MEP, 539:1230. "Lolo" in Chinese was often a broad term to indicate those ethnic groups in the northern mountainous areas of Yunnan.

21. MEP, 542:295 (28 August, 1875).

22. Dupuis, "Les Evenements du Tonkin," 87–90.

# Bibliography

"Ailao yixiong liezhuan" [Biographies of Ailao non-Han military leaders]. In Fang Guoyu, ed., *Yunnan shiliao congkan* [Series of Yunnan historical documents]. Kunming: Yunnan daxue chubanshe, 2001.

Allès, Elisabeth. *Musulmans de Chine: Une anthropologie des Hui du Henan*. Paris: Éditions de l'école des hautes études en sciences sociales, 2000.

Anderson, John. *A Report on the Expedition to Western Yunnan via Bhamô*. Calcutta: Office of the Superintendent of Government Printing, 1871.

——. *Mandalay to Momien: A Narrative of the Two Expeditions to Western China of 1868 and 1875 under Colonel Edward B. Sladen and Colonel Horace Brown*. London: MacMillan & Company, 1876.

Archives d'outre-mer [French National Archives Overseas Colonies]. Aix-en-Provence.

Armijo, Jacqueline. "Narratives Engendering Survival: How the Muslims of Southwest China Remember the Massacres of 1873." In Meaghan Morris and Brett de Bary, eds., *"Race" Panic and the Memory of Migration*. Hong Kong: Hong Kong University Press, 2001.

Armijo-Hussein, Jaqueline M. "Sayyid 'Ajall Shams Al-Din: A Muslim From Central Asia, Serving the Mongols in China, and Bringing 'Civilization' to Yunnan." Unpublished Ph.D. dissertation, Harvard University, 1997.

Atabaki, Touraj, and John O'Kane, eds. *Post-Soviet Central Asia*. Leiden: Tauris Academic Studies in Association with the International Institute of Asian Studies, 1998.

Atwill, David G. "Trading Places: Resistance, Ethnicity, and Governance in Nineteenth-Century Yunnan." In Robert Antony and Jane Kate Leonard, eds. *Dragons, Tigers and Dogs: Essays on Qing Crisis Management*. Cornell East Asia Series, no. 114. Ithaca, NY: East Asia Program, Cornell University, 2002.

Baber, Edward Colborne. "Report by Mr. Baber on the route followed by Mr. Grosvenor's mission between Tali-fu and Momein: with itinerary and map of road from Yünnan-fu." *British Parliamentary Papers: Journeys and Expeditions in China, 1869–1904*. London: Harrison and Sons, 1877.

Backus, Charles. *The Nan-chao Kingdom and T'ang China's Southwestern Frontier*. Cambridge: Cambridge University Press, 1981.

Bai Shouyi, ed. *Huimin qiyi* [Hui rebellions]. 4 vols. Shanghai: Zhongguo shenzhou guoguang chubanshe, 1953.

——. *Huizu renwuzhi (Mingdai)* [A collection of Hui biographies, Ming era]. Yinchuan: Ningxia renmin chubanshe, 1988.

——. *Huizu renwuzhi (Qingdai)* [A collection of Hui biographies, Qing era]. Yinchuan: Ningxia renmin chubanshe, 1992.

————. *Huizu renwuzhi (Jindai)* [A collection of Hui biographies, Modern era]. Yinchuan: Ningxia renmin chubanshe, 1997.

————. *Minzu zongjiao lunji* [Collected essays on ethnicity and religion]. Beijing: Beijing shifan daxue chubanshe, 1992.

————. "Diannan conghua" [Assorted thoughts on Yunnan]. In Bai Shouyi, ed., *Minzu zongjiao lunji [Essays on minority religion]*. Shijiazhuang: Hebei jiaoyou chubanshe, 2001.

————. "Guanyu Huizu shi de jige wenti" [Regarding several questions on Hui history]. In Bai Shouyi, ed., *Minzu zongjiao lunji [Essays on minority religion]*. Shijiazhuang: Hebei jiaoyou chubanshe, 2001.

————. "Guanyu Huizushi gongzuo de jige yijian" [A few opinions regarding the work on Hui history]. In Bai Shouyi, ed., *Minzu zongjiao lunyi [Essays on minority religion]*. Shijiazhuang: Hebei jiaoyou chubanshe, 2001.

Barth, Fredrik. "Introduction." In Barth, ed., *Ethnic Groups and Boundaries: The Social Organization of Cultural Difference*. Boston: Little, Brown, 1969.

Benedict, Carol. *Bubonic Plague in Nineteenth Century China*. Stanford, CA: Stanford University Press, 1996.

Bodde, Derek. *Chinese Thought, Society, and Science: The Intellectual and Social Background of Science and Technology in Pre-Modern China*. Honolulu: University of Hawaii Press, 1991.

Bourne, Frederick Samuel Augustus. "Report by F.S.A. Bourne of a Journey in South-Western China." *British Parliamentary Papers: Journeys and Expeditions in China, 1869–1904*. London: Harrison and Sons, 1888.

Bowers, A. *Bhamô Expedition Report on the Practicability of Re-opening the Trade Route Between Burma and Western China*. Rangoon: American Mission Press, 1869.

Broomhall, Marshall. *Islam in China: A Neglected Problem*. New York: Paragon Book Co., 1910.

Brunnert, Ippolit Semenovich, and V.V. Hagelstrom. *Present Day Political Organization of China*. Shanghai: Kelly and Walsh, 1912.

Cao Kun,"Tengyue duluan jishi" [A history of the Panthay Rebellion in Tengyue]. In HMQY, II:217–38.

Carné, Louis de. "Exploration du Mékong." *Revue des deux mondes*, vols. 85–87 (1870).

————. *Travels in Indochina and the Chinese Empire*. London: Chapman and Hall, 1872.

Cen Yuying. *Cen Xiangqing gong nianpu* [A chronological biography of Cen (Yuying) Xiangqing]. Taibei: Wenhai Chubanshe, 1967 (1899).

————. *Cen xiangqin gong yiji* [Writings of Cen Yuying]. Reprint, Taibei: Wenhai chubanshe, 1976.

Chan, Wellington K.K. "Ma Ju-Lung: From Rebel to Turncoat in the Yunnan Rebellion." Papers on China, vol. 20. Cambridge: East Asian Research Center (distributed by Harvard University Press), 1966.

————. "The 'Panthay Embassy' to Britain, 1872." *Far Eastern Affairs* 20, no. 4 (1967): 100–17.

Chen Bisheng. *Dianbian sanyi* [Remembrance of the tribal life along the border of Yunnan]. Taibei: Dongfang wenhua shuju, 1941.

Cheng Xiayu. *Qing shengxun xinan minzu shiliao* [Materials found concerning the ethnic minorities in the southwest in precepts issued by Qing emperors]. Chengdu: Sichuan chubanshe, 1988.

Chiang, Tao-chang. "The Salt Trade in Ch'ing China." *Modern Asian Studies* 17, no. 2 (1983): 197–219.

*Chuxiong xianzhi*. Compiled by Zhong Jian. Taibei: Chengwen Chubanshe, 1910.

Clarke, George W. *The Province of Yunnan: Past, Present and Future.* Shanghai: Shanghai Mercury Press, 1885.

———. *Kwiechow and Yün-nan Provinces.* Shanghai: Shanghai Mercury Press, 1894.

Clendinnen, Inga. *Reading the Holocaust.* Cambridge: Cambridge University Press, 1999.

Colquhoun, Archibald R. *Across Chrysê, A Journey of Exploration through the South China Border Lands from Canton to Mandalay.* London: William Clowes and Sons, Ltd, 1883.

Cooper, Thomas Thornville. *Travels of a Pioneer of Commerce: In Pigtail and Petticoats, or, An Overland Journey from China Towards India.* London: J. Murray, 1871.

Cordier, Georges. "Les musulmans du Yunnan: leur attitude." *Revue du monde musulman* 24 (1913): 318–26.

———. "Les mosques du Yunnanfu." *Revue du monde musulman* 27: 140–61 (1914).

———. "Le musée de Yunnan-fou." *Bulletin de l'école française d'extreme-Orient* 15, no. 3 (1916).

———. *Les musulmans du Yunnan.* Hanoi: Imprimerie tonkinoise, 1927.

Crossley, Pamela. "Thinking about Ethnicity in Early Modern China." *Late Imperial China* 11, no. 1 (1990): 1–35.

Cui Jingming, and Lu Ren. "Yuan, Ming, Qing shiqi Yunnan bianjiang minzu diqu de duiwai jingji jiaowang" [Borderland trade and contact of Yunnan ethnic groups during the Yuan, Ming, and Qing periods]. *Sixiang zhanxian* 4 (1998): 42–46.

*Dali xianzhigao* [Revised gazetteer of Dali district]. Compiled by Zhang Peijue and Zhou Zonglin. Taibei: Chengwen chubanshe, 1973 (1916).

Daniels, Christian. "Environmental Degradation, Forest Protection and Ethnohistory in Yunnan: The Uprising by Swidden Agriculturists in 1821." *Chinese Environmental History Newsletter* (November 1994): 7–13.

*Dao-Xian-Tong-Guang sichao zouyi* [Four reigns of imperial memorials]. 2 vols. Compiled by Wang Yunwu. Taibei: Taiwan shangwu yinshuguan faxing. 1970.

Davenport, Arthur. "Report by Mr. Davenport upon the Trading Capabilities of the Country Traversed by the Yunnan Mission." *British Parliamentary Papers.* London, Harrison and Sons, 1877.

Davies, Henry Rudolph. *Yün-nan, the Link between India and the Yangtze.* Cambridge: The University Press, 1909.

*Dayao xianzhi* [Gazetteer of Dayao district]. Compiled by Liu Rongfu. 1845.

de Jong, Frederick, and Bernd Radtke, eds. *Islamic Mysticism Contested: Thirteen Centuries of Controversies and Polemics.* Leiden: Brill, 1999.

Deng Baohua and Wang Huaide. *Yisilanjiao shi* [A history of Islam]. Yinchuan: Ningxia renmin chubanshe, 1992.

*Dengchuan zhouzhi* [Gazetteer of Dengchuan department]. Compiled by Hou Yunjin. Taibei: Chengwen Chubanshe, 1968 (1854).

Desgodins, August. *Le Thibet: d'apres la correspondance des missionaries.* Paris: Librairie catholique de l'œuvre de saint Paul, 1885.

Dessaint, William. *Au Sud des nuages: mythes et contés recueillis oralement chez les Lissou (Tibéto-Burman).* Paris: Gallimard, 1994.

Deveria, Gabriel. *Origine de l'islamisme en Chine: deux légendes musulmanes chinoises, pèlerinages de Ma Fou-tch'ou.* Paris: Imprimerie nationale, 1895.

"Dianhui jiluan" [A record of the Muslim Yunnanese rebellion]. In Jing Dexin, ed., YHQS, 270–311.

"Diannan zaji" [Narrative of southern Yunnan]. In HMQY, II:243–68.

"Dianxi bianluan xiaoshi" [A brief narrative of western Yunnan disturbances]. In HMQY, II:81–96.

Dillion, Michael. *China's Muslim Hui Community: Migration, Settlement and Sects.* Surrey: Curzon Press, 1999.

*Dianzhi* [Yunnan gazetteer]. Kunming: Yunnan jiaoyu chubanshe. Compiled by Liu Wenzheng. 1991 (1627).

Dubernard, Jules, and Auguste Desgodins. "Les sauvages Lyssous du Lou-tse-kiang." *Bulletin de la société de géographie* 10 (1875–76): 63–64.

Dupuis, Jean. "Voyage au Yun-nan," *Bulletin de société geographique,* July 1877.

———. *L'ouverture du fleuve Rouge au commerce et les événements du Tong-kin, 1872–1873.* Paris: Challamel Ainé, 1879.

Dupuis, Jean. *L'ouverture du fleuve rouge au commerce et les événements du Tonkin, 1872–1873.* Paris: Challamel Ainé, 1879.

Du Wenxiu. "Guanli junzhen tiaoli" [Rules of civil and military administration]. In HMQY, I:109–20.

———. "Fu Yang zhenpeng shu" [A reply to Yang Zhenpeng]. In HMQY, I:103–08.

———. "Shishi wen" [Declaration of war]. In HMQY, II:125–28.

———. "Shuaifu bugao" [Proclamation from the headquarters of the generalissimo]. In HMQY, II:121–24.

———. "Xingshi xiwen" [Summons to arms]. In HMQY, II:129–32.

"Du Wenxiu tongshu tizhiguan minglu" [Du Wenxiu's administrative officials' roster]. In HMQY, II:183–200.

Eickelman, Dale F., and James Piscatori, eds. *Muslim Travellers: Pilgrimage, Migration and the Religious Imagination.* Berkeley: University of California Press, 1990.

Elliot, Mark C. *The Manchu Way: The Eight Banners and Ethnic Identity in Late Imperial China.* Stanford, CA: Stanford University Press, 2001.

Elman, Benjamin A., and Alexander Woodside, eds. *Education and Society in Late Imperial China, 1600–1900.* Berkeley: University of California Press, 1994.

Esherick, Joseph W., and Mary Backus Rankin. *Chinese Local Elites and Patterns of Dominance.* Berkeley: University of California Press, 1990.

Evans, Brian. "Panthay Mission of 1872 and Its Legacies." *Journal of Southeast Asian Studies* 16, no. 1 (1985): 117–29.

Fairbank, John K., Edwin O. Reischauer, and Albert Craig. *East Asia: Tradition and Transformation.* Boston: Houghton Mifflin, 1989.

Fang Guoyu, Xu Wende, and Mu Qin, eds. *Yunnan shiliao congkan* [Series of Chinese Documents on Yunnan], 13 vols. Kunming: Yunnan daxue chubanshe, 2001.

Fan Jianhua. "Xi'nan gudao yu Han Tang wangchao shengbian" [The ancient southwest route and the new frontier of the Han and Tang]. *Sixiang zhanxian* 6 (1991): 72–84.

Fitzgerald, Charles P. *The Tower of Five Glories.* London: The Cresset Press, 1941.

Fletcher, Joseph. "A History of the Naqshbandiyya in China." In B. Manz, ed., *Studies on Chinese and Islamic Inner Asia.* London: Variorum, 1995.

Forbes, Andrew D.W. "The 'Cin-Ho' (Yunnanese Chinese) Muslims of North Thailand." *Journal Institute of Muslim Minority Affairs* 7, no. 1 (1986): 173–86.

———. "The Cin-Ho (Yunnanese Chinese) Caravan Trade." *Journal of Asian History* (W.Ger.) 21, no. 1 (1987): 1–47.

———. "The Yunnanese ('Ho') Muslims of North Thailand." In *The Muslims of Thailand,* vol. 1. Bihar, India: Centre for Southeast Asian Studies, 1988.

Fusaji, Takeuchi. "Sindai Unnan yakihatamin no hanran: 1820 nen Eihoku Risu zoku hoki o chushin ni" [Rebellions by swidden cultivators in Yunnan during the Qing: the Lisu uprising in Yongbei in 1820]. *Kumatsu shu* 7 (1992): 276–88.

Gao Fayuan, ed. *Du Wenxiu qiyi lunji* [Collected essays on the Du Wenxiu uprising]. Kunming: Yunnan daxue chubanshe, 1993.

Garnier, Francis. *Voyage d'exploration en Indo-Chine: effectué pendant les annés 1866, 1867, et 1868.* Paris: Hachette et cie., 1873.

Gervais-Courtellemont, Jules. *Voyage au Yunnan.* Paris: Librairie Plon, 1904.

Giersch, Charles Patterson. "Qing China's Reluctant Subjects: Indigenous Communities and Empire along the Yunnan Frontier." Unpublished Ph.D. dissertation, Yale University, 1998.

———. "'A Motley Throng': Social Change on Southwest China's Early Modern Frontier, 1700–1880." *Journal of Asian Studies* 60, no. 1 (2001): 67–94.

Gill, William. *The River of Golden Sand: The Narrative of a Journey through China and Eastern Tibet to Burmah.* London: John Murray, 1880.

Gillette, Maris B. *Between Mecca and Beijing: Modernization and Consumption among Urban Chinese Muslims.* Stanford, CA: Stanford University Press, 2000.

Gladney, Dru C. *Muslim Chinese: Ethnic Nationalism in the People's Republic.* Cambridge: Harvard University Press, Council on East Asia Studies, 1991.

———. "Nations Transgressing Nation-States: Constructing Dungan, Uygur and Kazakh Identities across China, Central Asia and Turkey." In Touraj Atabaki and John O'Kane, eds., *Post-Soviet Asia.* London and New York: Tauris Academic Studies, 1998.

———. *Dislocating China: Muslims, Minorities, and other Subaltern Subjects.* Chicago: University of Chicago Press, 2004.

———. "The New Central Asians and Turkey: Transnational Identities of the Kazakh, Uygur, and Dungan between China, Central Asia and Turkey." Unpublished paper.

Gong Yin. *Zhongguo tusi zhidu* [China's native chieftain system]. Kunming: Yunnan minzu chubanshe, 1992.

Gongzhongdang [Palace memorial archive]. National Palace Museum Archives, Taiwan.

*Guangnan fuzhi* [Gazetteer of Guangnan prefecture]. Compiled by Li Xiling. Taibei: Chengwen chubanshe, 1905 (1967).

Gui Liang. "Chiti Ma Wenzhao zousu mengmianting wenwu guanyuan mosha Huimin'an beigaoren zhengzha" [Mandate regarding Ma Wenzhao's petition of grievance regarding the case of the Mianning military and civil officials plot to kill Hui]. In HMQY, I:67–80.

Hall, John. "Notes on Early Ch'ing Copper Trade with Japan." *Harvard Journal of Asiatic Studies* 12, nos. 3–4 (1949): 444–61.

Hanna, A.C. "The Panthays of Yunnan." *The Moslem World* 21 (1931): 69–74.

Han Pengri. "Yixi Hanhui shilue" [A record of the Han–Hui incidents of western Yunnan]. In HMQY, I:175–82.

Harrell, Stevan. "Ethnicity, Local Interests, and the State." *Comparative Studies of Society and History* 32 (1990): 515–48.

———, ed. *Cultural Encounters on China's Ethnic Frontiers.* Seattle: University of Washington Press, 1995.

———. "The History of the Yi." In Harrell, ed., *Cultural Encounters on China's Ethnic Frontiers.* Seattle: University of Washington Press, 1995.

———. *Ways of Being Ethnic in Southwest China.* Seattle: University of Washington Press, 2001.

He Changling. *Naian zouyi* [The memorials of He Changling]. Taibei: Chengwen chubanshe 1882 (1968).

He Huiqing. "Yunnan Du Wenxiu jianguo shibanian shimo" [The narrative of the eighteen-year-long struggle of Du Wenxiu's Yunnan regime]. Parts I–V. *I jing wenshi banyue kan* (1937): 12:9–12, 13:34–36, 14:36–39, 15:32–38, 16:28–33.

"Heqing jiwen" [Chronicle of Heqing]. In HMQY, II:207–12.

*Heqing zhouzhi* [Gazetteer of Heqing department]. Compiled by Wang Baoyi. Taibei: Taiwan xuesheng shuju. 1968 (1895).

Herman, John. "Empire in the Southwest: Early Qing Reforms to the Native Chieftain System." *Journal of Asian Studies* 56, no. 1 (1997): 47–74.

Hill, Ann Maxwell. "Chinese Dominance of the Xishuangbanna Tea Trade." *Modern China* 15, no. 3 (1989): 321–345.

———. *Merchants and Migrants: Ethnicity and Trade among Yunnanese Chinese in Southeast Asia.* New Haven, CT: Yale University Southeast Asia Studies, 1998.

Ho Ping-ti. *Studies on the Population of China, 1368–1953.* Cambridge, MA: Harvard University Press, 1959.

Hosie, Alexander. "Report by Mr. Hosie of a Journey through the Provinces of Ssu-Ch'uan, Yünnan, and Kuei Chou: February 11 to June 14, 1883." *British Parliamentary Papers: Journeys and Expeditions in China, 1869–1904.* London: Harrison and Sons, 1888.

———. *Three Years in Western China: A Narrative of Three Journeys in Ssu-ch'uan, Kuei-chow, and Yün-nan.* London: George Philip & Son, 1890.

Hou Yunjin. *Dengchuan zhouzhi* [Gazetteer of Dengchuan department]. Taibei shi: Wenhai chubanshe, 1966 (1854).

Hsiao, Kung-chuan. *Rural China: Imperial Control in the Nineteenth Century*. Seattle: University of Washington Press, 1960.

Hsieh Shi-Chung. "Ethnic-Political Adaptation and Ethnic Change of the Sipsong Panna Dai: An Ethnohistorical Analysis." Ph.D. dissertation, University of Washington, 1989.

———. "On the Dynamics of Tai/Dai-Lue Ethnicity: An Ethnohistorical Analysis." In Harrell, ed., *Cultural Encounters on China's Ethnic Frontiers*. Seattle: University of Washington Press, 1995.

Hsü, Immanuel C.Y. *The Rise of Modern China*. New York: Oxford University Press, 2000.

Hua Li. "Qingdai baojia zhidu jianlun" [A preliminary discussion of the registration system during the Qing]. *Qingshi yanjiu ji* 6 (1988).

Huang, Philip C.C. *Code, Custom, and Legal Practice in China: The Qing and Republic Compared*. Stanford, CA: Stanford University Press, 2002.

Hummel, Arthur W. *Eminent Chinese of the Ch'ing Period (1644–1912)*. 2 vols. Washington: U.S. Government Printing Office, 1943–44.

Israeli, Raphael. "Muslims in China: The Incompatibility Between Islam and the Chinese Order." *T'oung Pao* 63, nos. 4–5 (July 1977): 296–323.

———. "Islam in the Chinese Context." *Contributions to Asian Studies* 17 (1982): 79–94.

Jenks, Robert D. *Insurgency and Social Disorder in Guizhou: The "Miao" Rebellion, 1854–1873*. Honolulu: University of Hawaii Press, 1994.

Jest, Corneille. "Kha-che and Gya-Kha-che, Muslim Communities in Lhasa." *Tibet Journal* 20, no. 3 (1995): 8–11.

Jing Dexin, comp. *Yunnan Huimin qiyi shiliao* [Historical documents relating to the Muslim Yunnanese uprising]. Kunming: Yunnan minzu chubanshe, 1986.

———. *Du Wenxiu qiyi* [The Uprising of Du Wenxiu]. Kunming: Yunnan minzu chubanshe, 1991.

Jin Shaoping. "Du Wenxiu Dali zhengquan jingji zhengce shixi" [A preliminary study of the economic policy of the Du Wenxiu regime in Dali]. In Jing Dexin, ed., Du Wenxiu Qiyi Lunji [Essays on the Du Wenxiu uprising]. Kunming: Yunnan Daxue Chubanshe, 1996: 114–24.

Kim Hodong. *Holy War in China: The Muslim Rebellion and State in Chinese Central Asia, 1864–1877*. Stanford, CA: Stanford University Press, 2004.

Kuhn, Philip A. *Soulstealers: The Chinese Sorcery Scare of 1768*. Cambridge, MA: Harvard University Press, 1990.

Kwong, Luke S.K. "The T'i-Yung Dichotomy and the Search for Talent in Late-Ch'ing China." *Modern Asian Studies* 27, no. 2 (1993): 253–279.

Lamley, Harry. "Hsieh-Tou: The Pathology of Violence in Southeastern China." *Ch'ing-shih wen-t'i* 3, no. 7 (November 1977): 1–37.

———. "Lineage Feuding in Southern Fujian and Eastern Guangdong under Qing Rule." In Lipman and Harrell, eds., *Violence in China: Essays in Culture and Counterculture*. Albany: State University of New York Press, 1990.

*Langqiong xianzhilue* [Records of Langqiong county]. Compiled by Zhou Hang. Taibei: Chengwen chubanshe, 1975 (1903).

Launay, Adrien. *Histoire de la mission du Thibet*. Lille–Paris: Desclee de Brouwer et cie, 1903.

Leach, Edmund. *Political Systems of Highland Burma: A Study of Kachin Social Structure*. London: Athlone Press, 1964 (1954).

Lee, James Z. "Food Supply and Population Growth in Southwest China, 1250–1850." *Journal of Asian Studies* 41, no. 4 (1982): 711–46.

———. "The Legacy of Immigration in Southwest China, 1250–1850." *Annales de démographie historique* (1982): 279–304.

———. "The Southwest: Yunnan and Guizhou." In Will and Wong, eds., *Nourish the People: The State Civilian Granary System in China, 1650–1850*. Ann Arbor: Center for Chinese Studies, University of Michigan, 1991.

Le May, Reginald S. *An Asian Arcady: The Land and Peoples of Northern Siam*. Cambridge, UK: W. Heffer, 1926.

Leong, Sow-Theng. *Migration and Ethnicity in Chinese History: Hakkas, Pengmin and Their Neighbors*, ed. Tim Wright. Stanford, CA: Stanford University Press, 1997.

Levanthes, Louise. *When China Ruled the Seas: The Treasure Fleet of the Dragon Throne, 1405–1433*. New York and Oxford: Oxford University Press, 1994.

Li Bingyuan. "Yongchangfu Baoshanxian Han-Hui hudou ji Du Wenxiu shixing geming zhi yuanqi" [The Yongchang-Baoshan Han-Hui incident and origins of the rise of Du Wenxiu's uprising]. In HMQY, I:4–5. Shanghai: Zhongguo shenzhou guogang chubanshe, 1953.

Li Gui. *Yunnan jindai jingjishi* [A modern economic history of Yunnan]. Kunming: Yunnan minzu chubanshe, 1995.

Ling Ti'an. *Xian-Tong Guizhou junshi shi* [A military history of Guizhou in the Xianfeng-Tongzhi period]. Shanghai: Cihui tushuguan, 1932.

Lin Changkuan. "Chinese Muslims of Yunnan, Southwest China, with Special Reference to their Revolt 1855–1873." Ph.D. dissertation, Aberdeen University, 1991.

———. "The Etymological History of Panthay: Chinese-Yunnanese Muslims." *Journal of the Institute of Muslim Minority Affairs* 12, no. 2 (July 1991): 346–54.

———. "Three Eminent 'Ulama' of Yunnan." *Journal of the Institute of Muslim Minority Affairs* 11, no. 1 (1992): 100–17

———. *Zhongguo Huijiao zhi fazhan jiqi yundong* [The development and movements of Muslim Chinese]. Taibei: Zhonghua minguo alabo wenhua jingji xiehui yinxing, 1996.

Lin Xinghua and Feng Jinyuan, eds. *Zhongguo yisilan jiao shi cankai ziliao xuanuji*. Yinchuan: Ningxia Renmin Chubanshe, 1985.

Lin Zexu. *Lin Wenzhong gong zhengshu* [The memorials of Lin Zexu]. 2 vols. Shanghai: Shangwu yinshukuan, 1935.

Lipman, Jonathan N. *Familiar Strangers: A History of Muslims in Northwest China*. Seattle: University of Washington Press, 1997.

———. "Sufism in the Chinese Courts: Islam and Qing Law in the Eighteenth and Nineteenth Century." In de Jong and Radtke, eds., *Islamic Mysticism Contested: Thirteen Centuries of Controversies and Polemics*. Leiden: Brill, 1999.

Li Shou and Su Peiming, eds. *Yunnan lishi renwen dili* [Yunnan history, culture, and geography]. Kunming: Yunnan daxue chubanshe, 1996.

Li Shoukong. "Xianfeng liunian Yunnan shengcheng miehui kaoshi" [An investigation of the 1856 Kunming massacre]. *Dalu Zazhi* 20, no. 6 (1960): 174–77.

———. "Ma Rulong xiangqing zhi yanjiu" [An examination of Ma Rulong's surrender]. *Dalu zazhi* 20, no. 1 (1960): 14–18.

———. "Wanqing Yunnan huibian shimo" [The rise and fall of the late Qing Yunnan Muslim rebellion]. In *Zhongguo jindai xiandai shi lunji* [Collected essays on modern and contemporary Chinese history]. Taibei: Taiwan shangwu yinshuguan, 1985–86.

Litton, George John. *Report by Acting Consul Litton on a Journey in North-West Yünnan.* London: Harrison and Sons, 1903.

Li Xiaoyou, ed. *Kunming fengwuzhi* [A collection of local stories and history]. Kunming: Yunnan minzu chubanshe, 1985.

Li Xinghua and Feng Jinyuan, eds. *Zhongguo yisilanjiao shi cankao ziliao xuanji* [Selected documents on Chinese Islam]. Yinchuan: Ningxia renmin chubanshe, 1985.

Li Xingyuan. *Li wengong gong zouyi* [The memorials of Li Xingyuan]. Taibei: Wenhai chubanshe 1969 (1865).

Liu Yaohan. "Yunnan Ailaoshan chu Yizu fanqing douzheng diaocha jilu" [An investigation of Yizu Ailao region anti-Qing resistance]. In *Jindaishi ziliao* 3:111–42. Beijing: Kexue chubanshe, 1957.

Li Youcheng. "Jianshui Huimin xiwen" [Jianshui Hui proclamation]. In HMQY, II:53–56.

Li Yuanbing. "Yongchangfu Baoshanxian Han-Hui hudou ji Du Wenxiu shixing geming zhi yuanqi" [The Han–Hui conflict in Baoshan district of Yongchang prefecture and the reasons for Du Wenxiu's revolution]. In HMQY, I:1–10.

Liu Yuezhao. *Dian-Qian zouyi* [Memorials on Yunnan and Guizhou]. Taibei: Wenhai chubanshe, 1968 (1888).

Li Yuzhen. "Dianshi shuwen" [A description of the Yunnan affair]. In YHQZ, 184–228.

*Longling Xianzhi* [Gazetteer of Longling district]. Compiled by Zhang Jian'an. Taibei: Chengwen chubanshe, 1975 (1917).

Luckert, Karl W., and Li Shujiang. *Mythology and Folklore of the Hui, a Muslim Chinese People.* Albany: State University of New York Press, 1994.

*Luoping Xianzhi* [Gazetteer of Luoping district]. Taibei: Taiwan Xuesheng Shuju, 1968 (1932).

Luo Qirui (compiler). *Yunnan zhanggu* [Historical anecdotes of Yunnan]. Kunming: Yunnan minzu chubanshe, 1996.

Lu Ren. *Bianqian yu jiaorong: Mingdai Yunnan Hanzu yimin yanjiu* [Change and assimilation along the borders: Research into Ming era Yunnan Han immigration]. Kunming: Yunnan jiaoyou chubanshe, 2001.

Ma Chaolin, "Ruijishugao zhaiyao dishisan ben [Volume thirteen in the summary of Rui's testimony]" In HMQY, I:173–96.

Mackerras, Colin. "Aspects of Bai Culture: Change and Continuity in a Yunnan Nationality." *Modern China* 14, no. 1 (1988): 51–84.

Ma Futu. "Ma Futu siji" [Private account of Ma Futu]. In HMQY, II:365–408.

*Maguan xianzhi* [Gazetter of Maguan district]. Compiled by Zhang Ziming. Taibei: Chengwen chubanshe, 1967 (1932).

Ma Guanzheng. "Dianyuan shisinian dahuo ji" [A record of the fourteen years of tragedy in Yunnan]. In HMQY, I:291–302.

Margary, Augustus Raymond. *Notes of a Journey from Hankow to Ta-lifu*. Shanghai: F. & C. Walsh, 1875.

Ma Rulong. "Shaoyu dianyuan shenmin" [Announcement to the people at the provincial capital]. In HMQY, II:69–74.

———. "Zhi Du wenxiushu" [A letter to Du Wenxiu]. In HMQY, II:97–102.

———. "Fu dasiping Ma Xingtang shu" [A response to General Ma Xingtang]. In HMQY, II:147–56.

Ma Shaoxiong and Zhao Rusong. "Du Wenxiu zhengquan shiqi de Qiaohou yanjin" [Qiaohou salt wells during the period of Du Wenxiu government]. In Yunnansheng Bianjizu, eds., *Yunnan Huizu shehui lishi diaocha* [Investigations of Yunnanese Hui society and history], IV:103–4. Kunming: Yunnan minzu chubanshe, 1985–88.

Ma Shengfeng. "Wuding shilue" [An account of the Wuding incident]. In HMQY, II:15–42.

Ma Tong. *Zhongguo yisilan jiaopai menhuan suyuan [A history of Muslim factions and the Menhuan system in China]*. Yinchuan: Ningxia renmin chubanshe, 1986.

Ma Weiliang. "Qingdai chuzhongqi Yunnan Huizu de kuangyeye" [The mining and metalurgical industry of the Muslim Yunnanese during the early and middle period of the Qing Dynasty]. *Huizu yanjiu* 13, no. 1 (1991): 31–39.

———. "Yunnan Daizu, Zangzu, Baizu he Xiaoliang shan Yizu diqu de Huizu" [Yunnan Dai, Tibetan, Bai, and Xiaoliang mountain area Hui peoples]. In *Yunnan yisilan wenhua lunwen yiji* [Proceedings of Islamic culture in Yunnan]. Kunming: Yunnan renmin chubanshe, 1993.

———. *Yunnan Huizu lishi yu wenhua yanjiu* [Research on Yunnan Hui history and culture]. Kunming: Yunnan daxue chubanshe, 1999.

Ma Zhu. *Qingzhen zhinan* [Islamic compass]. Kunming: Yunnan minzu chubanshe, 1990.

*Menghua xianzhi* [Gazetteer of Menghua district]. Compiled by Liang Yuyi. Taibei: Taibei: Chengwen chubanshe, 1974 (1919).

*Mianning Huimin kouhun gao* [Draft statement of a grievance of the Mianning Hui]. In HQMY, I:81–86.

Miao Yongling. *Ma Liansheng zhuanlüe* [Biographical account of Ma Liansheng]. In YHQS, 351–55.

Millward, James. *Beyond the Pass: Economy, Ethnicity and Empire in Qing Xinjiang, 1759–1894*. Stanford, CA: Stanford University Press, 1998.

Moerman, Michael. "Ethnic Identification in a Complex Civilization: Who Are the Lue?" *American Anthropologist* 67 (1965): 1215–25.

Mueggler, Eric. *The Age of Wild Ghosts: Memory, Violence, and Place in Southwest China*. Berkeley: University of California Press, 2001.

Murray, Dian H., and Qin Baoqi. *The Origins of the Tiandihui: The Chinese Triads in Legend and History*. Stanford, CA: Stanford University Press, 1994.

Na Lanzhen. "Ma Liansheng qiyi yu Dali zhengquan" [The Ma Liansheng Uprising and Dali regime]. In DWQL, 244–48. Kunming: Yunnan daxue chubanshe,
1993.

d'Ollone, Henri M.D. *Recherches sur les musulmans chinois*. Paris: E. Leroux, 1911.

———. "Les musulmans du Yun-nan." *Revue du monde musulman* 4, no. 2 (1908).

Olsen, James. *An Ethnohistorical Dictionary of China*. Westport, CT: Greenwood
Press, 1998.

Ortner, Sherry. "Resistance and Ethnographic Refusal." *Comparative Study of Society and History* 37, no. 1 (1995): 173–93.

Ownby, David. "Introduction: Secret Societies Reconsidered." In Ownby and Heid-
hues, eds., *"Secret Societies" Reconsidered: Perspectives on the Social History of
Modern South China and Southeast Asia*. Armonk, NY: M.E. Sharpe, 1993.

Palmer, Michael J.E. "The Surface–Subsoil Form of Divided Ownership in Late Imperial China: Some Examples from the New Territories of Hong Kong." *Modern
Asian Studies* 21, no. 1 (1987): 1–119.

Pasquet, Sylvie. "Entre Chine et Birmanie, Un mineur-diplomate au royaume de
Hulu, 1743–1752." *Études chinoises* 8, nos. 1 et 2 (printemps et automne 1989).

———. "Image et réalité du système tributaire: l'exemple des confins sino-birmans
au XVIIIe siècle." *Historiens-géographes* 340 (1993): 147–56.

Pichon, Louis. *Un Voyage au Yunnan*. Paris: Librarie Plon, 1893.

Pillsbury, Barbara. "Pig and Policy: Maintenance of Boundaries between Han and
Muslim Chinese." *Ethnic Groups* 1 (1976): 151–62.

*Ping qian jilue* [A record of the pacification of Guizhou]. Compiled by Luo Wenbin
and Wang Bing'en. 1938. Shanghai: Shanghai shu dian 1989 (n.d.).

Pourais, Émile René. *La Chine: huit ans au Yun-nan, récit d'un missionaire*. Lille:
Société de saint Augustin, 1888.

"Poxi shilue" [An account of the Poxi incident]. In HQMY, II: 41–52.

Proschan, Frank. "Peoples of the Gourd: Imagined Ethnicites in Highland Southeast
Asia." *Journal of Asian Studies* 60, no. 4 (2001): 999–1032.

———. "Cheuang in Kmhmu Folklore, History, and Memory." In Sumitr Pitiphat,
ed., *Tamnan keokap thao hung thao chuang: miti thang prawattisat lae watta-
natham* [Proceedings of the First International Conference on the Literary, Historical, and Cultural Aspects of Thao Hung Thao Cheuang]. Bangkok: Tham-
masat University, Thai Khadi Research Institute, 1998.

*Qinding pingding Huifei fanglüe* [Imperially commissioned record of the campaign
to pacify the Hui rebels]. Compiled by Yixin. Taibei: Wenhai Chubanshe, 1972
(1896).

*Qingshengxun xinan minzu shiliao* [Materials concerning the ethnic minorities in
the southwest from the precepts issued by Qing emperors]. 4 vols. Compiled by
Cheng Xiayu. Chengdu: Sichuan chubanshe, 1988.

*Qingshi liezhuan* [Qing biographies]. Shanghai: Zhonghua shuju. 1928.

*Qing shilu youguan Miandian Taiguo Laowo shiliao zhaichao* [Historical materials
on Vietnam, Burma, Thailand, and Laos excerpted from the Qing veritable
records]. Vol. V. Compiled by the Yunnan Provincial History Institute. Kunming:
Yunnan renmin chubanshe, 1986.

*Qing shilu youguan Yunnan shiliao Huibian* [Collection from the veritable records regarding Yunnan]. 4 vols. Kunming: Yunnan renmin chubanshe. Compiled by the Yunnan Provincial History Institute, 1984.

Qiu Lijuan. "Qingdai Yunnan tongkuang de jingying" [Management of Yunnan copper mines during the Qing]. Unpublished M.A. thesis, Taiwan Normal University, 1993.

Qiu Shusen, ed. *Zhongguo Huizu Shi* [A history of the Chinese Hui]. Yinchuan: Ningxia renmin chubanshe.

Rawski, Evelyn. *The Last Emperors: A Social History of Qing Imperial Institutions.* Berkeley: University of California Press, 1998.

Reid, Anthony. *Southeast Asia in the Age of Commerce 1450–1680, II: Expansion and Crisis.* New Haven, CT: Yale University Press, 1993.

Rocher, Émile. *La Province chinoise du Yün-nan.* 2 vols. Paris: Libraire de la société asiatique, 1879.

Rossabi, Morris. "The Muslims in the Early Yuan Dynasty." In John D. Langlois, Jr., ed., *China under Mongol Rule.* Princeton, NJ: Princeton University Press, 1981.

Rowe, William T. "Education and Empire in Southwest China: Ch'en Hung-mou in Yunnan, 1733–38." In Benjamin Elman and Alexander Woodside, eds., *Education and Society in Late Imperial China, 1600–1900.* Berkeley: University of California Press, 1994.

———. "Ancestral Rites and Political Authority in Late Imperial China: Chen Hongmou in Jiangxi." *Modern China* 24, no. 4 (1998): 378–407.

———. *Saving the World: Chen Hongmou and Elite Consciousness in Eighteenth-Century China.* Stanford, CA: Stanford University Press, 2001.

*Ruan Yuan nianpu* [A chronology of Ruan Yuan's life]. Compiled by Zhang Jin. Beijing: Xinhua shuju chubanshe, 1890 (1995).

Luo, Guanzhong. *Sanguo yenyi* [Tale of the three kingdoms]. Beijing: Wenhua yishu chubanshe, 1991.

Schoppa, Keith. "Local Self-Government in Zhejiang, 1909–1927." *Modern China* 2, no. 4 (1976): 503–30.

Schwartz, Henry G. "Some Notes of the Mongols of Yunnan." *Central Asiatic Journal* 28, nos. 1–2 (1987): 101–18.

Scott, James G., and J.P. Hardiman. *Gazetteer of Upper Burma and the Shan States* 2, no. 2 (Rangoon: Superintendent, Government Printing, Burma, 1900–01).

Sheng Yuhua. "Yongchang Hanhui hudouan jielue" [A record of the conflict between the Han and Hui in Yongchang]. In YHQS, 63–74.

Shepherd, John. *Statecraft and Political Economy on the Taiwan Frontier.* Stanford, CA: Stanford University Press, 1993.

She Yize. *Zhongguo tusi zhidu* [The native chieftain system of China]. Chongqing: Zhengzhong shuju, 1944.

Shimada Kenji. *Pioneer of the Chinese Revolution: Zhang Binglin and Confucianism.* Stanford: Stanford University Press, 1990.

Sladen, Edward. "Exploration via the Irrawaddy and Bhamo." *Proceedings of the Royal Geographical Society* 15, no. 5 (December 18, 1871): 151–64.

Société des missions-étrangères de Paris [Paris society of foreign missions]. Archives of the Société des missions-étrangères de Paris. Paris.

Song Guangyu, ed. *Hua'nan bianjiang minzu tulu* [An illustrated album of Chinese border peoples]. Taibei: Guoli zhongyang tushuguan chubanshe, 1991.

Sow-Theng Leong. *Migration and Ethnicity in Chinese History: Hakkas, Pengmin and Their Neighbors*. Stanford, CA: Stanford University Press, 1997.

Spence, Jonathan. *God's Chinese Son: The Taiping Heavenly Kingdom of Hong Xiuquan*. New York: W.W. Norton, 1996.

Spencer, Joseph Earle. "Kueichou: an Internal Chinese Colony." *Pacific Affairs* 13, no. 2 (June 1940): 162–72.

Struve, Lynn. *The Southern Ming, 1644–1662*. New Haven, CT: Yale University Press, 1984.

Sun, E-tu Zen. "The Board of Revenue in Nineteenth-Century China." *Harvard Journal of Asiatic Studies* 24 (1962–63): 175–228.

———. "The Copper of Yunnan: A Historical Sketch." *Mining Engineering* (July 1964): 118–24.

———. "Ch'ing Government and the Mineral Industries Before 1800." *Journal of Asian Studies* 27, no. 4 (1968): 835–45.

———. "The Transportation of Yunnan Copper to Peking in the Ch'ing Period." *Journal of Oriental Studies* 9, no. 1 (January 1971): 132–48.

Taeuber, Irene B., and Nai-Chi Wang. "Population Reports in the Ch'ing Dynasty." *Journal of Asian Studies* 19, no. 4: 403–17.

"Talang Nan'an zhengkuang ji" [A record of the Talang, Nan'an, mining incident]. In HMQY 1:249–62.

Tambiah, Stanley J. *Culture, Thought, and Social Action: An Anthropological Perspective*. Cambridge, MA: Harvard University Press, 1985.

*Tengyue tingzhi* [Gazetteer of Tengyue subprefecture]. Compiled by Zhao Duanli. Taibei: Chengwen Chubanshe, (1887).

Thongchai, Winichakul. *Siam Mapped: A History of the Geo-Body of a Nation*. Honolulu: University of Hawaii Press, 1994.

Tian Rukang. "Youguan Du Wenxiu duiwai guanxi de jige wenti" [Regarding some questions of Du Wenxiu's foreign relations]. *Lishi Yanjiu* 4 (1963): 133–46.

T'ien Ju-k'ang. *Moslem Rebellion in China: A Yunnan Controversy*. Canberra: The Australian National University Press, 1981.

———. "New Light on the Yün-nan Rebellion and the Panthay Mission." *Memoirs of the Toyo Bunko* 40 (1982): 19–56.

Tooker, Deborah E. "Putting the Mandala in its Place: A Practice-Based Approach to the Spatialization of Power on the Southeastern 'Periphery'—the Case of the Akha." *Journal of Asian Studies* 55, no. 2 (1996): 323–58.

Tsai Yuan-lin. "Confucian Orthodoxy vs. Muslim Resistance in Late Imperial China: the Ideological Origin and the Development of the Hui Rebellion in Yunnan under Qing Dynasty (1644–1911)." Unpublished Ph.D. dissertation, Temple University, 1997.

Van Spengen, Wim. "The Geo-History of Long-Distance Trade in Tibet, 1850–1950." *Tibet Journal* 20, no. 2 (1995): 18–63.

Wade, Geoff. "The Zheng He Voyages: A Reassessment," ARI Working Paper, No. 31, October 2004, www.ari.edu.sg/pub/wps.htm.

Wang Dingan. "Pingdian bian" [A record of the pacification of Yunnan]. In YHQS, 253–69.

Wang Dingchen. "Qing Xiantongjian Yunnan Huibian jiwen" [Chronicle of the Xianfeng-Tongzhi era Hui uprising in Yunnan]. In HMQY, II:297–306.

Wang Jianping. *Concord and Conflict: The Hui Communities of Yunnan Society.* Stockholm: Almqvist & Wiksell, 1996.

Wang Mingda, and Zhang Shilu. *Mabang wenhua* [Caravan culture]. Kunming: Yunnan renmin chubanshe, 1993.

Wang Shuhuai. *Xiantong Yunnan Huimin shibian* [The Muslim uprising in Yunnan, 1856–1873]. Nangang: Academia Sinica, 1974.

Wang Shulin. "Dianxi Huiluan jilue" [A record of the Western Yunnan Hui rebellion]. In YHQS, 229–52. Kunming: Yunnan minzu chubanshe, 1986.

Wang Song. *Daoguang Yunnan zhichao [An selected record of Yunnan during the Daoguang reign].* Kunming: Yunnan Shehui Kexueyuan, 1829 (1995).

Wang, S.T. *The Margary Affair and the Chefoo Agreement.* London: Oxford University Press, 1940.

Wang Wenguang. *Zhongguo gudai de minzu shibie* [A categorization of ancient China's ethnic peoples]. Kunming: Yunnan daxue chubanshe, 1997.

Wang Yunwu (compiler). *Dao-Xian-Tong-Guang sichao zouyi* [Collected memorials from the four reigns of the Daoguang, Xianfeng, Tongzhi, and Guangxu emperors]. 12 vols. Taibei Shi: Taiwan shangwu yinshuguan, 1970.

Wang Zhusheng. *The Jingpo Kachin of the Yunnan Plateau.* Tempe, AZ: Program for Southeast Asian Studies Monograph Series, 1977.

Wei, Alice Bihyun Gan. "The Moslem Rebellion in Yunnan." Ph.D. dissertation, University of Chicago, 1974.

Wei, Hsiu-mei. *Qingji zhiguanbiao* [A listing of Qing officials and offices]. Taibei: Zhongyang yanjiuyuan jindaishi yanjiusuo, 1977.

Wei Zhizhen. *Qingshilu Yizu shiliao jiyao* [Excerpts regarding Yi from the veritable records]. Kunming: Yunna minzu chubanshe, 1986.

Wien, Harold. *China's March toward The Tropics; a Discussion of the Southward Penetration of China's Culture, Peoples, and Political Control in Relation to the Non-Han-Chinese Peoples of South China and in the Perspective of Historical and Cultural Geography.* Hamden, CT: Shoe String Press, 1954.

Wijeyewardene, Gehan. "Thailand and the Tai: Versions of Ethnic Identity." In Wijeyewardene, ed., *Ethnic Groups across National Boundaries in Mainland Southeast Asia.* Singapore: Institute of Southeast Asian Studies, 1990.

Will, Pierre-Étienne, and R. Bin Wong, eds. *Nourish the People: The State Civilian Granary System in China, 1650–1850.* Ann Arbor: Center for Chinese Studies, University of Michigan, 1991.

Wright, Mary C. *The Last Stand of Chinese Conservatism: The T'ung-Chih Restoration, 1862–1874.* Forge Village, MA: Atheneum, 1967 (1957).

Wu Guangfan. *Yunnan diming tanyuan* [The origins of Yunnan place names]. Kunming: Yunnan renmin chubanshe, 1988.

Wu Qian, "Yongchang Huimin xiwen" [Official proclamation by the Hui of Yongchang]. In HMQY, 1:87–92. Shanghai: Zhongguo shenzhou guogang chubanshe, 1953.

Wu Qianjiu. "Yunnan Huizu de lishi yu xiankuang" [A history and current status of Yunnan Hui." *Yanjiu jikan* 16, no. 1 (1982).

Wu Xinfu. "Shilun Qingchao qianqi dui nanfang shaoshu minzu de liuzhi zhengce" [Early Qing Dynasty policies toward minorities in southern China]. *Guizhou wenshi congkan* 2 (1986).

Wu Xingnan. "Qingdai qianqi de Yunnan duiwai maoyi" [Yunnan foreign trade during the early Qing Dynasty]. *Yunnan shehui kexue* 2 (1997): 74–77.

Wyatt, David K. *Thailand: A Short History*. New Haven, CT: Yale University Press, 1982.

"Xianfeng bingchen jiluan liji" [Record of the Xianfeng bingchen (1856) uprising]. In YHQS, 175–78. Kunming: Yunnan minzu chubanshe, 1986.

Xiao Minghua (compiler). *Yunnan shaoshu minzu guanyin ji* [A collection of official seals from Yunnan minority groups]. Kunming: Yunnan minzu chubanshe, 1986.

*Xinping xianzhi* [Gazetteer of Xinping district]. Compiled by Ma Taiyuan. Taibei: Chengwen chubanshe, 1967 (1934).

*Xuanwei xianzhigao* [Gazetteer of Xuanwei county]. Compiled by Chen Jitong. Taibei: Chengwen chubanshe, 1967 (1934).

*Xuanwei zhouzhi* [Gazetteer of Xuanwei department]. Compiled by Liu Beilin. Taibei: Chengwen chubanshe, 1967 (1844).

*Xuxiu Jianshui xianzhi* [Revised gazetteer of Jianshui district]. Compiled by Ding Guoliang. Taibei: Chengwen chubanshe, 1975 (1920).

*Xuxiu Malong xianzhi* [Revised gazetteer of Malong district]. Compiled by Wang Mozhao. Taibei: Chengwen chubanshe, 1974(1917).

*Xuxiu Shunning fuzhi* [Revised gazetteer of Shunning prefecture]. Compiled by Tang Mengdeng. Taibei: Chengwen chubanshe, 1968 (1904).

*Xuxiu Songming zhouzi* [Revised gazetteer of Songming department]. Compiled by Wang Yiyuan. Taibei: Chengwen chubanshe, 1974 (1887).

Xu Yuanhua. "Xiantong yehuo bian" [A record of the reckless deeds of the Xiantong period]. In HMQY, 1:279–290. Shanghai: Zhongguo shenzhou guogang chubanshe, 1953.

*Xu Yunnan tongzhigao* [Revised comprehensive gazetteer of Yunnan]. Compiled by Wang Wenshao. Taibei: Wenhai chubanshe 1966 (1901).

Yang Shen. *Yang Shen ciqu ji [The words and writing of Yang Shen]*. Chengdu: Sichuan renmin chubanshe, 1984.

Yang Xifu. *Sizhitang wenji* [Collected essays by Yang Xifu]. Beijing: Beijing Chubanshe 1987 (1764).

Yang Zhaojun. *Yunnan Huizu shi* [A history of the Muslim Yunnanese]. Kunming: Yunnan minzu chubanshe, 1994.

Yan Zhongping. *Qingdai Yunnan tongzheng kao* [A draft survey of Yunnan copper mines during the Qing Dynasty]. Beijing: Zhonghua shuju chubanshe, 1957.

Yao Huating. "Chuxiong binchen kangbian shilue" [A record of the Chuxiong clash of 1856]. In HMQY, II:3–4. Shanghai: Zhongguo shenzhou guogang chubanshe, 1953.

Yao Jide. "Xi'nan xichou gudao yu yisilan jiao ru diankao" [The ancient silk road of the southwest and Islam's entry into Yunnan]. *Yi yu yan* 32, no. 1 (1994): 185–204.

Yaozhou zhi (Gazetter of Yaozhou). Comp by Gan Yu. Yaozhou: Yaozhou wenmiao zunjingge, 1885.

Yegar, Moshe. "The Panthay (Chinese Muslims) of Burma and Yunnan." *Journal of Southeast Asian History* 7, no. 1: 73–85.

Yen Ching-Hwang. "Ch'ing Changing Images of the Overseas Chinese (1644–1912)." *Modern Asian Studies* 15, no. 2 (1981): 261–85.

Ye Tong. *Dali Huizushi yu wenhua jilun* [A collection of essays on Dali Hui history and culture]. Dali: Dali musilin wenhua zhuanke xuexiao bianyin, 2000.

Yi Duanshan. "Zhiji cha liumin zhuoyi changcheng qin" [An investigation of the solutions to migrant population]. In Fang Guoyu, ed., *Yunnan shiliao congkan*, 13 vols. Kunming: Yunnan daxue chubanshe, 2001.

*Yingxuetang chaolu* [A record from the hall of brilliant snow]. In YHQS, 1–61.

*Yongchang fuzhi* [Gazetteer of Yongchang prefecture]. Compiled by Liu Yuke. Taibei: Chengwen Chubanshe 1967 (1886).

*Yongchang Huimin xiwen* [A proclamation of the Yongchang Hui]. In Bai Shouyi, ed., HMQY, I:87–92. Shanghai: Zhongguo shenzhou guogang chubanshe, 1953.

You Zhong. *Yunnan minzu shi* [A history of Yunnan minorities]. Kunming: Yunnan daxue chubanshe, 1994.

*Yuanmou jiwen* [A chronicle of Yuanmou]. In HMQY, II:213–16. Shanghai: Zhongguo shenzhou guogang chubanshe, 1953.

*Yunnan shaoshu minzu guanyin ji* [A collection of official seals from Yunnan minority groups]. Kunming: Yunnan Minzu Chubanshe, 1989.

*Yunnansheng bianjizu* [Yunnan editorial board]. 4 vols. *Yunnan Huizu shehui lishi diaocha* [Investigations of Yunnanese Hui society and history]. Kunming: Yunnan minzu Chubanshe, 1985–88.

*Yunnansheng dangan shiliao congbian: jindai Yunnan renkou shiliao (1909–1982)* [*Yunnan provincial archives: Modern Yunnan population records, 1909–1982*]. Kunming: Yunnan sheng dangan guan, 1987.

*Yunnan tongzhi* [Gazetteer of Yunnan]. Compiled by Jing Daomo. Taibei: Taiwan Shangwu Yinshuquan, 1983 (1736).

*Yunnan xianzhi* [Gazetteer of Yunnan district]. Comp. Huang Bingkun. Taibei: Chengwen Chubanshe, 1967 (1890)

*Yunnan yisilan wenhua lunwen yiji* [Proceedings of Islamic culture in Yunnan]. Kunming: Yunnan renmin chubanshe, 1993.

Zelin, Madeline. "The Rise and Fall of the Fu-Rong Salt-Yard Elite: Merchant Dominance in Late Qing China." In Esherick and Rankin, *Chinese Local Elites and Patterns of Dominance*. Berkeley: University of California Press, 1990. 82–109.

Zhang Chaoyu, ed. *Kunmingshi dimingzhi* [Place names of Kunming]. Kunming: Kunmingshi renmin chubanshe, 1987.

Zhang Mingqı. "Xiantong bianluan jingliji" [Record of the Xian-Tong uprising]. In YHQS, 81–82. Kunming: Yunnan minzu chubanshe, 1986.

Zhang Pengyuan, "Yun-Gui diqu shaoshu minzu de shehui bianye jiqi xianzhi" [A demographic study of the minorities of the Yun-Gui regions]. In *Zhongguo xiandai hualun wenji*, Taibei: Guoli tushuguan, 1991.

Zhang Qingfen. "Jiantan shijiu shiji zhongye yi Hui-Yi wei zhuti de Yunnan gezu renmin daqiyi" [Some notes on major Hui and Yi personages in mid-nineteenth-century era multiethnic uprisings]. In DWQL, 196–204. Kunming: Yunnan daxue chubanshe, 1993.

Zhang Tao. "Dianluan jilue" [A record of the Yunnan rebellion]. In HMQY, I:263–78. Shanghai: Zhongguo shenzhou guogang chubanshe, 1953.

Zhang Zhongfu. "Luyun jishi gao" [A record of Luyun]. In HMQY, II:421–84. Shanghai: Zhongguo shenzhou guogang chubanshe, 1953.

Zhao Fan. Cen Xiangqin gong nianpu [A chronology of Cen Yuying's life]. Taibei: Chengwen chubanshe, 1968.

———. Cen Xiangqin gong xude jiefu tu [An album of Cen Yuying's illustrious career: presented on his 60th birthday by the gentry of Yunnan]. Private lithograph print, 1890.

Zhao Qing. "Bianyuan jieyuan lu" [A record of justifying the wrongs]. In HMQY, I:43–66. Shanghai: Zhongguo shenzhou guogang chubanshe, 1953.

Zhaotong xianzhi [Gazetteer of Zhaotong district]. Compiled by Yang Lujian. Taibei: Chengwen Chubanshe, 1967 (1924).

Zhongguo yisilan baike quanshu [Chinese encyclopaedia of Islam]. Chengdu: Sichuan zishu chubanshe, 1994.

Zhu Bingce. "Yuanren Hunan tidu Ma Gong Yufeng zhuan" [The biography of the late incumbent Hunan provincial military commander Ma Yunfeng]. In HMQY, II:357–64. Shanghai: Zhongguo shenzhou guogang chubanshe, 1953.

# Index

Ailao, 113, 143
Allès, Elisabeth, 37
Anderson, Benedict, 40
Anderson, John: comment regarding visit to Dali 237n32; description of Tengyue, 151
Appeals to Qing court, 66, 74, 77, 95–96
Arabic, 143, 146–147, 166; and Ma Dexin, 222n130

Baber, Edward, 16, 18, 240
Bai (Minjia): general description of, 32; support of Hui rebels 112, 143
Bai Shouyi: 38, 206n21
Baiyang Mine Incident, 65–67
banditry: reputation of Yi as sources of, 31; differences between hanjian-ism and, 53;correlation between Hui, violence and, 81, 94
Baojia: 57, 62, 80, 81, 190; and mines, 22
Baoshan, 15, 41, 186
Baoshan Massacre (1845), 5, 70–76; government response to, 77–83, 92, 215n112; Zhang Liangji and, 95, 117, 219n72
Binchuan, 116, 118, 140, 141, 178
Black Flags, 186
Bolin, 27, 52, 59, 81;and Lin'an Uprising, 55–58
Bowers, Capt. A., 144
Burma, 10, 12, 15–16, 18, 21, 31–32, 44, 46, 48, 49, 144, 147, 149, 151, 165, 166, 169, 179, 184, 186, 188, 189

Cai Fachun, 117, 118, 120, 141
caravans: description of 18; Hui and 42–44; trade, 7, 12, 19, 32, 150
cattle protection associations (niucong), 71, 72, 80
Cen Yuying: early career 173–174; relations with Ma Rulong 127, 129, 136, 137, 174, 175; as governor and governor-general of Yunnan, 176–180; post-rebellion role of, 185, 188–189
Cheli, 33, 60

Chenggong, 105, 107, 165, 177
Chauveau, Joseph Pierre, 86, 88,112, 141
Chuxiong, 98, 178, 186; battle of 118–121, 131, 151;early violence in, 87–88, 91, 101, 118
Clendinnen, Inga, 114
communal violence (xiedou), 69
conditional land sales (dian), 58, 210n45
Cooper, Thomas, 149, 168, 236n16
copper, 1, 19, 22
Crossley, Pamela, 8

Dai (Tai), 25, 112, 205n96, and Dao Shengwu Affair, 60–62
Dali, 13; description of, 21, 32; as focus of Qing military campaigns, 116–118, 140–141; French mission to, 166–168; Hui uprising (1856) in, 101–104; political symbols of, 145–150, surrender of, 182–184; transregional ties, 44; as capital of the sultanate, 146, 148, 161
Dali Kingdom (937-1253), 2, 7, 34
Daniels, Christian, 59
Dao Shengwu, 60–62
de Carné, Louis, 106, 142, 149, 162, 165, 179, 185, 226n21
Disease, 44, 63, 175, 180; malaria, 11, 12, 61, 80; plague, 178
Dong Jialan, 140, 141
Dongchuan, 15, 21, 92, 96, 109, 110, 113, 136, 166, 177,
Dupuis, Jean, 29, 187, 255n129
Du Wenxiu, 9; differentiating between Hui and Muslim, 155–159; early life, 104; and emphasis on trade, 150-152; and final campaign against the Qing, 162–165, 175–178; multiethnic orientation, 40, 103, 112, 139, 144, 146; relations with other Hui leaders, 119–121,128, 130, 131, 133, 141, 152–155, 172, 173; religious orientation, 131–134, 147; as ruler of Dali Sultanate, 142–144; relations with Europeans, 144, 165–169; surrender of, 181–183